Lecture Notes in Computer Science

Lecture Notes in Computer Science

Edited by G. Goos and J. Hartmanis

16

Operating Systems

Proceedings of an International Symposium
held at Rocquencourt, April 23–25, 1974

Edited by E. Gelenbe and C. Kaiser

Springer-Verlag
Berlin Heidelberg GmbH 1974

Dr. E. Gelenbe
Dr. C. Kaiser
IRIA LABORIA
Domaine de Voluceau
Rocquencourt
F–78150 Le Chesnay/France

Library of Congress Cataloging in Publication Data
Main entry under title:

Operating systems.

(Lecture notes in computer science, no. 16)
Sponsored by the Institut de recherche d'informatique
et d'automatique with the participation of the Association française pour la cybernétique économique et
technique and others.
English and French.
1. Electronic digital computers--Congresses.
2. Electronic digital computers--Programming--Con-
gresses. I. Gelenbe, E., 1945-   ed. II. Kaiser,
Claude, ed. III. Institut de recherche d'information
et d'automatique. IV. Association française de
cybernétique économique et technique. V. Series.
QA76.5.058   001.6'4'044   74-14991

AMS Subject Classifications (1970): 68-00, 68-02
CR Subject Classifications (1974):   4.3, 8.1

ISBN 978-3-540-06849-5   ISBN 978-3-540-37805-1 (eBook)
DOI 10.1007/978-3-540-37805-1

Originally published by Springer-Verlag Berlin Heidelberg New York in 1974.

Offsetdruck: Julius Beltz, Hemsbach/Bergstr.

PREFACE

Le présent volume rassemble les travaux présentés au colloque international sur les aspects théoriques et pratiques des systèmes d'exploitation des ordinateurs. Cette réunion a été organisée par l'IRIA-
LABORIA* du 23 au 25 avril 1974 et a bénéficié du patronage de
l' "Association Française pour la Cybernétique Economique et Technique",
de l' "Association for Computing Machinery", du "Chapitre Français"
de cette dernière association, de la "Computer Society of the Institute of Electrical and Electronics Engineers" et de la "Society for
Industrial and Applied Mathematics".

Ce colloque a réuni à Rocquencourt près de 200 chercheurs et ingénieurs
de nombreux pays. L'originalité des travaux présentés et la qualité
de l'auditoire attestent de la vigueur de cette branche de l'informatique et de l'extrême intérêt scientifique et technique qui s'attache
aux méthodes d'exploitation des ordinateurs.

Nous tenons à remercier tout particulièrement:
    Monsieur André Danzin, Directeur de l'IRIA,
    Monsieur J.L.Lions, Directeur du LABORIA,
    Mademoiselle T.Bricheteau et le service des relations extérieures
    de l'IRIA qui ont permis l'organisation de ce colloque.

Notre gratitude va également au président et à nos collègues du comité
de programme ainsi qu'aux commentateurs qui ont contribué à animer
d'intéressantes discussions:
    MM. B.Arden, A.N.Habermann, S.Krakowiak, B.Lampson, R.Mahl,
    D.Parnas, L.Pouzin, B.Randell, J.P.Verjus.

Enfin, nous adressons nos remerciements aux rapporteurs, aux con-
férenciers et à tous les participants.

                            E. GELENBE,   C.KAISER

---

*) Institut de Recherche d'Informatique et d'Automatique-Laboratoire
de l'IRIA BP n° 5 - 78150 LE CHESNAY - France.

TABLE OF CONTENTS

COMITÉ DU PROGRAMME
PROGRAMME COMMITTEE

Président
Chairman

B. ARDEN   Princeton University, U.S.A.

Membres
Members

E. GELENBE   IRIA-LABORIA, France
N. HABERMANN   Canergie Mellon University, U.S.A.
C. KAISER   IRIA-LABORIA, France
S. KRAKOWIAK   Université Grenoble I, France
B. RANDELL   University of Newcastle-Upon-Tyne. U.K.

Le Colloque International sur les aspects théoriques et pratiques des
Systèmes d'Exploitation est organisé par l'Institut de Recherche
d'Informatique et d'Automatique (IRIA) sous le patronage de:

- Association Française poùr la Cybernétique Economique et Tech-
  nique (AFCET)
- Association for Computing Machinery (ACM)
- Chapitre Français de l'A.C.M.
- Computer Society of the Institute of Electrical and Electronics
  Engineers (IEEE)
- Society for Industrial and Applied Mathematics (SIAM)

The International Symposium on Operating Systems is organized by the
Institut de Recherche d'Informatique et d'Automatique (IRIA) with the
participation of the Association Française pour la Cybernétique Econo-
mique et Technique (AFCET), the Association for Computing Machinery
(ACM), the French Chapter of the ACM, the Computer Society of the
Institute of Electrical and Electronics Engineers (IEEE) and the
Society for Industrial and Applied Mathematics (SIAM).

REFERES
REFEREES

M.	ALEXANDER	Etats-Unis
J.	BELLINO	France
C.	BETOURNE	France
L.	BOLLIET	France
A.	BRANDWAJN	France
B.	COCHI	France
E.	COFFMANN	Etats-Unis
S.	CRESPI-REGHIZZI	Italie
P.J.	DENNING	Etats-Unis
J.C.	DERNIAME	France
P.H.	DORN	Etats-Unis
E.W.	DYKSTRA	Pays Bas
J.	FERRIE	France
H.	GALLAIRE	France
B.A.	GALLER	Etats-Unis
J.	GEORGES	Belgique
C.	GIRAULT	France
R.A.	GUEDJ	France
D.F.	HARTHLEY	Grande-Bretagne
J.D.	ICHBIAH	France
G.	KAHN	France
B.W.	LAMPSON	Etats-Unis
H.C.	LAUER	Grande-Bretagne
J.	LENFANT	France
J.	LEROUDIER	France
J.J.	LEVY	France
M.C.	LYNCH	Etats-Unis
R.	MAHL	France
A.G.	MERTEN	Etats-Unis
J.	MOSSIERE	France
D.	POTIER	France
L.	POUZIN	France
M.D.	SCHROEDER	Etats-Unis
G.S.	SHEDLER	Etats-Unis
T.J.	TEOREY	Etats-Unis
H.	VANTILBORGH	Belgique
J.P.	VERJUS	France
W.A.	WULF	Etats-Unis

CORRECTNESS OF REALIZATIONS OF LEVELS
OF ABSTRACTION IN OPERATING SYSTEMS

G. Belpaire, J.P. Wilmotte

·Université de Louvain, Belgique

———

ABSTRACT.

This paper presents a method of proving properties of the implementation of levels
of abstraction in a hierarchically structured Operating System. For any two
adjacent levels L (low) and H (high), the processes of level L are seen as
(virtual) processors realizing the processes of level H. A Scheduling program is
assumed to implement the realization of level H by level L. Means of defining
properties of this realization are studied, together with a formal method of
proving these properties. The proofs are carried out on the basis of two kinds
of hypotheses : (1) assumptions about the behaviour of the processors, and
(2) properties of the scheduling program. The hierarchy of the system is taken
into account to proceed step by step to the proofs of the realization of the last
level and, consequently, of the whole system. Advantages and inconveniences of
the method are discussed.

1. INTRODUCTION.

This paper presents a method of proving properties of the implementation of levels
of abstraction in hierarchically structured Operating Systems [6,8,15].

Within such systems a given level of abstraction is a representation for data
types and information structures and for operations on these types and structures.
Processes can be seen as computations of these operations.

Processes of level 1 are realized by the processors of level 0 (the hardware
processors). For any two adjacent levels L (low) and H (high), the processes of
level L are seen as (virtual) processors realizing the processes of level H.

This work is supported by a grant of the Belgian Government, Programme National
d'Impulsion à le Recherche en Informatique, Contrat n° I-14.5/11.

Processors at level L can be specialized processors (e.g. the I/O handler) able to realize only specific operations. Processes at level H can consist of operations of different kinds, needing to be realized by specific processors. Usually, the number of level L processors is smaller than the number of level H processes. A scheduling of the realization of level H by level L is therefore necessary : for every pair of adjacent levels, there must be a scheduling program whose function is to assign processors to processes and to establish the necessary queues. This scheduling program must not necessarily be a program in the usual sense (cf. for instance the multiprogramming of sixteen concurrent processes in the Venus machine [15]).

This paper studies formal means of defining properties of realizations of level H by level L, together with a formal method of proving these properties. These proofs are carried out on the basis of two kinds of hypotheses :
1.   assumptions about the behaviour of the processors, and
2.   properties of the scheduling program.

For a system with many levels (numbered from 0 to n), such proofs should be carried out for every pair of adjacent levels (i,i+1). The behaviour of the level 0 processors realized by hardware is assumed to have some given properties. A proof of the properties of the realization of level 1 can then be built on the properties of level 0 and of the scheduling program. Then, these proven properties are taken as hypotheses for the behaviour of level 1 to prove properties of level 2, and so on. Therefore, one can proceed to prove properties of the realization of the last level and, consequently, of the whole system.

The structuring of a system in a hierarchy of levels of abstraction provides a means of "modularizing" the proofs. This advantage was outlined by Dijkstra for the T.H.E. System [8]. One part of the formal method used in this paper is an application of the Hoare/Wirth axiomatic method of defining the semantics of a programming language [12], another part consists of an approach similar to the mathematical semantics method that Scott and Strachey have defined for programming languages [17].

2.   THE METHOD.

Figure 1 outlines the method for a given pair of adjacent levels. We distinguish three fields (instead of "field", the words "domain" or "level" might be used but would lead to confusion) : the program field, the program semantics field and the system semantics field.

The program field contains the scheduling program written in some programming language (PASCAL [20] in the illustration developed in section 5). Within this field there are statements, and data types and variables. The program is assumed to operate on process description blocks and on queues in order to implement the realizations.

The semantics of the program is formalized in the program semantics field by an axiomatic approach similar to Hoare/Wirth's [12]. The program semantics field consits of :
1.   domains of values and variables wich correspond to the types and variables of the PASCAL programs, and
2.   logical assertions establishing relations between properties of domains before and after the execution of the statements.
The interpretation of the domains of values in the program semantics field is the usual one for PASCAL types. There is no further interpretation in terms of processes or of levels.

The system semantics field is a formal representation of properties of levels of abstraction, processes, processors, and realizations. Every term in this field denotes a concept or an object relevant to the realization of a level by another adjacent one. This being done for each pair of levels gives a model of properties of the complete system.

The link between the program field and the program semantics field is made of :
1.   axioms about the domains of values, and
2.   rules of inference associated with the statements of the programming language.
The way this is done is an application of the principles given by Hoare (e.g., see [10,11,12]). Only the results are given in the example in section 5.

The link between the program semantics field and the system semantics field is made of valuation functions Φ . The domain of these functions is built from :
1.   the domains of values of the program semantics field, and
2.   the logical assertions of the program semantics field.
Their range is :
1.   the sets of objects of the system semantics field, and
2.   the relations between these objects.
By mapping the program semantics field into the system semantics field, the valuation functions attribute the meaning defined by the system semantics field to the terms of the program semantics field.

Proofs of the following type can be obtained :
1.   For every pair of adjacent levels L and H, properties of the realization are deduced from the particular scheduling program by means of the successive mappings.
2.   Using the latter properties and assuming some hypotheses about the behaviour of processors at level L, properties of the processes at level H can be proven. This gives a means of proving, for instance, the concurrent activity at all levels by assuming the concurrent activity at level O.

The advantages of this method are the following :
1.   Objects and concepts belonging to the same conceptual universe are grouped in the same semantic field, and mappings are defined between pairs of fields.
2.   The hierarchy of the system is taken into account to divide in simple steps the task of proving the properties.
3.   At any step of the proof one can see exactly what is being proven and what is to be done next.

3.   BASIC CONCEPTS IN THE SYSTEM SEMANTICS FIELD.

3.1.   Processes.

Processes are considered to be the basic objects which form a computing system. Usually, a process is defined by three kinds of objects (see e.g. [9,14]) :
1.   states S ,
2.   transformations (also called transitions or actions) which are mappings from S to S ,
3.   initial states.
In this paper the characterization of the system is made of properties which deal only with actions and not with states. For this reason, we will adopt a definition of a process where actions are the basic elements and where states do not appear explicitly. This point of view is taken here merely for the sake of simplicity. Furthermore, we consider only sequential processes, and we introduce an explicit specification in time of the evolution of the processes. Events and instants are defined in relation with actions of processes.

Definition 3.1.1.   E is a set of elements called *events*.
The *time* is a totally ordered set T , whose elements are called *instants*.
The ordering relation is denoted ⩽ .
(e,t) ∈ E X T is called the *occurrence* of the event e at instant t, and is
denoted (e)$_t$.   Note that this definition allows for different occurrences of
the same event.

Definition 3.1.2.   A *sequential process* p is made of :

1.   A$_p$ a finite set of elements called *actions*.

2.   S$_p$ ⊆ A$_p$ X A$_p$ a total ordering relation called the *sequencing relation*
(of the actions).

3.   begin$_p$ = inf A$_p$ the *initial action*.

4.   end$_p$ = sup A$_p$ the *final action*.

5.   E$_p$ ⊆ E   For every action a ∈ A$_p$, $\bar{a}$ ∈ E$_p$ denotes a unique event called the
initiation event of a , and $\underline{a}$ ∈ E$_p$ denotes a unique event called the
termination event of a . The only elements of E$_p$ are the initiation and
termination events of the actions of p . For two different actions a$_1$ and a$_2$
of p , $\underline{a}_1$, $\bar{a}_1$, $\underline{a}_2$, and $\bar{a}_2$ denote four distinct events.
Remark.   Since we consider only sequential processes throughout this paper,
the term *process* will be used from now on for sequential process.

Definition 3.1.3.   An *evolution* of a process p is a relation C$_p$ ⊆ E$_p$ X T
with the following properties :

1.   to every e ∈ E$_p$ corresponds one and only one t ∈ T

2.   if a ∈ A$_p$ and $(\bar{a})_{t_1}$, $(\underline{a})_{t_2}$ ∈ C$_p$ then t₁ ⩽ t₂

3.   if (a$_1$,a$_2$) ∈ S$_p$ and $(\underline{a}_1)_{t_1}$, $(\bar{a}_2)_{t_2}$ ∈ C$_p$ then t₁ ⩽ t₂

Remark.   To be logically rigorous, the sequencing relation should involve a
logical modality : for any couple of actions (a$_1$,a$_2$) , if (a$_1$,a$_2$) ∈ S$_p$ then
a$_2$ must follow a$_1$ but the occurrence of $\bar{a}_2$ may happen at an unspecified
finite time after the occurrence of $\underline{a}_1$. This condition is similar to the
asynchronous permissiveness of Slutz [18] and to the event possibility described
in [1].

3.2.   Procedures and executions.

Any process is closely related to a procedure as Dennis and Van Horn stated it in
[7] : *A process is a locus of control within an instruction sequence. That is,
a process is that abstract entity which moves through the instructions of a
procedure as the procedure is executed by a processor.*   Thus, if a procedure is
considered as a sequence of instructions (or operations), to one process
corresponds one and only one procedure, and to each action of that process
corresponds one and only one operation of the procedure. Several processes are
allowed to execute the same procedure. In this case, they form a class of
processes (e.g. cf. [1,4]).

Within a procedure, the operations forming the sequence are not necessarily
different from each other and, in this case, they are considered as different

instances of the same operations (e.g. in a loop). In the formal definitions given below the *operations* are distinct elements and should be understood as the above instances of operations. This is done to enhance a certain simplicity of the definitions and does not harm the coherence of the whole system of definitions.

Definition 3.2.1. A *sequential procedure* s or, for short, a *procedure* s is made of :

1. K_s a set of elements called *operations*.
2. $S_s \subseteq K_s \times K_s$ a total ordering relation.
3. $begin_s = \inf K_s$
4. $end_s = \sup K_s$

Definition 3.2.2. Let Σ be a set of procedures, and P a set of processes. Ex : $P \rightarrow \Sigma$ is a function on P to Σ . For every $p \in P$, $s = Ex(p)$ is called the procedure *executed* by the process p .

Definition 3.2.3. Let p be a process and $s = Ex(p)$. $Ex_p : A_p \rightarrow K_s$ is an isomorphism for the ordering relations. For every $a \in A_p$, $k = Ex_p(a)$ is called the operation *executed* by the action a .

A process is seen as a dynamic evolution in time of a number of actions. A procedure is a symbolic description of these actions. At any instant a process is associated with one operation of one procedure and is said to execute it. In this paper, it is not necessary to give further interpretation for the operations of a procedure.

The above definition of a procedure does not allow for a representation of conditional and other control statements. More general models of procedures exist, e.g. [5] , but our simple model is sufficient for our present purpose.

3.3. Levels and Realizations.

The concept of realization arises from the generalization of the concept of nucleus or of supervisor in Operating System*s.*

In a paper by Brinch Hansen [3], the *nucleus* of a system is presented as a means of providing a virtual environment within which processes and the communications between processes can exist. The nucleus implements fundamental primitives whose functions are to dynamically create and remove processes and to allow for communications between them. This environment can be seen as a virtual processor upon which the processes and the communication functions can be executed. The nucleus realizes these functions and these concepts in the same way as a real processor realizes the functions of the machine code.

Stockton Gaines [19] introduces the concept of supervisory computer programs as complex supervisory functions. Each time a program (or a process) calls for a function of the supervisor, it can specify a sequence of functions to be executed by the *supervisory computer* (i.e. that part of the supervisor which executes the supervisory computer programs). Thus a supervisory call does not request the supervisory computer to execute a single function but a sequence of functions. This supervisory computer is a step further towards the concept of a virtual processor which realizes functions available to processes.

In hierarchical systems, levels of abstraction are used to enhance a better design of the system. This includes objectives of comprehension, correctness, modularity and manageability of design decisions. The definition of a level of abstraction with respect to the others can be best understood in a statement by Liskov [15] : *A level is defined not only by the abstraction which it supports (for example, virtual memories) but also by the resources which it uses to realize that abstraction. Lower levels (those closer to the machine) are not aware of the resources of higher levels; higher levels may apply the resources of lower levels only by appealing to the functions of the lower level.* For a pair of adjacent levels L and H, the level H is implemented by the functions of level L. The processes of level H are allowed to use the functions of level L and, in some sense, they provide new functions for a higher level. In some cases the supervisory function can be microprogrammed (as in [15]) and an object originally seen as a process (like the nucleus in [3]) becomes independently realized and is considered as a processor.

Processes of level number i will be seen as processes for the level number i-1 and as processors for the level number i+1 . Thus we can generalize the concept of realization and say that each level i is realized by the level i-1 .

The notion of realization of a process is given in several papers, e.g. [14,16], although it is not presented as a key concept in the hierarchy of levels of abstraction. Our purpose is to give a conceptual basis for the formalization of realizations of processes. This does not include all kinds of hierarchically orderings of computing systems (for example, memory hierarchies).

Definition 3.3.1. The *L level* is a set Π whose m elements are named *processors*. $\Pi = \{\pi_1, \pi_2, ..., \pi_m\}$
The *H level* is a set P of processes, such that, for every $p \in P$ the set A_p of actions of p is partitioned into m subsets $A_p^1, A_p^2, ..., A_p^m$.
The *realization* of a process of the H level by processors of the L level is a relation $R_p \subseteq A_p \times \Pi$, such that :

1. $R_p = \bigsqcup_1^m R_p^i$ with $R_p^i = \{(a_p, \pi_i) \,|\, a_p \in A_p^i\}$, $1 \leqslant i \leqslant m$

2. $R_p \subseteq E$ i.e. the elements of R_p are events.

An *evolution* of a realization R_p is a relation $L_p \subseteq R_p \times T$.
An element $((a_p, \pi), t)$ of L_p is noted $(a_p, \pi)_t$.
Assumption. For every $p \in P$ and for a given evolution C_p and a given evolution of realization L_p ,
If $a_p \in A_p^i$, $(a_p, \pi_i)_t \in L_p$, and $(\overline{a}_p)_{t_1}, (\underline{a}_p)_{t_2} \in C_p$ then $t_1 \leqslant t \leqslant t_2$,
that is, any event of the evolution of a realization of a process occurs between the occurrences of the initiation and termination events of the realized action.

4. ILLUSTRATION OF THE CONCEPTS.

An illustration of the concepts defined so far is shown on figure 2, where a box represents a process at a given level. An arrow going from one box X to another box Y means that process X needs processor Y for its realization. When several arrows go from one box A to boxes B,C,...,D (figure 3), this means that process A will be realized with processors B,C,...,and D. Note that, since process A is sequential, it needs only one of these processors at a time for its realization. When several arrows go to one box E from boxes F,G,...,H (figure 4), this means that processes F,G,...,and H will be realized with the same processor E, and that a scheduling program must be established for the sharing of processor E. A "earth" sign attached to a box means that the corresponding processor is physically realized.

Figure 2 could represent the resource management part of a computing system. In Operating Systems, the resources are usually separated into three categories namely, (1) CPU's, (2) core and (disk and drum) paging memories, and (3) input/output and file sytems. In our model we do not make any dicrimination between CPU's and other (virtual or real) processors, because in this model, resources are seen as processors at some level L for some processes at level H. As a consequence, CPU's must be introduced explicitly at some level, and it is possible to specify explicitly which processes need them (shared or not) for their realization. This proves to be particularly useful when we want to study a multiprocessing system. For instance, in figure 2, CPU2 is used only for the computation of user processes, and CPU0 is used only for the realization of the classical supervisory functions of the system.

It is essential that no arrow can go across any level. This is the only way to obtain a step by step proof of the realization between successive pairs of levels, as it was pointed out in the introduction. In practice however, there are cases where such a condition is not satisfied. One or more intermediate processes must be introduced to model these cases. There is no contradiction between the model and the reality if one admits that the intermediate processes will be realized by identification. For example, CPU1 in figure 2 is such an intermediate process and the relation of realization between CPU1 and CPU0 is an identity.

5. ILLUSTRATION OF THE METHOD.

5.1. Description of a subsystem.

The subsystem upon which the method is demonstrated is represented in the figure 5. This is a subsystem in the sense that it could be considered to be a part of a (more complex) real system. It consists of two processors at level L and two processes at level H. PROCESS1 needs PROCESSOR1 for its realization, and PROCESS2 needs both PROCESSOR1 and PROCESSOR2, alternatively, for its realization. The realization of the two level H processes with the two level L processors is implemented by a scheduling program which is made of procedures activated by "interrupts". In a general hierarchical system, we consider that each L level is able to issue some signals which play the same role as classical interrupts of hardware processors. We call these signals, interrupts.

Usually, scheduling programs are seen as elements of the system, and they have a status similar to the processes status, e.g. they can compete for system resources. In our framework, a scheduling program is not a part of the system semantics field. Scheduling programs constitute the program field, and their actual execution is a problem that we do not treat here. It has been treated explicitly in the detailed study of a complete example [2].

However, in general, it is illusory to think that whenever an interrupt occurs, the scheduling program is run on one of the processors PROCESSOR1 or PROCESSOR2, for it is possible that neither PROCESSOR1 nor PROCESSOR2 are able to run the scheduling program.

In the remaining part of this section, we give only the elements necessary to the proof of one theorem one can obtain for such a subsystem.

5.2. The program field.

The scheduling program could be written, for example, in PASCAL [20]. The program field comprises some types and variables, and two procedures.

For the subsystem considered here we declare, for example :

```
type aprocess = record state : (running, waiting, completed);
                       instruction : ↑instruction
            end;
```

This is the description block of a process. The state field describes the execution status of the process i.e. running on a processor, waiting for a processor, or completed. The instruction field either points to the currently executed instruction if the state is 'running', or (if the state is 'waiting') it points to the instruction to be executed. The last instruction of a sequence is assumed to be 'end'.

```
var π1-owner,π2-owner : ↑aprocess;
```

These variables are pointing to process description blocks. When a process is running on a processor the corresponding pointer is assumed to point to this process.

```
var p1,p2 : aprocess;
```

These are the description blocks of processes PROCESS1 and PROCESS2.

The two procedures correspond to the two processors, and they are activated by the issuing of an interrupt by the corresponding processors. The execution of these procedures is indivisible (for details about indivisibility see e.g. [1,8]). This can be achieved, for example, by delaying the interrupts when necessary.

```
        interrupt procedure π1-interrupt;
        begin if π1-owner↑ = p1
            then begin p1.state := completed;
                       π1-owner := nil
                 end
            else if p2.instruction↑ = end
                 then begin p2.state = completed;
                            if p1.state = completed
                            then π1-owner := nil
                            else begin π1-owner↑ := p1;
                                       p1.state := running
                                 end
                      end
                 else begin π2-owner↑ := p2;
                            π1-owner↑ := p1;
                            p1.state := running
                      end
        end

        interrupt procedure π2-interrupt;
        begin p1.state := waiting;
              π1-owner↑ := p2;
              π2-owner  := nil
        end
```

5.3. The program semantics field.

Notations. 1. Let a be a variable, $(a)_t$ is the value of a at time t.
2. Let A and B be logical formulas, and $\perp$ a logical connector.
$(A)_t$ means A is true at time t, and $((A) \perp (B))_t = (A)_t \perp (B)_t$.
Particularly, $(a=b)_t = (a)_t = (b)_t$ and $(A \longrightarrow B)_t = (A)_t \longrightarrow (B)_t$,
$\longrightarrow$ being the implication sign.
3. In what follows, the notation introduced by Hoare [12] :

$$\textit{Predicate-1} \ \{\pi1\text{-interrupt}\} \textit{Predicate-2}$$

becomes :

$$(\textit{Predicate-1})_t \wedge (\textit{int1})_t \longrightarrow (\textit{Predicate-2})_{t+\tau}$$

where t is the time of activation and $t+\tau$ the time of end of execution of the interrupt procedure. $\textit{int1}$ is defined below.

5.3.1. Domains.

T time

K set of instructions

$K = K_1 \cup K_2$ partition

$P = \{p1, p2\}$ They correspond to the variables p1 and p2 of the program field.

The sequence of instructions executed by $p1$ has the form $a \ end$

and the sequence executed by $p2$ has the form $a_1 \ b_1 \ a_2 \ b_2 \ \dots \ b_{n-1} \ a_n \ end \ (n > 0)$

where $end, a, a_1, \dots, a_n \in K_1$, $b_1, \dots b_{n-1} \in K_2$

$L = \{\pi1\text{-}owner, \pi2\text{-}owner\}$ Their values range over P . They correspond to the variables π1-owner and π2-owner of the program field.

$U = \{\textit{int1}, \textit{int2}\}$ They are predicates. $(\textit{int1})_t$ means that π1-interrupt is activated at time t (and the same for $(\textit{int2})_t$).

nil denotes <u>nil</u> .

Notation. If pp has the value $p \in P$ then the notation pp = "p" corresponds to $pp\uparrow$ = p in the program field.

5.3.2. Axioms and assertions.

We define τ as the execution time of π1-interrupt.
<u>Axioms about the instructions.</u>
Let $k_1 \ k_2 \ \dots \ k_m$ be the instruction sequence of $p2$. We have the following axiom :

$(X1) \Vdash \ ((\pi1\text{-}owner = "p2") \wedge (p2.\textit{instruction} = "k_i") \wedge (\textit{int1}))_t$
    $\longrightarrow (p2.\textit{instruction} = "k_{i+1}")_{t+\tau}$, $k_i \neq end$

We have similar axioms for π1-$owner$ and $p1$, and for π2-$owner$ and $p2$.
<u>Assertions about the procedures.</u>

We give only the assertions related to π1-interrupt.

Let $q1$ be the predicate   π1-$owner$ = "p1" ,
    $q2$ $p2.\textit{instruction}$ = "end" , and
    $q3$ $p1.\textit{state}$ = completed .

We have :

(A1) $\vdash ((int1) \wedge (q1))_t \longrightarrow ((q3) \wedge (\pi1\text{-}owner = nil))_{t+\tau}$

(A2) $\vdash ((int1) \wedge (\neg q1) \wedge (q2))_t \longrightarrow (p2.state = completed)_{t+\tau}$

(A3) $\vdash ((int1) \wedge (\neg q1) \wedge (q2) \wedge (q3))_t \longrightarrow ((\pi1\text{-}owner = nil))_{t+\tau}$

(A4) $\vdash ((int1) \wedge (\neg q1) \wedge (q2) \wedge (\neg q3))_t \longrightarrow ((\pi1\text{-}owner = "p1") \wedge$

$(p1.state = running))_{t+\tau}$

(A5) $\vdash ((int1) \wedge (\neg q1))_t \wedge (\neg q2)_{t+\tau} \longrightarrow ((\pi1\text{-}owner = "p1") \wedge (p1.state = running)$

$\wedge (\pi2\text{-}owner = "p2"))_{t+\tau}$

5.4. The system semantics field.

5.4.1. Domains.

T   time

P = {p1,p2}   The set of processes

K   the set of operations , $K = K_1 \cup K_2$ partition

K^+ = {s1,s2}   s1 is a sequence of the form a end , and s2 is a sequence of the

form $a_1 b_1 a_2 b_2 \ldots b_{n-1} a_n$ end , (n > 0), where :

$\qquad end, a, a_1, \ldots, a_n \in K_1$, $b_1, \ldots, b_{n-1} \in K_2$

Ex : $P \rightarrow K^+$ relation of execution, Ex(p1) = s1 ,   Ex(p2) = s2 .

$Ex_p : A_p \rightarrow Ex(p)$ A_p is the set of actions of process p , Ex_p is a bijection.

$\Pi = \{\pi1, \pi2\}$ the set of processors.

R_p is defined as in the definition 3.3.1.

$R \subseteq P \times \Pi$,$(p,\pi) \in R \leftrightarrow \exists a_p, a_p \in A_p, (a_p,\pi) \in R_p$

5.4.2. Valuation functions.

$\qquad \Phi[\![A \rightarrow B]\!]$ is a notation for a function from A to B

$\qquad \Phi[\![x]\!]$ is the value of Φ for the argument x .

$\qquad \Phi[\![T \rightarrow T]\!]$ is an homomorphism for the ordering relation.

$\qquad \Phi[\![K \rightarrow K]\!]$ is a bijection, $\Phi[\![end]\!] = end_p$, $p \in P$.

$\qquad \Phi[\![P \rightarrow P]\!]$ is a bijection.

We define now the valuation functions for some predicates : we write the only functions we need for our present purpose. For some application of functions, the effect of valuation is manifested by the change of the typographical font, e.g. $\Phi[\![t]\!] = t$. We will use this commodity whenever there is no confusion.

(V1) $\Phi[\![(\pi1\text{-}owner = "p")_t]\!] = (p,\pi1)_t$

(V2) $\Phi[\![(p.instruction = "k")_t]\!] = (a_p)_t$, $a_p = Ex_p^{-1}(k)$

(V3) $\Phi[\![(p.state = completed)_t]\!] = (end_p)_t$

(V4) $\Phi[\![(int1)_t]\!] = (a_{\underline{p}})_t \wedge (a_p, \pi)_t$

  if $(\pi 1\text{-}owner = "p")_t$, $(p.instruction = "k_i")_{t+\tau}$, and $Ex(a_p) = k_{i-1}$

This means that an interrupt is interpreted as the end of the realization of an action. If an interrupt occurs at time t , the valuation of $(p.instruction = "k")$ is undefined between the time t and $t+\tau$. This is justified by the fact that the scheduling program is not in the system semantics field and that between t and $t+\tau$ only the scheduling program is in activity. Thus, if $(int1)_t$, the valuation of $(p.instruction = "k")$ can be done only at at time t and $t+\tau$.

Note that V4 can be seen as the precise definition of an interrupt in the system semantics field. The valuation function is conditional i.e. an interrupt is meaningful only if some other conditions are satisfied.

(V5)   If X and Y are logical expressions and $\perp$ is a logical connector then

  $\Phi[\![X \perp Y]\!] = \Phi[\![X]\!] \perp \Phi[\![Y]\!]$ if $\Phi[\![X]\!]$ and $\Phi[\![Y]\!]$ exist.

5.4.3. Assumptions about the processors.

(H1) $\Vdash \forall t\ (p,\pi)_t \longrightarrow \ \exists\ t'\ ,\text{finite},\ ((a_p,\pi)_{t'} \wedge (a_{\underline{p}})_{t'})$

(H2) $\Vdash \Diamond\ ((p1,\pi1)_{T_1} \wedge (p2,\pi2)_{T_2} \wedge (T_1 \cap T_2 \neq \emptyset))$

$\Diamond$ is a logical sign for the modal possibility ("it is possible that ..") T_1 and T_2 are intervals of T .

By this, we assume that (1) a processor completes any activity within a finite and (2) two processors can be active concurrently.

5.4.4. Theorems.

From the axioms and assertions in the program semantics field and the valuation functions defined in the system semantics field, it is possible to state some theorems about the realizations of actions and processes in the system semantics field.
For example (informally stated) :
1. Any action is realized within a finite time.
2. An action which has to be realized by one type of processor is actually realized by a processor of this type.
3. The realization of process p2 takes a finite time.

We show below how one can prove the last theorem. To do so, it is sufficient to prove that, if an action of p2 is realized at time t then the following action of p2 is realized within a finite time after t, since the sequence of actions of p2 is finite. Formally :

(T1) $\Vdash\ \forall\ a_i \neq end_{p2}\ ((p2,\pi1) \wedge (a_i,\pi1))_t$

  $\longrightarrow\ \ \exists\ t'\ \text{finite},\ ((p2,\pi2) \wedge (a_{i+1},\pi2))_{t'}$

(T2) $\Vdash\ \forall\ a_j\ ((p2,\pi2) \wedge (a_j,\pi2))_t \longrightarrow \exists\ t'\ \text{finite}\ ((p1,\pi1) \wedge (a_{j+1},\pi1))_{t'}$

The proofs of (T1) and (T2) are similar. We give the proof of (T1) below.

By applying (V1), (V2) and (V4) to (X1) and (A5) we obtain :

(L1) $((p2,\pi1) \wedge (a_i) \wedge (a_i,\pi1) \wedge (\underline{a}_i))_t \longrightarrow (a_{i+1})_{t+\tau}$, $a_i = Ex_{p2}^{-1}(\Phi[\![k_i]\!])$
$\neq end_{p2}$

and

(L2) $((p2,\pi1) \wedge (a_j))_t \wedge \neg(end_{p2})_{t+\tau} \wedge ((a_j,\pi1) \wedge (\underline{a}_j))_t$

$\longrightarrow ((p1,\pi1) \wedge (p2,\pi2))_{t+\tau}$, $a_j = Ex_{p2}^{-1}(\Phi[\![k_j]\!])$

From (L1) and (L2) one can deduce :

$((p2,\pi1) \wedge (a_i) \wedge (a_i,\pi1) \wedge (\underline{a}_i))_t \longrightarrow ((a_{i+1}) \wedge (p2,\pi2))_{t+\tau}$

if a_i and a_{i+1} different from end_{p2}

With the assumption in section 3.3. this reduces to (T1) with the condition
that $a_{i+1} \neq end_{p2}$. For $a_{i+1} = end_{p2}$, (A2) and (A3) lead to the same result.

6. CONCLUSION.

What we have presented in this paper is to be considered as a proposal for a
theoretical tool rather than as an exhaustive development of such a tool
applicable to a large class of system correctness problems. The simple
subsystem that we have studied here gives a feeling for the kind of properties
than one can prove about the realizations of levels of abstraction. It is clear
that the bulkiness of the definitions and the complexity of the proofs increase
rapidly with the number of processes at every level but this seems to be a
general characteristic of formalizations rather than a peculiarity of our method.
As a consequence, it is likely that the study of a real system would require as
many steps as possible to be automatized. Furthermore, in order to go further
in the development of the theory, it is necessary to introduce more systematic
and more general definitions of parts of this theory, e.g. for the valuation
functions.

However, the concepts and the method introduced so far seem to be useful for the
treatment of the subsystem of section 5 and for the example described in [2].
They also seem to be general enough to deal with a real hierarchical system,
in such a way that the advantages outlined in the introduction are verified :
1.   The objects and concepts belonging to the same conceptual universe are
grouped in the same semantic field, and mappings are defined between each pair
of fields.
2.   The hierarchy of the system is taken into account to divide in simple steps
the task of proving properties of that system.
3.   The proof itself is systematic : it is composed of a sequence of predefined
steps; at any step of the proof, one knows exactly what is being proven and one
knows what is to be done next.

REFERENCES.

1.   Belpaire, G., and Wilmotte, J.P. A Semantic Approach to the Theory of
Parallel Processes. International Computing Symposium 1973, A. Günther et al.
eds., North-Holland Publ. Co., 1974, pp. 159-164.

2.   _____ A Proof of the Correctness of a Simple
Hierarchical System. Unpublished Report, University of Louvain, 1974.

3.   Brinch Hansen, P. The Nucleus of a Multiprogramming System. Comm. ACM 13, 4, (April 1970), 238-241, 250.

4.   Courtois, P.J., Heymans, F., and Parnas, D.L. Concurrent Control with Readers and Writers. Comm. ACM 14, 10, (October 1971), 667-668.

5.   De Bakker, J.W., and Meertens, L.G.L.T. Simple Recursive Program Schemes and Inductive Assertions. Report MR 142, Mathematische Centrum, Amsterdam, 1972.

6.   Dennis, J.B. The Construction and Design of Software Systems. In Advanced Course on Software Engineering. F.L. Bauer, Ed. , Springer Verlag, Berlin, 1973, pp. 12-28.

7.   Dennis, J.B., and Van Horn, E.C. Programming Semantics for Multiprogrammed Computations. Comm. ACM 9, 3, (March 1966), 143-155.

8.   Dijkstra, E.W. The Structure of the "THE"-multiprogramming System. Comm. ACM 11, 5, (May 1968), 341-346.

9.   Gilbert, G., and Chandler, W.J. Interference between Communicating Parallel Processes. Comm. ACM 15, 6, (June 1972), 427-437.

10. Hoare, C.A.R. Notes on Data Structuring. In Structured Programming. Academic Press, New York, 1972, pp. 83-174.

11. _____ Proof of Correctness of Data Representations. Acta Informatica 1, 4, (1972), 271-281.

12. Hoare, C.A.R., and Wirth, N. An Axiomatic Definition of the Programming Language PASCAL. Eidg. Technische Hochschule, Zürich, November 1972.

13. Holt, A.W., and Commoner, F. Events and Conditions. Record of the Project MAC Conference on Concurrent Systems and Parallel Computation. ACM, Decembre 1970, pp. 3-52.

14. Horning, J.J., and Randell, B. Process Structuring. Computing Surveys 5, 1, (March 1973), 5-30.

15. Liskov, B.H. The Design of the Venus Operating System. Comm. ACM 15, 3, (March 1972), 144-149.

16. Olszewski, J. On a Structure of Operating System Schedulers. Proc. IFIP Congress 1971, TA-3, 163-167.

17. Scott, D., and Strachey, C. Toward a Mathematical Semantics for Computer Languages. Proc. of the Symposium on Computers and Automata, Microwave Research Institute Symposia Series Volume 21, Polytechnic Institute of Brooklyn.

18. Slutz, D.R. The Flow Graph Schemata Model of Parallel Computation. Ph.D Thesis, M.I.T., September 1968.

19. Stockton Gaines, R. An Operating System based on the Concept of Supervisory Computer. Comm. ACM 15, 3, (March 1972), 150-156.

20. Wirth, N. The Programming Language PASCAL (Revised Report) Eidg. Technische Hochschule, Zürich, November 1973.

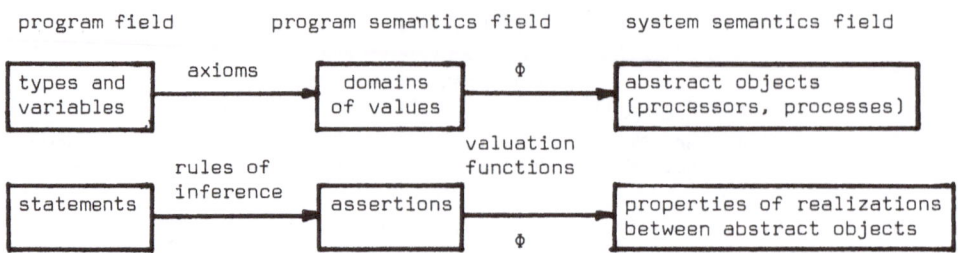

Fig. 1. The method for a given pair of adjacent levels.

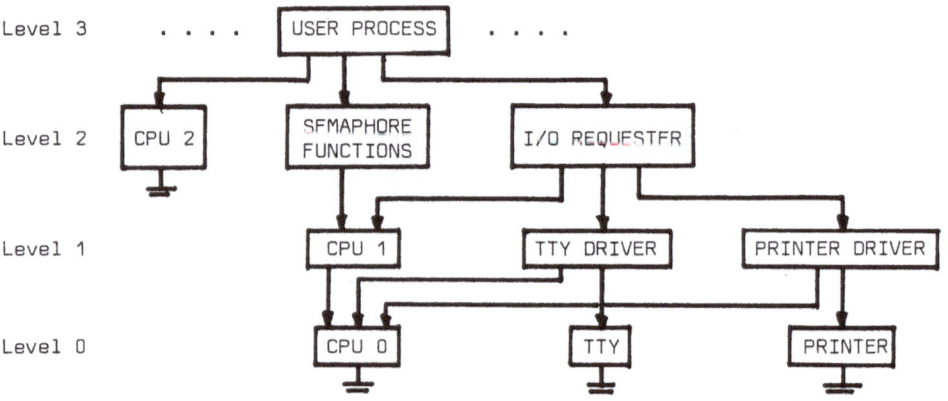

Fig. 2.

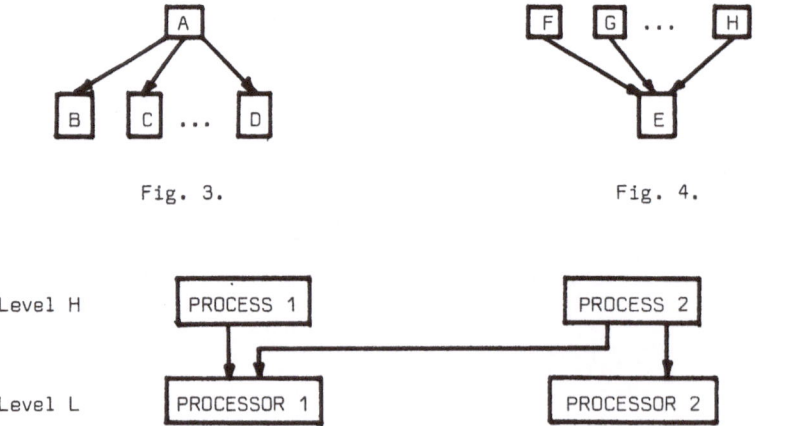

Fig. 3.   Fig. 4.

Fig. 5.

A SIMULATION MODEL REPRESENTING THE OS/VS2
RELEASE 2 CONTROL PROGRAM

T. Beretvas

I.B.M., New-York

Abstract

Traditionally, successful simulation modeling as a design evaluation tool and a performance evaluation vehicle has been confined to
small subsystems of an operating system. The effort involved in
modeling a total operating system usually has been prohibitive.
Those models that were created tended to be too complex to use, and
their architectures reflected existing systems rather than future
systems.

This paper describes techniques used for CSS modeling of the
OS/VS2 Release 2 Control Program prior to the existence of the full
systems. The model was conceived to operate at the system level,
representing a functional rather than an imitative approach to
simulation. It gives a general overview of the modelling techniques
used and then discusses a salient feature of the model, representation of the relocate environment (paging). A section is devoted to
discussion of the novel tracing methodology used with the model.
The validation approach used for the model is described, the basis
for which is a comparison of comparable real system runs and trace
driven model runs.

Introduction

Previous efforts at modeling software have generally been limited to
subsystems rather than to an entire operating system.[1] Alternatively, models of operational systems were created, viewing the system
only from a high-level overall performance viewpoint, not modeling
the software in any detail.[2,3] Most models of entire systems were
too expensive to create and were difficult, if not impossible, to
maintain.[4] A notable exception was the FSD HOST model of OS/360
MVT Release 18 created by IBM Houston.[5] Encouraged by this success,
a project was started to model the OS/VS2 Release 2 before the

operating system was actually built. The model, a system-level model written in CSS,[6] represents a functional rather than an imitative approach to simulation. It simulates most major components of, and interfaces in, OS/VS2-2. By limiting efforts to functional level simulation, it was hoped that model maintenance due to changes in the operating system would be considerably reduced.

This paper contains a brief discussion of the development environment in which the model was built and of the overall architecture of the model, including a technical description of the modeling aspects of a relocate environment, of the tracing technology used, and of the first-level validation that took place.

The model is a "hybrid" in that it can be run in trace mode, in self-driven mode, or in a combination of the two. Both modes of loading use the same system model structure.

In the past, trace programs monitored both system and problem program activities.[7] In the new tracing technology implemented by the model,[8] only problem program activities are monitored. With this advance in the technology, conceptually the problem program activities can be monitored on any system, with any hardware configuration, and with any software belonging to the same family of operating systems. The contents of the trace are invariant from system to system and can be used to predict the performance of a totally different system. Also, tracing at the problem program level is easily understandable, since this is the interface level seen by the application programmer.

Acronyms used in this report are defined in the Glossary. IBM does not intend to make this model available outside of IBM.

The Model Development

The model was built concurrently with the development of OS/VS2 Release 2 as a tool to aid the design/development process. In many instances, only gross design specifications and occasional flow-charts were available; thus, at the writing of this report, it does not represent the mature operating system.

Objectives

The major objectives of the model were to provide performance information about VS2-2 operation and to provide feedback to the designers in the form of recommendations.

Operational Characteristics of the Model

Conceptual description of the operating system environment. Application programs executed on computers normally interface with the software, the operating system provided by the computer manufacturer. In the OS/360 family of operating systems, the operating system control program schedules, initiates, and supervises the work performed by the computing system.[9] The use of the computer must describe the work to be done and the resources needed. This information is conveyed through the use of job control language. (See Figure 1.)

When executing, the application program uses control program services, which may be the establishment of priorities, task creation, the passing and sharing of main storage, etc. These requests are communicated to the control program by the supervisor call (SVC) interruption. The SVCs corresponding to the control program services enumerated above are CHAP, ATTACH, GETMAIN, FREEMAIN, etc. Once an SVC is issued, the computer operates in supervisor mode until the control program returns to the application program, which operates in a problem program mode.

The application programs usually rely on control program services for moving data between external and main storage. The data management routines of the operating system and of the access methods are used for this purpose. The application programs issue OPEN and CLOSE SVCs for the data sets to start and finish the data accessing operations. The actual data access takes place either through the control program itself via EXCP SVCs and WAIT SVCs, if the user has written his own channel programs, or via the data management macro instructions GET, PUT, READ, WRITE, and CHECK, which transfer control to the access methods. The access methods in turn translate the data management macros requests into EXCP and WAIT SVCs.

Application program modeling. The application program (the problem program) code execution consumes problem program time. These time intervals are delineated by requests for supervisor or data management service.

Similarly, the application program model contains a time ordered series of events which represent the load exerted on the system. Problem program time events, supervisory call, and data management events alternate in the series. (Note that the internal logic of an application program between invocation of control program services is not modeled.) This series of events can be represented by explicit application model code (self-driven model) or by trace data obtained on a real system (application program job profiles) which is read by a general trace-driven application model that exerts the load on the model of the control program. (See Figure 2)

In the real system, job control language is required to describe the work and resources needed. The model job control language plays a similar role in the modeling environment.

The control program model. In the real world the control program schedules, initiates, and supervises the work performed by the computing system. Thus, analogously, the control program model must perform the same functions for the simulated workload.

Basically this means that the main operating system functions must be functionally modeled in the control program. Decisions taken by the model must parallel the important real decisions taken in the operating system. The key part of the control program model is the simulation of the SVCs, since the application program models (trace or self-driven) communicate with the control program model via simulated SVCs. In addition, modeled dispatching and job selection functions must simulate real system decisions. The model of these major functions must incorporate the decision making logic for the system. Since the execution of these functions consumes CPU time and may require additional services (I/O operation, execution of other operating system functions), the invocation of these secondary services must also be properly represented.

The crucial decision to be made in the process of modeling is the level of detail at which a particular operating system function should be simulated. Since the model is performance-oriented, individual decisions on the detail level are prompted by performance considerations. If superficial representation of the function is is satisfactory from a system performance viewpoint, then detail is omitted in order to speed up the model. In contrast, paging functions must be modeled in greater detail, since their operation is crucial from a system performance point of view.

Modeling virtual and real memory. In modeling the VS2-2 functional flow, it was essential to simulate the virtual/real storage relationship. Therefore, a simulation technique was required to represent multiple virtual memories and real storage page frames.

At model initialization, a CSS entity is created for each frame (4K) of real storage allotted for paging. A table is created for each active virtual memory (initiator/TSO user), with an entry for each virtual page of that memory. The page frame entities and virtual memory tables are then the basic elements manipulated by the model.

As illustrated in Figure 3, briefly stated:

1. Each virtual memory is represented by a REFTL (a CSS entity, short for "reference table"). There is an entry in the REFTL for each virtual page. Each entry contains flag bits to characterize the page states and a page frame number field for associating a valid virtual page with a real frame.

2. NOTEs (another CSS entity) are used to represent real core page frames because they can be queued and because queuing statistics are automatically kept by CSS. A NOTE contains paging status and the virtual address, which is virtual memory identification, and an offset entry number of the virtual page in the assigned memory.

3. For each virtual memory, a NOTE entity--the address space control block (ASCB)--is used as the memory descriptor and queue anchor. The ASCB NOTEs exist on a system ASCB queue (as tasks were queued in MVT).

The paging process is triggered by the time handling mechanism (associated with a CSS PROCESS statement) of the model. This portion of the model was designed to enable the requestor of modeled CPU time to specify the relationship between a time interval T and a set of pages X_i referenced during the time interval.

In the most general case, two random variables based on statistical distributions are used to generate the sequence of page sets corresponding to a 10 msec subinterval T_i of T. For each interval T_i, the first variable is used to define N, the size of X_i; the second variable is then used N times to define the members of X_i (Figure 4). This set X_i will be the pages referenced for interval T_i.

As a first approximation, these variables were defined on a system-wide basis to provide a statistical approximation of the real page reference patterns. Later, for several kinds of job steps and TSO sessions, problem program paging reference patterns were obtained experimentally and reduced to statistical distribution patterns for a more refined approximation.

Tracing Inputs to the Model

In the implementation of the trace mechanism (see Figure 5), the job or jobstream is run on an OS/MVT system with the Generalized Trace Facility (GTF) active for tracing at least the dispatcher and SVC system events.[10]

The trace tape produced is then edited by the filter program, which retains only the problem program state SVC events (that is, SVCs issued by a problem program) and problem program execution time events, then transforms them into formatted records that can be read by the application program model. Each job step is represented by a "job step profile" consisting of a series of ordered records in the profile library. The application program model reads the job step profiles. The job steps are executed (modeled) in a sequence determined by the scheduler portion of the control program model and by the model JCL input. (See Figure 1.)

It was mentioned earlier that application programs rely on control program services and on access methods to transfer data between external and main storage. Ideally, therefore, tracing should have taken place at the access method interface; that is, the trace should have recorded all READ, WRITE macros issued by application programs. (See Figure 1.) In the actual tracing implementation, tracing took place at the EXCP level; the access method functions were assumed to be part of the application program. This caused major difficulties in the model validation.

Model Validation

A simulation model is of little use for prediction unless it is validated. Validation of an operating system model means that key parameters are represented within well-defined error ranges. Validation is a systematic and long process.[11]

Complete validation of the model must await the availability of the mature VS2-2 system. The validation performed so far could be described as a first-level validation effort. In the process, we have tried to assure that the model is structurally sound, that it correctly represents the functional flow of OS/VS2-2. Since the model output represents performance projection, it was essential that this numerical performance projection be checked for "reasonableness." Gross extremes in the performance numbers obtained in the model, such as very high CPU channel or device utilizations, had to be checked carefully and their cause corrected if, as usually was the case, the extremes were due to modeling errors.

Structural validation. Since the model was built concurrently with the real system, a close working relationship had to be maintained with system component designers and developers. In this way, the component models were changed as their design evolved. In fact, the process of evolution was due in part to design changes suggested by the model itself.

The modeling function had to be coupled with an instruction count required for the execution of the function in the real world. (The instruction count translates into CPU time when a given CPU model with a specific instruction execution rate is assumed.) These instruction counts were obtained from developers, estimates, measurements of similar functions in OS/VS2-1, and instruction counts in available OS/VS2-2 code and were upgraded as more precise information became available.

Numerical validation. There were two alternatives for validating the model, using synthetic or real jobs. The advantage of simple synthetic jobs is that they can be easily coded and modeled, using event-driven simulation. Real jobs must be traced on a real system and the trace used in the model. In either case, measurements must be made on the real system and compared with modeling results, the cause of discrepancies identified and eliminated.

Trace-drive validation was chosen primarily so that the model could be used to project the performance of the real jobstreams. This was a major cause of our validation problems because of the limitations of the tracing approach.

Because there was neither a VS2-2 prototype nor running VS2-2 code against which measurements could be made, the basic premise for validation was to evaluate figures for "reasonableness." This was done by comparing the model results with OS/VS2-1 measurements. Discrepancies in the figures were explained in terms of differences between the operating systems or were corrected by changes in the model.

Validation was performed against batch jobstreams and TSO sessions. Since the multiprogramming environment on the measured OS/VS2 Release 1 is significantly different from the modeled OS/VS2 Release 2, only single initiator, uniprogramming environments were measured and modeled. It was believed that in such a sterile environment operating systems could be most directly compared and problems most easily identified and resolved.

Data available for comparison included elapsed time, CPU supervisor state busy time, CPU problem program state busy time, bytes transferred across the channels, channel utilization, number and type of SVCs, and SVC sequence.

Problems encountered during validation and remedial actions taken. The process of validation identified many problems which were then eliminated. The following were some of the key problems encountered.

- The use of multiple scratch packs made measurements nearly unrepeatable. Therefore, instead single scratch pack environments were measured and modeled.

- Discrepancies between modeled and measured results were reduced when scratch datasets were specifically allocated on the device used in the model to reflect the measured configuration.

- In the real system, EXCPs were sometimes followed by WAITs if the I/O device to be used was busy. Thus, the model had to reflect an appropriate ratio of WAITs to EXCPs, since only EXCPs appeared in the trace. Several adjustments were made in the model and ultimately logic was modeled to resemble the access method logic in the control program. Access method level tracing and modeling would have eliminated this problem.

- Since the trace data did not contain information about the number of bytes transferred, the blocksizes used, and the actual location of retrieved blocks on the direct access devices, these input parameters had to be adjusted experimentally. The adjustments included variations in blocksizes used and in specific allocation of datasets.

- The modeled problem program time had to be adjusted repeatedly to reflect the measured problem program time. This discrepancy was due to a shortcoming of the trace mechanism because tracing overhead was included in the problem program time recorded. The measured problem program times were adjusted by calculating and removing tracing overhead.

- The size and direct access residence location of the operating system modules loaded into main storage turned out to be an unanticipated but significant performance factor. Adjustment to the model was made by adding a detailed representation of the operating system fetching function.

- Discrepancies in measured and modeled SVC counts and sequences had to be accounted for. (Some SVCs considered of small significance were not modeled.) An apparent major discrepancy between measured and modeled results was in the number of GETMAIN/FREEMAIN and MODESET SVCs executed in the control program itself. In fact, the OS/VS2-2 control program was designed to reduce the number of these SVCs; thus part of the discrepancy could be and was attributed to differences between OS/VS2-1 measured and OS/VS2-2 modeled. Another source of the discrepancy was insufficient detail level in parts of the model, which were modeled in a gross fashion; i.e., some SVCs in these paths were omitted. The most appropriate remedy would have been more detailed modeling representation. Since this approach was not practical, a compromise had to be chosen which consisted of representing supervisory overhead associated with the paths not modeled in detail without representing every actual SVC issued.

Validation results. To illustrate the final results of the validation work, three tables are presented, with validation results:

Table 1 compares measured and modeled SVC counts for a particular job, JOB3. The table lists SVCs issued by the problem program and by the system itself. The table shows that most of the major SVCs were modeled (EXCP, WAIT, EXIT, LINK, XCTL, LOAD, DELETE, OPEN, CLOSE, GETMAIN/FREEMAIN). Since the frequency of their occurrence is much smaller in the real system, it was not considered necessary to model such SVCs as TIME, SYNCH, SPIE, and PURGE. The discrepancy in the number of GETMAIN/FREEMAINs and the lack of modeled MODESET SVCs have already been explained partly by the differences in the modeled and measured systems, partly by lack of detail in some cases. The model contains more OPEN/CLOSE SVCs than the real system because multiple dataset OPEN/CLOSE SVCs were not modeled and were replaced with single dataset OPEN/CLOSE SVCs.

Table 2 compares measured and modeled statistics in a single initiator environment. The measured and modeled numbers show reasonable correspondence. The model inputs, problem program busy time, and count of bytes transmitted are very close to the measured statistics. The model outputs such as supervisory busy time and elapsed times show close correlation to the measured figures. These results indicate that the corrections and adjustments described above have in fact eliminated most discrepancies in the model representation. Some unexplained discrepancies (such as problem program busy time for JOB1, STEP5) still remain, however.

Table 3 compares measured and modeled statistics for a TSO session. Again, the numbers appear reasonable. In the TSO environment, however, the impact of the SVCs not modeled was higher than in the batch environment, which is manifested in the modeled supervisory instruction count being significantly lower than the measured count. Consequently, TSO projections were optimistic in omitting some operating system overhead. The TSO results indicate that more model detail would have to be present for an accurate representation of the TSO environment.

Table 1. Comparison of measured and modeled SVC counts for JOB3
STEP1

| | ATTACH TO DETACH | | | |
| | Total Count | | Problem Program Count | |
SVC	VS2-1	VS2-2 Model	VS2-1	VS2-2 Model
EXCP/EXCPVR	219	305	47	88
WAIT	426	291	30	22
POST	3	–	–	–
EXIT	502	343	20	8
GETMAIN/FREEMAIN	427	85	2	2
LINK	8	8	8	8
XCTL	191	200	–	–
LOAD	54	44	–	–
DELETE	54	44	–	–
TIME	4	–	1	–
SYNCH	11	–	–	–
SPIE	2	–	2	–
PURGE	19	–	–	–
OPEN	4	12	4	12
CLOSE	4	15	4	15
CLOSET	5	–	5	–
DEVTYPE	4	–	4	–
TRKBAL	7	–	7	–
WTO	3	–	–	–
TTIMER	1	–	1	–
STIMER	1	–	1	–
DLQ	3	–	–	–
EOV	8	–	8	0
ENQ	3	–	–	–
CHATR	5	–	–	–
STATUS	1	–	1	–
XQMNGR	5	–	–	–
MODESET	310	–	–	–
ESR	63	–	–	–
Totals	2037	1347	145	105

Table 2. Comparison of measured and modeled statistics for a batch jobstream run in single initiator environment on VS2-1 system and VS2-2 model

	Elapsed Time (secs)		Supervisor Busy Time (secs)		Problem Program Busy Time (secs)		Channel Busy Time (secs)		Bytes Transmitted (thousands)	
	VS2-1	VS2-2 Model	VS2-1	VS2-2 Model	VS2-1	VS2-2 Model	VS2-1	VS2-2 Model	VS2-1	VS2-2 Model
JOB1										
STEP1	14.87	15.94	4.56	5.86	5.30	4.87	3.06	1.80	802	742
STEP2	2.24	1.73	.86	.73	.22	.17	.46	.32	171	104
STEP3	11.32	11.71	3.09	4.20	1.79	1.76	1.72	4.43	425	414
STEP4	29.52	31.86	9.23	10.39	2.57	2.59	7.25	7.55	1863	1779
STEP5	14.69	15.52	9.42	5.82	9.30	4.63	3.04	1.72	706	722
STEP6	1.98	1.67	.80	.73	.22	.15	.45	.31	114	104
JOB2										
STEP1	22.42	23.04	5.52	6.87	4.22	4.36	2.15	7.47	469	451
STEP2	36.79	38.20	8.81	11.37	1.49	1.73	3.68	7.00	824	798
STEP3	17.04	18.49	5.14	5.77	2.00	2.04	1.56	3.70	282	264
STEP4	21.81	24.96	5.39	6.61	1.69	1.70	2.42	3.75	595	576
STEP5	41.74	42.12	9.26	11.26	2.46	2.68	4.38	10.50	1131	1115
JOB3										
STEP1	10.18	7.93	3.19	3.63	.72	.66	5.13	1.02	580	559
STEP2	1.83	1.23	.72	.61	.11	.11	.65	.17	106	98
STEP3	53.13	30.27	7.52	9.41	.41	.43	2.11	10.35	274	327
JOB4										
STEP1	4.49	4.17	.81	.97	2.91	2.27	.52	.22	125	115
STEP2	3.77	3.67	1.33	1.33	1.06	1.07	.64	.27	78	115
JOB5										
STEP1	13.67	11.70	4.05	4.47	1.04	1.47	3.01	3.39	383	283
STEP2	7.56	4.96	2.48	2.16	.16	.30	2.46	.88	297	190

Table 3. Comparison of measured and modeled statistics for TSO SCRIPT run on VS2-1 system and VS2-2 model

	Measured on VS2-1	Modeled by VS2-2 Model
Elapsed time	776.66 sec	739.76 sec
CPU busy %	20.42	15.55
Supervisor busy %	18.02	12.89
Problem program busy %	2.34	2.66
Supervisor instructions	10.37 M	7.86 M
Bytes transferred	1262 K	490 K
Channel busy time	10.46 sec	1.26 sec
Response time	1.09 sec	.69 sec

Validation summary. In summary, the following validation steps were performed:

1. Structural validation. Model paths were carefully checked and adjusted to assure that the flow paths were functionally correctly represented and that instruction counts were accurately included. In addition, the dynamic behavior of the model was examined repeatedly to see whether it corresponded to the expected behavior of OS/VS2 Release 2.

2. Tracing technology validation. Both the tracing programs and the model were refined until the modeled problem program time, EXCP count, SVC counts, and count of bytes transferred matched the measured counts, or until the deviations were considered generally either insignificant or explainable.

3. Numerical validation. The model projections of elapsed times, supervisor busy time, and channel busy times were checked against OS/VS2-1 measurements. When no further gross discrepancies were found for the jobstream and the TSO sessions modeled, the first-level validation was completed.

The validation process showed that many of the validation problems arose because of inadequate level of detail in the modeling representation. Thus the validation difficulties illustrated the difficulty of determining the required modeling level prior to the actual implementation. Therefore the conclusion was inevitable that in a large simulation project either most parts of the system must be modeled in great detail initially or subsequently significant resources must be devoted to corrections in the implemented level of detail. A fuller conclusion is that model validation is a long, arduous, iterative process which is usually underestimated in difficulty and in resources.

Desirable additional validation. The model can be validated against the mature OS/VS2-2 system. In this case structural validation must be repeated and numerical validation performed against the real system. Structural validation and single initiator measurements would yield second-level validation, while measurement of a complex multi-initiator, multi-terminal environment would yield third-level validation.

Conclusion

A brief description of a model of OS/VS2 Release 2 has been presented. The project has proved that though it is possible to create a model of a yet-unbuilt operating system, it is a difficult and complicated process. In addition to dealing with the customary program bugs, the modelers must work in a continuously changing design environment.

A first-level validation effort was fairly successful. Through structural and numerical validation, model discrepancies were discovered and corrected until performance projections for the single initiator (uniprogramming) environment appeared reasonable. This scheme allowed use of the model for performance projections in a multi-initiator (multiprogramming) environment.

REFERENCES

1. A fairly complete bibliography of non-IBM literature is provided in H. C. Lucas, Jr., Performance Evaluation and Testing (ACM Computing Surveys, Vol. 3, No. 3, Sept. 1971). See also bibliography in "Techniques of Computer Performance: Analysis," Computers (IEEE Computer Society, Sept./Oct. 1972), pp. 35-67.

2. Thomas A. Byrne, Alan V. Piercey, and Frank L. Myers, "Prototype II: A Job Selection Model," Proceedings of Symposium on the Simulation of Computer Systems, ACM/SIGSIM (June 1973), pp. 3-14.

3. Arthur C. Traub, Jr. and William F. Zachman, "A GPSS Model of a Complex On-Line Computer System," Proceedings, pp. 17-37.

4. P. H. Seaman and R. C. Soucy, "Simulating Operating Systems," IBM Systems Journal, Vol. 8, No. 4 (1969), pp. 264-279.

5. Houston Operation Simulations Technique, User's Guide, IBM FSD, Houston (Feb. 1971).

6. Computer System Simulation II (CSS/II) Program Description and Operations Manual, IBM Form SH20-0875.

7. S. W. Sherman and J. C. Browne, "Trace-Driven Modeling: Review and Overview," Proceedings, pp. 201-207.

8. Thomas Beretvas, "System-Independent Tracing for Prediction of System Performance," Proceedings, pp. 209-213.

9. IBM System/360 Operating System Concepts and Facilities, IBM Form GC28-6535.

10. IBM System/360 Operating System Service Aids, Generalized Trace Facility, IBM Form C28-6719.

11. M. Beilner and G. Waldbaum, "Statistical Methodology for Calibrating a Trace-Driven Simulator of a Batch Computer System," IBM Technical Report RC 3855 (IBM Research, Yorktown Heights, N.Y., May 1973).

GLOSSARY OF ACRONYMS

ASCB	Address space control block
CPU	Central processing unit
CSS	Computer systems simulator language
GTF	Generalized trace facility
JCL	Job control language
LPA	Link pack area
OS/360	Operating System/360
MVT	Multiple variable tasks
REFTL	Reference table
SQA	System queue area
SVC	Supervisory call
TSO	Time Sharing Option
VS2	Virtual Storage Version 2
VS2-1	Virtual Storage Version 2 Release 1
VS2-2	Virtual Storage Version 2 Release 2

Figure 1. User interfaces with the operating system control program

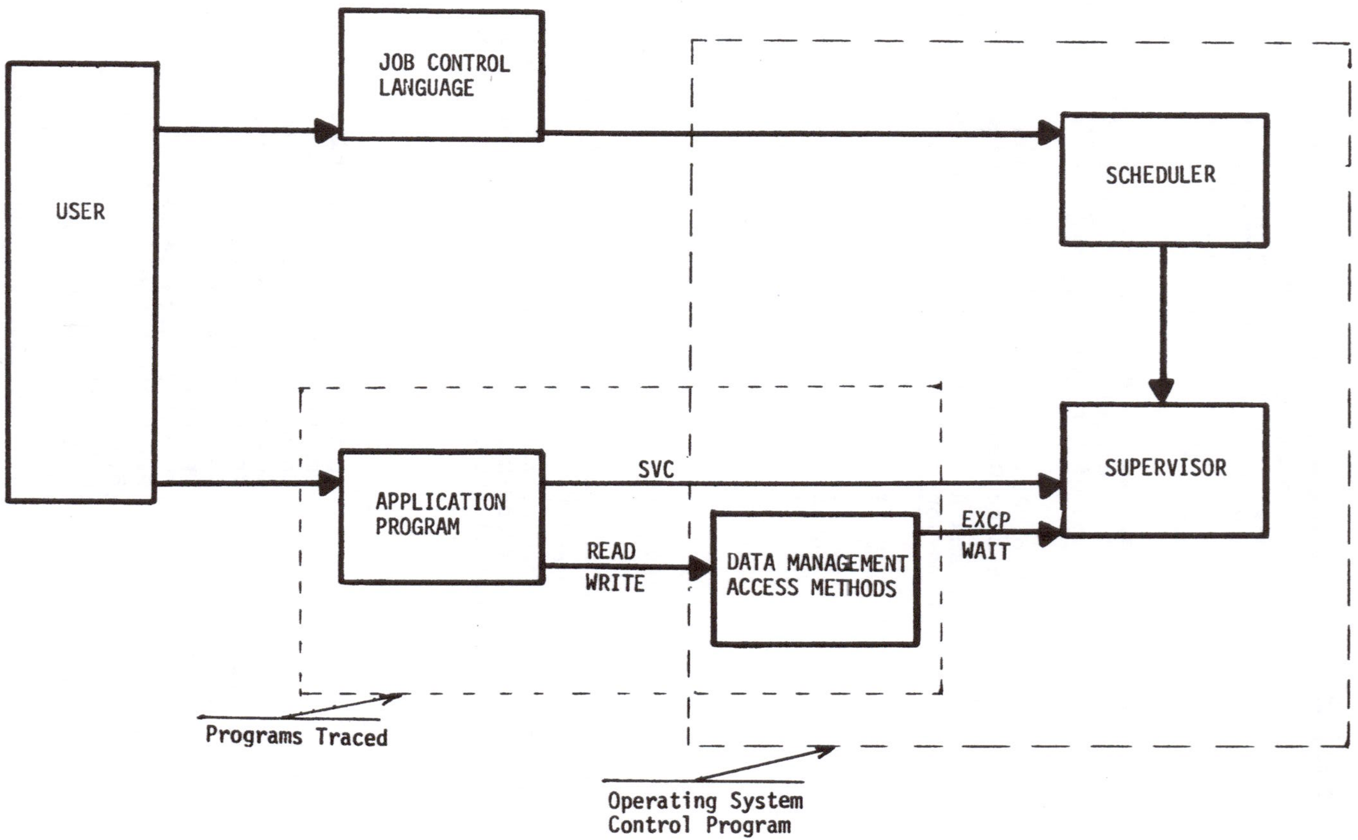

Figure 2. Model interfaces

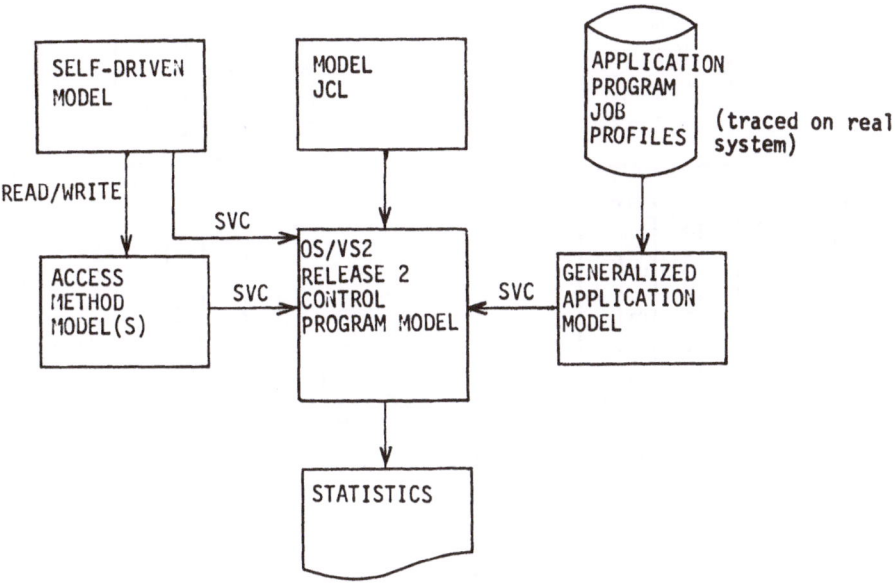

28

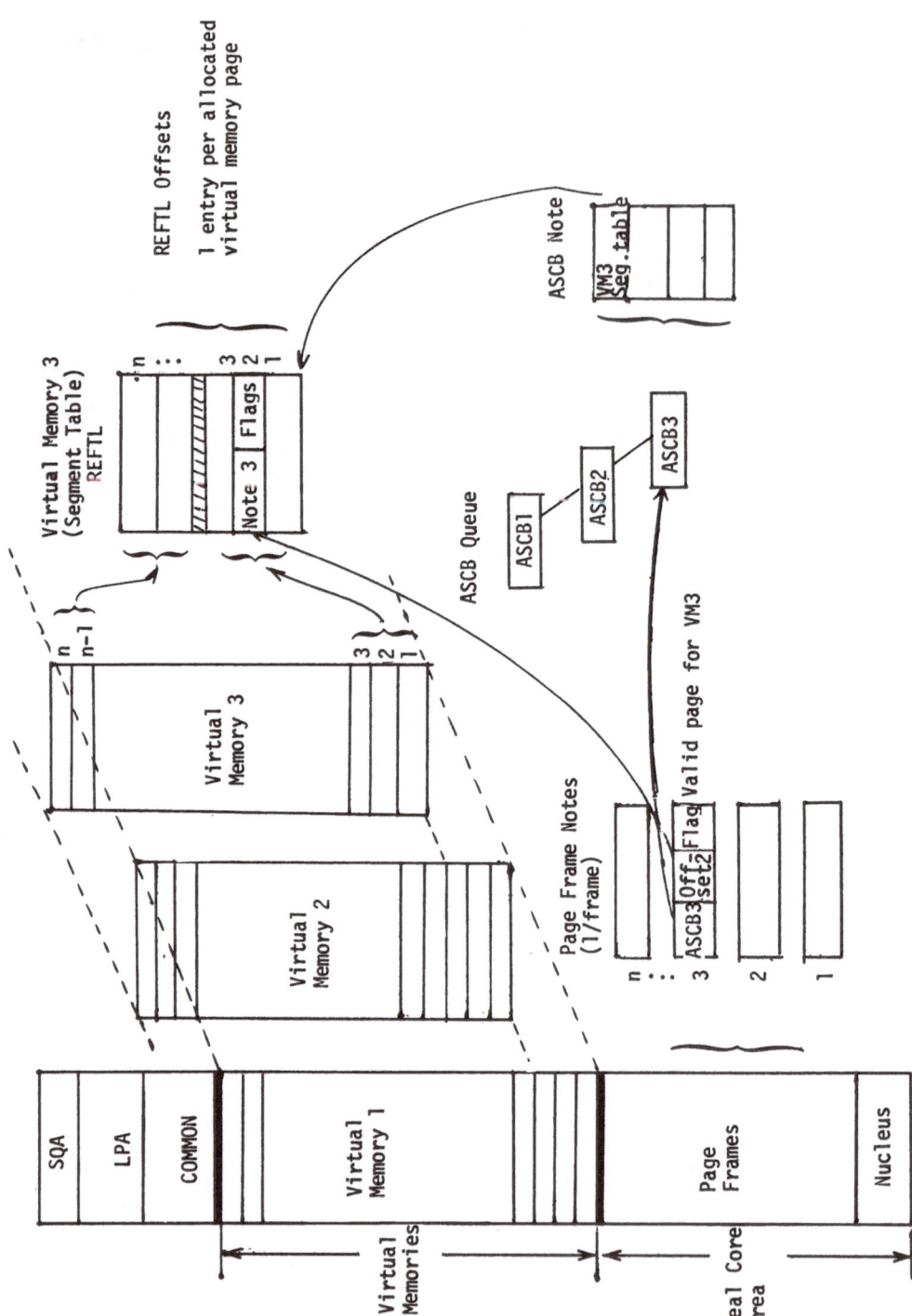

Figure 3. Virtual memory representation in the model

Figure 4. Paging variables

TIME INTERVAL T

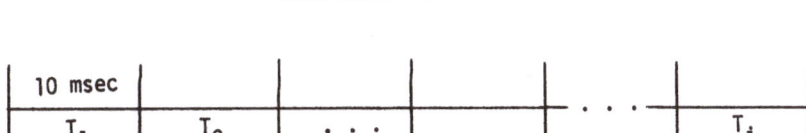

To determine the set of pages X_i, referenced in time interval T_i, two variables are evaluated:

   Variable 1: Number of pages referenced = N, the size of X_i

   Variable 2: Virtual address of page referenced, variable used N
            times to determine the members of X_i

Figure 5. Trace profile construction and use

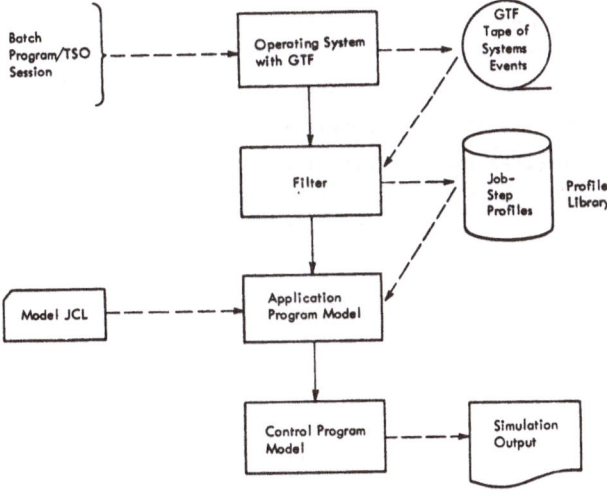

UNE ANALYSE DE SYSTEME PAR TYPOLOGIE

D. Borrione
ENSIMAG, Grenoble

I - INTRODUCTION

Il est courant, lors de la conception d'un système batch fonctionnant en multiprogrammation (OS, SIRIS 7, etc...) de prévoir des classes d'utilisateurs. On distingue ainsi, par exemple, les programmes qui sont essentiellement consommateurs de mémoire centrale de ceux dont la caractéristiques est de demander un temps de calcul important, ou de ceux qui font surtout beaucoup d'entrées-sorties. L'utilisateur déclare à quelle classe son programme appartient (des classes par défaut sont parfois prévues) et le système, dans la mesure du possible, charge en mémoire simultanément des programmes de classes différentes, dans le but d'optimiser l'utilisation des ressources de l'installation. Notons cependant la vulnerabilité de cette politique, qui n'est efficace que dans la mesure où l'utilisateur ne se trompe pas, ou ne tente pas de tricher.

De même, dans les systèmes conversationnels, on divise souvent les utilisateurs en deux groupes : les interactifs, qui dialoguent fréquemment avec l'ordinateur, et que l'on cherche à favoriser, et les non interactifs, considérés comme moins prioritaires. Ainsi, dans le système CP/CMS que nous avons analysé, et dont nous reparlerons plus loin, après toute entrée-sortie à sa console, l'utilisateur est considéré comme interactif. Ce n'est qu'après épuisement du premier quantum de temps que l'utilisateur change de groupe, s'il n'a pas provoqué de réponse à son terminal. Il est donc possible, là aussi, de tricher, en créant des entrées-sorties parasites qui permettent de rester dans le groupe le plus prioritaire.

Partant de cet état de fait, notre but était de trouver un critère objectif de classement. Nous nous sommes attachés à mettre en lumière non pas des types d'utilisateurs (car ces types peuvent varier rapidement dans le temps) mais des types de commandes du système, qui sont caractéristiques du système lui-même, et ne changent que si l'on réécrit des composants de celui-ci.

Les commande dont dispose un utilisateur sont généralement réparties en catégories logiques (14) :
- manipulations de fichiers
- éditions de fichiers
- assemblages et compilations
- chargements, mises au point et exécutions
-divers.

Nous avons, pour notre part, cherché à classer les commandes en fonction des ressources qu'elles utilisent. L'intérêt d'un tel mode de regroupement est double :
- intérêt explicatif : d'après les groupes obtenus, on sait quelles commandes mettent en jeu les mêmes ressources, ou des quantités analogues de certaines ressources.
- intérêt prédictif : lorsqu'un utilisateur frappe un nom de commande, le système s'il a été conçu dans cette optique, sait à priori quelles ressources seront nécessaires à la satisfaction de cette commande, et peut en tenir compte pour la gestion des files d'attente du "dispatcher".

Pour réaliser ce travail, il nous fallait disposer de mesures sur les commandes du système étudié. Puis considérant une commande comme un point dans un espace à n dimensions, nous devions définir sur le nuage de points une métrique intéressante, et un algorithme de regroupement. Nous avons choisi d'appliquer une méthode statistique, à ce jour peut utilisée en informatique : la typologie.

II - ALGORITHMES DE TYPOLOGIE

Au cours des dix dernières années, de nombreuses techniques de typologie ont été développées. Nous en avons expérimenté deux, sous forme de deux programmes écrits en Fortran, que des modifications mineures ont permis d'adapter à nos données.

Le premier, écrit par Monsieur FAGES, de l'Université de Lyon 1, est basé sur l'optimisation d'un critère d'agrégation des classes. Aucune documentation n'est malheureusement parue, à ce jour, expliquant en détail l'algorithme utilisé. Nous nous contenterons donc d'en exposer brièvement le principe en A.

Le second, dont l'auteur est Monsieur DIDAY, de L'IRIA, repose sur un algorithme qui sera développé au paragraphe B.

A - LE PROGRAMME DE FAGES

1) Introduction

Soit E un ensemble fini d'objets à classer. Card (E) = Imax.

Soit P l'ensemble des parties de E.

Chaque élément de E est défini par Jmax paramètres réels.
$$E \subset R^{Jmax}$$
$$\forall \ x \ \epsilon \ E, \ x = (x_1, \ x_2, \ldots \ x_{Jmax})$$
On cherche une partition de E en Kmax classes, qui possède les propriétés suivantes :

- les objets d'une même classe se ressemblent le plus possible, au sens du problème posé.

- les objets de deux classes différentes se ressemblent le moins possible.

Un critère donnant une valeur à chaque partition traduit les propriétés précédentes.

La méthode consistera, à partir d'une partition donnée, à en trouver une "voisine" qui ait une meilleure valeur.

On itère cette opération tant qu'elle est possible, ce qui conduit à un optimum local selon le voisinage considéré.

Les caractéristiques principales de ce programme sont de :

- chercher des partitions dont le nombre de classes est croissant (au sens large).

- progresser suivant un ordre assez "économique".

2) Notations

On notera :

L_k l'ensemble des partitions de E en k classes.

l_k un élément de L_k : $l_k = (C_1, C_2, \ldots C_k)$.

Soit x un élément de E. On dira que deux partitions de E en k classes l_k et l_k' sont voisines par déplacement de x si on passe de l'une à l'autre en changeant de classe l'élément x au plus.

Soit G le critère d'agrégation des classes que la typologie doit optimiser
$$G : \bigcup_{k=1}^{Kmax} L_K \rightarrow \mathbb{R}^+$$

On définit une transformation par
$$Z_K : E \ x \ L_K \rightarrow L_K$$

$\qquad (x, \ l_k) \rightarrow l_k'$ voisine de l_k par déplacement de x

avec $G(l_k') = \max (G(l_k''))$

$\qquad\qquad\qquad l_k''$ voisine de l_k par déplacement de x.

Z_K est la transformation qui, pour un élément x de E fixé, fait correspondre à la partition de départ, la "meilleure" partition (pour le critère G) obtenue en déplaçant au plus l'élément x.

3) L'algorithme

L'algorithme est basé sur l'heuristique suivante :
- on procède par itérations, en partageant l'ensemble E en deux, puis trois, jusqu'à Kmax classes.
- a chaque étape, pour un nombre k de classes fixé, on parcourt successivement tous les éléments de E, en cherchant pour la partition courante, sa meilleure voisine par déplacement de l'élément considéré.

On construit donc une suite l_k^1, l_k^2,... l_k^m vérifiant $l_k^i = Z_k(j, l_k^{i-1})$ avec j = i-1 modulo Imax.
- lorsqu'on a parcouru une fois entière l'ensemble E sans déplacer d'éléments, c'est à dire lorsqu'on a obtenu la partition l_k^m telle que :
$$\forall \ x \ \epsilon \ E, \ Z_k \ (x, \ l_k^m) = l_k^m$$

On a trouvé un optimum local, au sens du voisinage défini ci-dessus. On augmente alors de un le nombre de classes.

4) Remarques

L'impression de la valeur $G(l_k)$, à chaque itération, permet de sélectionner le nombre de classes le mieux adapté au nuage de points considéré.

On choisit le nombre de classes à partir duquel la création d'une classe supplémentaire cesse d'induire une augmentation sensible du critère.

L'algorithme est très efficace, car de nombreux calculs intermédiaires ne sont effectués qu'une fois. D'autre part, on obtient directement la typologie demandée, même si l'on n'a à priori aucune indication sur le nombre et la forme des classes.

La méthode a cependant l'inconvénient de faire d'un point isolé une classe à lui seul.

La version du programme que nous avons expérimentée ne permettait de faire qu'une typologie selon distance euclidienne. Nous avons donc complété notre étude grâce au programme de M. DIDAY.

Il se peut que les deux remarques ci-dessus soient caduques. Nous avons appris, en cours de rédaction de cet article, qu'une version améliorée du programme de M. FAGES venait d'être écrite.

B - LA METHODE DES "NUEES DYNAMIQUES" (3,5)

1) Notations

Reprenons les notations du chapitre précédent : $E \subset R^{Jmax}$: ensemble des objets à classer. Card (E) = I max.

K max : nombre de classes désirées. On appellera étalons d'une classe l'ensemble des éléments les plus représentatifs de cette classe.

On suppose qu'au départ, les éléments sont rangés dans un certain ordre. E sera représenté par la matrice T. T(i,j) est la valeur du jième paramètre pour le ième objet. Dans la suite, on confondra un élément de E avec son rang dans T.

Soit C_K la Kième classe dans E, et m_k le nombre d'étalons de C_K.

On notera : étal (i) : le numéro de l'objet, parmi les Imax de E, qui est le ième étalon de C_K.

L'algorithme fait intervenir trois fonctions :

- $d : E \times E \rightarrow \mathbb{R}^+$

d est une distance entre éléments de E, par exemple la distance euclidienne, la distance du Khi2, la somme des valeurs absolue de la différence entre les coordonnées des deux éléments etc...

- $D : E \times P \rightarrow \mathbb{R}^+$

D est une distance entre un élément de E et un sous-ensemble de E. Le choix de D dépend de celui de d.

Par exemple, si d est la distance euclidienne, on prendra :

$$\forall i \in E, \forall C_K \subset E, D(i,C_K) = \sum_{1}^{m_k} \sum_{j=1}^{Jmax} (T(i,j) - T(\text{étal}(1),j))^2$$

- une fonction d'agrégation-écartement R définie de la façon suivante :

Soit I = {1,2... Kmax} l'ensemble des numéros des classes, et m l'application qui, à chaque numéro de classe, fait correspondre le nombre d'étalons fixé pour cette classe.

$m : I \rightarrow N$

$\qquad K \rightarrow m (k) = m_k$

Si $L_{Kmax, m}$ représente l'ensemble des répartitions possibles des étalons dans les Kmax classes, pour une application m donnée, on aura :

$R : E \times I \times L_{Kmax, m} \rightarrow \mathbb{R}^+$

R dépend de la distance D.

Etant donnée une classe C_k, les éléments les plus représentatifs de C_K sont ceux qui minimisent R.

Exemple :

$$\forall i \in E, \forall k \in I, \forall L \in L_{Kmax, m}, R(i,k,L) = D(i,C_k)$$

2) L'algorithme

a) - lecture des données :

- le tableau $T(i,j)$, $(i = 1,...\ Imax; j = 1...\ Jmax)$ $T(i,j)$ étant la valeur du jième paramètre pour le ième objet.

- Kmax le nombre de classes que l'on veut former

- les nombres m_k d'étalons par classe

- la liste des étalons, si on connaît à priori la forme des classes. Sinon, les étalons sont tirés au hasard.

On a donc une répartition $L = (E_1, E_2, ... E_{Kmax})$

- la distance d choisie.

b) - on calcule la distance de chaque élément à l'ensemble des étalons de chaque classe.

$D(i, C_k)$ $(i=1,..., Imax; k = 1,...\ Kmax)$

c) - on forme les classes

L'élément i est rangé dans la classe dont il est le plus proche

$i \in C_k \iff \forall k' \in \{1,...\ Kmax\}$, $k' \neq k$, $D(i, C_k) < D(i, C_{k'})$.

d) - pour chaque classe C_k, on calcule $R(i,k,L)$.

e) - pour chaque classe C_k, on cherche l'ensemble E_k' des nouveaux étalons. Ce sont les m objets qui rendent R minimum.

f) - si les étalons n'ont pas changé, c'est à dire si

$\forall k \in \{1,2,...\ Kmax\}$, $E_k = E_k'$

la convergence est atteinte. On va en h, sinon on va en g.

g) - on remplace l'ancienne répartition L d'étalons par la nouvelle.

$\forall k \in \{1,2,...\ Kmax\}$ $E_k \leftarrow E_k'$

On va en b.

h) - fin.

3) Remarques

E. DIDAY (5) a établi une condition nécessaire de convergence du processus, portant sur une propriété de la fonction R. En pratique, l'algorithme converge généralement, et de manière rapide. Sur nos données, pour 146 points, la convergence est atteinte après un nombre d'itérations variant entre 3 et 8, suivant le tirage au hasard des étalons de départ.

Le choix des étalons initiaux peut être déterminant pour la partition finale, la convergence étant atteinte pour un optimum local de la suite L des répartitions, qui n'est pas nécessairement l'optimum absolu. Il est donc nécessaire, dans le cas où l'on n'a aucune information sur la typologie à obtenir, de procéder à plusieurs tirages aléatoires des étalons.

Si,quel que soit le tirage des étalons, un groupe d'objets se trouve tou-jours dans une même classe, celui-ci est appelé "forme forte". Ces formes fortes sont en fait l'un des résultats les plus significatifs du programme de typolo-gie. En particulier, elles aident l'expérimentateur à fixer le nombre de classes qui décrivent le mieux l'ensemble considéré.

Si le nombre Kmax est supérieur au nombre de classes qui existent effecti-vement, l'algorithme forme des classes vides.

III - APPLICATION AU SYSTEME CP-CMS

1) Introduction

Le système CP, fonctionnant sur IBM 360/67 est un système à partage de temps qui simule pour chaque utilisateur un ordinateur IBM 360 classique. Ainsi, l'utilisateur dispose d'un certain nombre de ressources partagées (unité de cal-cul, mémoire centrale), simulées (pupitre opérateur : son propre terminal, lec-teur de carte, imprimante) ou lui appartenant en propre en permanence (cylindres de disque) ou temporairement (dérouleurs de bandes magnétiques). Cependant, tout se passe pour lui comme s'il possédait son propre calculateur, sur lequel il peut installer le système de son choix.

Prévu pour être implanté sur ces ordinateurs simulés, le système CMS offre à l'utilisateur une soixantaine de commandes lui permettant, de manière conver-sationnelle, de modifier des fichiers, faire compiler ses programmes, les exécu-ter, les mettre au point etc...

Pour éviter toute ambiguité, nous appellerons ordre l'envoi, à partir d'un terminal, d'un nom de commande (suivi d'un certain nombre de paramètres, selon le cas). Ainsi, si un utilisateur compile séparément deux programmes fortran, il frappera deux fois la même commande : FORTRAN, mais ce seront pour le système deux ordres différents.

Jacques LEROUDIER a réalisé un outil permettant de recueillir, pour chaque ordre émis par un utilisateur à son terminal, les renseignements suivants :

- nom de la machine virtuelle émettrice
- nom de la commande
- nombre d'E/S disque
- nombre d'E/S console
- nom et type du fichier concerné
- longueur du fichier s'il y a lieu
- temps CMS (temps d'exécution sur un calculateur véritable)

- temps CP+CMS (temps tenant compte de l'overhead de simulation des ressources).
- temps passé par l'utilisateur devant sa console
- indication d'erreur, ou non, pour la commande
- nombre d'utilisateurs sur le système
- fichier existant, ou en création (pour la commande EDIT)
- niveau de récursion de la commande (CMS permet de définir des macro-commandes).

Deux prises de mesures sur ce système ont permis d'obtenir un échantillon de 60.000 ordres. Il n'était cependant pas possible de faire directement une typologie sur cet échantillon, pour les raisons suivantes :

- les paramètres ne sont pas de même nature : noms, booléens, nombres
- le temps d'exécution de l'algorithme croît très vite avec le nombre de points à classer (il est proportionnel à $Imax^P$, $1 < P < 2$).
- l'encombrement en mémoire centrale pour la partie "donnée" du programme FORTRAN, compté en cellules mémoire nécessaires au codage des nombres réels, est de l'ordre de :

    Imax x Jmax + 5. Imax pour le programme de DIDAY.

    Imax x Jmax + 2. Imax + (Jmax + 2) x Kmax pour le programme de FAGES.

Deux travaux préliminaires ont donc dû être effectués :
- une réduction des données
- un choix des variables explicatives servant de coordonnées aux points.

2) Réduction des données

De l'ensemble E des 60.000 ordres dont nous disposons, nous avons déduit un ensemble F de moins de 150 points. Chaque élément de F est le barycentre d'un groupe d'ordres portant sur le même nom de commande, par rapport à des paramètres choisis. Ce barycentre est obtenu par programme, après avoir procédé à une typologie partielle sur tous les ordres invoquant la commande considérée.

Lorsqu'une commande a été mise trop peu de fois pour qu'une typologie soit significative, un seul point représente cette commande.

Certaines commandes ne retournent jamais de code d'erreur. Pour les autres, nous avons toujours traité séparément celles qui s'étaient déroulées normalement de celles qui avaient renvoyé un code d'erreur.

Ainsi, sur les 60.000 ordres, 969 étaient la commande de compilation FORTRAN. Deux typologies partielles ont permis d'en extraire 7 groupes, représentés dans F par leur barycentre : 4 groupes pour les ordres sans erreur (voir figure 1), 3 pour ceux qui ont retourné un code d'erreur.

Cette réduction de données peut être résumée par les résultats suivants :

- nombre de commandes représentées par un seul point : 25
- nombre de commandes représentées par deux points (fin normale, erreur):18
- nombre de commandes sur lesquelles a porté une typologie partielle : 14
- nombre de points de l'ensemble résultant : 144 pour le premier jeu de paramètres, 146 pour le second (les typologies partielles ont été recommencées lorsque nous avons pris d'autres variables explicatives, et le nombre de groupes représentatifs de chaque commande n'est pas toujours resté identique).

Chaque fois que cela était possible, et avait un sens, nous avons caractérisé les éléments de l'ensemble F par :

- le nom de la commande
- présence ou absence d'une erreur
- longueur du fichier concerné par la commande

Remarques

Nous aurions pû réduire nos données en procédant à un échantillonnage. Nous avons rejeté cette solution pour les raisons suivantes :

- certaines commandes, peu appelées, risquaient de ne pas être représentées.
- l'échantillonnage aurait conservé la disproportion des appels de certaines commandes par rapport à d'autres. Or ce n'était pas la population des utilisateurs du système qui faisait l'objet de cette étude, mais les composants de ce système. Une typologie partielle, au contraire, égalisait la représentation des commandes.
- les résultats d'une typologie partielle permettaient, par eux-mêmes, de mieux comprendre le comportement de la commande à laquelle cette typologie était appliquée.

La méthode que nous avons employée pose cependant un problème théorique en ce qui concerne la typologie selon la distance du khi2. En effet, les typologies partielles et les barycentres des groupes obtenus ont été calculés en utilisant la distance euclidienne (le barycentre d'un nuage de points selon la norme du khi2 n'a pas de signification). C'est grâce à la forme particulière de nos nuages de points, à l'intérieur de chaque commande, que nous avons pû, sans craindre d'obtenir des résultats aberrants par rapport à une typologie qui aurait traité l'ensemble des 60.000 points de départ, appliquer à l'ensemble réduit une typologie selon la norme du khi2. Nous ne pouvons cependant pas justifier cette méthode de façon formelle, pour un nuage de points quelconque.

3) Choix des variables explicatives

Notre but était de caractériser les groupes de commandes par les ressources consommées. Nous disposions donc de mesures sur les ressources suivantes :

- E/S console
- E/S disque
- temps d'unité centrale (temps CP+CMS).

Les intervalles de variation de ces paramètres sont très différents : le nombre d'E/S console est compris entre 0 et 560, le nombre d'E/S disque entre 0 et 6200, le temps d'UC (exprimé en centièmes de secondes) entre 0 et 25600. Une solution consisterait à normaliser ces paramètres, qui serait tout à fait satisfaisante du point de vue statistique, mais qui semble parfaitement arbitraire en ce qui concerne l'interprétation que l'on pourrait donner des résultats. Les échelles doivent donc être choisies en fonction du critère que l'on veut étudier. Par exemple, si l'on cherche à favoriser les commandes très intéractives, comme c'est en général le cas pour les systèmes conversationnels, il faut trouver une unité de temps d'UC compatible avec l'intervalle de variation des E/S console.

Cette étude voulant s'appliquer à un plus large éventail de systèmes, nous avons décidé de considérer les consommations de ressources physiques, en nous appuyant sur des considérations économiques.

Choix de l'unité de temps

Prenons le couple de paramètres temps CP+CMS et nombre d'E/S disque. Ils correspondent aux ressources physiques unité centrale d'une part, unité de contrôle du disque d'autre part. On peut envisager de faire payer à l'utilisateur un prix fixe de location de la portion de disque qui lui est réservée pour ranger ses fichiers permanents. Outre cette location on peut imaginer de facturer non pas (comme cela est pratiqué dans notre centre de calcul pour CP/CMS) le temps d'unité centrale seul, mais toutes les ressources physiques consommées, proportionnellement à leur prix d'achat ou de location.

Dans notre installation, un canal simple est relié à une unité 2314 de 8 disques avec leur unité de contrôle.

Le prix de l'unité centrale est 10 fois celui du canal, qui est lui-même 2 fois celui du disque avec l'unité de contrôle. Le temps moyen d'une E/S disque est t = temps moyen de déplacement du bras

+ temps moyen de recherche sur la piste (durée d'un demi-tour)

+ temps de transfert.

Le temps moyen de déplacement du bras est de 60 millisecondes lorsque les demandes sont uniformément réparties sur le disque. Des mesures sur des systèmes analogues à CP montrent que cette hypothèse n'est pas vérifiée, à cause du faible degré de multiprogrammation par rapport au nombre de disques. Nous prendrons 30 millisecondes pour fixer les idées.

Le disque fait 1 tour en 25 millisecondes. Le délai moyen de positionnement rotationnel est donc 12,5 millisecondes.

Le disque débite à 312 K octets par seconde. CP fait des E/S par blocs de 800 octets. Un transfert dure donc 2,5 millisecondes.

Soit a le prix de la milliseconde de travail de l'unité de contrôle du disque. La milliseconde de travail du canal coûte donc 2a, celle de l'unité centrale 20 a.

Le temps de déplacement du bras n'occupe que le contrôle du disque (coûtant a par milliseconde) alors que les deux temps suivants occupent le contrôle et le canal (coûtant 3a par milliseconde). Le coût d'une E/S disque est donc :

$$C = 30 \times a + (12,5 + 2,5) \times 3 a = 75 a$$

ce qui correspond à un temps de travail de l'unité centrale inférieur à 4 millisecondes.

A titre de comparaison, nous avons refait ce calcul à partir des prix de matériel CII équivalent : unité centrale IRIS 80, disque MD 50, débitant à 312000 octets par seconde, canal double débitant à 800000 octets par seconde. Une E/S disque d'un bloc de 1 K octets coûte autant que 7 millisecondes de travail de l'unité centrale.

Ces chiffres justifient, de notre point de vue économique, le choix d'exprimer le temps CP+CMS en centièmes de seconde. La précision des mesures ne permettait pas de prendre une unité plus petite, ce qui est d'ailleurs sans grande importance, puisque la typologie est déjà terminée par la composante temps d'unité centrale.

Il n'est pas impossible qu'avec l'évolution de la technologie, un autre rapport de prix intervienne, et justifie un changement d'échelle correspondant pour la typologie.

En appliquant le même type de raisonnement, dont nous ne répéterons pas tous les détails, pour comparer les importances relatives des paramètres E/S console et E/S disque, il est apparu que cette deuxième composante devrait être prépondérante.

C'est pourquoi, compte tenu des disproportions entre les trois variables explicatives, nous avons choisi , non pas de faire porter une typologie sur les trois dimensions, mais de travailler sur les deux couples de paramètres les plus proches :

D'une part : - nombre d'E/S console
              - nombre d'E/S disque

D'autre part : - temps CP/CMS
               - nombre d'E/S disque

Pour chaque doublet de paramètres, deux typologies ont été faites. La première, utilisant la distance euclidienne, regroupe les points dont les coordonnées sont proches, au sens de la norme habituelle sur R^2. La deuxième typologie,
selon la distance du Khi2, forme des classes allongées, dont les points se si-
tuent autour d'une droite. Dans ce dernier cas, nous avons calculé les droites
qui approximent le mieux chaque classe, au sens des moindres carrés.

Les résultats complets de chaque typologie sont donnés dans (4).

4) <u>Résultats et interprétation des typologies sur les E/S console et les</u>
   <u>E/S disque</u>

a) <u>typologie selon la norme euclidienne</u>

L'intervalle de variation des E/S disque étant dix fois celui des
E/S console, la typologie suivant la norme euclidienne est déterminée uniquement par la composante E/S disque (voir figure 2).

- <u>Type 1</u>

Commandes faisant moins de 155 E/S disque.

Toutes les commandes utilitaires consommant très peu de ressources.

Toutes les commandes d'édition et de manipulation de fichier avec erreurs,
et toutes celles, sans erreur, qui portent sur des fichiers de moins de 700 cartes.

Les compilations peu coûteuses, soit parce qu'elles portent sur de petits
programmes (FORTRAN, LISP, ALGOL W), soit parce que le compilateur fait peu
d'E/S disque (PL 360, BRUIN).

Tous les appels de bibliothèque.

La plupart des chargements et des exécutions.

En fait ce type regroupe 86% des ordres de notre échantillon.

- <u>Type 2</u>

Commandes faisant entre 160 et 430 E/S disque.

Les utilitaires les plus coûteux.

Les éditions de fichiers de plus de 700 cartes.

Les lectures ou écritures de fichiers ayant entre 800 et 3900 cartes.

Les compilations moyennement coûteuses (FORTRAN sur de gros programmes,
ALGOL 60).

Des chargements et exécutions.

- Type 3

    Commandes faisant entre 450 et 490 E/S disque.

    Les éditions et les manipulations de fichiers exceptionnelles.

    Les assemblages et compilations coûteux :

        . assembleur G sur des fichiers de moins de 500 cartes,

        . compilations PL/1 de petits programmes.

    Peu de chargements et exécutions.

    Les deux derniers types sont très réduits, (entre 1400 et 2500 E/S disque, et entre 2800 et 6200 E/S disque). On y trouve les compilations PL/1 et les assemblages de gros fichiers, et quelques rares exécutions.

    b) typologie selon la norme du Khi2

    La typologie selon la norme du Khi2 fait apparaître le rapport entre le nombre d'E/S console et disque (voir figure 3). Aussi, lorsqu'une même commande est représentée par plusieurs points distribués dans deux types distincts (FORTRAN par exemple), le facteur déterminant n'est plus la longueur du fichier, mais le fait que la commande a retourné ou non un code d'erreur (la plupart des commandes inscrivent les messages d'erreur à la console).

    Pour chaque type, on donne la pente A de la droite des moindres carrés: E/S disque = A. E/S console + B.

- Type 1 : A = 33,48

    Ce type est caractérisé par un nombre d'E/S console négligeable devant les E/S disque.

    Tous les ordres d'appels d'un assembleur ou d'un compilateur (à l'exclusion des interpréteurs) ne retournant pas de code d'erreur, et la plupart de ceux qui retournent un code d'erreur (FORTRAN et PL360 exceptés).

    Tous les appels de bibliothèque, tous les chargement, très peu d'exécutions. (Il est d'ailleurs logique de penser que l'utilisateur d'un système interactif préférera avoir sur sa console le résultat de l'exécution de son programme).

Editions et manipulations de fichiers : Celles qui consistent à concaténer deux fichiers, à changer le nom d'un fichier, ou à l'envoyer sur le "spooling" de CP, ainsi que la commande d'édition réservée aux gros fichiers, entrainant un nombre important d'E/S disque.

Divers : Les commandes de définitions de caractère, de transfert de fichiers CMS d'un disque à l'autre, ou de disque à bande magnétique sans erreur.

- Type 2 : A = 7,68

    Compilations ayant retourné un code d'erreur : FORTRAN, PL360.

    De nombreuses exécutions, notamment la plupart de celles qui ont eu une fin anormale.

On trouve aussi, dans ce type les commandes de transfert de disque à bande pour lesquelles l'utilisateur doit préciser de nombreux paramètres.

- Type 3 : A = 3,5

Ce type est très réduit. Il contient les ordres d'édition des très gros fichiers (plus de 700 cartes) et quelques ordres divers avec des codes d'erreur.

- Type 4 : A = 1,25

Mises à part quelques commandes très peu employées et faisant moins de 10 E/S disque, ce type est composé essentiellement des éditions de fichiers usuelles et des exécutions (avec lecture et écriture sur la console pour un grand nombre d'entre elles). Ce sont des commandes considérées comme intéractives.

- Type 5 : A = 0,23

Ce type se décompose en deux parties :

. Les commandes qui écrivent sur la console des informations rangées sur le disque. Un enregistrement sur disque peut faire jusqu'à 800 caractères, alors qu'une ligne de terminal contient au plus 132 caractères et souvent moins de 80; ces commandes dont donc plus d'E/S console que d'E/S disque.

. Les commandes très intéractives faisant peu d'E/S disque : les commandes servant à la mise au point et les interpréteurs.

5) Résultat et interprétation des typologies sur le temps CP+CMS et les E/S disque

A titre indicatif, et pour bien montrer la difficulté d'emploi de cette méthode, nous avons fait, pour la norme euclidienne et la norme du Khi2, deux typologies : pour la première, les temps sont exprimés en 1/100 secondes; pour la deuxième ils sont exprimés en 1/25 secondes.

Lorsque l'on considère les typologies selon la norme du Khi2, les groupes obtenus ne sont pas identiques, mais offrent cependant de grandes similitudes. Par contre, la distance euclidienne induit des regroupements radicalement différents. Lorsque l'unité de temps est la centième de seconde, les types sont (graphiquement) séparés par des parallèles à l'axe des E/S disque : seule la composante temps influe sur le résultat. (figure 4). Lorsque l'unité de temps est le vingt cinquième de secondes, les types sont séparés par des parallèles à la seconde bissectrice : les deux composantes ont des rôles équivalents (figure 5).

Pour les raisons que nous avons développées plus haut, nous avons estimé que l'unité de temps réaliste était la centième de seconde. Par conséquent, nous ne commenterons ici que les typologies suivant cette unité.

a) typologie selon la norme euclidienne

La typologie selon la distance euclidienne permet donc de définir, pour chaque classe, des bornes de temps d'exécution.

- Type 1 : commandes courtes

Moins de 7 secondes d'unité centrale. Moins de 500 E/S disque.

La plupart des utilitaires.

Les concaténations de fichiers de moins de 1800 cartes, les lectures et écritures de fichiers de moins de 1250 cartes, la commande de mise en page de texte portant sur des fichiers de moins de 500 cartes, et toutes les autres commandes de manipulation de fichiers.

La commande d'édition de fichiers usuels. Les interpréteurs (BRUIN, LISP) et les compilateurs rapides ou ayant traité dans notre échantillon de petits programmes seulement (PL360, ALGOL W, ALGOL 60, FORTRAN pour des programmes de moins de 150 cartes).

Tous les appels de bibliothèque et les chargements. La très grande majorité des exécutions.

Ce type contient en fait 85% des ordres de notre échantillon.

- Type 2 : commandes moyennement longues

De 7 à 24 secondes d'unité centrale. Moins de 800 E/S disque.

Les éditions de gros fichiers et certaines manipulations de gros fichiers.

Des compilations de fichiers de moins de 500 cartes (FORTRAN, PL1, assembleur G).

Quelques rares exécutions de modules, ayant renvoyé un code d'erreur.

- Type 3 : commandes longues

De 25 à 60 secondes d'unité centrale.

Les assemblages et compilations (PL1, FORTRAN) importants.

La commande qui recopie des fichiers d'une bande magnétique sur une autre.

Les grosses exécutions.

- Type 4 : commandes exceptionnelles

Plus de 60 secondes d'unité centrale.

Les très gros assemblages (plus de 700 cartes) et compilations (FORTRAN : plus de 900 cartes, PL1 : plus de 1100 cartes).

Quelques très grosses exécutions de fichiers modules.

b) typologie selon la norme du Khi2

Dans le système considéré, le nombre d'E/S disque influe de façon non négligeable sur le temps CP+CMS. En effet, un programme canal est d'abord écrit au niveau CMS, comme si l'E/S devait s'effectuer sur une machine nue.

Puis ce programme canal est repris au niveau CP, et traduit de façon à tenir compte du partage des disques et de la mémoire (compilation des programmes canaux).

BARD (2) a estimé, par des méthodes de régression, le coût d'une E/S disque à 5 millisecondes d'unité centrale, en moyenne.

La droite des moindres carrés. Temps CP+CMS = A x E/S disque + B que nous avons calculée pour chaque type permet d'évaluer la part des E/S dans le temps d'exécution des ordres regroupés par la typologie. (Fig. 6).

- Type 1 : A = 1,3

Nombreuses E/S disque, très peu de calcul.

Parmi les manipulations de fichiers, on trouve les commandes de concaténation, changement de l'entête, suppression du fichier.

Les éditions de gros fichiers.

Assemblages et compilations : l'assembleur G, ALGOL 60, PL1 sur des fichiers de moins de 250 cartes.

Le compilateur ALGOL et l'assembleur G n'ont pas été conçus pour un système à mémoire virtuelle illimitée. Ils font de nombreux transferts de mémoire à disque. Le compilateur PL1, de par sa structure, effectue un nombre minimal d'E/S disque situé entre 400 et 500. Pour les petits programmes, le traitement de ces E/S disque représente une grande partie du temps de compilation.

Chargements et exécutions : les appels de bibliothèque, les chargements de fichiers "text", les générations de fichiers "module" quelques exécutions ayant renvoyé un code d'erreur.

Sous la rubrique divers : les échanges de disque à bande magnétique sans erreur, les spécifications de bibliothèque, la commande LOGIN implicite ou non.

- Type 2 : A = 2,1

Nombreuses E/S disque, mais calculs proportionnellement deux fois plus importants que dans le type précédent.

Les éditions de fichiers qui existaient déjà.

Les compilations PL360 sans erreur, et PL1 sur des fichiers allant jusqu'à 620 cartes.

Les chargements de modules non translatables.

De nombreuses exécutions.

Les échanges entre disque et bande magnétique avec code d'erreur.

Quelques commandes diverses.

- Type 3 : A = 4,3

Pas de fortes E/S disque. Temps de calcul beaucoup plus long.

Les éditions de nouveaux fichiers, les lectures, écritures et perforations de fichiers.

Les compilations ALGOL W, PL360 avec erreur, PL1 sur de gros fichiers.

La plupart des exécutions de fichiers de type module, sans erreur.

Parmi les divers : les échanges de disque à disque, les tris.

On peut remarquer que ce type contient les principales commandes de transmission de fichiers par l'intermédiaire du "spooling" de CP : une cause possible du temps de calcul relativement long pour exécuter ces commandes est la présence dans CP, de la routine PACK, qui comprime les blancs des fichiers lus, ou au contraire, restitue ces blancs avant d'imprimer ou de perforer le fichier.

- Type 4 : A = 6,1

E/S disque qui peuvent être assez nombreuses, mais aussi fort temps de calcul.

Les compilations FORTRAN de petits programmes, PL1 de très gros programmes (plus de 1100 cartes) et l'interpréteur BRUIN.

Pour les manipulations de fichiers : la commande d'impression de gros fichiers sur la console. Il est difficile de donner une explication sur la présence de cette commande dans ce type.

Quelques exécutions, essentiellement de modules non translatables.

- Type 5 : A = 25,5

Les commandes de ce groupe, soit font peu d'E/S disque, soit ont un temps d'exécution exceptionnellement long.

Dans les manipulations de fichiers, la commande d'écriture avec mise en page a un temps d'exécution assez long dû au décodage des symboles de contrôle.

Les compilations de programmes FORTRAN de plus de 180 cartes, et l'interprétation des programmes LISP.

La commande DEBUG, de mise au point, qui ne fait pas d'E/S disque.

Des exécutions de fichiers module peu nombreuses, mais extrêmement longues, et toutes les exécutions classiques sans erreur.

Dans les divers : les définitions de caractères de contrôle et quelques commandes courtes faisant très peu d'E/S disque.

REMARQUE :

On aurait pû faire une typologie différente sur les temps de calcul et les E/S disque, faisant apparaître non plus la consommation de ressources physiques, mais la consommation de ressources logiques. Les paramètres considérés auraient alors été le temps CMS (virtuel) d'une part, le temps d'unité centrale équivalent au coût d'une E/S disque d'autre part. (4 millisecondes correspondant au travail du canal et de l'unité de contrôle + 5 millisecondes de traitement de l'E/S par CP en mode superviseur). Cette typologie aurait été plus intéressante du point de vue de l'utilisateur, mais aurait moins bien reflété la charge effective des composants du système.

CONCLUSION

Les résultats que nous avons obtenus montrent que les classifications à priori sont en général peu fondées. Ainsi, chacun des groupes logiques de Scherr a été éclaté dans nos différents types. Par exemple, dans la typologie selon la norme euclidienne sur le temps CP+CMS et les E/S disque, les éditions et manipulations de gros fichiers sont regroupées dans la classe des commandes moyennement longues, avec de nombreuses exécutions et les compilations FORTRAN et PL1 de petits fichiers.

L'analyse d'un système par typologie est longue et coûteuse, notamment à cause de toutes les typologies partielles nécessaires à la réduction de l'échantillon de mesures. Nous pensons cependant que ce travail mérite d'être fait, en particulier peu de temps après la mise en service d'un nouveau système. En effet, pendant cette phase d'expérimentation, on s'attache beaucoup à prélever des mesures, évaluer les performances, fixer certains paramètres, confirmer ou infirmer les hypothèses de fonctionnement qui avaient été formulées. La typologie, qui regroupe les commandes ayant des comportements internes analogues, permet une vision plus globale de l'ensemble des composants du système.

On pourrait donc tirer, des résultats d'une typologie, des conseils d'utilisations, livrés avec le système. Ainsi, il est très parlant, pour un utilisateur, de savoir que la recopie d'un fichier d'une bande magnétique sur une autre est aussi coûteuse que la compilation d'un gros programme FORTRAN.

Nous devons toutefois tirer quelques conclusions négatives de cette étude. Il nous a été impossible, pour les commandes de chargement et d'exécution, pour lesquelles des typologies partielles ont été effectuées, de trouver une caractérisation (par une longueur de fichier ou tout autre paramètre objectif, c'est à dire ne tenant pas compte de la personne qui a issu la commande) des types internes à ces commandes. De plus, dans bien des cas, une commande qui a renvoyé un code d'erreur ne se trouve pas dans le même type que la même commande qui s'est déroulée normalement. Or, excepté l'oubli d'un paramètre que l'on détecte au décodage d'un ordre, on ne peut pas savoir à priori s'il y aura ou non un code d'erreur. Dans ces conditions, il nous paraît bien improbable de réussir à élaborer des algorithmes de gestion des ressources efficaces, basés sur les seuls résultats de typologies.

Cependant, on peut imaginer de prévoir, rajoutée au descripteur des fichiers que les utilisateurs conservent sur disque, la liste des commandes qui peuvent s'appliquer à ces fichiers et dont le type ne peut pas être connu de façon suffisamment précise. Lors du premier appel d'une telle commande, on lui affecterait son type le plus probable. A la fin de l'exécution de la commande, on ré-évaluerait son type, que l'on conserverait dans le descripteur du fichier.

Il faudrait, par conséquent, prévoir des outils de mesure intégrés au système (12). Les mesures recueillies permettraient de faire, en temps réel, un
schéduler adaptatif par la procédure que nous proposons; et en différé, on pourrait recalculer le type des commandes mal représentées dans l'échantillon de départ, et connaître le pourcentage de mauvaises affectations de types, ainsi que
l'efficacité d'un tel algorithme. Précisons que nous n'avons pas évalué le coût
d'un tel schéduler; en particulier, l'overhead qu'il induirait ne risquerait-il
pas d'annuler les avantages escomptés ? Le problème reste ouvert.

Ce travail a été financé par le contrat DRME N° 72.34.601.00.480.75.01.

49

BIBLIOGRAPHIE

1) A. AUROUS, C. HANS : "Introduction aux systèmes CP-67 et CMS", Monographies
   informatiques - AFCET, les systèmes conversationnels : L. BOLLIET-
   DUNOD.

2) Y. BARD : "CP-67 Measurement and analysis : overhead and throughput". Workshop on system performance evaluation, April 1971 - HARWARD.

3) J. BARRE : "Programme de la méthode des nuées dynamiques", Fascicule IRIA,
   Décembre 1971, ROCQUENCOURT.

4) D. BORRIONE : "Une analyse du système CP-CMS par typologie", note IMAG -
   Grenoble, Octobre 1973.

5) E. DIDAY : "Une nouvelle méthode en classification automatique et reconnais-
   sance des formes, la méthode des nuées dynamiques". Revue de statistique appliquée 1971, vol XIX, n° 2.

6) I.B.M. Corp : "CMS program logic manual", Form GU20 - 0591.

7) I.B.M. Corp : "CP-67 Program Logic Manual", Form GY20-0590.

8) I. LEBART et J.P. FENELON : "Statistiques et informatique appliquées", DUNOD
   Paris 1971.

9) J. LE FAOU : "Mesure et analyse de l'utilisation d'un système informatique",
   Thèse de 3e cycle, Rennes 1973.

10) J. LEROUDIER : "Analyse de la demande d'un système", Note IMAG - Grenoble
    juin 1972.

11) J. LEROUDIER : "Analyse d'un système à partage de ressources", Séminaires
    IRIA, décembre 1972, PARIS.

12) J. LEROUDIER : "Une analyse de système", Thèse de 3e cycle, Grenoble 1973.

13) Y.V. LINNIK : "Méthode des moindres carrés", DUNOD - PARIS.

14) A.L. SCHERR : "An analysis of time-shared computer system", Thesis - Project
    MAC, MIT 1965.

FORTRAN SANS ERREUR

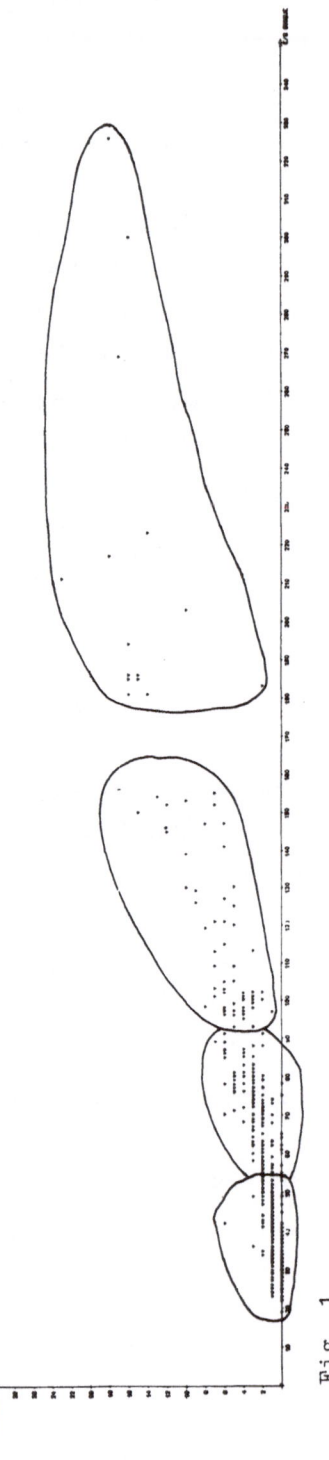

Fig. 1

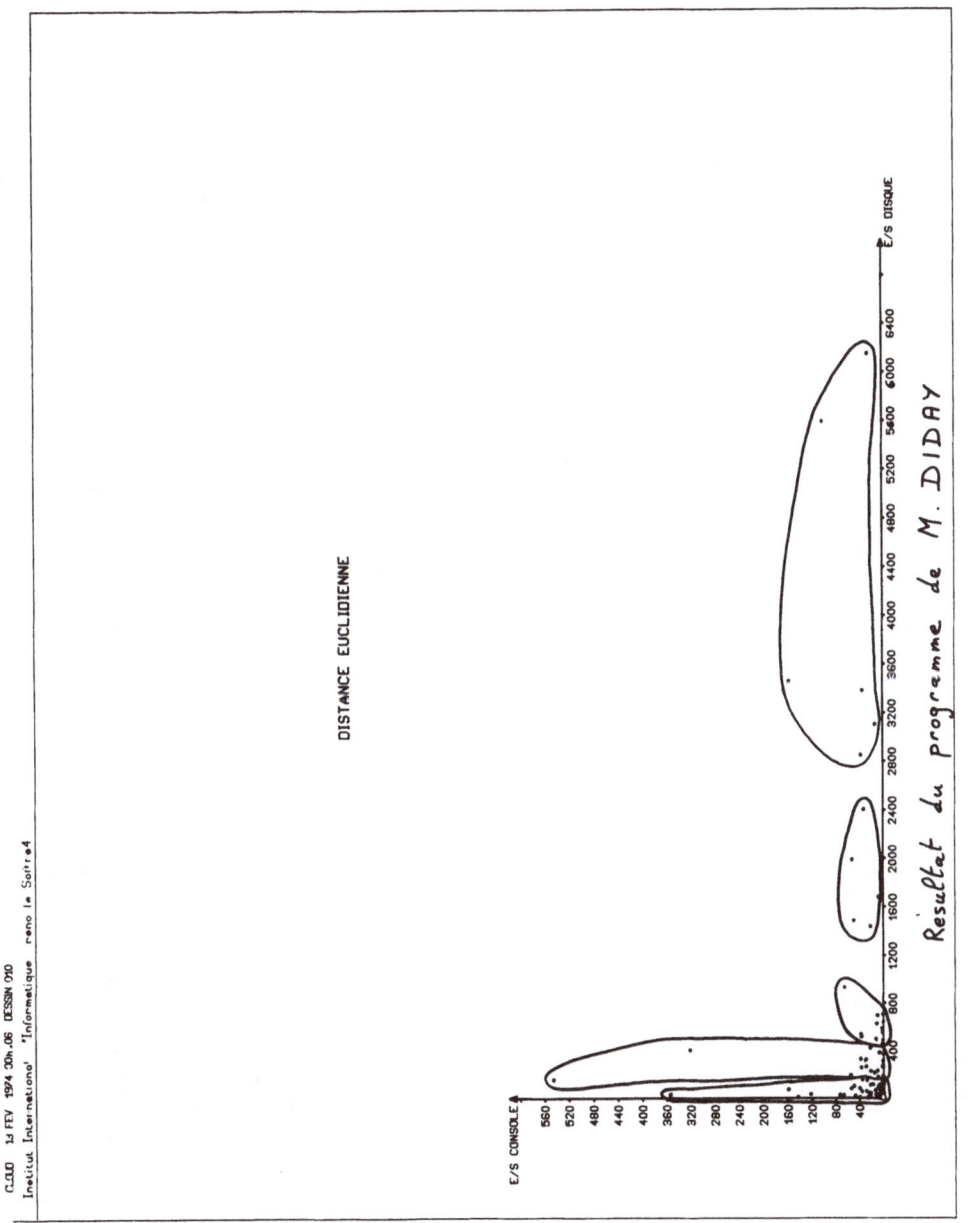

DISTANCE EUCLIDIENNE

E/S CONSOLE

E/S DISQUE

Resultat du Programme de M. DIDAY

Fig. 2

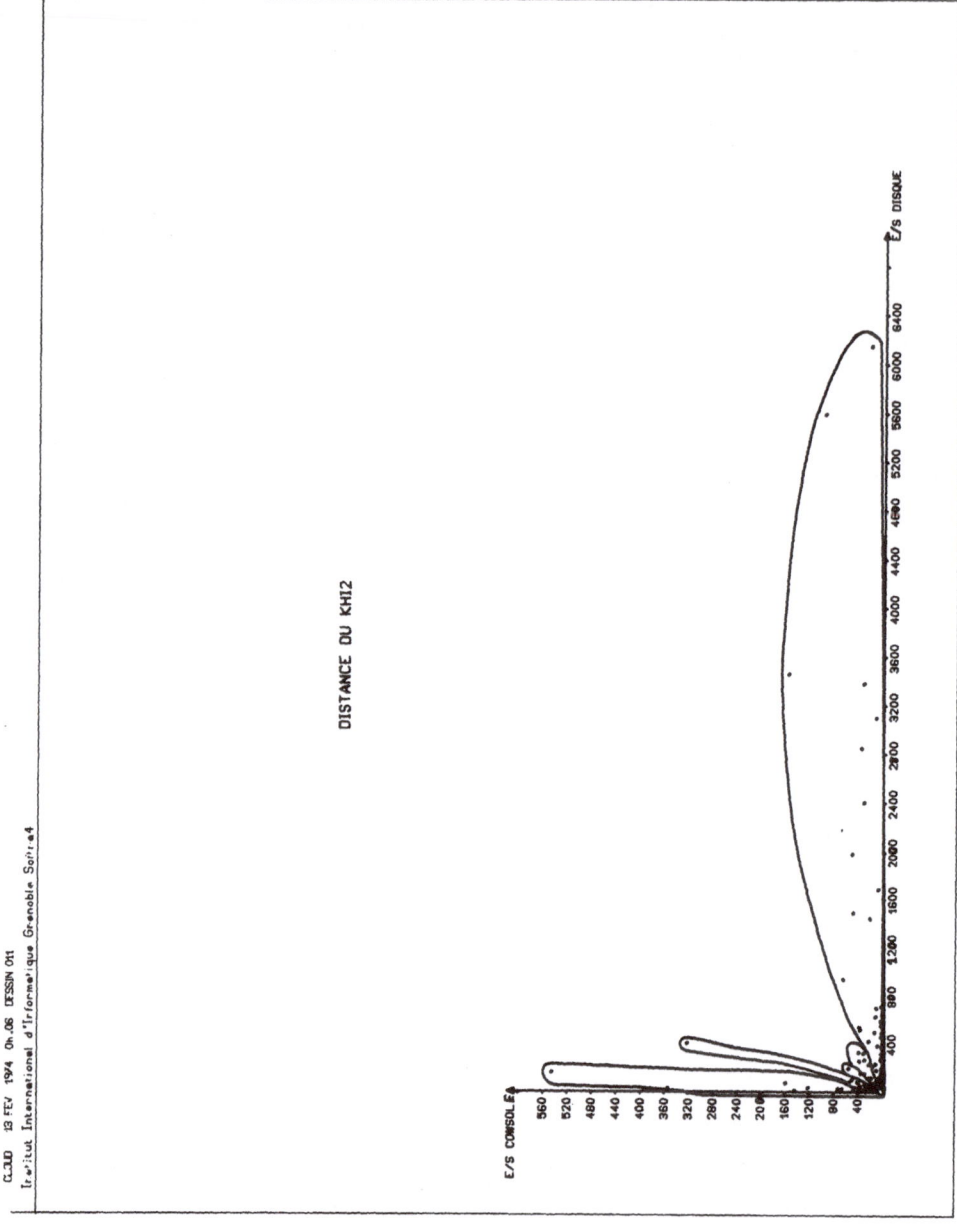

Fig. 3

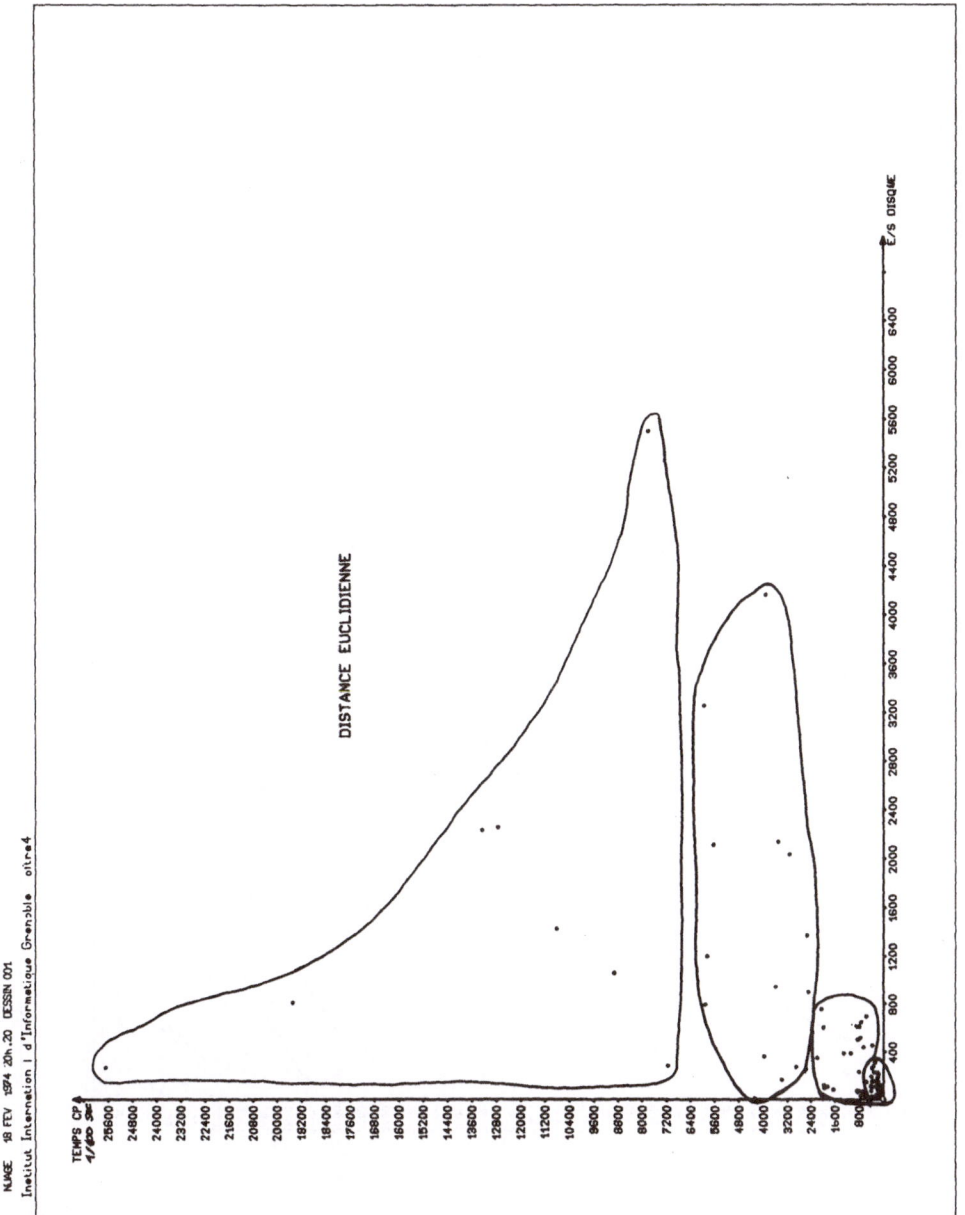

NUAGE   18 FEV 1974 20h.20 DESSIN 001
Institut International d'Informatique Grenoble   oitre4

TEMPS CP
1/60 sec

DISTANCE EUCLIDIENNE

E/S DISQUE

Fig. 4

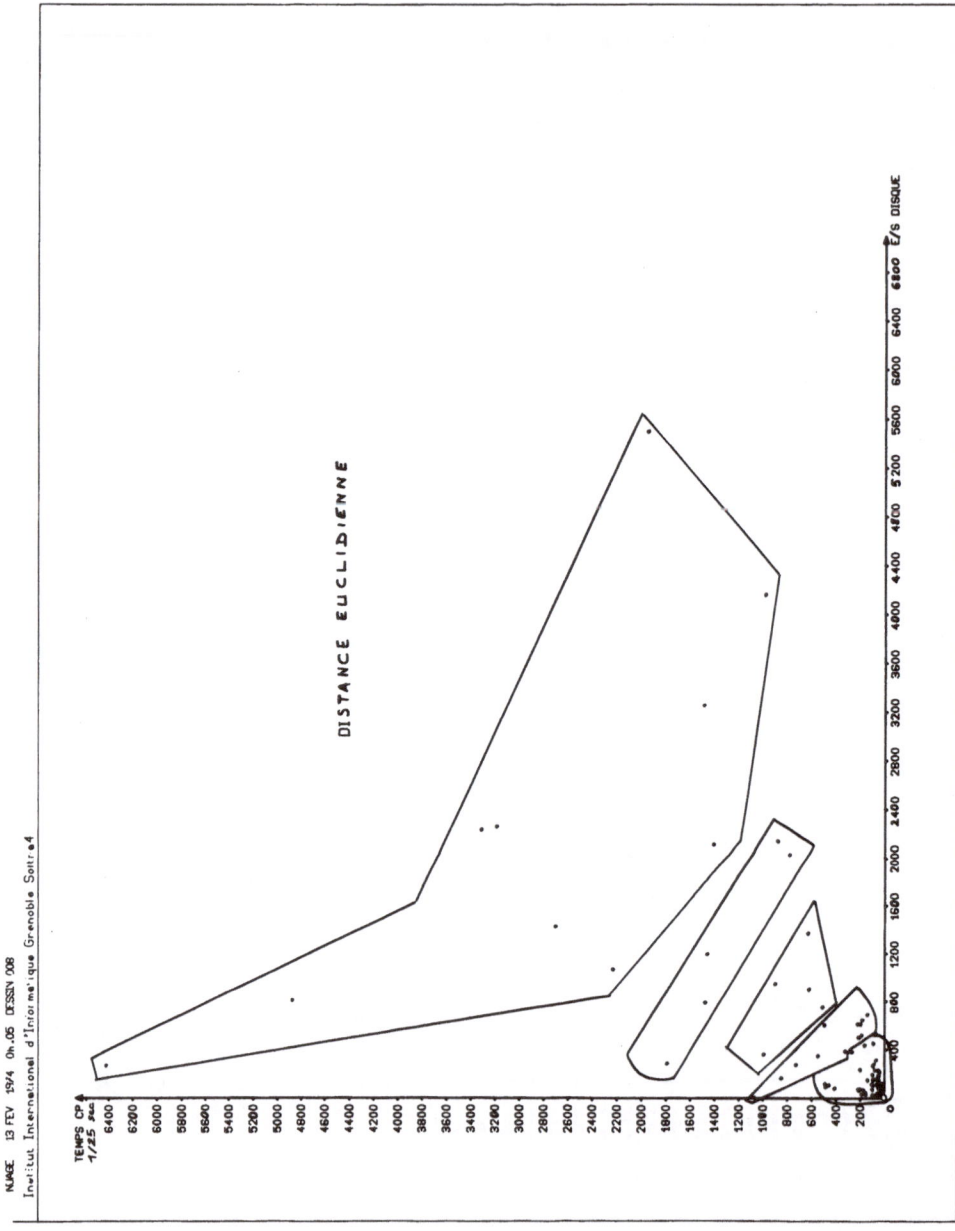

NUAGE   13 FEV 1974   0h .05 DESSIN 008
Institut International d'Informatique Grenoble Sortie4

TEMPS CP
1/25 sec

DISTANCE EUCLIDIENNE

E/S DISQUE

Fig. 5

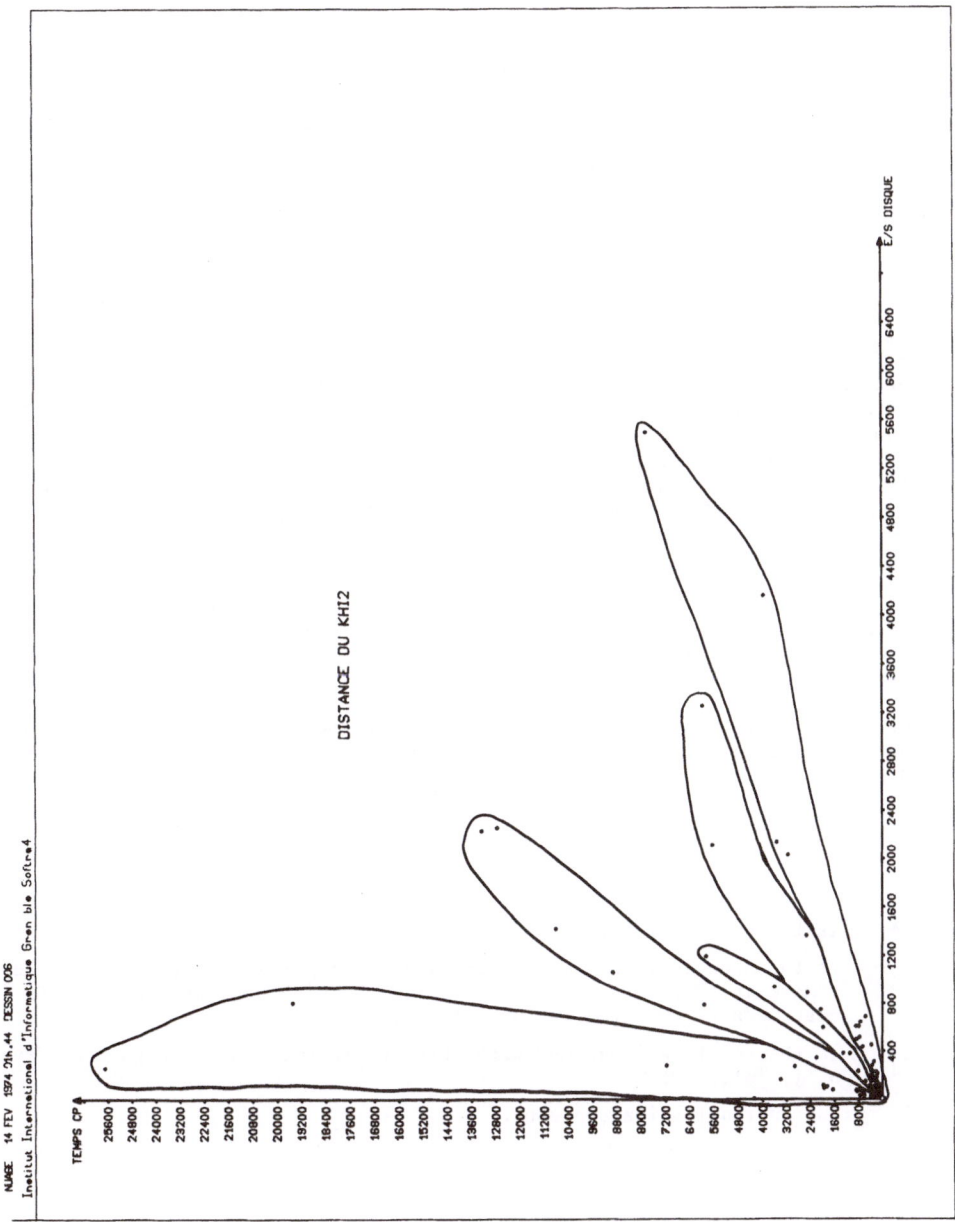

NUAGE 14 FEV 1974 21h.44 DESSIN 006
Institut International d'Informatique Gren ble Softre4

DISTANCE DU KHI2

TEMPS CP

25600
24800
24000
23200
22400
21600
20800
20000
19200
18400
17600
16800
16000
15200
14400
13600
12800
12000
11200
10400
9600
8800
8000
7200
6400
5600
4800
4000
3200
2400
1600
800

E/S DISQUE

400 800 1200 1600 2000 2400 2800 3200 3600 4000 4400 4800 5200 5600 6000 6400

Fig. 6

EQUIVALENCE AND DECOMPOSITION METHODS WITH APPLICATION TO A MODEL OF A TIME-SHARING VIRTUAL MEMORY SYSTEM

A. Brandwajn
IRIA - LABORIA

I - INTRODUCTION

Queueing network models have been applied by several authors to the analysis and the prediction of computer system performance [1], [2], [3], [4], [5], [17]. The results obtained from these models appear to match well measurements done on real systems [1][4].

The basic result for queueing networks has been given by JACKSON [6]. He considers open and closed networks of arbitrarily interconnected exponential servers. The mean service time of a server is allowed to be an almost arbitrary function of the number of customers in the queue of the server (such a server will be called henceforth a Jackson server). A customer leaving a server has constant probabilities of directing itself to any server of the network (or of leaving the system in an open network).

In open networks the arrival process is assumed to be Poisson ; its parameter may be an almost arbitrary function of the current total number of customers in the system.

For closed (i.e. with no arrivals from outside and no departures) networks the stationary probability distribution for the number of customers at each server always exists and is given by

$$p(k_1,\ldots,k_1)=G \prod_{j=1}^{\ell} \prod_{i=1}^{k_j} \frac{e_j}{u_j(i)}$$

where

ℓ is the number of servers,

$\dfrac{1}{u_j(i)}$ is the mean service time of server j, $1\leq j \leq \ell$ when the number of customers at this server is i, $i=1,\ldots,N$, N being the total number of customers circulating in the network,

e_j is the relative frequency with which customers pass through the server n° j, $j=1,\ldots,\ell$,

and   G   is a normalization constant.

More recently MUNTZ and BASKETT [7] have presented an extension of this solution to networks with different classes of customers and, for some service disciplines, to servers with more general service time distributions.

In this paper, we shall present an approach distinct from the preceding work. We characterize the random variable representing uninterrupted computation at the CPU for a given process, and the routing probabilities in the network, as functions of program behaviour parameters. This introduces the possibility of examining the effect of sharing of memory between processes on CPU utilization and expected response time of the system. The model leads to a queueing network which is not a particular case of Jackson's networks. Standard numerical methods turn out to be inefficient when applied to our model, probably because the transition rate matrix is ill-conditioned : elements which correspond to the user's behaviour at a terminal are up to 10^6 times smaller than elements corresponding to internal transitions in the system.

We show that the whole processing part of the model is equivalent, as far as the current total number of processes in it is concerned, to a single Jackson server, and we obtain an approximate expression for the stationary solution.

We also consider two ways of controlling the degree of multiprogramming in order to prevent thrashing. The equivalence is still valid for such systems and we give the stationary state probability distributions.

II - THE MODEL

2.1 - General description

Consider the model described in Figure 1. It represents the system architecture of the time-sharing multiprogrammed paged virtual memory computer under consideration. The system consists of a set of terminals from which a set of users (whose number is equal to that of the terminals) generate commands, a CPU, a secondary memory device (SM) (e.g. drum or fixed head disk, LCS, etc.) and a filing disk (FD). A queue of requests is associated with each device ; the order in which these requests are satisfied is not taken into consideration. When a command is generated, the user at the terminal will remain inactive until the system provides the proper response. Symbolically, a user having generated a command enters the CPU queue. The terms "user" and "user process" or just "process" will be used interchangeably.

We assume that all the processes are statistically identical and independent. Let N and n be the total member of users and the current degree of multiprogramming, respectively. If at any time n_o, n_1, n_2 are the numbers of processes in the CPU, SM, FD queue respectively, then

$$(1) \qquad\qquad n = n_o + n_1 + n_2 , \qquad 0 \leq n \leq N.$$

In the model, the behaviour of a user at a terminal is described by his think time i.e. the time elapsed between the last response of the system to the user's command and the next command be generates. The behaviour of processes in the system is characterized by a compute time followed by either a page fault (after which the process enters the SM queue) or an input-output (file request) in which case the process enters the FD queue. Processes which terminate their service at the SM or at the FD return to the CPU queue. Symbolically, the completion of a command is represented by a departure of a process form the CPU to the terminals.

n being the degree of multiprogramming, let $\tau(n)$ be the random variable representing uninterrupted computation at the CPU. Let $t_1(n)$, $t_2(n)$ be the random variables representing the compute time between two successive page faults, or I/O operations, respectively. Suppose that $t_1(n)$, $t_2(n)$ have probability distribution functions $F_1^n(t)$, $F_2^n(t)$. Let also $t_3(n)$ be the random variable representing total compute time of a process, with distribution function $F_3^n(t)$. We shall assume, in order to make use of the "memoryless" property of the exponential distribution function, that

$$(2) \quad \begin{cases} F_1^n(t) = 1 - e^{\dfrac{t}{q(n)}} \\[2em] F_2^n(t) = 1 - e^{\dfrac{t}{r(n)}} \\[2em] F_3^n(t) = 1 - e^{\dfrac{t}{c(n)}} \end{cases}$$

the assumption being that $t_1(n)$, $t_2(n)$, $t_3(n)$ are independent. Because of the memoryless property of the exponential distribution, the random variable $\tau(n)$ is distributed as

$$\min_{\substack{i \\ i=1,2,3}} \{t_1(n),\ t_2(n),\ t_3(n)\}$$

Let us add a few words of clarification. Suppose that n being maintained constant a given process begins its execution at the CPU (in one of its passes) at time x, and is interrupted at time y. Then $\tau(n)=x-y$, and if one considers the realizations of the three random variables $t_1(n)$, $t_2(n)$, $t_3(n)$, $\tau(n)$ will correspond to the smallest residual at each trial (i.e. each time that a process executes at the CPU). We then obtain

$$(3) \quad \begin{cases} F^n(t) = \text{Prob}\ [\ \tau(n) \leq t\ ] \\[1em] \quad = 1 - \text{Prob}\ [t_1(n) > t \& t_2(n) > t \& t_3(n) > t\ ] \\[1em] \quad = 1 - [1 - F_1^n(t)]\ [1 - F_2^n(t)][1 - F_3^n(t)] \\[1em] \quad = 1 - e^{-t\left(\frac{1}{q(n)} + \frac{1}{r(n)} + \frac{1}{c(n)}\right)} \end{cases}$$

Thus $\tau(n)$ is exponentially distributed with expected value

$$(4) \quad E\{\tau(n)\} = \frac{1}{u_o(n)} = \frac{1}{\frac{1}{q(n)} + \frac{1}{r(n)} + \frac{1}{c(n)}}$$

Note that $\tau(n)$ is the service time at the "server" representing the CPU when the degree of multiprogramming is n in the queueing network model of Figure 1.

To obtain $p_1(n)$ and $p_2(n)$, the probabilities that a process leaving the CPU will direct itself to the SM device or to the FD, respectively, the current number of processes that execute in the system being n, we proceed as follows :

$$(5) \quad p_1(n) = \int_0^\infty \text{Prob}\ [t-dt < t_1(n) \leq t\ \&\ t_2(n) > t\ \&\ t_3(n) > t]$$

where the integral is over all values of time t, since it is the probability that $\tau(n)$ and $t_1(n)$ coincide. We then obtain

$$(6) \quad p_1(n) = \int_0^\infty dt\ \frac{1}{q(n)}\ e^{-\frac{t}{q(n)}}\ e^{-\frac{t}{r(n)}}\ e^{-\frac{t}{c(n)}}$$

$$= \frac{1}{u_o(n)q(n)}$$

where $1/u_o(n)$ is the mean service time at the CPU when the degree of multiprogramming is n.

Similarly, we shall have

(7)
$$p_2(n) = \int_0^\infty dt \frac{1}{r(n)} e^{-\frac{t}{r(n)}} e^{-\frac{t}{q(n)}} e^{-\frac{t}{c(n)}}$$

$$= \frac{1}{u_0(n)r(n)}$$

and

$$p_0(n) = 1 - p_1(n) - p_2(n) = \frac{1}{u_0(n)c(n)}$$

We assume that the service times at the SM and the FD as well as the user think time are exponentially distributed with expected values $\frac{1}{u_1}, \frac{1}{u_2}$ and $\frac{1}{\lambda}$, respectively.

2.2 - The effect of memory sharing

We propose to use our model to analyze the effect of memory sharing in the system. We therefore need a model relating $F_1^n(n)$ to the amount of space allocated to each process.

Experimental evidence [8] indicate that the mean compute time between page faults, q for a process executing in memory space m (called the lifetime function) has the general shape shown in Figure 2. q may be approximated by a function of the form
$$q_1 = \alpha m^k$$
where depends on the processing speed as well as on program characteristics while k depends on program locality and on the memory management strategy (e.g. the page replacement algorithm). BELADY and KUEHNER [8] indicate that k is in the range $1.5 < k < 2.5$, while SALTZER [9] claims that it is close to unity.

Recently, CHAMBERLIN, FULLER and LIU [10] have proposed another fit for the lifetime function
$$q_2 = \frac{2b}{1+(\frac{d}{m})^2}$$
where d is a relative measure of the memory space needed to enable the process to be executed efficiently i.e. the number of pages that provides the process with half of its largest possible lifetime ; b is the expected execution time between page faults when the process is allocated a memory space d.

We shall assume that total primary memory available is of size M and that it is equally shared among processes currently executing in the system :

(8)
$$m = \frac{M}{n} .$$

This yields for the mean compute time between two successive page faults

(9)
$$q(n) = \alpha (\frac{M}{n})^k$$
with the Belady lifetime function and

(10)
$$q(n) = \frac{2b}{1+(\frac{dn}{M})^2}$$

using q_2.

r and c are assumed independent of m, n or N, which seems reasonable.

2.3 - The equations describing system behaviour

We would like to use the preceding assumptions regarding the service time distributions, and their relationship to program behaviour, in order to compute the expected responde time of the system and the CPU utilization as representative measures of system performance.

The behaviour of the system is completely characterized by the joint probability distribution

$$p(n_o, n_1; n_2, n_c, t)$$

of the number of processes in the three queues and of active users at the terminals at time t ; notice that $n_c = N - n_o - n_1 - n_2 = N - n$. The differential-difference equations for the system are :

$$
(11) \begin{cases}
\frac{d}{dt} p(n_o, n_1, n_2, n_c, t) = -\left[V_o + V_1 + V_2 + n_c \lambda \right] p(n_o, n_1, n_2, n_c, t) + \\[2mm]
+ (n_c + 1)\lambda p(n_o - 1, n_1, n_2, n_c + 1, t) + p_o(n+1) u_o(n+1) p(n_o + 1, n_1, n_2, n_c - 1, t) + \\[2mm]
+ u_1 p(n_o - 1, n_1 + 1, n_2, n_c, t) + u_2 p(n_o - 1, n_1, n_2 + 1, n_c, t) + \\[2mm]
+ p_1(n) u_o(n) p(n_o + 1, n_1 - 1, n_2, n_c, t) + p_2(n) u_o(n) p(n_o + 1, n_1, n_2 - 1, n_c, t)
\end{cases}
$$

where for any i, j, k, ℓ negative or greater than N we have

$$(12) \qquad p(i, j, k, \ell, t) = 0 \quad \text{for all } t.$$

$$(13) \qquad V_m = \begin{cases} u_m & \text{if } n_m > 0 \\[4mm] 0 & \text{otherwise} \end{cases}$$

for $m = 0, 1, 2$.

These equations are easily obtained using the exponential assumptions on service time ; due to the "memoryless" property of the exponential distribution, at any time t, the probability that a process executing at the CPU will leave it during the time interval $(t, t+dt]$ and direct itself for example to the SM queue is $p_1(n) u_o(n) dt + 0(dt)$, n being the number of processes in the system at time t, regarless of how much CPU time the process has already obtained and what the previous values of the degree of multiprogramming have been. $O(\delta t)$ is a function of δt such that

$$\lim_{\delta t \to 0} \frac{O(\delta t)}{\delta t} = 0.$$

The stationary solution of (11) is defined as

$$(14) \qquad p(n_o, n_1, n_2, n_c) = \lim_{t \to \infty} p(n_o, n_1, n_2, n_c, t).$$

It can be shown that (14) exists for the system considered and that it is independent of the initial conditions.

It is easy to see (because of the dependence of the CPU service time distribution parameter on n which is the sum of the number of processes in the three queues) that this model is not a particular case of JACKSON's networks [6] so that the stationary solution cannot be obtained by direct application of his result. Thus another approach must be sought.

In the next section we state several theorems which applied to our model give an approximate solution for the stationary state of the system.

III - EQUIVALENT SERVERS AND NEAR COMPLETE DECOMPOSABILITY IN EXCHANGE SERVER QUEUEING NETWORKS.

3.1 - Equivalent server

Definition 1

Two queueing systems are __equivalent__ if the probability distributions of the __total__ number of customers in each of these systems are identical.

Consider now the closed queueing network of Figure 3. The subsystems C and A consist of k and L-k Jackson servers, respectively (labelled 1 to k and k+1 to L) arbitrarily interconnected within each subsystem but interacting with the outside world only through the __exchange server__. The service time of the latter is assumed to be an exponentially distributed random variable with mean $1/u_o(n)$ when the number of customers in the subsystem B (exchange server and subsystem C) is n. At any instant of time, the state of A will be given by the vector $\bar{s} = (i_{k+1}, \ldots, i_L)$, where i_j, $k+1 \leq j \leq L$, is the number of customers at the server j of A.

Theorem 1

In the system considered, at the stationary state (which always exists the network being closed), the subsystem B is equivalent as regards the probability distribution of the total number of customers in B, i.e. in the sense of Definition 1, to a single exponential server with routing probabilities normalized with respect to $p_o(n)$ and service rate $A_o(n,\bar{s})p_o(n)u_o(n)$ (see Figure 4), where

(15)

$A_o(n,\bar{s})$ is the stationary conditional probability of the exchange server being busy given that there are n customers in the subsystem B and that the state of the subsystem A is $\bar{s}$,

$p_o(n)$ is the probability that a customer finishing service at the exchange server will direct itself to the subsystem A when the number of customers in B is n.

The proof of this theorem is given in [19].

Note that if A consist of a single server the equivalent network is a particular case of Jackson's network [6].

3.2 - Near-complete-decomposability.

Consider again the subsystem B in Figure 3. Intuitively, if B interacts weakly with the outside world (e.g. if the relaxation time of B after a change in the number of customers n in it is much smaller than the mean time between two successive changes), the conditional probability of the exchange server being busy $A_o(n)$ (or $A_o(n,\bar{s})$) should not be much different from the probability of the exchange server being busy in the closed network obtained by cutting off the links between B and the outside world.

Systems in which all variables can somehow be clustered into a small number of groups so that : (i) the interactions among the variables of each single group may be studied as if interactions among groups did not exist and (ii) interactions among groups may the studied without reference to the interactions within groups, are called Nearly Completely Decomposable Systems. SIMON and ANDO [11][12] who investigated these systems proved two theorems. They state that, provided __inter-group__ dependencies are sufficiently weak as compared to __intragroups__ ones, in the short run the system may be considered as a set of independent subsystems which may approximately be analyzed separately from one another. In the long run the whole system appears to evolve keeping roughly the state of equilibrium within each subsystem.

The theory of near-complete-decomposability has been applied by COURTOIS [13] to a subclass of Jackson's stochastic networks of interconnected queues. We shall investigate the circumstances under which the network considered in Theorem 2, the subsystem A being specialized to a single exponential server as in Figure 5, is nearly-completely-decomposable.

Let n_0 and n_ℓ, $\ell = 1,\ldots,k$, be the number of customers at the exchange server and at the k servers of the subsystem C, respectively. Let also $u_\ell(n_\ell)$ be the service rate at server ℓ, $1 \leq \ell \leq k$ when the number of customers at it is n_ℓ and $u_0(n)$, $n = \sum_{j=0}^{k} n_j$, the service rate of the exchange server when there are n customers in the subsystem B.

The mean service time of the unique server of A, labelled L, is $1/\Lambda(i_L)$ when the number of customers at that server is i_L. We have

$$i_L + \sum_{j=0}^{k} n_j = N,$$ where N is the total number of customers in the network.

The transfer probabilities are for the exchange server :
$p_{om}(n)$, $m = 0,1,\ldots,k,L$, when the number of customers in the subsystem B is n ;
$$\sum_{m} p_{om}(n) = 1, \quad n = 1,\ldots,N$$

for the server of C :

$p_{\ell j}(n_\ell)$, $1 \leq \ell \leq k$, $0 \leq j \leq k$, when the number of customers at the server $n\%$ is n_ℓ ;
$$\sum_{j=0}^{k} p_{\ell j}(n_\ell) = 1, \quad n_\ell = 1,\ldots,N$$
for the server of A :

$p_{Lq}(i_L)$, $q = 0$ or L, i_L being the number of customers at the server.

Theorem 2   If
$$(16) \quad \begin{cases} x(i_L)\lambda(i_L)(1-p_{LL}(i_L)) + x(n_0)u_0(n)p_{oL}(n) << \sum_{\ell=1}^{k} x(n_\ell)u_\ell(n_\ell)(1-p_{\ell\ell}(n_\ell)) + \\ + x(n_0)u_0(n) \sum_{m=\ell}^{k} p_{om}(n), \quad \text{for } i_L = 0,\ldots,N, \quad x(j) = \begin{cases} 0, & \text{if } j=0 \text{ or } N+1 \\ 1, & \text{otherwise,} \end{cases} \end{cases}$$

the stochastic matrix $Q(N,L)$, $N > 0$, $L > 1$, defines a system nearly completely decomposable into (N+1) systems which may be represented by stochastic matrices $Q(x)$ of order
$$\binom{N+L-X-1}{L-1}, \quad X = 0,\ldots,N,$$

corresponding to all possible interactions among $(n_0,\ldots,n_k)$ states with $i_L = X$.
The proof of this theorem can be found in [19].

Theorem 2 gives a sufficient condition under which the network of Figure 5 is nearly completely decomposable. The stochastic matrices Q(X) describe in fact the behaviour of a closed network obtained by cutting off the links between subsystem B and A.

3.3 - Application to the model

We shall now use the preceding results in order to obtain an approximate solution for the stationary behaviour of the time-sharing multiprogrammed virtual memory computer system of Section 2.

It is easy to see that our model is a particular case of the network represented in Figure 3. The set of terminals may be considered as a single exponential server with service rate $\lambda(n_c) = \lambda n_c$, when the number of active users at the terminals is n_c ; this server constitutes the subsystem A. The CPU is the exchange server, and the subsystem C consists of the SM and FD. Therefore, Theorem 1 applies and the CPU along with the SM and FD may be replaced by a single exponential server with service rate $u(n,\bar{s}) = A_0(n,\bar{s})p_0(n)u_0(n)$, according to (15). In our case,

$\bar{s} = (n_c) = (N-n)$, i.e. the state of A is completely defined by the number n of processes in the system. Hence, we obtain an equivalent queueing network (see Figure 6) consisting of two Jackson servers with service rates λn_c and

$$u(n) = A_o(n) p_o(n) u_o(n), \quad n_c + n = N, \quad \text{respectively.}$$

The stationary probability distribution of the number of processes executing in the system n is known to be

(17)
$$p(n) = \frac{1}{H} \frac{\lambda^n}{(N-n)! \prod_{i=1}^{n} u(i)}$$

where

$$H = \sum_{n=0}^{N} \frac{\lambda^n}{(N-n)! \prod_{i=1}^{n} u(i)}$$

Using (7) we write

$$\prod_{i=1}^{n} u(i) = \prod_{i=1}^{n} A_o(i) p_o(i) u_o(i) = \frac{1}{c^n} \prod_{i=1}^{n} A_o(i)$$

which after substitution into (17) yields

(18)
$$\begin{cases} p(n) = \dfrac{1}{H} \dfrac{(\lambda c)^n}{(N-n)! \prod\limits_{i=1}^{n} A_o(i)} \\[20pt] H = \sum\limits_{n=0}^{N} \dfrac{(\lambda c)^n}{(N-n)! \prod\limits_{i=1}^{n} A_o(i)} . \end{cases}$$

In the solution given by (18) there is still an unknown function $A_o(i) =$ Prob $\{$CPU busy $|$ i processes in the system$\}$, i=1,...,N. In order to compute $A_o(i)$, we shall make use of the physical nature of the problem, i.e. the values of the model parameters. The mean think time of a user at a terminal is of order of

$$1/\lambda = 10 \text{ sec}$$

Current values for the mean service times of the SM and the FD could be

$$1/u_1 = 10 \text{ msec.}$$
and
$$1/u_2 = 50 \text{ msec.}$$

Assume that the mean compute time of a process c is 1 sec and that there are N=50 terminals. We then have

$$(N-i)\lambda + p_o(i) u_o(i) \leq 0.006 \quad , \quad \text{for all } i=1,...,N$$
and
$$u_1 + u_2 + u_o(i)(1-p_o(i)) \geq 0.02 , \quad \text{for all } i=1,...,N$$

taking for the mean compute time between two successive I/O requests r 50 ms. Therefore, we shall be able to assume, for practically all values of model parameters which are of interest, that

$$(19) \quad \left\{ (N-i)\lambda + x(n_o)u_o(i)p_o(i) \ll \sum_{\ell=1}^{2} x(n_\ell)u_\ell + x(n_o)u_o(i) \sum_{\ell=1}^{2} p_\ell(i), \quad i=1,\ldots,N \,; \right.$$

$$\forall\, n_o \,,\, n_\ell = 0,\ldots,N \,.$$

But then, according to Theorem 2, the system is nearly completely decomposable and $A_o(i)$ is approximately equal to the probability of the CPU being busy in the closed queueing network of Figure 7 with a total of i processes executing in it.

We write p_1u_o, p_1u_o, p_2u_o for $p_o(i)\,u_o(i)$, $p_1(i)u_o(i)$ and $p_2(i)u_o(i)$, given by (6) and (7), respectively, and also u_o for $u_o(i)$.

The model is a particular case of Jackson's network [6] so that we have the stationary solution defined as

$$p^i(n_o,n_1,n_2) = \lim_{t\to\infty} p^i(n_o,n_1,n_2,t)$$

$$(20) \quad p^i(n_o,n_1,n_2) = \frac{1}{G(i)} \left(\frac{p_1u_o}{u_1}\right)^{n_1} \left(\frac{p_2u_o}{u_2}\right)^{n_2}$$

where

$$(21) \quad G(i) = \sum_{n_1,n_2} \left(\frac{p_1u_o}{u_1}\right)^{n_1} \left(\frac{p_2u_o}{u_2}\right)^{n_2} \qquad 0 \le n_1+n_2 \le i.$$

A_o^i is the probability of a non-empty CPU queue given by

$$A_o^i = \sum_{\substack{1 \le n_o \le i \\ 0 \le n_1 < i}} p^i(n_o,n_1,n_2)$$

and is obtained directly from (21) (see [2]) as

$$(22) \quad A_o^i = \frac{G(i-1)}{G(i)} \,.$$

It results from Theorem 2 that

$$(23) \quad A_o(i) \approx A_o^i$$

which, together with (18), yields an approximate solution for the total number of processes in the three queues.

We also remark that $p^i(n_o,n_1,n_2)$ given by (20) is approximately equal to the probability of having (n_o,n_1,n_2) processes in the three queues of the original model conditioned on the fact that $n_o+n_1+n_2 = i$, i.e.

$$(24) \quad p(n_o,n_1,n_2 \mid \sum_{j=0}^{2} n_j = i) \approx p^i(n_o,n_1,n_2)$$

We therefore may compute approximate values for the state probabilities $p(n_o,n_1,n_2,n_c)$ as

$$(25) \quad p(n_o,n_1,n_2,n_c) = p(N-n_c)p^{N-n_c}(n_o,n_1,n_2)$$

The expected response time W obtained from the Little's formula (see [14]) is given by

$$W = \frac{\bar{n}}{\lambda(N-\bar{n})}$$

where $\bar{n}$ is the mean total number of processes in the three queues, so that considering $\bar{n}$ as a variable we have

$$\frac{\Delta W}{W} \approx \frac{N}{N-\bar{n}} \frac{\Delta \bar{n}}{\bar{n}} \quad .$$

We see that for $\bar{n}$ close to N a small relative error in $\bar{n}$ will produce an important error in W, e.g. let

$$N = 20$$

$$\bar{n} = 19$$

$$\frac{\Delta \bar{n}}{\bar{n}} = 0,5 \ \%$$

then

$$\frac{\Delta W}{W} \approx \frac{20}{20-19} \ 0.5 \ \% = 10 \ \%.$$

Therefore, when the system saturates ($\bar{n}$ becomes close to N) the values obtained for the expected response time may not be reliable.

Numerical results obtained from our model with the Belady lifetime function (9) are reported in Figures 8 to 13 in which the CPU utilization and the mean response time of the system versus N (the number of terminals) are shown for a wide range of model parameters. The mean compute time of a process c and the mean think time of a user $\frac{1}{\lambda}$ are kept constant throughout the examples at 500 msec. and 10 sec., respectively. α is set to $\alpha=0.01$ and the mean compute time between two successive I/O requests r is set to r=20 msec.

In Figures 8 and 9 the effect of the number of terminals N on the CPU utilization and the expected response time, respectively is shown for a set of system parameters with a primary memory size M=128 pages. We see that an improvement in program behaviour (increasing k from 1.5 to 2.0 and 2.5) can produce a dramatic increase in the CPU utilization as well as an improvement of the mean response time of the system. We also see that there is an optimal number of terminals which maximizes CPU utilization and when N exceeds this number the CPU utilization decreases dramatically while the average response time goes up very rapidly. The same curves are drawn in Figures 10 and 11 with M=256 pages but with the other parameters unchanged. We observe a marked increase of CPU utilization and of the optimal number of terminals and an important improvement in the expected response time. The effect of the mean service time of the paging secondary memory device

($t_{SM}=\frac{1}{u_1}$) is illustrated in Figures 12, 13 and 10, 11 where t_{SM} is reduced from

10 ms (in Figures 12, 13) to 5 ms without modifying the remaining parameters.

The same numerical results obtained with the Chamberlin lifetime function are shown in Figures 14 to 19. The curves labelled 1, 2 and 3 in each figure correspond to the following values of parameters b and d in (10) :

$$b = 20 \ ms, \quad d = 60 \ pages$$

$$b = 25 \ ms, \quad d = 50 \ pages$$

$$b = 10 \ ms, \quad d = 15 \ pages.$$

These values are taken from [10]. The mean compute time of a process and the mean think time of a user are set to c=500 ms and $\frac{1}{\lambda}$ = 10 s, respectively.

We see that the curves obtained exhibit the same behaviour as for the Belady lifetime function. This is probably due to the fact that in the region where the two approximations differ, the paging device is under light load and thus the response time is determined by CPU and I/O demand.

As a whole, it appears that the expected response time of the system increases relatively slowly with N (the number of terminals) until the value of N which maximizes CPU utilization is reached ; when the number of terminals exceeds this value the response time "explodes". Therefore a good operation point for the system seems to be slightly below the number of terminals which maximizes CPU utilization.

IV - SYSTEMS WITH CONTROL OF THE DEGREE OF MULTIPROGRAMMING

In the time-sharing system studied in the preceding sections a user command arriving to the system was unconditionally admitted into the CPU queue, i.e. allowed to share real core. Intuitively, this seems to be the reason why the system thrashes (the CPU utilization drops down dramatically and the response time explodes) when the number of active terminals increases over a certain value. In this section we investigate two ways of controlling the degree of multiprogramming in a time-sharing virtual memory computer.

A study of the application of optimal control mechanisms can be found in [18]. The approach we shall present here is essentially different from [18] in that we give analytical results for control mechanisms which are not necessarily optimal with respect to some performance criterion.

Consider the system described in Figure 20. It consists like the system of Section 2 of a set of terminals, a CPU, a secondary memory device (SM) and a filing disk (FD). The latter three devices, each having a queue of requests associated with it, constitute the processing part of the system (R) in which users share real core.

A command generated by a user has now to pass first through the queue Q and a control switch K before being admitted to share real memory.

K is characterized by a function $f(k,n)$ which may take only two values 0 and 1 :

$$f(k,n) = \begin{cases} 0 \\ 1 \end{cases} \quad \text{if the switch is} \quad \begin{cases} \text{open} \\ \text{closed} \end{cases} \quad ,$$

when there are k and n processes in Q and R, respectively.

The function $f(k,n)$ will be called the control function.

Suppose that at a given instant of time t there are k and n processes in Q and R, respectively. Suppose also that an arrival of a command from a terminal occurs. The state of the system becomes $(k+1,n)$ and the control switch K is instantaneously placed in the position corresponding to $f(k+1,n)$. Assume that $f(k+1,n)=1$; then a process of Q (e.g. the first process in the queue) will instantaneously enter the queue R, the state of the system thus becoming $(k,n+1)$. If $f(k,n+1) = 1$ another process will be admitted into R, but if $f(k,n+1) = 0$, k will remain open at least until another arrival of a command from the terminals or a departure of a process from R occurs.

It is assumed that changes in the control switch position and introduction of a user from Q to R take place in zero time.

We make the same assumption regarding the service times as in Section 2 so that, formulae (6), (7), (9) and (10) remain valid.

Clearly, certain states, although possible, will have a zero probability because of the assumption of instantaneous position changes for the control switch K. These unstable states will not be considered in the stationary probability distribution.

It can be shown (see [19]) that the processing part R of the model of Figure 20 is equivalent in the sense of Definition 1 to a single exponential server with service rate
(26) $$u(k,n) = A_0(k,n)p_0(n)u_0(n) = A_0(k,n)/c$$

where $A_0(k,n)$ is the stationary probability of the CPU being busy conditioned on the fact that there are k and n processes in Q and R, respectively.

Let the behaviour of the control switch be described by the control function $f_1(k,n)$ (27).

$$(27) \qquad f(k,n) = f_1(k,n) = \begin{cases} 1, & \text{if } 0 \leq n \leq n_o - 1 \qquad 0 < n_o \leq N \\ \\ 0, & \text{otherwise} \end{cases}$$

Clearly, if conditions (16) hold, the system of Figure 20 enjoys the property of near complete decomposability : for $n=0,\ldots,n_o-1$ k is zero and the system behaves as if the queue Q and the control switch did not exist ; for $n=n_o$ and $k \neq 0$ the number of processes in R is maintained constant ; Q acts as a separation buffer between the terminals and the processing part R.

The rigorous proof of the near complete decomposability property of the system is easy to carry out and will not be presented.

Note that for each value of n_c there is only one possible pair (k,n) and we have

$$(28) \qquad A_o(k,n) \approx A_o(n) = A_o^n$$

A_o^n in (28) is the probability of the CPU being busy in the closed system of Figure 7 and is given by (22).

Let $p(k,n)$ be the stationary probability of having k and n processes in Q and R, respectively

$$(29) \quad \begin{cases} p(k,n) = G \dfrac{(\lambda c)^k}{(N-n_o-k)! \left[A_o(n_o)\right]^k} \dfrac{(\lambda c)^n}{(N-n)! \prod\limits_{i=1}^{n} A_o(i)} \\ \\ \dfrac{1}{G} = \dfrac{1}{(N-n_o)!} \sum\limits_{n=0}^{n_o-1} \dfrac{(\lambda c)^n}{(N-n)! \prod\limits_{i=1}^{n} A_o(i)} + \dfrac{(\lambda c)^{n_o}}{(N-n_o)! \prod\limits_{i=1}^{n_o} A_o(i)} \sum\limits_{k=0}^{N-n_o} \dfrac{(\lambda c)^k}{(N-n_o-k)! \left[A_o(n_o)\right]^k}. \end{cases}$$

The efficiency of the control is illustrated in Figures 21 and 22 where the mean response time versus N (the number of terminals) is shown for a set of system parameters. In Figure 21 the effect of varying the maximum degree of multiprogramming n_o is examined for the model with the Belady lifetime function the locality exponent k being set to 2.0. We see that there exists an optimal value of n_o which minimizes the expected response time and makes it increase with N much more slowly than in a system without control of the degree of multiprogramming. The same conclusions may be drawn from the curves of Figure 22 which shows the effect of varying n_o for our model with the Chamberlin function with parameters b=20 ms and d=60 pages.

An explicit expression can also be obtained (see [15] and [19]) for the stationary state probability distribution of k and n with another control function :

$$(30) \qquad f_2(k,n) = \begin{cases} 1 \ , & \text{if } 0 \leq n \leq n_o - 1 \\ \\ 0 \ , & \text{if } n = n_o \text{ and } k = 0,1,\ldots,k_o \ , \\ \\ 1 \ , & \text{if } k > k_o \\ \\ 0 \ , & \text{otherwise} \end{cases}$$

$$(31) \qquad p(k,n) = G \dfrac{(\lambda c)^k (N-n_o)!}{(N-n_o-k)! \left[A_o(n_o)\right]^k} \dfrac{(\lambda c)^n}{(N-n)! \prod\limits_{i=1}^{n} A_o(i)} \qquad \begin{array}{l} \text{for } n = 0,\ldots,n_o \\ k = 0,\ldots,k_o \end{array}$$

$$(31) \quad p(k,n) = G \frac{(\lambda c)^{k_o}}{\left[A_o(n_o)\right]^{k_o}} \frac{(\lambda c)^n}{(N-k_o-n)! \prod_{i=1}^{n} A_o(i)} \text{ for } n=n_o,\ldots,N-k_o \quad k=k_o$$

G is the normalization constant.

Numerical results obtained for the control function $f_2(k,n)$ are reported in Figure 23 where the effect of varying k_o (the maximum stable state length of the queue Q) is shown for a value of n_o which is optimum when the control function $f_1(k,n)$ is used. We see that the mean response time of the system passes monotonically from the curve for the system with no control of the degree of multiprogramming ($k_o=0$) to the curve for the control function $f_1(k,n)$ (k=N).

It may be shown (see [15]) that if $A_o(n)$ is a unimodal function of n with only one maximum for $n=n_1$, then among all control functions $f_1(k,n)$ the one with $n_o=n_1$ yields the minimum expected response time for all N, and no control function $f_2(k,n)$ can ensure better response time. Therefore, the optimum value for n_o in a control function $f_1(k,n)$ is approximately equal (for a system which is nearly completely decomposable) to the value of i which maximizes CPU utilization A_o^i ((22)) for the system of Figure 7 :

$$n_o \approx i_1$$

$$A_o^{i_1} \geq A_o^i \ , \ \forall \ i=1,\ldots,N.$$

Note that the control function $f_1(k,n)$ with $n_o=i_1$ ensures a near optimal CPU utilization and thus prevents thrashing.

An optimization mechanism which periodically estimates $A_o(n)$ and determines the n_o to be applied in the control function $f_1(k,n)$, has been implemented by the author in an experimental system and its performance is currently under study.

ACKNOWLEDGMENTS

I would like to thank all the members of the research group on modelling and performance evaluation at I.R.I.A. for providing the pleasant atmosphere in which this work was done. I would also like to thank Professor E. GELENBE for his encouragement and advice in the preparation of this paper, and Dr. J. LEROUDIER and Mr. D. BASTIN whose simulation and numerical results validated the approximation methods we have presented.

BIBLIOGRAPHY

[1] C.G. Moore, Network Models for Large Scale Time-Sharing Systems, Ph. D. Thesis, University of Michigan, 1971.

[2] J. Buzen, Queueing Network Models of Multiprogramming, Ph. D. Thesis, Harvard University, 1971.

[3] S.R. Arora and A. Gallo, The Optimal Organization of Multiprogrammed Multi-Level Memory, Proc. ACM-SIGOPS Workshop on System Performance Evaluation, April 1971, 104-141.

[4] A.L. Scherr, An Analysis of Time-Shared Computer Systems, M.I.T. Press, Cambridge, Mass., 1967.

[5] A. Sekino, Throughput Analysis of Multiprogrammed Virtual-Memory Computer Systems, 1st Annual SIGME Symposium on Measurement and Evaluation, 1973, 47-53.

[6] J.R. Jackson, Jobshop-Like Queueing Systems, Management Science, 10, 1, October 1963, 131-142.

[7] R.R. Muntz and F. Baskett, Open, Closed and Mixed Networks of Queues with different Classes of Customers, Stanford Electronic Laboratories, Technical Report, N°33, August 1972.

[8] L. Belady and C.J. Kuehner, Dynamic Space Sharing in Computer Systems, Comm. ACM, Vol. 12, N°5, May 1969, 282-288.

[9] J.H. Saltzer, A simple linear model of demand paging performance, Massachusetts Institute of Technology Project MAC Report (To appear).

[10] D. Chamberlin, S. Fuller, L. Liu, An Analysis of Page Allocation Strategies for Multiprogramming Systems with Virtual Memory I.B.M. J. Res. Develop., September 1973.

[11] H. Simon and A. Ando, Aggregation of Variables in Dynamic Systems,Econometrica, Vol. 20, N°2, April 1961.

[12] A. Ando and F.M. Fisher, Near-Decomposability, Partition and Aggregation, and the Relevance of Stability Discussions, International Economic Review vol. 4, n°1, January 1963.

[13] P. Courtois, On the Near-Complete-Decomposability of Networks of Queues and of Stochastic Models of Multiprogramming Computing Systems,Carnegie Melon Report, November 1971.

[14] J.D. Little, A proof of the queueing formula L=λW, Oper. Res. 9, 1961, 383-387.

[15] A. Brandwajn, Control Schemes in Queueing networks (to appear).

[16] T.L. Saaty, Elements of Queueing theory, Mac Graw-hill, New York, 1961.

[17] A. Brandwajn, E. Gelenbe, D. Potier, J. Lenfant, Modèle de système multiprogrammé à mémoire virtuelle paginée, Compte Rendu des journées d'études sur les recherches en mesure, simulation, modélisation de systèmes informatiques, IRIA, Toulouse, juin 1973.

[18] E. Gelenbe, D. Potier, A. Brandwajn, J. Lenfant, Gestion d'un ordinateur multiprogrammé à mémoire virtuelle, 5th Conference on Optimization Techniques, Springer, Berlin, 1973.

[19] A. Brandwajn, A model of a time-sharing virtual memory system solved using equivalence and decomposition methods, (to appear).

TERMINALS

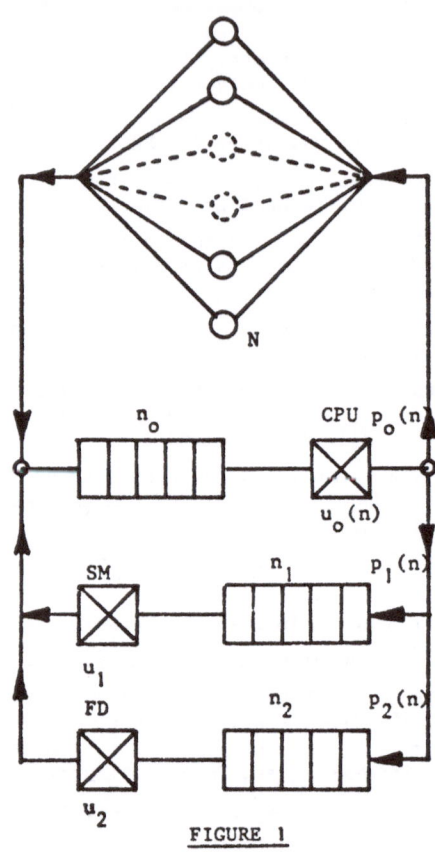

FIGURE 1

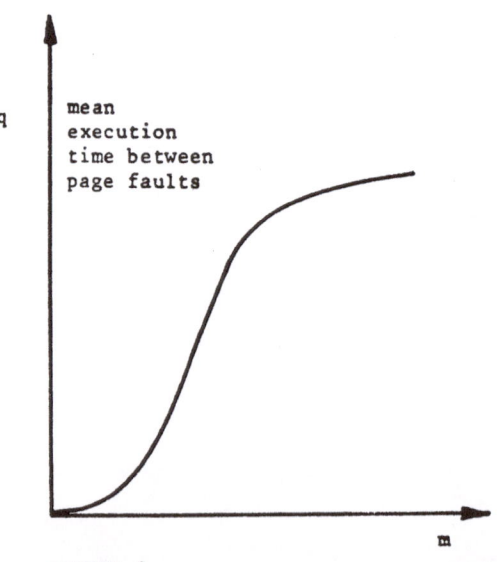

FIGURE 2

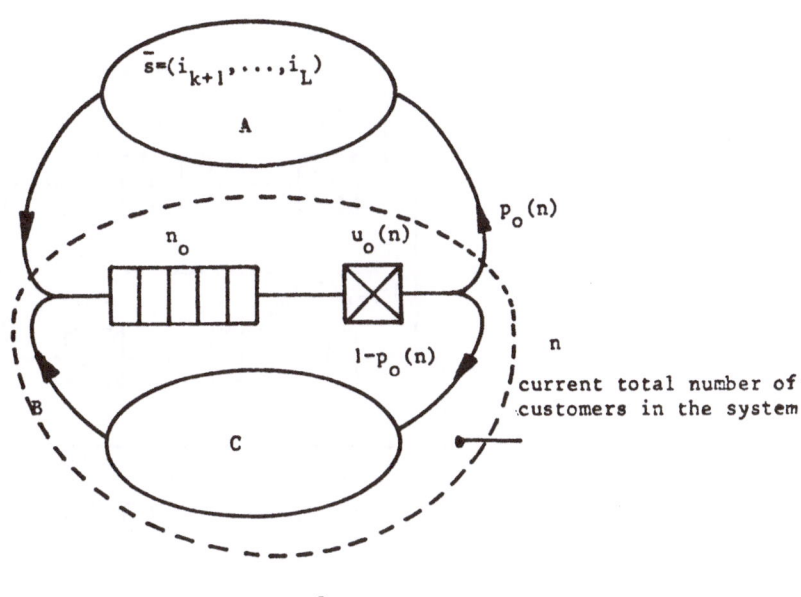

FIGURE 3

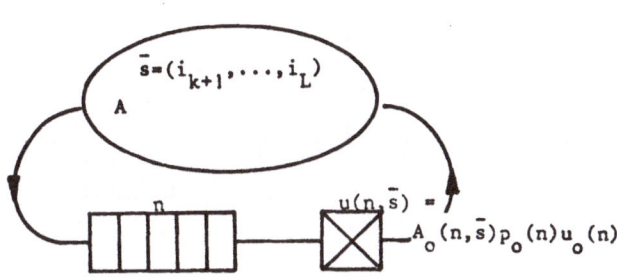

FIGURE 4

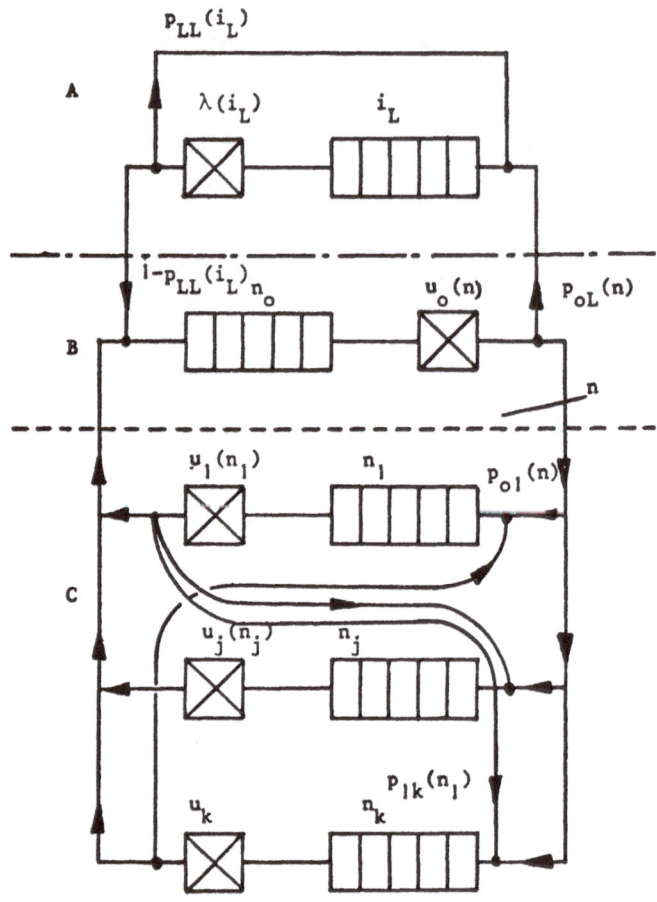

FIGURE 5

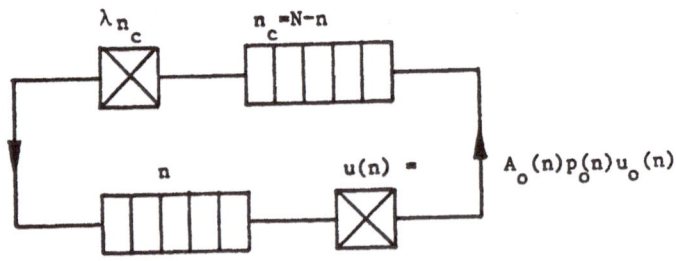

FIGURE 6

n1
SM
u1
p0
p1
n0
CPU
n2
FD
u0
p2
u2

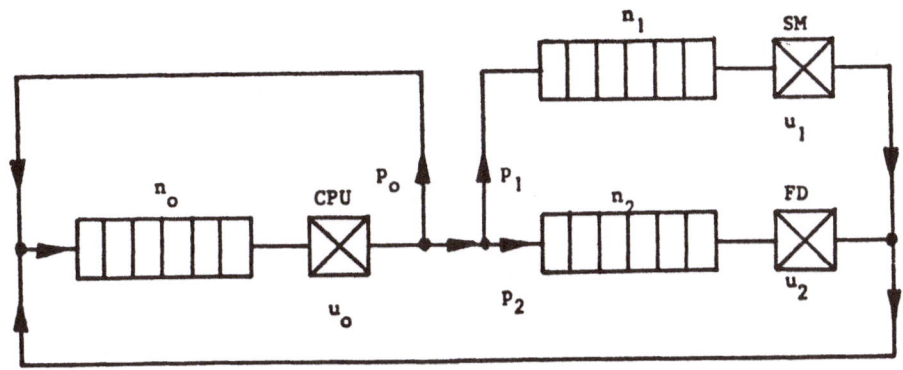

FIGURE 7

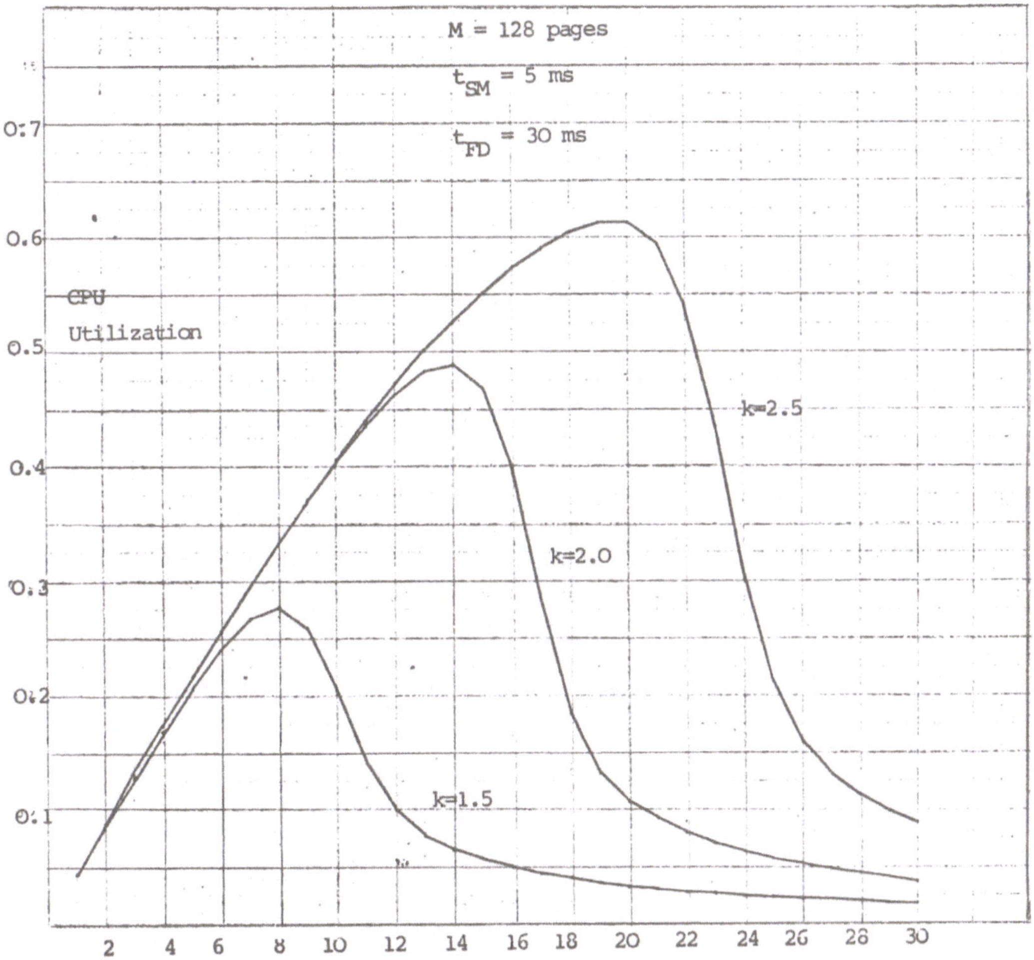

M = 128 pages
tSM = 5 ms
tFD = 30 ms
CPU
Utilization
0.7
0.6
0.5
0.4
0.3
0.2
0.1
k=2.5
k=2.0
k=1.5
2
4
6
8
10
12
14
16
18
20
22
24
26
28
30

Figure 8

Number of terminals N

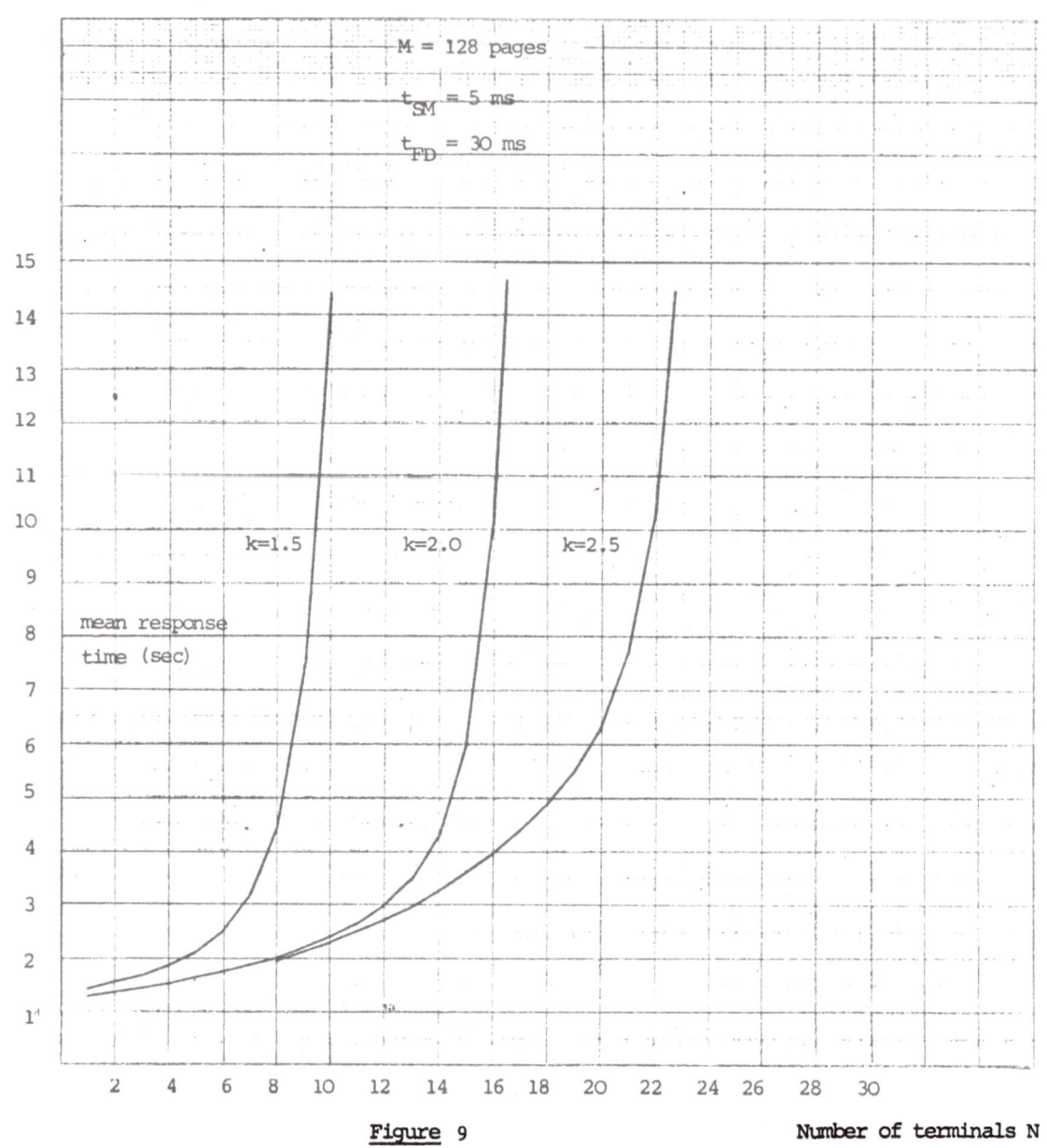

Figure 9   Number of terminals N

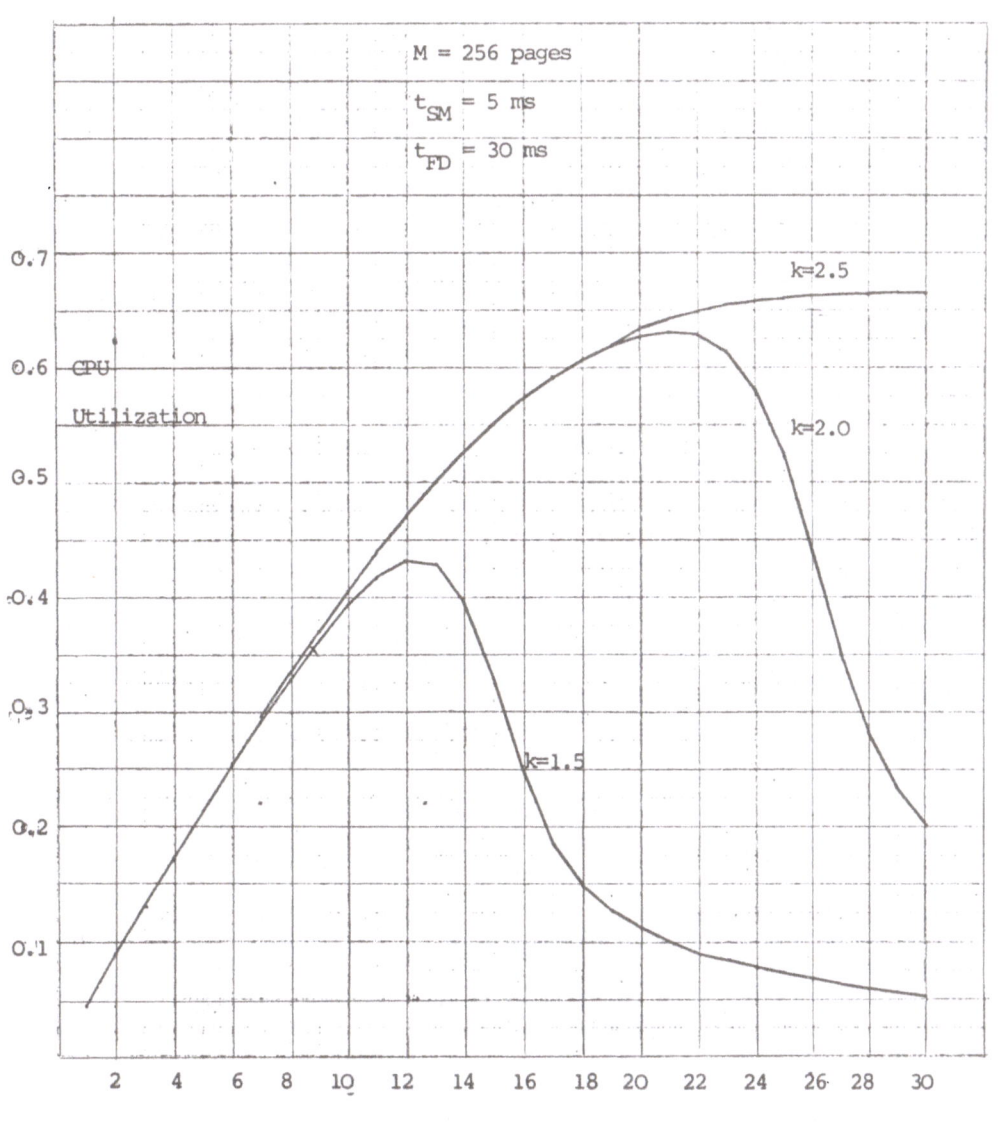

Figure 10

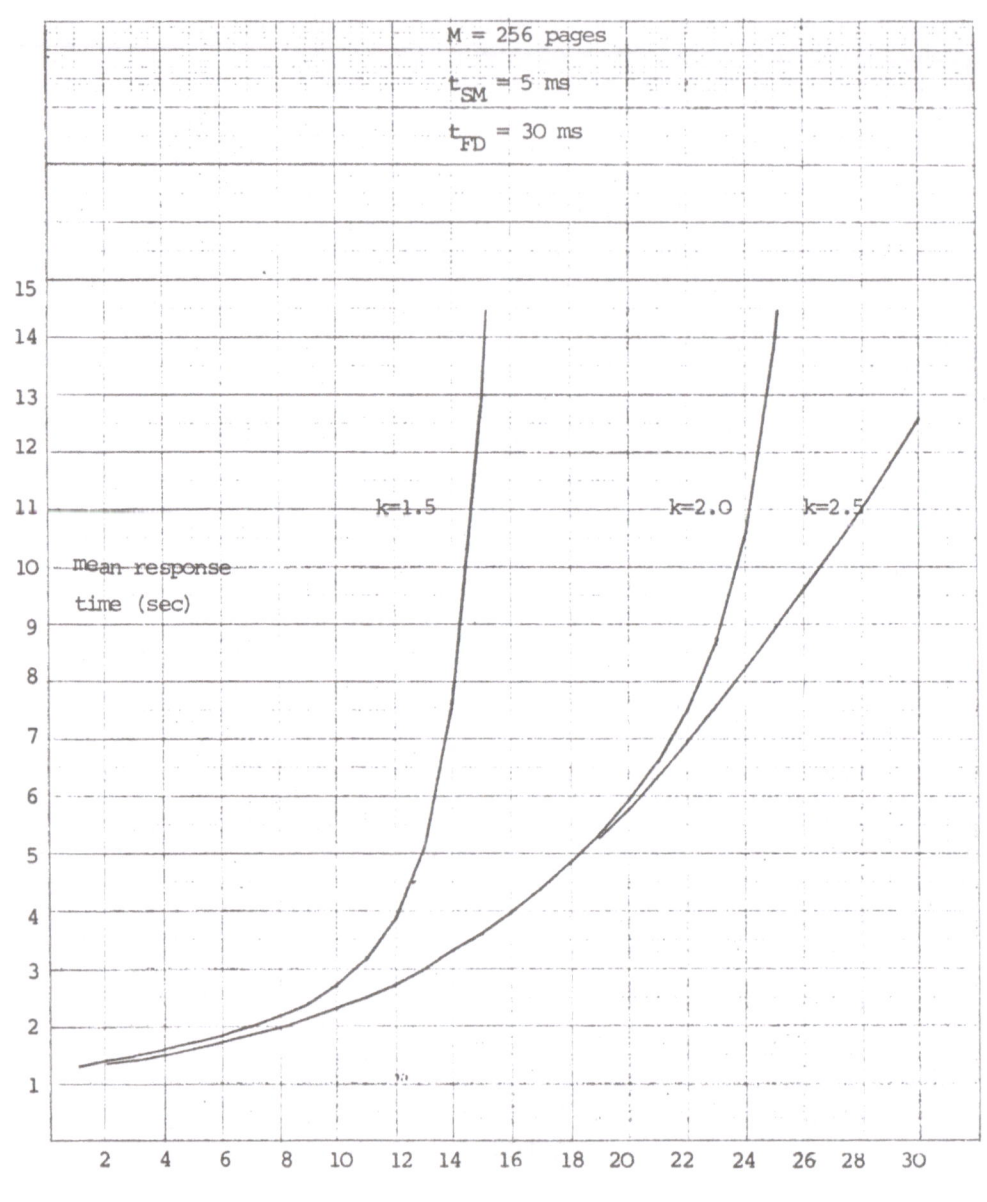

<u>Figure</u> 11

Number of terminals N

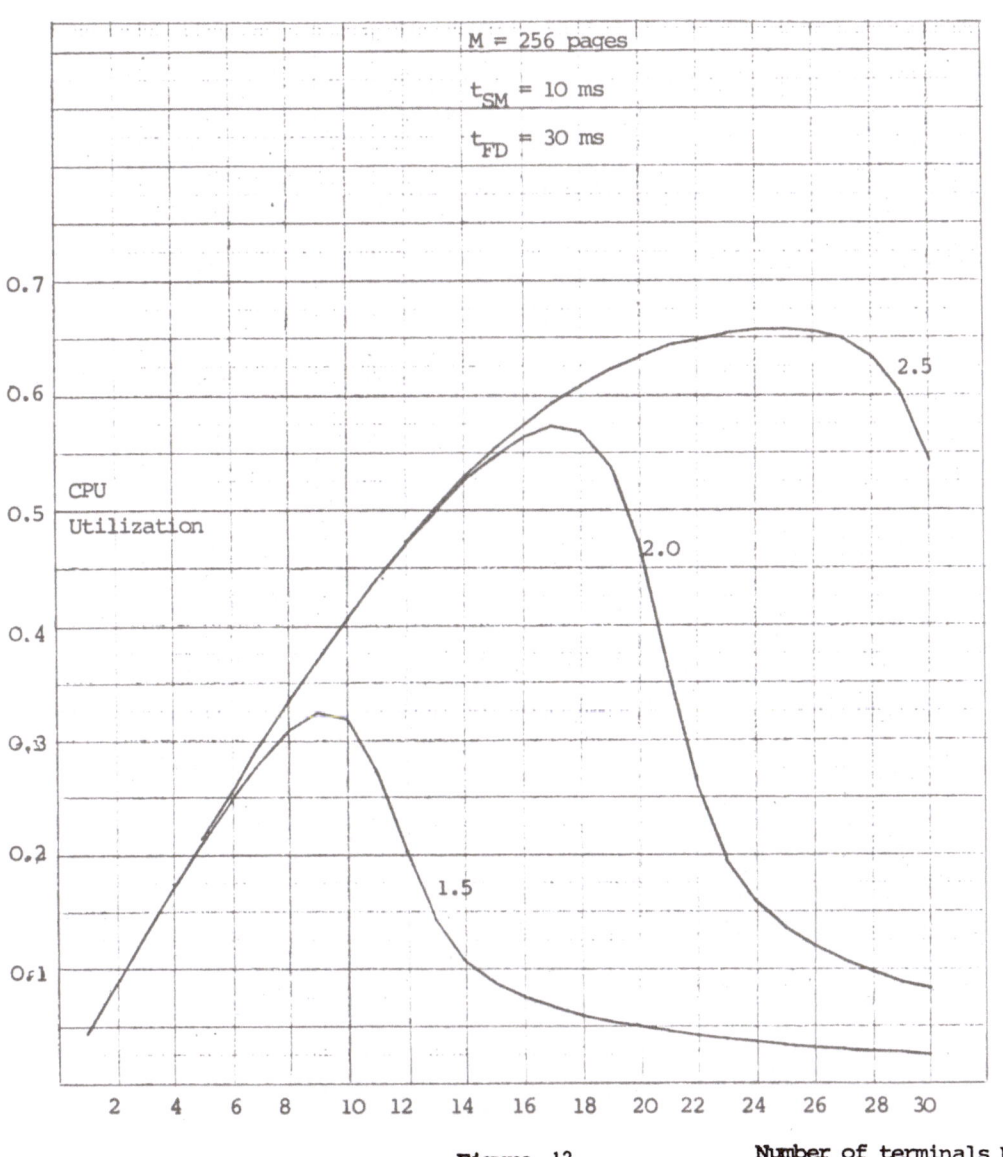

M = 256 pages

t_{SM} = 10 ms

t_{FD} = 30 ms

CPU
Utilization

2.5

2.0

1.5

Figure 12

Number of terminals N

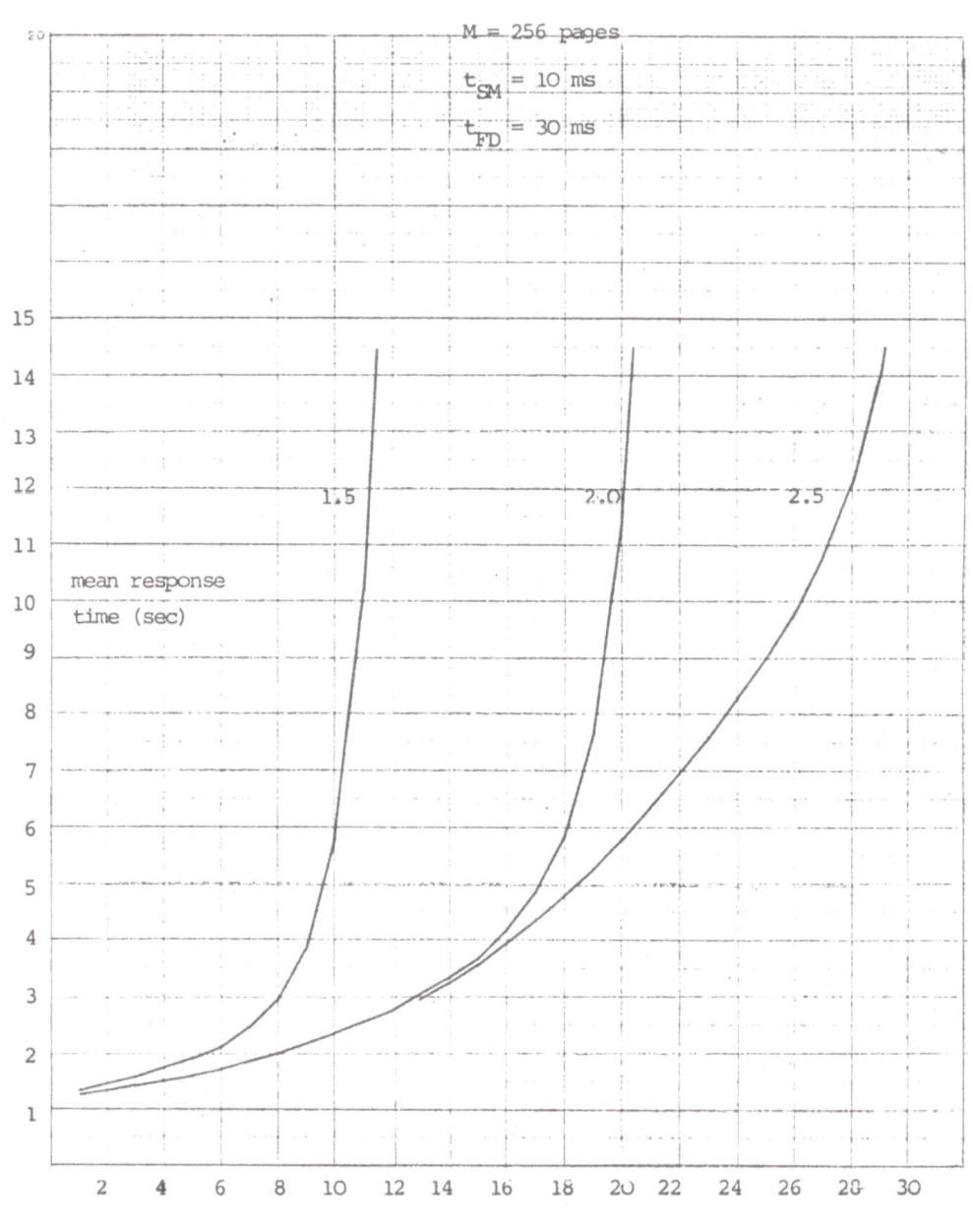

Figure 13   Number of terminals N

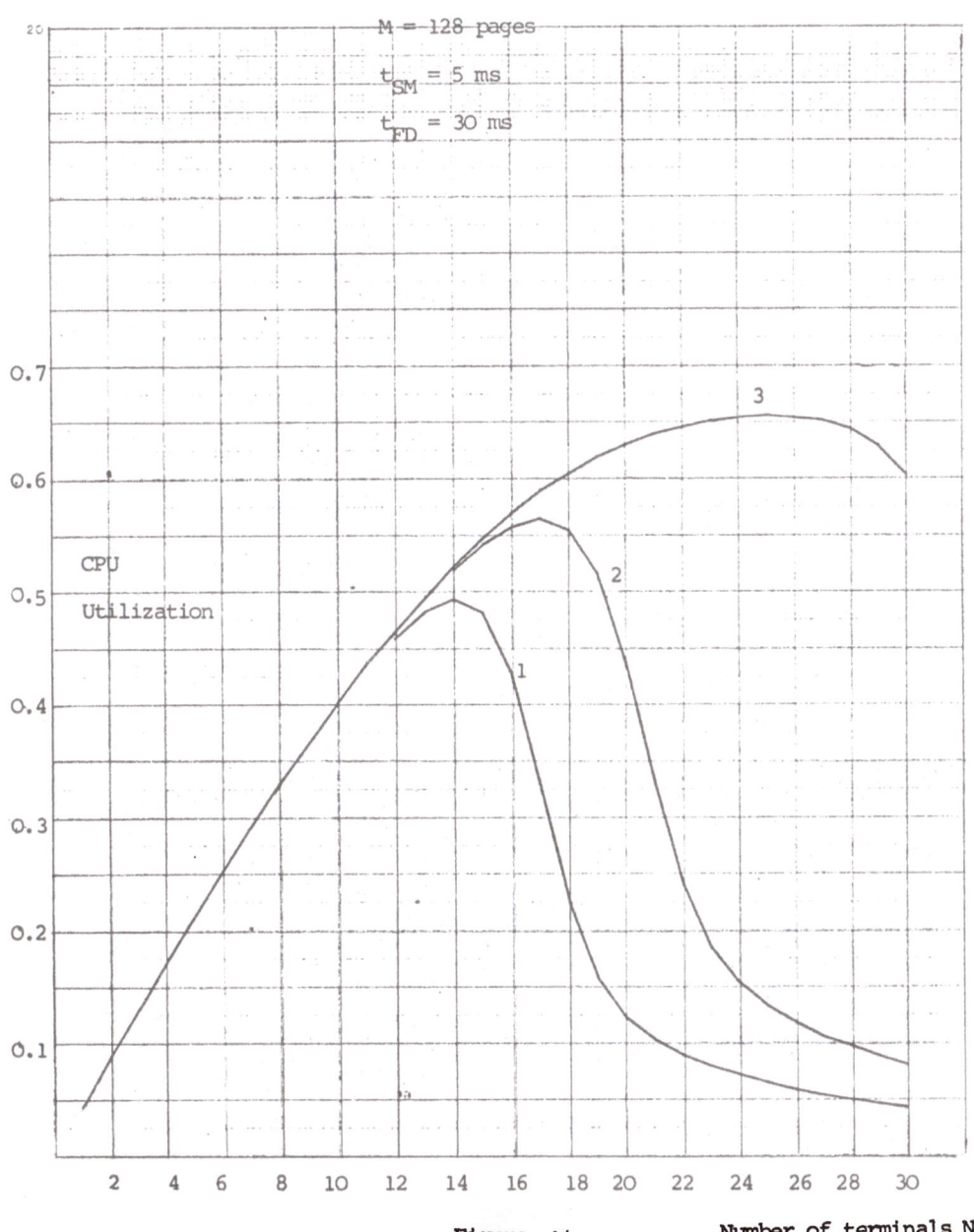

Figure   14

Number of terminals N

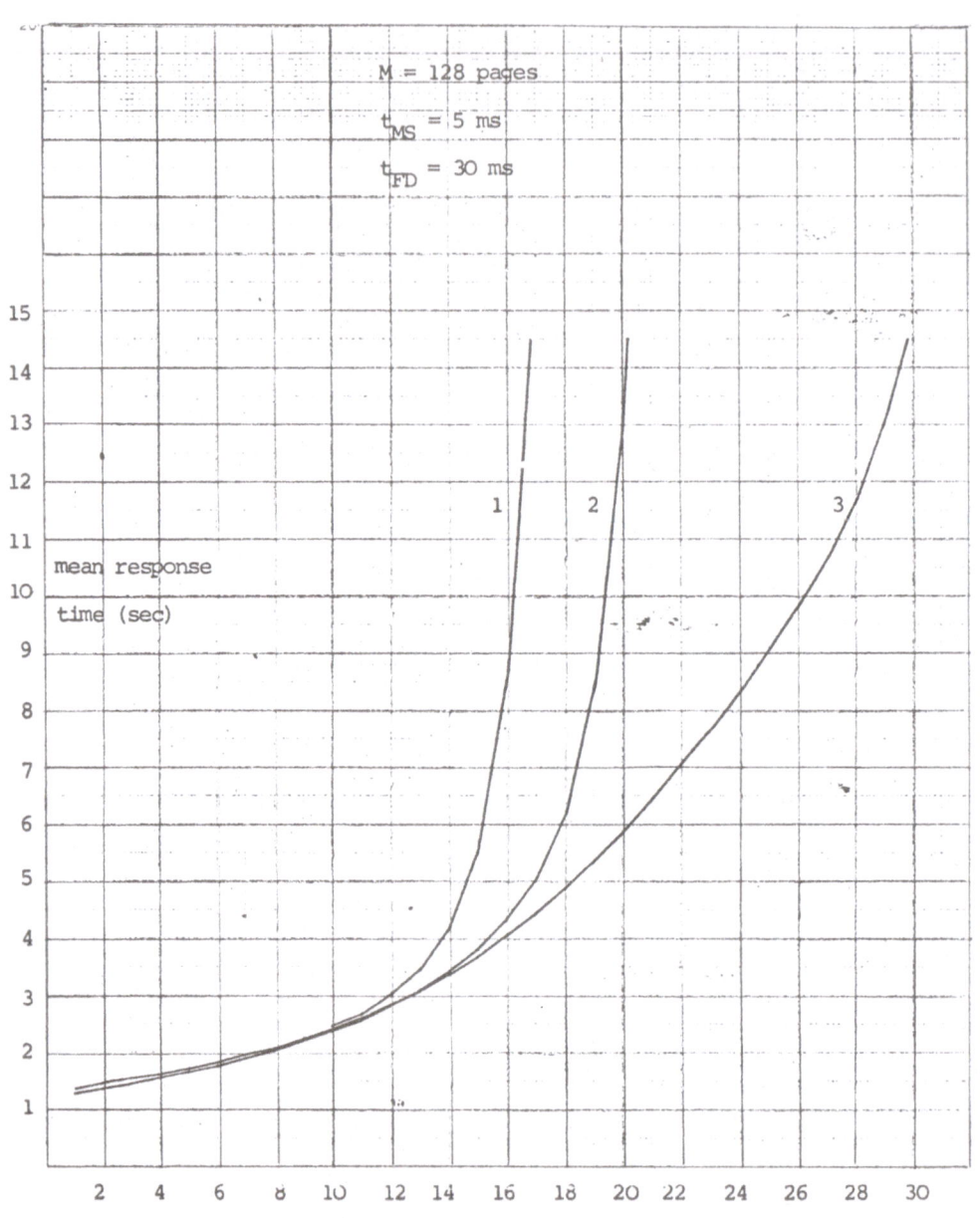

Figure 15   Number of terminals N

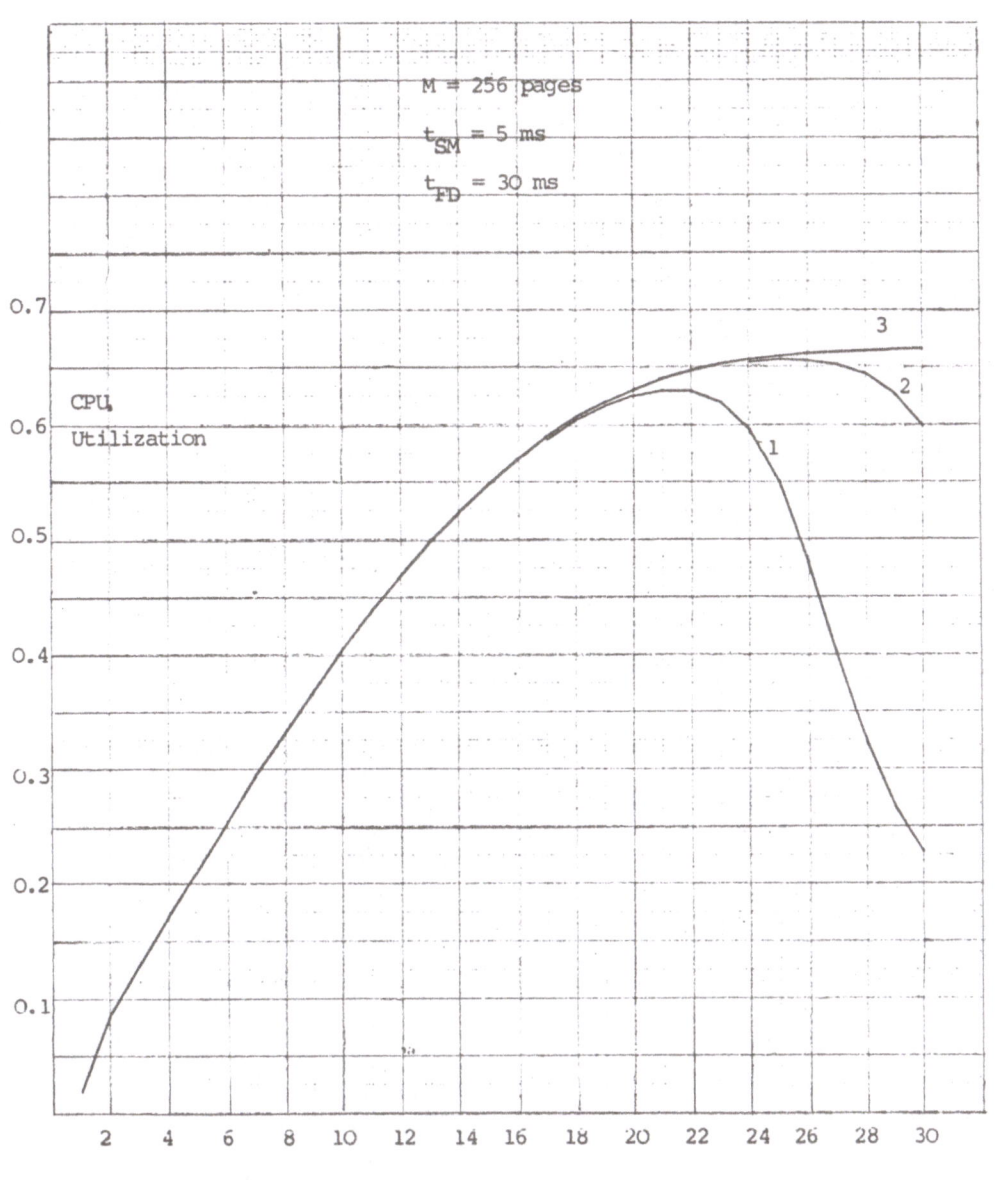

M = 256 pages

t_{SM} = 5 ms

t_{FD} = 30 ms

Figure 16

Number of terminals N

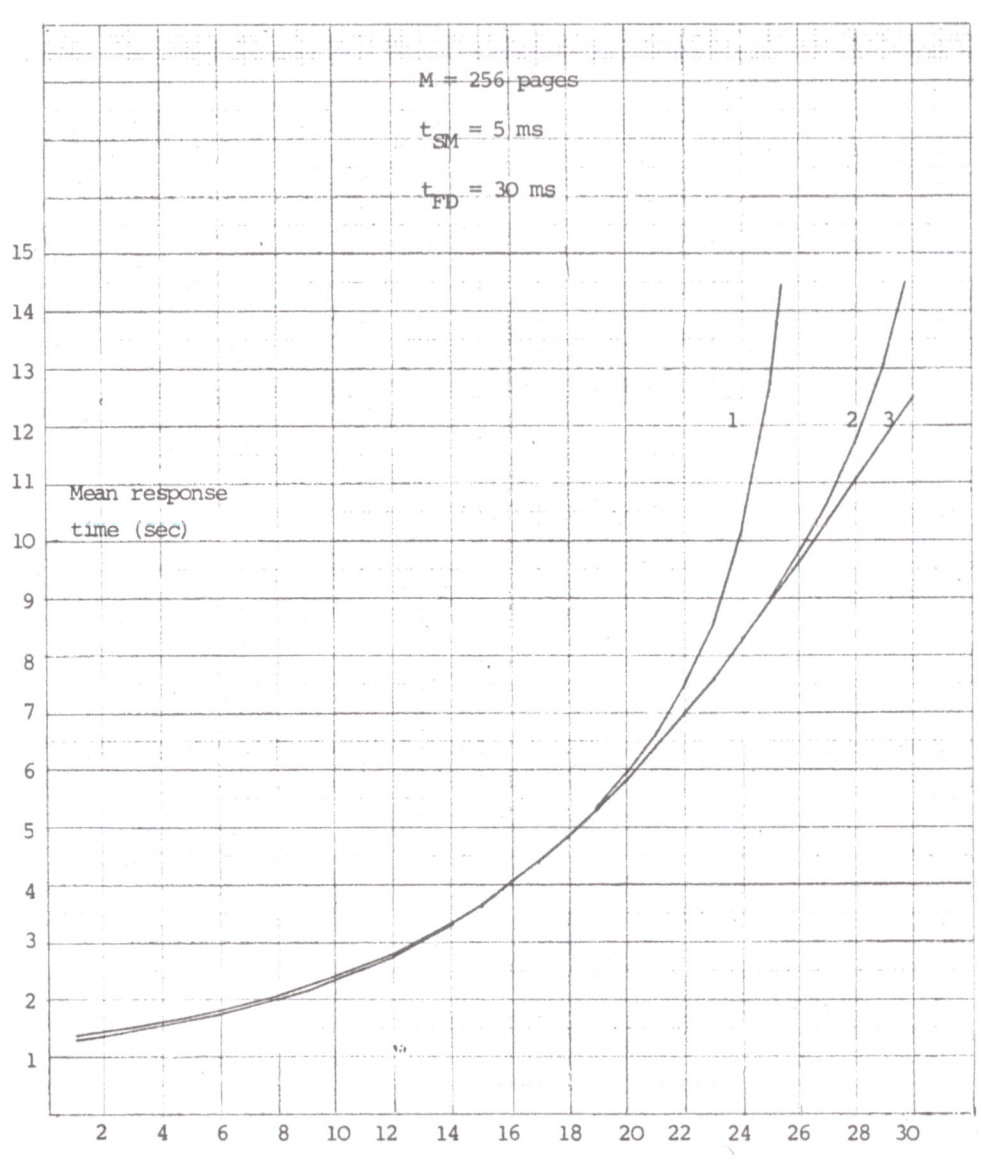

Figure 17   Number of terminals N

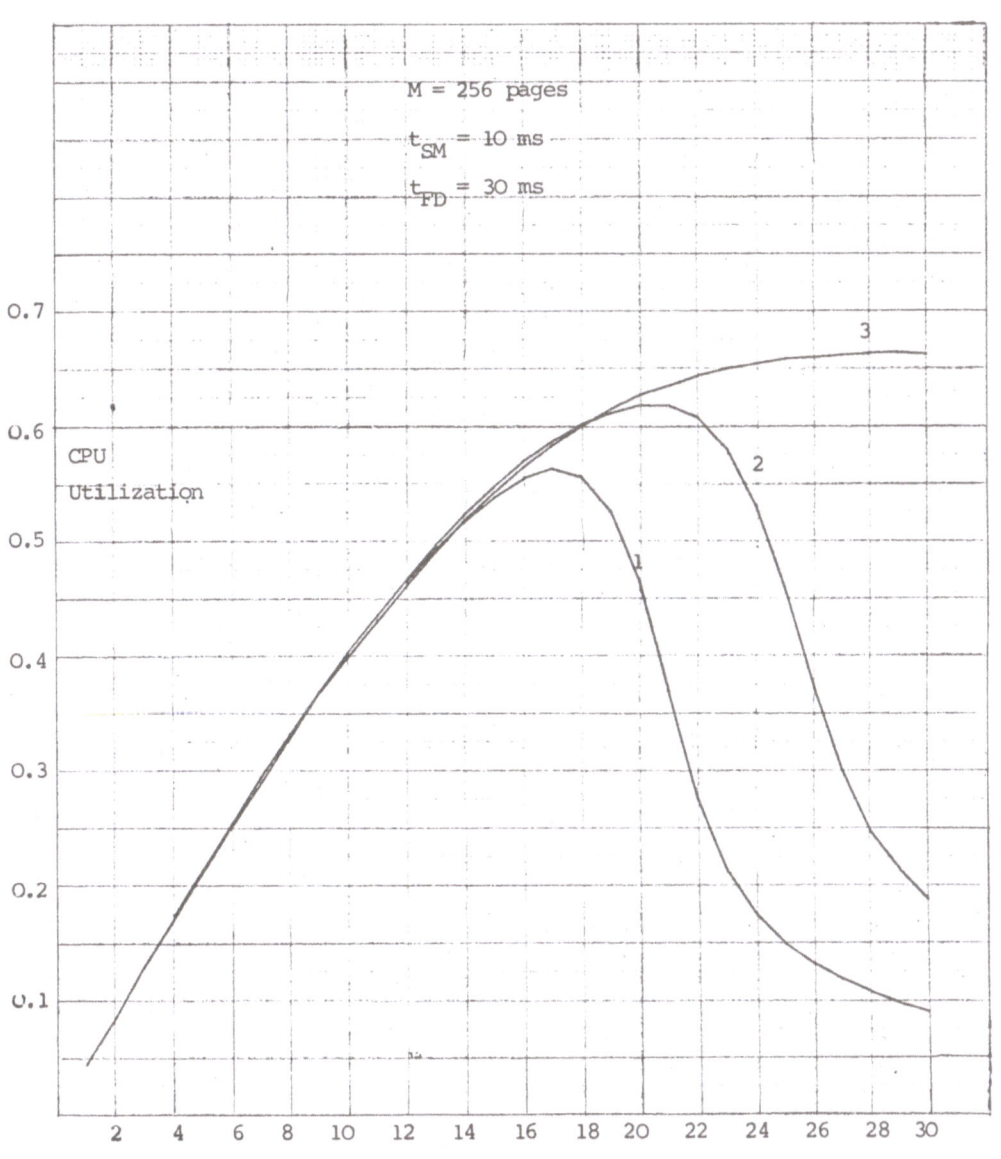

Figure 18   Number of terminals N

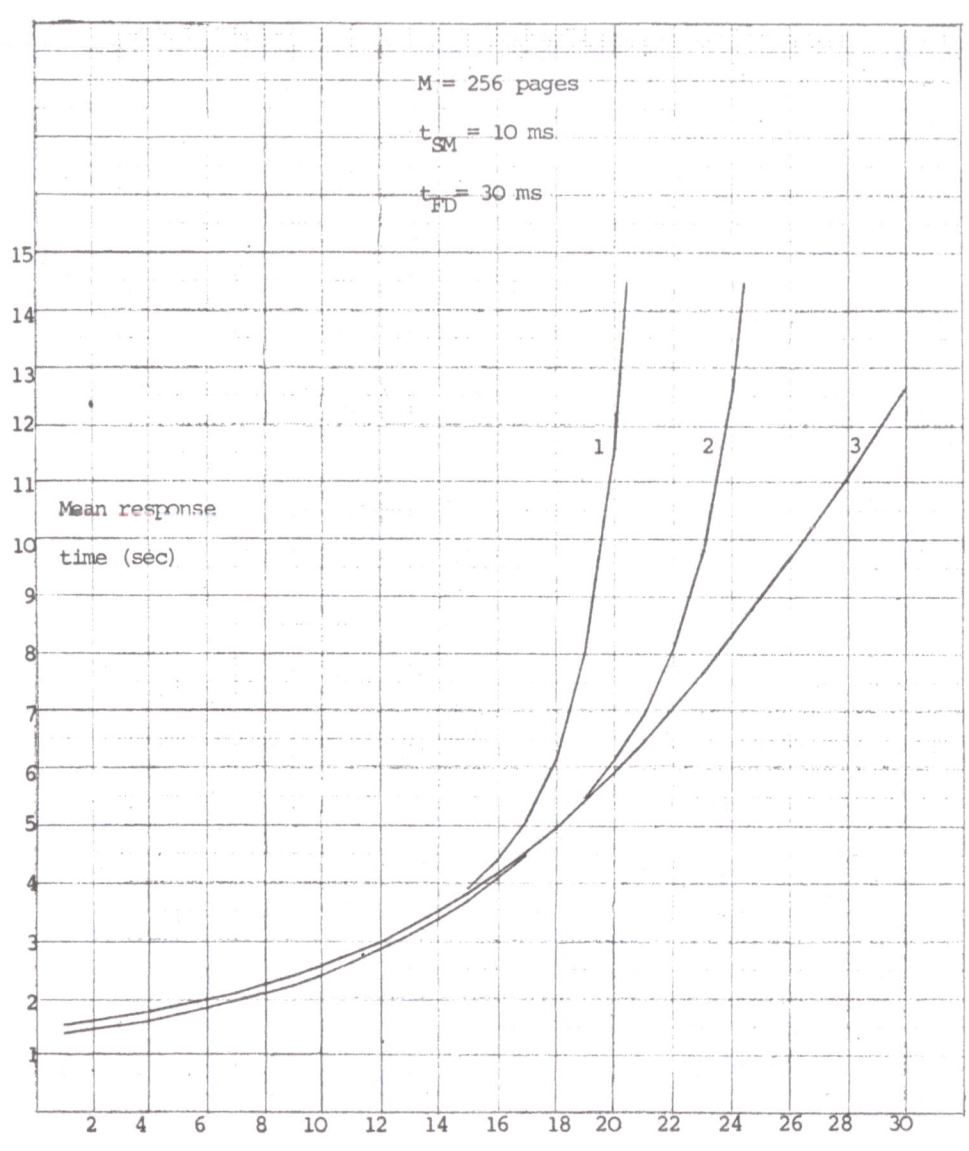

Figure 19   Number of terminals N

TERMINALS

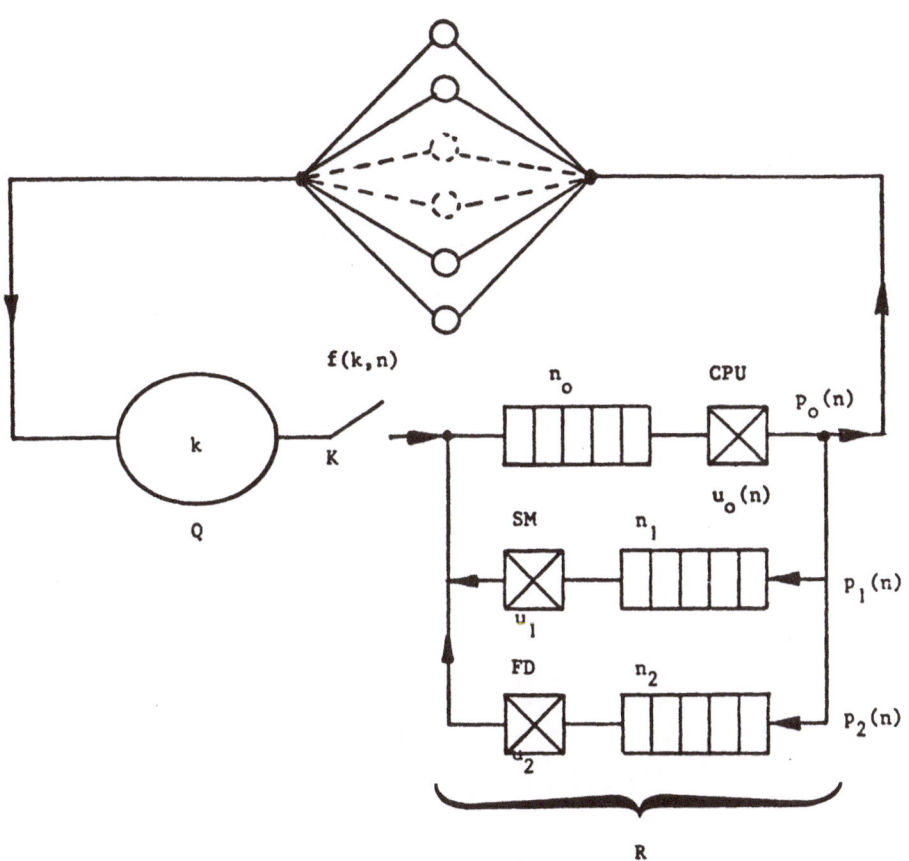

FIGURE 20

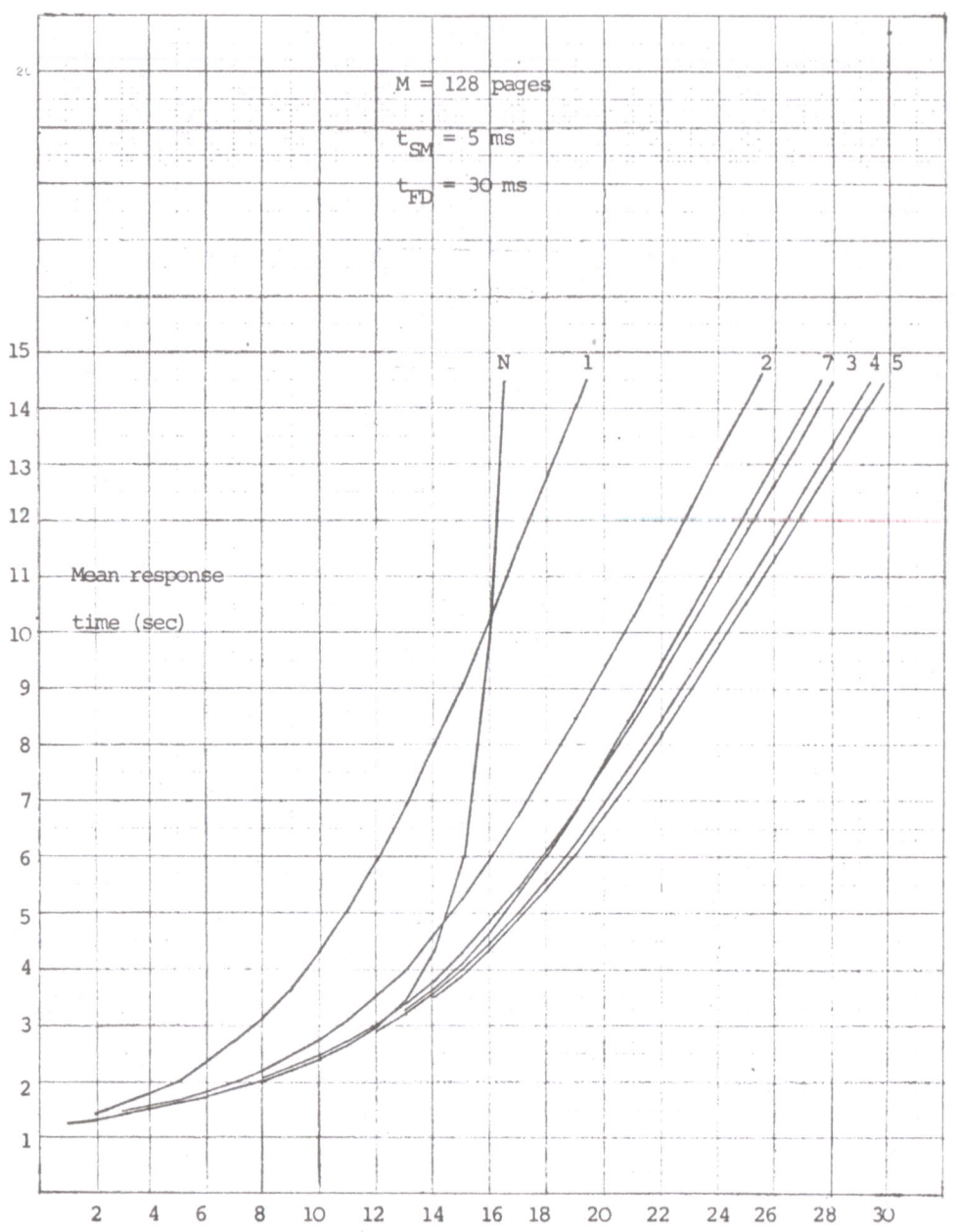

Figure 21

Number of terminals N

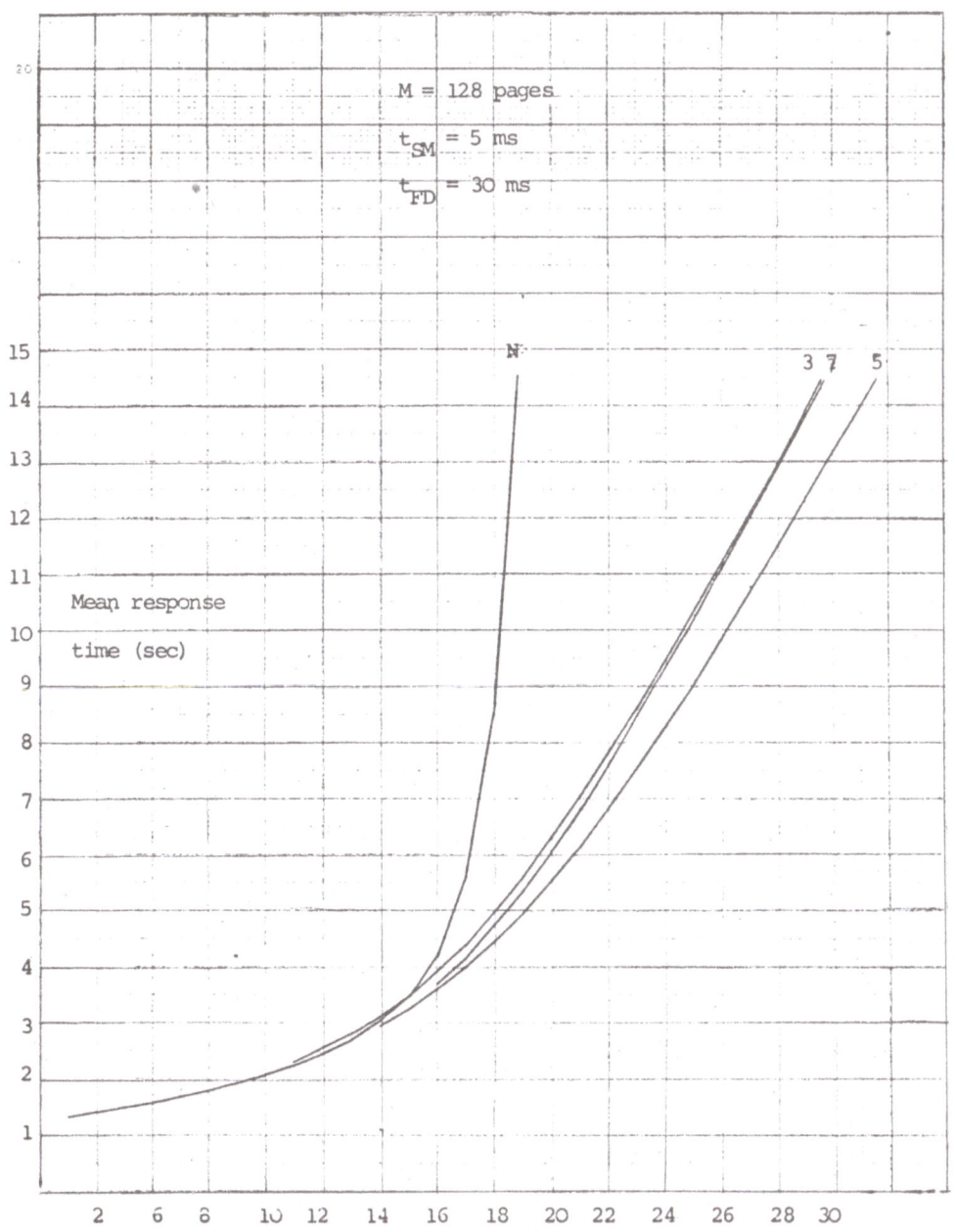

M = 128 pages

t_{SM} = 5 ms

t_{FD} = 30 ms

Mean response

time (sec)

Figure 22   Number of terminals N

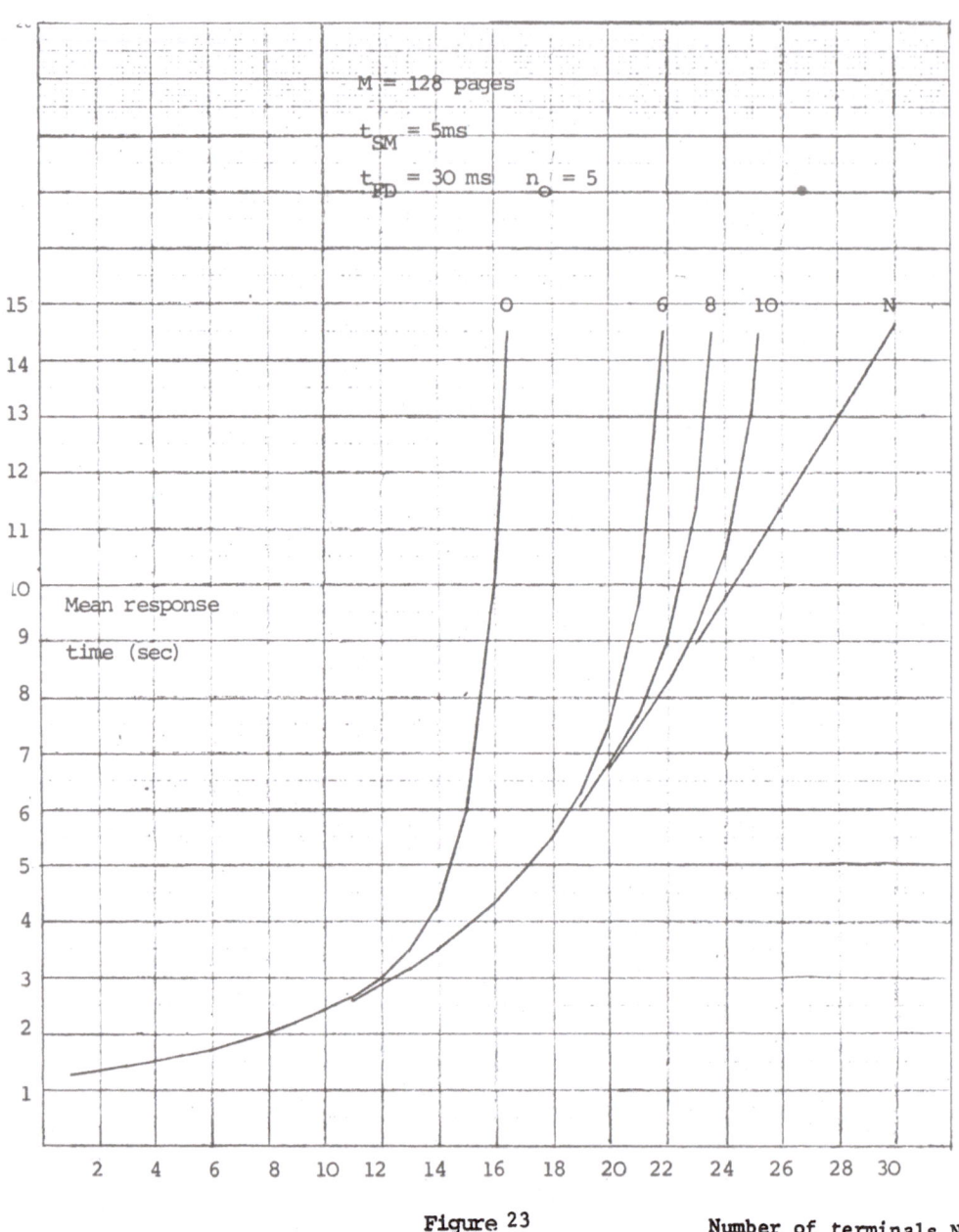

Figure 23

Number of terminals N

THE SPECIFICATION OF PROCESS SYNCHRONIZATION BY PATH EXPRESSIONS

R.H. Campbell
University of Newcastle Upon Tyne (G.B.)

A. N. Habermann
Carnegie-Mellon University, Pittsburg

Abstract

    A new method of expressing synchronization is presented and the
motivations and considerations which led to this method are explained.
Synchronization rules, given by 'path expressions', are incorporated into
the type definitions which are used to introduce data objects shared by
several asynchronous processes. It is shown that the method's ability to
express synchronization rules is equivalent to that of P and V operations,
and a means of automatically translating path expressions to existing
primitive synchronization operations is given.

12th December, 1973.

1. Introduction

The design and construction of the co-operation and co-ordination of concurrent processes is a difficult task, particularly in large operating systems. One major problem is the synchronization of actions belonging to separate processes. Some present methods, such as P and V [1] and Wait and Signal [2], are extremely primitive and subject to many hazards in programming. Other methods such as Monitors [3], Message Passing Systems [4] and Secretaries [5] are attempts to overcome some of these hazards.

We consider a process as operating, by a sequence of actions, on a known set of objects. Synchronization is required in order to maintain the integrity of objects which are shared between different processes. The explicit programming of critical sections and of communication of processes using P, V operations has the effect of spreading the implementation of synchronization of operations on shared data throughout the various programs of concurrent processes. Dijkstra's idea of the secretaries [5] controlling the operations on shared data can be viewed as a step in the direction of associating the specification of synchronization with the shared object. This paper proposes a general mechanism for representing synchronization rules in a consistent and coherent manner. It advocates the further step of combining those rules with "type definitions" that are used to introduce each class of object.

The new mechanism describes synchronization at the level of procedures. That is, if we want to synchronize two actions, each must be provided by a separate procedure invocation. The mechanism allows one to state what action sequencing is permissable, which is in direct contrast with synchronization schemes in which the main function is to prohibit or delay actions. Our proposal is that the synchronization be specified directly by describing how the body of one procedure, as a unit, is allowed to execute in relation to others, irrespective of when invoked by processes. The mechanism will specifically describe the synchronization permissible between executions of procedures and prohibit all others. That is, a process trying to execute one of the procedures must wait until the combination of circumstances specified in the synchronization has occurred.

The type definition we shall describe has two divisions; the first consists of the internal structure (for example data declarations and internal functions), the second, called its operations, consists of the procedures known to the outside program which are permitted to alter the internal structure. Together, the type definition and synchronization mechanism describe which procedures (operations) may be invoked by a program to access data objects and how these procedures are to be synchronized to allow the objects to be shared among separate processes.

First we shall describe our synchronization method and notation with several solutions of well known synchronization problems used as illustrations. Then we shall describe our notion of type and discuss, with the aid of examples, how it complements the synchronization method. Finally we shall show that our synchronization method is equivalent to P,V operations in terms of its ability to express synchronization, and describe an automatic method of translating our notation into existing primitive synchronization operations.

2. The Synchronization Mechanism

The proposed mechanism allows the synchronization between executions of procedures by separate processes to be specified by means of a path expression. Later we shall show how these path expressions may be used within a type declaration to describe the synchronization which will allow an object of that type to be shared by several processes. First, however, we shall identify what we think are fundamental synchronization schemes and describe how they may be combined to describe complex synchronization.

The notation, although somewhat arbitrary, is based on regular expressions, which we feel provide a familiar framework and allows path expressions
to be represented by finite state machines. We have also placed certain
restrictions upon the notation which enable us later to describe an implementation of path expressions in terms of other synchronization primitives. We
shall indicate the decisions we have made and attempt to justify them by
example or by argument.

The idea underlying the mechanism can be envisaged as follows:- A path
expression names the procedures whose execution by processes are to be
synchronized. It includes a specification which describes exactly the way in
which the synchronization is to be organized. Each path expression is
implemented by a <u>controller</u>. Given that an individual synchronized procedure
has been invoked by a process, the controller decides when the procedure
execution should be allowed to commence, and therefore the process to continue.

The controller mechanism could operate as follows:- Each procedure
commences with a prologue and finishes with an epilogue. A process executing
the prologue of a synchronized procedure enquires of the controller whether
it may proceed. The controller, using the synchronization specification, may
decide either to delay execution or to allow it to continue. Finally, when
the process executes the epilogue of the procedure, it notifies the controller
which may now be able to release other delayed processes.

The notation we have adopted is designed to simplify the construction of
these controllers; we show that they might, for example, take the form of
finite state machines constructed from P, V operations and semaphores [1].

The first two fundamental synchronization schemes we shall identify are
the <u>sequence</u> of <u>actions</u> and the <u>selection</u> from a set of actions. (By <u>action</u>
we mean the execution by a process of a procedure). A <u>sequence</u> of actions
permits each one to occur in the order specified. Suppose the executions of
three procedures p, q and r are to be sequentially synchronized. Then

$$p \; ; \; q \; ; \; r$$

is an example of a path expression which would, in our notation, express that
procedures p, q and r are to be executed one after the other in the sequence
given. The procedures may have been invoked by separate processes, in a
different order and with possible intermediate delays. If an invocation of q
occurs first, the invoking process will be delayed until procedure p has been
executed. A <u>selection</u> from a set of actions permits only one to occur.
Suppose the executions of the three procedures p, q and r.are to be selectively
synchronized.

Then

$$p, \; q, \; r$$

is an example of a path expression which would specify that a selection of one
procedure is to be made from p, q and r. The process attempting to execute the
procedure selected is allowed to continue, while processes attempting to execute
those procedures not selected are delayed until a new selection is made from
p, q and r. The selection of a procedure is made from amongst those procedures
which have been invoked by processes. The selection is made using an unspecified
rule which ensures fair random order [1] (and which caters for any possible
simultaneity).

These two basic schemes may be combined to form more complex path
expressions.

Thus the path expression

$$p \; ; \; (q, \; r); \; s$$

synchronizes the executions of procedures, p, q, r and s. Executions of q
and r are synchronized selectively. The executions of procedure p, the
selected procedure from q or r, and the procedure s are synchronized sequentially, Thus the path expression permits two possible series of executions:-
Either the execution of p precedes that of q which precedes that of s or the
execution of p precedes that of r which precedes that of s.

For simplicity in the design of controllers for our notation, we allow
a procedure name to occur once only in any path expression. This is not very
restrictive because a procedure can always be renamed by embedding it inside
another procedure.

There are two additional synchronization concepts which we find practical
to represent. These are <u>repetition</u> and <u>simultaneous execution</u>.

<u>Repetition</u> permits a path expression once completed to be repeated.
Many processes are cyclic in behaviour and this needs to be reflected in our
synchronization notation. We represent repetition by enclosing a path
expression between the key words <u>path</u> <u>end</u>. Again, for simplicity in design
of controllers for our notation, we make the restriction that repeated path
expressions may not be embedded within other path expressions. We have not
found this restriction to be very important in the examples for which we have
so far written synchronization rules and there are certainly ways in which
this restriction may be relaxed. The path expression

<u>path</u> P1 <u>end</u>

synchronizes the procedure P1 so that it may be executed by processes repeat -
edly. If many processes invoke P1, one of them at a time will be allowed to
execute P1 while the remainder are delayed until their turn comes. The path
expression

<u>path</u> P1, (P2 ; (P3, P4)) <u>end</u>

is an example of a complex synchronization scheme involving the procedures
P1, P2, P3 and P4. At first either procedure P1 or P2 may be selected to
execute. If P1 is selected then, when execution by the process of P1 is
complete, repetition will occur and a new selection made between procedures
P1 and P2. If P2 is selected then, when execution by the process of P2 is
complete, a selection will be made between procedures P3 and P4. In this
case, when the procedure P3 or P4 which is selected has been executed by its
invoking process, repetition will occur and a new selection made between
procedures P1 and P2.

<u>Simultaneous Execution</u> permits several processes to execute given
procedures concurrently. In many synchronization problems it is often
desirable that a body of code can be simultaneously executed by several
processes provided that by doing so the processes do not infringe other
synchronization restrictions. The notation representing simultaneous
execution is a bracket pair { } placed around a regular expression. These
brackets may not be nested. One view of simultaneous execution is that it
generates as many instances of the enclosed expression as there are requests
for it until all instances have been completed. The path expression

{ P1 }

synchronizes the procedure P1 so that it may be executed by many processes
simultaneously. Once one process begins to execute P1, other processes may
do the same without delay, providing that there are outstanding (uncompleted)
executions of P1. As soon as the last of these is finished, the path
expression is considered to be complete and further processes invoking P1 will
be delayed.

The path expression

<u>path</u> A ; { B ; C } <u>end</u>

synchronizes the procedures A, B and C using a combination of several basic
synchronization schemes. Procedure A may be executed first by a process. On
the completion of procedure A by a process, the sequence B ; C can be executed
by many processes simultaneously. A process invoking procedure C will be
delayed until the execution is completed by some other process of procedure B.
Procedures B and C may be executed simultaneously by many processes, however the
number of processes executing and which have executed procedure C can never
exceed the number of processes which have executed B. If at some time all
requests by processes for the sequence B ; C have been completed (the number of
executed procedures B equals the number of executed procedures C and there are
no more invocations of B) then repetition will enable a new invocation of A by
a process to execute.

In our opinion, path expressions provide a clear and compact method for
describing synchronization problems. For example, the path expression

<u>path</u> read, write <u>end</u>

specifies a series of executions by processes of the procedures read and write
in unpredictable order, none of which overlap in time.

The path expression

<u>path</u> {read}, write <u>end</u>

specifies a series of executions by processes of the procedures read and write
in unpredictable order. Read executions may overlap other read executions but
write executions may not overlap other read or write executions. Reading, once
started, will continue for as long as there are processes invoking read and at
least one process executing read.

The above path specifications can be used, for instance, for programming
file processing, and we shall now demonstrate how they may be adapted so that
a particular access priority can be implemented and localized in one central
place. In the last example, once reading commences, all processes requesting
reading may proceed. It is therefore conceivable that one wants a policy in
which, once writing commences, all processes requesting writing will proceed
provided that they do so one at a time. This can be implemented by means of
two path expressions.

<u>path</u> {read}, {WRITE} <u>end</u>

<u>path</u> write <u>end</u>

where WRITE is a procedure defined by

WRITE = <u>begin</u> write <u>end</u>

The internally defined procedure write actually performs the writing action.
The first path ensures that if the read procedure begins to execute, all reading requests are accepted, and similarly with WRITE. The second path ensures
that the actions of writing are mutually exclusive. Thus executions of WRITE
are synchronized with respect to the first path and executions of its body
(write) are synchronized with respect to the second path. The synchronization
specification given by each path can be understood separately since, in the
present proposal, a particular procedure name can appear in only a single path
expression. (In other words there can be a separate controller with respect to
each path).

Another strategy is to give individual read and write invocations by
processes an equal chance of executing first. This can be achieved by having
each process invoke a READ or a WRITE procedure which first obtains permission
before performing the read or write. A construct with such properties is:

<u>path</u> requestread, requestwrite <u>end</u>

<u>path</u> {openread; read}, write <u>end</u>

where requestread = <u>begin</u> openread <u>end</u>

    requestwrite = <u>begin</u> write   <u>end</u>

    READ   = <u>begin</u> requestread; read <u>end</u>

    WRITE   = <u>begin</u> requestwrite <u>end</u>

The first path gives reading and writing an equal chance of starting. Once a read request has been granted, a read has been opened, thus the second path disables writing until the read has been executed. The braces in the second path make sure that reading can overlap if no writing is requested at all.

Suppose we require the strategy that writing should have priority over reading. This is the readers and writers problem solved by Courtois,Heymans and Parnas [9] and requires that when writing is requested, no further reading should be granted and writing should start as soon as the current reading is finished. The following construct has these properties:-

    <u>path</u> readattempt   <u>end</u>

    <u>path</u> requestread, {requestwrite} <u>end</u>

    <u>path</u> {openread; read}, write <u>end</u>

where

    readattempt = <u>begin</u> requestread <u>end</u>

    requestread = <u>begin</u> openread <u>end</u>

    requestwrite = <u>begin</u> write <u>end</u>

    READ = <u>begin</u> readattempt ; read <u>end</u>

    WRITE = <u>begin</u> requestwrite <u>end</u>

The purpose of the first path is to let only one read request occur at a time. While one process requests reading, all others have to wait until they can initiate a read attempt. This assures that a write request is granted in the second path at the earliest possible moment. The braces in the second path expression serve the purpose of immediately granting all write requests as long as writing is still going on. The braces in the third path allow, as before, read operations to overlap.

Finally, let reading have priority over writing, i.e., when reading is requested, from that moment no further write requests should be granted and reading should begin as soon as the current writing has been finished. A write request, on the other hand, should not stop the flow of reading. This can be written as:-

    <u>path</u> writeattempt   <u>end</u>

    <u>path</u> {requestread}, requestwrite <u>end</u>

    <u>path</u> {read} , (openwrite ; write) <u>end</u>

where requestwrite = <u>begin</u> openwrite <u>end</u>

    writeattempt = <u>begin</u> requestwrite <u>end</u>

    requestread = <u>begin</u> read <u>end</u>

    READ = <u>begin</u> requestread <u>end</u>

    WRITE = <u>begin</u> writeattempt ; write <u>end</u>

The first path insures that only one prospective writer can request
writing. The braces in the second path serve the purpose of letting all
subsequent read requests through so that reading will not be interrupted by
writing. The braces in the third path allow (as usual) an overlap in reading.

While not actually proving the correctness of our solutions above, we
have been able to make assertions about their behaviour. The similarity
between path expressions and finite state machines suggest that it might be
possible to automatically prove or disprove assertions about solutions using
them. These examples serve to demonstrate the synchronization facilities that
path expressions provide and give an idea as to their power. We shall return
to this point in the next section where it is shown that P & V operations can
be simply programmed using path expressions.

3.   Structuring Synchronization with Types

Types, under one name or another, have been used in programming languages
for many purposes. Notable instances of their use are for checking as in
Pascal [6], for describing building blocks as in extensible languages (for
example ECL [11]) and for implementing new data objects and operations as in
the classes of Simula 67 [8] or the modes of Algol 68 [7].

Programming languages have long provided an adequate tool for constructing
complicated operations out of simpler ones by means of a procedure mechanism.
An important aspect of such a tool from the designer's point of view is that it
allows the programmer to separate the definition of an operation from its use.
This has the advantage that, at the places where it is used, an operation can
be treated as an object whose properties are known by its specification.
Moreover, all implementation issues are now concentrated in one place and this
facilitates validation and modifications of the implementation. We believe
that type definitions should be used to accomplish on behalf of the construction of data objects the analogue of what procedure declarations do for
operations. Thus, at the place where it is used, the details of the
implementation of an object should be irrelevant and underlying structure
should not be accessible at that moment. The reasons why this should be so
are obviously the same as those that underly a procedure mechanism: separation
of specification and implementation, and concentration of implementation issues
so as to facilitate verification, debugging and modifications.

As a natural consequence of this point of view, a type definition is used
to create new data objects which appear as atomic entities at the places where
used. Drawing the parallel between type definitions and procedure declarations,
accessing a structural part of a typed object is similar to jumping into a
procedure body.

The primary function of a type definition in a program is to describe the
implementation of the operations on objects of this type in terms of earlier
defined operations on the structural parts of such objects (though being the
earliest of the three languages mentioned above, SIMULA 67 comes closest to
this idea of type definition). Thus, another part of a type definition ought
to be a description of the detailed structure that objects of this type will
have.

These two functions of a type definition are reflected in a notation which
we have devised to help us visualize our ideas. The syntax is purely arbitrary
and is not intended as a proposal for a new programming language or any part of
one.

For example we might have:-

> <u>type</u>   buffer;
>
> message   frame;
>
> <u>operations</u>
>
> > <u>procedure</u> read (<u>returns</u> message m) : m := frame;
> >
> > <u>procedure</u> write (<u>accepts</u> message m) : frame : = m;
>
> <u>endtype</u>

This example is a definition of a type of object called a <u>buffer</u>, whose structure consists of a variable <u>frame</u> of type <u>message</u>, and whose operations are the procedures <u>read</u> and <u>write</u>. (The type <u>message</u> is assumed to have been previously defined.) Instances of buffers can be declared or created in the scope of the type definition, and each one will contain its own instance of <u>frame</u>. The program using a <u>buffer</u> cannot, however, access <u>frame</u> directly but must use <u>read</u> and <u>write</u>. The procedures can be applied to them by means of the Simula 67 dot notation.

For example: buffer A;

> message T;
>
> A. read (T);
>
> A. write (T);

The type definition thus has two important properties:-

1. Protection of its structure by the scope rules.

2. Only a fixed, identifiable set of procedures is defined, giving carefully controlled access to the data of the objects of that type.

Objects created from type definitions can be common to the scope of two or more processes. The type buffer defined above is not satisfactory when various concurrent processes may simultaneously read and write a shared buffer and some form of synchronization is required.

In general, the sharing of objects of a type will be unsatisfactory if the data contained in the object can be corrupted by several processes executing procedures simultaneously or in invalid sequences. We will combine our path expressions with our notion of type to introduce some orderly structure in the sharing of objects.

The restrictions we must place on the operations read and write of our buffer example in order to preserve the integrity of the contained data are:-

1. Every read must be followed by a write.

2. Every write must be followed by a read.

3. A read and write must not execute simultaneously.

Provided the buffer obeys these rules we can assert that it will not lose or duplicate any information.

The following type definition ensures these three properties:-

```
type    buffer;
message frame;
path write; read end
operations
        procedure read (returns message m) : m : = frame;
        procedure write (accepts message m) : frame : = m;
endtype
```

The path is applied to the operations to produce the correct synchronization. A different instance of the synchronization path is associated with each instance of a buffer. Thus any declaration of a buffer will result in an atomic object which can be read or written alternately.

This type definition of a buffer may be used to build more complex data structures, for example objects of type "ring buffer". Suppose that a number of similar readers and writers wish to exchange information but are constrained by the amount of space available for buffers. One such device is demonstrated below and is designed to permit as much concurrency as possible. A ring of the above described buffers is declared. A send or receive request allocates a buffer to be read or written on a round-robin basis. The integrity of the buffers is assured by their type definition. Allocation is achieved by advancing pointers around the ring of buffers. Many requests to send or receive may occur simultaneously. However, each pointer may only be advanced by one process at a time if the integrity of the allocation mechanism is to be preserved. A type pointer is introduced which includes the necessary synchronization. Thus we have:-

```
type ring-buffer;
array 0 to N - 1 buffer R;
        type pointer;
        integer P = 0; path next end;
        operations
        procedure next (returns integer I):
            begin P: = (P + 1) mod N; I: = P; end;
        endtype;
pointer write-slot, read-slot;
operations
procedure send (accepts message M):
    begin integer J; J: = write-slot.next; R[J].write (M); end;
procedure receive (returns message M):
    begin integer J; J: = read-slot.next; M: = R[J].read; end;
endtype;
```

The implementations of the buffers and the pointers are separated from the ring-buffer mechanism. Similarly the readers and writers can be programmed independently of the implementation of the buffering system.

The examples we have described above encourage us in our belief that the method is worth studying and is a potential contribution to better structured and safer synchronization methods. We shall now show that it is at least as powerful as the more primitive synchronization operations such as P and V [1] or Signal and Wait [2]. For example the path path {V;P} end provides the synchronization necessary to implement P and V operations. The number of executed Ps can never be greater than the number of completely executed Vs. This path may be embedded within the type description for a semaphore. Thus:-

> type semaphore;
>
> path {V;P} end ;
>
> operations
>
> > procedure V : null;
> >
> > procedure P : null;
>
> endtype ;

Variables of type semaphore may be declared and each instance will have its own synchronizing path. The value of the semaphore can only be changed by executing either a P or a V. In the example above, semaphores are always initialized to zero. An extension to the above notation would be to include initialization in types and perhaps paths. Thus a program restricted to using our notation has lost none of the power of P, V operations but has gained the structuring facilities that the use of types and paths provide.

4.   Implementation

One important aspect of our notation is that it has a practical implementation. Controllers for our notation can be implemented using existing synchronization methods and these may be generated automatically from the path expressions, for example by a compiler. We will show one particular implementation in which path expressions are transformed into appropriate P and V operations for use in the prologues and epilogues of the procedures the path expressions name. (Incidentally, this will complete the equivalence between the two synchronization methods.)

The following recursive algorithm will translate path expressions composed of the synchronization schemes of Section 2) above . Each path expression is subjected to repeated transformations, the final result providing the prologues and epilogues for each of the procedures named in the path expression. At each stage of the algorithm the path expression yet to be translated is labelled <pathexpression>. In general, the <pathexpression> will be surrounded by two generated synchronization operations O_L and O_R which are on its left and right respectively. The operation O_L may be either a P or a PP operation. (To simplify the algorithm two operations PP and VV are introduced which take three parameters, a counter and two semaphores. These operations will be explained later in terms of P and V.) The operation O_R may be either a V or a VV operation.

> Stage 1)   Select a unique semaphore S1, initialized to one, and
>
> replace   path   <path expression> end by
>
> > P(S1)   <path expression> V(S1)
>
> Carry out stage 2) of the algorithm for <path expression>.
>
> > Finish.
>
> Stage 2)   Examine the <path expression> and depending upon the
>
> synchronization scheme of which it is composed do one of the following:-
>
> a)   A Sequence: The <path expression> is composed of:-
>
> > <path expression 1> ; <path expression 2>.
>
> Select a unique semaphore S2, initialized to zero and replace the
> <path expression> by:-

<path expression 1> V(S2) P(S2) <path expression 2>

Carry out stage 2) for <path expression 1> and <path expression 2>

Finish of stage 2).

b)　　**A selection**:　　The <path expression> is composed of:-

<path expression 1>, <path expression 2>

Using the two synchronizing operations O_L (which may either be a P or a PP operation) and O_R (which may be either a V or a VV operation) enclosing the <path expression> replace the <path expression> using the replacement rule:-

O_L <path expression 1>, <path expression 2> O_R is replaced by

O_L <path expression 1> O_R O_L <path expression 2> O_R

Carry out stage 2) for <path expression 1> and <path expression 2>

Finish of stage 2).

c)　　**Simultaneous Execution**:　　The <path expression> is composed of:-

{ <path expression> }

Select a unique counter C1, initialized to zero, and semaphore S3, initialized to one.　The operations O_L and O_R enclosing the <path expression> will be of the form

P(Si) { <path expression> } V(Sj)

Replace the operations and braces in the following way:-

PP(C1, S3, Si) <path expression> VV (C1, S3, Sj)

Carry out stage 2) for the remaining <path expression>.

Finish of stage 2).

d)　　**Procedure name**:　The path expression remaining is just the name of one of the procedures to be synchronized.　The synchronizing operation O_L (which may be a P or a PP operation) on the left of the procedure name is to be included in that procedure's prologue.　The operation O_R (which may be a V or VV operation) is to be included in the epilogue of that procedure.

Finish of stage 2).

The operations PP and VV implement the simultaneous execution synchronization.　Both operations share a counter C1 and a semaphore S3.　The semaphore S3 is used to exclude more than one process from changing the counter at a time. The PP operation increments the counter, the VV operation decrements it.　If the counter is increased from zero the operation P(Si) is invoked.(See below). If the counter is decreased to zero the operation V(Sj) is invoked.

100

```
procedure PP (counter C1; semaphore S3, Si);  procedure VV(counter C1;semaphore
                                                                        S3,Sj);

        begin                                     begin
          P  (S3);                                  P  (S3);
          C1 : = C1 + 1;                            C1 : = C1 - 1;
          if C1 = 1 then P(Si);                     if C1 = 0 then V(Sj);
          V (S3);                                   V (S3);
        end;                                      end;
```

The following example illustrates the translation of a path expression
into P, V operations. The translation is represented by a tree. Each step of
the algorithm corresponds to a node in that tree and the synchronization
operations which have been generated up to a given step are written on either
side of the corresponding node.

The path expression **path** ({A;B}), C **end** translates as:-

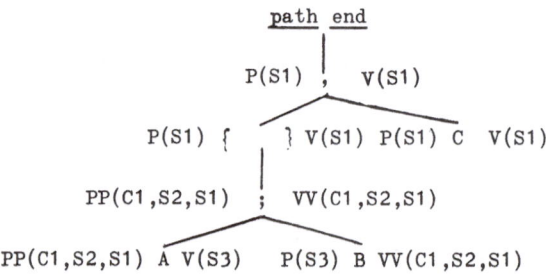

The resulting set of procedure prologues and epilogues which are created
by part d) of the algorithm are written below in program form.

    semaphore   S1 = 1, S2 = 1, S3 = 0; counter C1=0;
    procedures
        A : begin PP(C1, S2, S1) ; <body of A>; V(S3); end
        B : begin P(S3)   ; <body of B>; VV(C1,S2,S1) end
        C : begin P(S1)   ; <body of C>; V(S1) end
    end

The procedures A, B and C implement the path precisely. Execution by a
process of procedure A will set semaphore S1 to zero, (thus excluding the
execution of procedure C by processes), semaphore S3 to one and the counter
to one. Thus further processes may execute A and one process can execute B.
When there are an equal number of executed A and B procedures and no further
processes executing A the counter will have been reduced to zero and semaphore
S1 set to one permitting the repetition of the path expression. If a process
executes procedure C, it sets the semaphore S1 to zero to exclude processes
from executing A. When a process finishes executing C it resets semaphore S1
to one allowing repetition of the path expression.

The example described above also serves to show that the path expression
provides a structured synchronization technique which emphasizes what is needed,

not how it is to be achieved. The P, V implementation of the path expression does not directly express the synchronization it is used to create. (See also [10]).

Therefore, our mechanism can lead to automatically generated, well structured uses of synchronization primitives and the programmer is relieved of the problem of implementing his desired synchronization. Our choice of implementation is reflected in the constraints we have adopted in our notation. (See section 2). This aspect requires further investigation to ascertain what are the minimum set of constraints necessary to ensure unambiguous path expressions, and what are the minimum set of constraints for any given implementation.

Conclusion

We have introduced a new method of synchronization which provides a clear and structured approach to the description of shared data and the coordination and communication between concurrent processes. This method is equivalent to P and V operations with respect to its ability to express any given synchronization.

The path expression describes synchronization between executions of procedures by processes. It is a statement of all permissible synchronizations between the various procedures named within it. When combined with our type definition, it provides a powerful tool with which to design shared data objects. The type contributes the protection necessary to avoid carefully designed synchronization schemes from being upset by processes directly accessing the data and collects together in one place all the implementation details of a shared object. The path expression allows a specification of the synchronization needed to ensure the successful sharing of an object and does not require details of how that is to be done. Assertions can be made about the behaviour of path expressions. The resemblance of these expressions to finite state machines suggests that it may be possible to provide a means of automatically checking such assertions. Implementations of path expressions are possible using existing synchronization methods. In our notation we have restricted path expressions to allow for a simple implementation scheme, however this has seemed quite adequate for a variety of quite complicated synchronization problems. The algorithm which translates our notation into P and V operations has been used in a program to automatically generate code from path expressions. When the mechanism is used in this way the burden of implementing any given synchronization is removed from the programmer, eliminating the possibility of mistakes.

Acknowledgements

This work was carried out as part of R.H. Campbell's Ph.D. thesis at the Computing Laboratory of the University of Newcastle upon Tyne. We gratefully acknowledge the help of Dr. H.C. Lauer and Professor B. Randell for their help in preparing this paper. R.H. Campbell was financed by a grant from the Science Research Council.

References

[1]   E.W. Dijkstra, Co-operating Sequential processes.
       (in Programming Languages, F. Genuys, ed. Academic Press, New York, 1968).

[2]   A.N. Habermann, Synchronization of Communicating Processes.
       CACM 15, 3, (March 1972), pp. 171-176.

[3]   C.A.R. Hoare, Monitors, An operating system structuring concept.
       (To be published).

[4]   P. Brinch Hanson, Nucleus of a Multiprogramming System.
      CACM 13, 4, (April 1970), pp. 238-241.

[5]   E.W. Dijkstra, Hierarchical ordering of sequential processes.
      (in Operating Systems Techniques) ed. C.A.R. Hoare and R.H. Perrott,
      Academic Press. (1973).

[6]   The programming language PASCAL , Acta Informatica, Vol. 1,1, (May 1971),
      pp. 35-63.

[7]   Final Draft Report on the Algorithmic Language Algol 68.

[8]   O-J. Dahl, B. Myrhhaug and K. Nygaard, the Simula 67 Common Base Language.
      Norwegian Computing Centre.   (1970).

[9]   P.J. Courtois, F. Heymans and D.L. Parnas, Concurrent Control with
      "Readers" and "Writers". CACM 14, 10 (October 1971). pp.667-668.

[10] P. Brinch Hansen, Structured Multiprogramming. CACM 15,7 (July 1972)
      pp.574.

[11] W. Wegbreit, B. Brosgol, G. Holloway, C. Prenner and J. Spitzen,
      E.C.L. Programmers Manual. Center for Research in Computing Technology,
      Harvard University, Cambridge, Massachusetts. (1972).

A FOREGROUND - BACKGROUND TIME SHARING QUEUE
WITH GENERAL SERVICE TIMES

C. Guimaraes

Universidade Federal do Rio de Janeiro

———

ABSTRACT

A foreground-background queue with Poisson arrivals and independent
and identically distributed service times with a general distribution $H(x)$ is analysed using the method of the imbedded Markov
chain. The generating function of the stationary distribution of
queue sizes and the Laplace transform of the stationary distribution
of waiting times is obtained for two priority disciplines:preemptive
resume and non-preemptive or head-of-the-line. Numerical examples
indicate that when the coefficient of variation of service times is
high considerable reduction of total expected queue size can be
obtained over the first-come-first served discipline. The results
found for two queues and preemptive resume discipline can be extended
to a system with an arbitrary number of queues.

1. Introduction

Let's consider a single server queue with interrupted service
in the following way: jobs arrive according to a Poisson process of
density λ and join a first-come-first served "foreground" queue
where each job is processed for a fixed amount of time of length Q ;
if the job finishes within Q, it departs. Otherwise it joins a
"background" queue where it waits for further service. Jobs in the
first queue may have preemptive resume or non-preemptive priority
over the second queue. Each job requires a service time x with a
general distribution function $H(x)$ independent of the others and of
the arrival process.

Similar models have assumed geometric service times (Kleinrock

[6]) or exponential service times (Adiri & Avi-Itzhak [5]), (Coffman [1]) . It is well-known, however, that service times in computer
systems have large coefficients of variation(standard deviation over
mean) and are better characterized by distributions like the hyper-
exponential (Fife [3]) .

The method of imbedded Markov chains will be used to find the
stationa·y distributions of the queue size and waiting times.

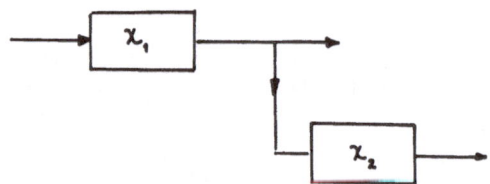

Figure 1   A   F-B   Queue

2. Definitions and Notation

Let's call a "quantum service" x_1 , the service time given to
a job in the first queue, and $H_1(x)$ its distribution function.
Then

$$P\{x_1 \le x\} \;=\; H_1(x) \;=\; \begin{cases} H(x) & \text{if } x < Q \\ 1 & \text{if } x \ge Q \end{cases}$$

Let x_2 be the remaining service time given that a job requires
more than Q units of time for service and $H_2(x)$ its distribution
function.
Then

$$P\{x_2 \le x\} = H_2(x) = \frac{H(x+Q)-H(Q)}{1-H(Q)}$$

Let

$$\Psi(s) = \int_0^\infty e^{-sx} dH(x) \quad Re(s) \ge 0$$

$$\Psi_i(s) = \int_0^\infty e^{-sx} dH_i(x) \quad (i=1,2) \quad Re(s) \ge 0$$

$$\alpha_r = \int_0^\infty x^r dH(x) \quad \alpha \equiv \alpha_1$$

$$a_r = \int_0^\infty x^r dH_1(x) \quad a \equiv a_1$$

$$b_r = \int_0^\infty x^r dH_2(x) \quad b \equiv b_1$$

Then

$$\Psi_1(s) = \int_0^{Q-0} e^{-sx} dH(x) + e^{-sQ}(1-H(Q))$$

$$\Psi_2(s) = \frac{e^{sQ}}{1-H(Q)} \int_Q^\infty e^{-sx} dH(x)$$

$$b = \frac{1}{1-H(Q)} (\alpha-a) = \frac{\alpha-a}{p} \qquad \text{where} \quad p=1-H(Q)$$

$$b_2 = \frac{-2Q(\alpha-a)+\alpha_2-a_2}{1-H(Q)}$$

3. Stationary Distribution of the Queue Size

CASE 1 : Preemptive Resume Priority Rule

In this case jobs in the first queue preempt jobs in the second queue that may be using the processor (server) when they arrive; jobs in the second queue may run only when the first queue is empty; a job in the second queue resumes its processing from the point where stopped with no loss of time.

The first queue behaves as if the second queue did not exist and results for queue size and waiting times follow immediately from the theory of the $M|G|1$ queue with Poisson input, general service time distribution and first-come-first-served service discipline.

In order to study the stochastic behavior of the second queue we observe the size of the second queue immediately after the completion time of a service in that queue and if at the last such epoch the second queue was empty, then we observe the size of the queue at the end of the following busy period of the first queue.

Let τ_n be the sequence of such epochs $(n=0,1,\ldots)$ and $\zeta_n^{(i)}$ be the size of the ith queue $(i=1,2)$ at τ_n. Then,

$$\zeta_n^{(1)} \equiv 0 \quad \text{and} \quad \{\zeta_n^{(2)}\} = \text{Markov Chain}$$

In order to determine the transition probabilities p_{ij} for this Markov Chain we note that if

$$\zeta_n^{(2)} = i , \quad i > 0 \quad \text{then} \quad \zeta_{n+1}^{(2)} = j \quad (j \geq i - 1) \quad \text{if}$$

k arriving jobs preempt the service of the job being processed in the second queue during $(\tau_n, \tau_{n+1}]$ initiating k busy periods in queue 1 and from all jobs served in these k busy periods $j-i+1$ join the second queue.

Let $f_j^{(k)}$ be the probability of j arrivals to the background queue during a busy period initiated by 1 job in queue 1 and let $F^{(k)}(w)$

be its generating function.

Then

$$f_j^{(1)} = \sum_{k=0}^{\infty} \int_0^Q P_k(t) dH(t) f_j^{(k)} + p P_k(Q) f_{j-1}^{(k)} \tag{1}$$

where

$$p = 1 - H(Q), \quad P_k(t) = \frac{e^{-\lambda t}(\lambda t)^k}{k!}$$

A busy period initiated by k jobs has the same distribution as the sum of k independent busy periods initiated by 1 job.   This implies:

$$F^{(k)}(w) = \left[F^{(1)}(w) \right]^k \tag{2}$$

and forming the generating function of (1) and writing $F(w) = F^{(1)}(w)$ for simplicity we get:

$$F(w) = \int_0^Q e^{-(1-F(w))\lambda t} dH(t) + p w e^{-\lambda Q(1-F(w))} \tag{3}$$

Now let

$b_j = P\{j$ arrivals to the background queue during the completion time of a background service$\}$

and let

$$G(w) = \sum_{j=0}^{\infty} b_j w^j \qquad |w| \le 1$$

Similarly to (1) and (3) we get:

$$b_j = \sum_{k=0}^{\infty} \int_0^{\infty} P_k(t) dH_2(t) f_j^{(k)} \tag{4}$$

$$G(w) = \Psi_2(\lambda - \lambda F(w)) \tag{5}$$

We can write the transition probabilities P_{ij} for the Markov Chain $\{\zeta_n^{(2)}\}$:

$$P_{ij} = b_{j-i+1} \qquad i > 0 \tag{6}$$

$$P_{0j} = f_j^{(1)}$$

Clearly this is an irreducible and aperiodic M.C.; therefore, if a stationary distribution $\{\Pi_j\}$ exists for this M.C. , it must satisfy:

$$\Pi_j = \sum_{i=0}^{\infty} \Pi_i P_{ij} , \quad \Pi_j > 0 , \quad j = 0, 1, 2 \ldots , \quad \sum_{j=0}^{\infty} \Pi_j = 1 \tag{6.1}$$

If we let $U(w)$ be the generating function of $\{\Pi_j\}$ we get from (5), (6) and (6.1):

$$U(w) = \sum_{j=0}^{\infty} \Pi_j w^j = F(w) U(0) + G(w) \cdot \frac{U(w) - U(0)}{w}$$

$$U(w) = U(0) \cdot \frac{wF(w) - G(w)}{w - G(w)} \tag{7}$$

In Section 7 we show that $F(w)$ is the transform of a proper distribution function if and only if $\lambda a \leq 1$.

We now want to compute $U(0)$ and $U'(1)$ from (7).

Let's assume that the first two moments of the distribution obtained from $f_j^{(1)}$ exist (if $\lambda a < 1$ they do exist as will be seen later). It is convenient to expand the numerator and denominator of (7) in a truncated power series:

$$U(w) = U(0)\left[1 + \frac{wF'(1) + \frac{w(w-1)}{2} F''(1) + o(w-1)}{1 - G'(1) - \frac{w-1}{2} G''(1) + o(w-1)}\right] \tag{8}$$

where

$$\frac{o(w-1)}{w-1} \longrightarrow 0 \qquad \text{as} \quad w \to 1$$

From (3) and (5) we get:

$$F'(1) = \frac{p}{1-\lambda a}$$

$$F''(1) = \left[\frac{\lambda^2 a_2}{1-\lambda a} + 2\lambda Q\right] F'(1)^2 \tag{9}$$

$$G'(1) = \lambda b F'(1)$$

$$G''(1) = \lambda b F''(1) + \lambda^2 b_2 F'(1)^2$$

so that for $w=1$ we get:

$$U(0) = \left[1 + \frac{F'(1)}{1-G'(1)}\right]^{-1} = \frac{1 - \lambda\alpha}{1 - \lambda\alpha + p} \tag{10}$$

and the condition $0 < U(0) < 1$ gives

$$\lambda\alpha < 1 \tag{11}$$

(note that $\alpha \geq a$)

$U'(1)$ can be computed from (8); it can be easily checked that the terms $o(w-1)$ in (8) do not contribute to $U'(1)$; the result is:

$$U'(1) = \frac{p}{1-\lambda\alpha+p}\left[1 + \frac{\lambda p Q}{1-\lambda a} + \frac{p\lambda^2 \alpha_2/2}{(1-\lambda\alpha)(1-\lambda a)}\right] \tag{12}$$

We have then shown:

Theorem 1:

If $\lambda\alpha < 1$ the MC $\{\zeta_n^{(2)}\}$ is ergodic and the generating function of its stationary distribution is

$$U(w) = \frac{1-\lambda\alpha}{1-\lambda\alpha+p} \cdot \frac{wF(w)-\Psi_2(\lambda-\lambda F(w))}{w-\Psi_2(\lambda-\lambda F(w))} \tag{13}$$

where $F(w)$ is the unique root of equation (3) for $|w|<1$, and $F(1) = 1$.

CASE 2 : Non-Preemptive Priority

As in Case 1, jobs in the background queue start processing only when the first (foreground) queue is empty; however, once a job is started in the background queue it is run to completion.

We will observe the size of both queues immediately after a departure from either queue.

Let
$\zeta_n^{(i)} = i^{th}$ queue size immediately after the nth departure ; $i=1,2$.

$\{\zeta_n^{(1)},\zeta_n^{(2)}\}$ is a Markov Chain for which the following transition probabilities $p(m,n \to j,k)$ hold:

$m>0$

$$p(m,k \to j,k) = \int_0^Q P_{j-m+1}(x)dH(x) \qquad j \geq m-1, \ k \geq 0$$

$$p(m,k-1 \to j,k) = P_{j-m+1}(Q) \cdot p \qquad j \geq m-1, \ k > 0$$

$m=0$

$$p(0,k+1 \to j,k) = \int_0^\infty P_j(x)dH_2(x) \qquad j \geq 0, \ k \geq 0 \tag{15}$$

$$p(0,0 \to j,0) = \int_0^Q P_j(x)dH(x) \qquad j \geq 0$$

$$p(0,0 \to j,1) = P_j(Q) \cdot p \qquad j \geq 0$$

From (15) it follows that $\{\zeta_n^{(1)},\zeta_n^{(2)}\}$ is an irreducible and aperiodic Markov Chain. Let $\Pi_{j,k}$ denote its stationary distribution and let $U(z,w)$ be its generating function:

$$U(z,w) = \sum_{j=0}^\infty \sum_{k=0}^\infty \Pi_{j,k} \ z^j w^k \tag{16}$$

Using (15) and (16) we get for $U(z,w)$:

$$U(z,w) = \frac{U(z,w)-U(0,w)}{z} g(z,w) + \frac{U(0,w)-U(0,0)}{w} \cdot \Psi_2(\lambda-\lambda z) +$$

$$+ U(0,0)g(z,w) \tag{17}$$

where

$$g(z,w) = \int_0^Q e^{-\lambda x(1-z)} dH(x) + wpe^{-\lambda Q(1-z)} \tag{18}$$

Rearranging terms in (17), we get:

$$U(z,w) = \frac{U(0,w)\left[z\Psi_2(\lambda-\lambda z)-wg(z,w)\right] +U(0,0)\left[wzg(z,w)-z\Psi_2(\lambda-\lambda z)\right]}{w\left[z-g(z,w)\right]}$$

$$\ldots\ldots \tag{19}$$

Now, from Lemma 1 (Section 7), $g(z,w)-z$ has exactly one zero (in z) in the region $|z| < 1$ and let $z(w)$ denote this root. Since $U(z,w)$ is regular in $|z| < 1$, $|w| < 1$, then $z(w)$ must also be a root of the numerator. Note that $z(w) = F(w)$, $z(1)=1$.

$$U(0,w) = U(0,0) \cdot \frac{wz(w)-\Psi_2(\lambda-\lambda z(w))}{w-\Psi_2(\lambda-\lambda z(w))} \tag{20}$$

In order to find $U(0,0)$ it is convenient to expand the numerator and denominator of (20) in a truncated power series; after canceling the common factor $w-1$ from the numerator and denominator of (20) we get:

$$U(0,1) = U(0,0) \cdot (1 + \frac{p}{1-\lambda\alpha}) \tag{21}$$

We need the following auxiliary relations, which follow immediately from the definition of $g(z,w)$:

$$g(1,1) = 1$$
$$g(z,1) = \Psi_1(\lambda-\lambda z)$$
$$g(1,w) = 1 + p(w-1)$$

Let $z=1$ in (19); after simplification we get:

$$U(1,w) = \left[U(0,w) - U(0,0)\right] \cdot \frac{1 + wp}{wp} \tag{22}$$

Now let $w=1$ and substitute (21) in (22):

$$U(1,1) = U(0,0) \frac{1 + p}{1 -\lambda\alpha} = 1 \tag{23}$$

and the condition $0 < U(0,0) < 1$ gives:

$$\lambda\alpha < 1 \tag{24}$$

We have then shown:

Theorem 2:

If $\lambda\alpha < 1$ then the M.C. $\{\zeta_n^{(1)}, \zeta_n^{(2)}\}$ is ergodic and its stationary distribution exists and has a double generating function given by (19) and (20), where $z(w)$ is the unique root in z of $g(z,w) - z = 0$ inside $|z| \leq 1$ for $w < 1$ and $z(1) = 1$.

The Expectation of the Queue Size

We want to compute the expectation of the marginal distribution for each queue; substituting (20) in (22), we get:

$$U(1,w) = U(0,0) \frac{1+wp}{p} \cdot \frac{F(w)-1}{w-\Psi_2(\lambda-\lambda F(w))} \tag{25}$$

Expanding the numerator and denominator of (25) in a truncated power series and canceling the term $w-1$ we get:

$$U(1,w) = U(0,0) \frac{1+wp}{p} \cdot \frac{F'(1)+F''(1)(w-1)/2+o(w-1)}{1-bF'(1)-\left[\lambda^2 b_2 F'(1)^2+\lambda b F''(1)\right]\frac{(w-1)}{2}+o(w-1)}$$

$$\dots\dots (26)$$

where the terms $o(w-1)$ are of the form: constant $\cdot \frac{(w-1)^2}{2}$

Taking derivatives with respect to w of (26) and setting $w=1$ we get:

$$E\{\zeta_n^{(2)}\} = U'(1,w)_{w=1} = \frac{p}{1+p} + \frac{\lambda pQ}{1-\lambda a} + \frac{\lambda^2 p\alpha_2/2}{(1-\lambda a)(1-\lambda\alpha)} \tag{27}$$

Similarly, if we let $w=1$ in (19), we get:

$$U(z,1) = \frac{U(0,1)\left[z\Psi_2(\lambda-\lambda z)-\Psi_1(\lambda-\lambda z)\right]+U(0,0)z\left[\Psi_1(\lambda-\lambda z)-\Psi_2(\lambda-\lambda z)\right]}{z - \Psi_1(\lambda-\lambda z)}$$

$$\dots\dots\dots (28)$$

Let $K = 1 + \frac{p}{1-\lambda\alpha}$ \qquad (29)

After expanding the numerator and denominator of (28), we get:

$$U(z,1) = U(0,0)\{K\left[1+\lambda bz-\lambda a+\frac{\lambda^2}{2}(b_2-a_2)(z-1)+o(z-1)\right] -$$

$$- z \cdot \left[\lambda(b-a) + \frac{\lambda^2}{2}(b_2-a_2)(z-1) + o(z-1) \right] \} \ /$$

$$\{ 1 - \lambda a - \frac{\lambda^2 a_2 (z-1)}{2} + o(z-1) \} \qquad (30)$$

Taking derivatives and letting $z=1$ we get after simplification:

$$E\{\zeta_n^{(1)}\} = \frac{1}{1+p} \left[\frac{\lambda(\alpha-a)(1-\lambda Q) + \lambda^2 \alpha_2/2}{1-\lambda a} + \lambda a \ \frac{1-\lambda \alpha}{1-\lambda a} \right] \qquad (31)$$

4. Stationary Distribution of Waiting Times

In what follows we only consider stationary processes; we shall give conditions in each case for the existence of such stationary processes.

Let

η_1 = waiting time in the first queue for a job arriving in a stationary process.

η_2 = waiting time in the first queue + Q + waiting time in the second queue for a job arriving in a stationary process which requires more than Q units of service time.

γ_t = total time in the system (also called response time or residence time) conditioned on a given service time requirement t; let $T_t(x)$ be its distribution function and $T_{r/t}$ its rth moment $(r=1,2,\ldots)$ and

$$T_t(s) = \int_0^\infty e^{-sx} \, dT(x) \qquad Re(s) \geq 0$$

Let's consider a modified process in which all jobs are served to completion first-come-first-served in a single queue.

Let η be the waiting time of a job for the stationary modified process.

Let's introduce the following notation:

$$W_i(x) = P\{\eta_i \leq x\}$$

$$\Omega_i(s) = \int_0^\infty e^{-sx} dW_i(x) \qquad Re(s) \geq 0 \qquad (i=1,2)$$

$$W(x) = P\{\eta \leq x\}$$

$$\Omega(s) = \int_0^\infty e^{-sx} dW(x)$$

$$w_r^{(i)} = \int_0^\infty x^r dW_i(x) \qquad (i=1,2) \qquad (r=1,2,\ldots)$$

$$w_r = \int_0^\infty x^r dW(x)$$

CASE 1 : <u>Preemptive Resume Priority</u>

In this case $W_1(x)$ can be easily obtained from the theory of the $M|G|1$ queue $H_1(x)$ as service time distribution. In particular if $\lambda a < 1$. Then $W_1(x)$ exists and

$$\Omega_1(s) = \frac{1-\lambda a}{1 - \dfrac{\lambda(1-\Psi_1(s))}{s}} \tag{32}$$

$$w_1^{(1)} = \frac{\lambda a_2}{2(1-\lambda a)}$$

The method for the derivation of equations (33) and (35) below can be found in Gaver[4], Takacs[10] and Schrage[8].

In order to determine $W_2(x)$ we observe that an arriving job that requires more than Q units of service time must wait for the total completion of all jobs which arrived before it (i.e., the waiting time in the modified process) + Q plus an additional delay due to the jobs arriving during this waiting time + Q; each such job generates a busy period in the first queue.
Therefore

$$W_2(x) = \sum_{j=0}^{\infty} \int_0^x e^{-\lambda y} \frac{(\lambda y)^j}{j!} G^{(j)}(x-y) d\widehat{W}(y) \tag{33}$$

where $G^{(j)}(x)$ is the jth convolution with itself of the busy period distribution in the first queue and $\widehat{W}(y) = W(y-Q)$

$$G^{(j)}(x) = \left[G(x)\right]^{*j}$$

Let

$$\Gamma(s) = \int_0^{\infty} e^{-sx} dG(x), \quad \widehat{\Omega}(s) = \int_0^{\infty} e^{-sx} d\widehat{W}(x) \tag{34}$$

Then from (33), we get

$$\Omega_2(s) = \widehat{\Omega}(s+\lambda-\lambda\Gamma(s)) = \Omega(s+\lambda-\lambda\Gamma(s)) \cdot e^{-Q(s+\lambda-\lambda\Gamma(s))} \tag{35}$$

On the other hand, $W(x)$ exists if and only if $\lambda\alpha < 1$ and

$$\Omega(s) = \frac{1-\lambda\alpha}{1-\lambda \dfrac{1-\Psi(s)}{s}} \tag{36}$$

Therefore $W_2(x)$ exists if and only if $\lambda\alpha<1$ and $\Omega_2(s)$ can be obtained from (35) and (36) as well as the moments $w_{(r)}^{(2)}$;in particular

$$w_1^{(2)} = \frac{w_1+Q}{1-\lambda a} = \frac{\lambda\alpha_2}{2(1-\lambda a(1-\lambda\alpha)} + \frac{Q}{1-\lambda a} \text{ , where} \tag{37}$$

$$w_1 = \frac{\lambda\alpha_2}{2(1-\lambda\alpha)}$$

Then

$$T_t(s) = \Omega_1(s) \; e^{-st} \qquad t \leq Q \tag{38}$$

$$T_t(s) = \Omega(s+\lambda-\lambda\Gamma(s)) \; e^{-t(s+\lambda-\lambda\Gamma(s))}, \quad t>Q \tag{39}$$

(38) follows from the fact that for $t \leq Q$, $\gamma_t = \eta_1 + t$, η_1 being independent of t and (39) can be derived using exactly the same arguments that led to (35) with t in place of Q .

Similarly, from (38) and (39), we get:

$$T_{1/t} = \frac{\lambda a_2}{2(1-\lambda a)} + t \qquad t \leq Q$$

$$\tag{40}$$

$$T_{1/t} = \frac{\lambda \alpha_2}{2(1-\lambda a)(1-\lambda\alpha)} + \frac{t}{1-\lambda a} \qquad t>Q$$

CASE 2 : <u>Non-Preemptive Priority</u>

In this case $\Omega_2(s)$ can be computed exactly as before, for a job requiring service in both queues has to wait for the completion of all jobs arriving before it (waiting time in the modified process) plus the additional delay caused by busy periods initiated in queue 1 by all jobs arriving during this waiting time + Q .

Therefore

$$\Omega_2(s) = \Omega(s+\lambda - \lambda\Gamma(s)) \cdot e^{-Q(s+\lambda-\lambda\Gamma(s))} \tag{41}$$

and

$$T_t(s) = \Omega_2(s) \cdot e^{-s(t-Q)}, \quad t>Q \tag{42}$$

In order to compute $\Omega_1(s)$ let's introduce an indicator random variable (see Takacs [10]).

$$X_n = \begin{cases} 1 & \text{if } n^{th} \text{ service was in queue 1} \\ 0 & \text{otherwise} \end{cases}$$

Now the number of jobs left in queue 1 after a job departing from queue 1 is equal to the number of jobs arriving during the waiting time plus service time of that job, i.e.,

$$P\{\zeta_n^{(1)} = j \,|\, x_n=1\} = \int_0^\infty e^{-\lambda x} \frac{(\lambda x)^j}{j!} \; d \; (W_1 * H_1)(x) \tag{43}$$

Let's assume $\lambda\alpha<1$;

$$P\{\zeta_n^{(1)} = j, x_n = 1\} = P\{x_n=1\} \cdot P\{\zeta_n^{(1)} = j \,|\, x_n=1\} =$$

$$U(o,o)P\{\nu_n^{(1)}=j\} + \sum_{k=1}^{\infty} P\{\zeta_{n-1}^{(1)} = k\}P\{\nu_n^{(1)}=j-k+1\}$$

where $\nu_n^{(i)}=$ no. of arrivals during a service in queue i (i=1,2).

$$\sum_{j=0}^{\infty} P\{x_n = 1\} \cdot P\{\zeta_n^{(1)} = j | x_n = 1\} z^j = U(o,o)\Psi_1(\lambda - \lambda z) + \frac{U(z,1) - U(o,1)}{z} \quad \cdot$$

$$\cdot \ \Psi_1(\lambda - \lambda z) \qquad\qquad |z| \le 1 \qquad\qquad\qquad (44)$$

Now

$$P\{x_n = 1\} = 1 - P\{\zeta_n^{(1)} = 0, \ \zeta_n^{(2)} > 0\}$$

$$= 1 - [U(0,1) - U(0,0)] \qquad\qquad\qquad (45)$$

Then from (43), (44) and (45)

$$[1 - U(0,1) + U(0,0)] \ \cdot \ \Omega_1(\lambda - \lambda z)\Psi_1(\lambda - \lambda z) =$$

$$U(0,0)\Psi_1(\lambda - \lambda z) + \frac{U(z,1) - U(0,1)}{z} \ \Psi_1(\lambda - \lambda z)$$

$$\Omega_1(\lambda - \lambda z) = \frac{z U(0,0) + U(z,1) - U(0,1)}{z(1 - U(0,1) + U(0,0))} \qquad\qquad (46)$$

From (46) we get:

$$w_1^{(1)} = \frac{1}{\lambda} \cdot \frac{U'(z,1) - (1 - U(0,1))}{1 - U(0,1) + U(0,0))}\Big|_{z=1} = \frac{1}{\lambda} \{(1+p)U'(z,1) - \lambda\alpha\}|z=1$$

$$= \frac{\lambda(\alpha_2 - 2Q(\alpha - a))}{2(1+p)(1 - \lambda a)}$$

Given $t \le Q$ $\gamma_t = \eta_1 + t$ and

$$T_t(s) = \Omega_1(s) \ e^{-st} \qquad\qquad\qquad (47)$$

$$T_{1/t} = w_1^{(1)} + t$$

If $\lambda\alpha > 1$ it may happen that the first queue remains bounded while the second queue is unbounded. Let's assume this is the case; we shall see that the additional condition needed is $\lambda a < 1$. Then

$$\zeta_{n+1}^{(1)} = \begin{cases} \zeta_n^{(1)} - 1 + \nu_{n+1}^{(1)} & \text{if } \zeta_n^{(1)} > 0 \\ \nu_{n+1}^{(2)} & \text{if } \zeta_n^{(1)} = 0 \end{cases} \qquad\qquad (48)$$

Let $\{\Pi_j \quad j=0,1,\ldots \}$ be the stationary distribution of $\{\zeta_n^{(1)}\}$ and

$$U_1(z) = \sum_{j=0}^{\infty} \Pi_j z^j \qquad\qquad |z| \le 1 \qquad\qquad (49)$$

Then from (48)

$$U_1(z) = \frac{U_1(z) - \Pi_o}{z} \ \Psi_1(\lambda - \lambda z) + \Pi_o\Psi_2(\lambda - \lambda z)$$

$$U_1(z) = \frac{\Pi_o[z\Psi_2(\lambda - \lambda z) - \Psi_1(\lambda - \lambda z)]}{z - \Psi_1(\lambda - \lambda z)} \qquad\qquad (50)$$

and the condition $U_1(1) = 1$ gives

$$\Pi_o = \frac{1-\lambda a}{1+\lambda b - \lambda a} \tag{51}$$

and the condition $0 < \Pi_o < 1$ gives

$$\lambda a < 1 \tag{52}$$

Now (44) becomes:

$$\sum_{j=0}^{\infty} P\{\chi_n = 1\} \cdot P\{\zeta_n^{(1)} = j | \chi_n = 1\} z^j = \frac{U_1(z) - U_1(0)}{z} \cdot \Psi_1(\lambda - \lambda z)$$

and

$$P\{\chi_n = 1\} = 1 - U_1(0)$$

$$\Omega_1(\lambda - \lambda z) = \frac{U_1(z) - U_1(0)}{(1 - U_1(0))z} \tag{53}$$

5. An application: Hyper-Exponential Service Time Distribution

Let's assume that

$$H(x) = \sum_{i=1}^{m} r_i H_i(x) \qquad \text{where}$$

$$H_i(x) = \begin{cases} 1 - e^{-\mu_i x} & x \geq 0 \\ 0 & x < 0 \end{cases} \qquad , \quad \sum_{i=1}^{m} r_i = 1 \quad r_i > 0$$

Then

$$H(x) = 1 - \sum_{i=1}^{m} r_i e^{-\mu_i x} \qquad x \geq 0$$

$$\alpha = \sum_{i=1}^{m} \frac{r_i}{\mu_i}$$

$$\alpha_2 = 2 \sum_{i=1}^{m} \frac{r_i}{\mu_i^2}$$

$$a_n = \sum_{i=1}^{m} \frac{n! r_i}{\mu_i^n} \left[1 - e^{-\mu_i Q} (1 + \mu_i Q + \ldots + \frac{(\mu_i Q)^{n-1}}{(n-1)!}) \right]$$

This formula for a_n can be obtained using the following relation

$$\int_0^Q x^n \mu e^{-\mu x} dx = \frac{n!}{\mu^n} \quad 1 - e^{-\mu Q} (1 + \mu Q + \ldots + \frac{(\mu Q)^n}{n!})$$

which can be easily proved by induction, and the fact that $H_1(x)$ has a jump of size $\sum_{i=1}^{m} r_i e^{-\mu_i Q}$ at $x = Q$.

$$H_2(x) = \sum_{i=1}^{m} \frac{r_i e^{-\mu_i Q}}{(\sum_{j=1}^{m} r_j e^{-\mu_j Q})} (1 - e^{-\mu_i x})$$

$$b = \sum_{i=1}^{m} \frac{\frac{r_i}{\mu_i} \cdot e^{-\mu_i Q}}{\sum_{j=1}^{m} r_j e^{-\mu_j Q}} \quad , \quad b_2 = \sum_{i=1}^{m} \frac{\frac{r_i}{\mu_{i2}} \cdot e^{-\mu_i Q}}{\sum_{j=1}^{m} r_j e^{-\mu_j Q}}$$

$$p = \sum_{i=1}^{m} r_i e^{-\mu_i Q}$$

One of the possible performance measures that can be asked from this model is the following optimization problem:

Given H(x) find Q such that

$E\{\zeta_n^{(1)} + \zeta_n^{(2)}\}$ is a minimum for a stationary process.

We have used gradient methods to find the optimal Q in the results presented in the graphs of Figure 6. Two distributions were used in the examples plotted:

(i) $H(x) = 0.99(1 - e^{-\frac{x}{4}}) + 0.01(1 - e^{-\frac{x}{4000}})$,
which has coefficient of variation $\tilde{=}12.8$, $\alpha \cong 44$

(ii) $H(x) = 0.99(1 - e^{-\frac{x}{4}}) + 0.01(1 - e^{-\frac{x}{40}})$
which has coefficient of variation $\cong 1.5$., $\alpha \cong 4.4$

It is interesting to observe from Figure 2 that for large coefficients of variation the expected queue size is close to the minimum for a wide range of values of Q .

In the figures 2 - 5   the y-ordinate represents the total expected queue size: $E\{\zeta_n^{(1)}\} + E\{\zeta_n^{(2)}\}$ as given by (31) and (27) for the non-preemptive discipline and for the preemptive-resume discipline :

$$(\lambda a + \frac{\lambda^2 a_2}{2 (1-\lambda a)}) + E\{\zeta_n^{(2)}\}$$

where the first term is the expected queue size in the foreground queue considered as an M|G|1 queue with $H_1(x)$ as service time distribution and $E\{\zeta_n^{(2)}\}$ is given by (12) and is the expected queue size of the imbedded Markov Chain constructed for the background queue.

The x-ordinate represents the quantum size Q in the same units of time (miliseconds , say) as the expected service time α. The

load factor   ρ   is equal to   λα   and the symbol   ∞   over   a
dashed line indicates the value of the total expected queue size for
the FCFS discipline (Q=∞).   It can be easily shown that (12) and
(27) tend to   0   as   Q → ∞   and that (31) tends to $\lambda\alpha + \frac{\lambda^2\alpha_2}{2(1-\lambda\alpha)}$
as   Q → ∞.

6. Extensions and Conclusions

It is desirable to extend the Foreground-Background model to K
queues with K>2; with regard to waiting times this has been carried
out by Schrage [8] and lately by Kleinrock and Muntz[7] for various
priority disciplines; for a non-preemptive discipline this leads to
the analysis of a complex Markov Chain, but for the preemptive -
resume case the same method used for computing the waiting times can
be used for the calculation of queue sizes; the method consists in
constructing a modified process form the original one using the
notion of completion times introduced by Gaver[4] : due to the
preemptive-resume policy, as far as the kth queue is concerned
(k=1,2,...,K), queues k+1,...,K do not exist; also, any job in the
k^{th} queue has to wait for the completion of all jobs in queues
1,2,...,k-1 , plus service of jobs in front of it in the kth queue
plus a delay caused by arrivals during these waiting times; the
order in which jobs are served in queues 1,2,...,k-1 is irrelevant
(with respect to the job in the kth queue) and the modified process
consists in serving all jobs in queues 1,2,...,k-1 on a First-
Come-First-Served basis; this reduces the problem to the Foreground-
Background case treated in Section 3 with the distribution of the
quantum service time in the modified foreground queue given by

$$H_{1,2...k-1}(x) = \begin{cases} H(x) & \text{if } x < Q_1+Q_2+...+Q_{k-1} \\ 1 & \text{if } x \geq Q_1+Q_2+...+Q_{k-1} \end{cases} \tag{54}$$

(where Q_i is the quantum size for the ith queue , i=1,2,...,K),and
the distribution of the quantum service time for the background
queue (the kth queue) given by:

$$H_k(x) = \begin{cases} \dfrac{H(x+Q_1+...+Q_{k-1})-H(Q_1+...+Q_{k-1})}{1-H(Q_1+...+Q_{k-1})} & x<Q_k \\ \\ 1 & x \geq Q_k \end{cases} \tag{55}$$

In other words, for each   k=2,...,K , we consider the imbedded
Markov Chain given by the size of the kth queue at every quantum

completion time for the kth queue, or, if at the last such epoch the kth queue was empty, then we look at the kth queue size at the termination of the busy period initiated by the next arrival and with service time distribution given by $H_{1,2,\ldots,k-1}(x)$; the method of section 3 carries through with (54) used in place of $H_1(x)$ and (55) used in place of $H_2(x)$.

7. Supplementary Section

We want to generalize slightly equations (1) and (3) in order to be able to include in the model set-up times, (Guimarães [11]).

Accordingly let

$$f_j^{(1)} = (1-p) \sum_{k=0}^{\infty} \int_0^{\infty} P_k(t) d\hat{K}_1(t) f_j^{(k)}$$

$$+ p \sum_{k=0}^{\infty} \int_0^{\infty} P_k(t) d\hat{K}_2(t) f_{j-1}^{(k)} \tag{56}$$

where $0 < p \leq 1$ and $\hat{K}_1(t)$, $\hat{K}_2(t)$ are arbitrary distribution functions of positive random variables with Laplace-Stieltjes transform $K_1(s)$ and $K_2(s)$ respectively; we interpret (56) as follows:

p is the probability that a job initiating a busy period in the foreground queue joins the background queue and receives a quantum sevice with distribution $\hat{K}_2(t)$;

1-p is the probability that a job initiating a busy period in the foreground queue does not join the background queue and receives a quantum service with distribution $\hat{K}_1(t)$. (56) reduces to (1) if we put

$$p = 1 - H(Q)$$

$$\hat{K}_1(x) = \begin{cases} \dfrac{H(x)}{1-p} & x \leq Q \\ 1 & x > Q \end{cases}$$

$$\hat{K}_2(x) = \begin{cases} 0 & \text{if} \quad x < Q \\ 1 & \text{if} \quad x \geq Q \end{cases}$$

Forming the generating function of (56) using the same arguments as in (2) we get:

$$F(w) = (1-p)K_1(\lambda - \lambda F(w)) + pwK_2(\lambda - \lambda F(w)) \tag{57}$$

Lemma 1:

Let $K_1(s)$, $K_2(s)$ be Laplace-Stieltjes Transforms of distribution functions of non-negative random variables with expectations a_1 and a_2 respectively; let $0 < p \leq 1$ and denote $K(s) = (1-p)K_1(s) + pK_2(s)$, $a = (1-p)a_1 + pa_2$.

Then, the equation in z,

$$z = (1-p)K_1(\lambda - \lambda z) + wpK_2(\lambda - \lambda z), \tag{58}$$

(i) has a unique root $z(w)$ in the unit circle $|z| < 1$ for $|w| < 1$ or $|w| \geq 1$ and $\lambda a > 1$.

(ii) if $\lambda a \leq 1$ then $z(1) = 1$;

(iii) if $\lambda a > 1$ then $z(1) < 1$.

Proof:

(This proof is essentially equivalent to the proof of Takacs' Lemma presented in his book [9] or in the book of J.W. Cohen [2]. If $p=1$ the lemma reduces to Takacs' Lemma).

If $|w| < 1$ then $|(1-p)K_1(\lambda - \lambda z) + wpK_2(\lambda - \lambda z)| \leq |w| < 1 - \varepsilon$ for $\varepsilon < 1 - |w|$ and (i) follows from Rouche's Theorem.

Similarly if $|w| \leq 1$ and $\lambda a > 1$ then

$$|(1-p)K_1(\lambda - \lambda z) + wpK_2(\lambda - \lambda z)| \leq |K(\lambda - \lambda z)| \leq K(\lambda|1-z|) \leq K(\lambda(1-|z|)) =$$

$$= K(\lambda \varepsilon) < 1 - \varepsilon \quad \text{if} \quad |z| = 1 - \varepsilon \quad \text{and} \quad \varepsilon > 0 \quad \text{is sufficiently small};$$

then (i) follows from Rouche's Theorem. In order to prove (ii) and (iii) we note that $F(w)$ satisfies (58), then $F(w) = z(w)$ for $|w| < 1$; further $F(w)$ is analytic in $|w| < 1$ and continuous in $|w| \leq 1$.

Now let $w=1$ and $\lambda a \leq 1$.
Then, for $|z| \neq 1$, $|z| \leq 1$

$$|K'(\lambda - \lambda z)| < |K'(\lambda - \lambda z)|_{z=1} = \lambda a \leq 1$$

Therefore,

$$|K(\lambda - \lambda z) - 1| < |z - 1|$$

and (58) has no root in $|z| < 1$;
Now let z_0 with $|z_0| = 1$ be a root of (58);
then

$$1 = |K(\lambda - \lambda z_0)| \qquad \text{implies} \quad z_0 = 1$$

and from the continuity of $z(w)$ it follows that $z(1) = z_0 = 1$.
Now let $w=1$ and $\lambda a > 1$; since $K(\lambda - \lambda z)$ is monotone increasing on

$0 \leq z \leq 1$ it follows that (58) has a unique real root $0<z<1$ and from (i) this is the only root in $|z|<1$; therefore $z(1)<1$.

Acknowledgment:

I would like to thank the referee for the helpful suggestions to clarify the presentation of the numerical examples presented in the figures 2 through 6.

REFERENCES

1. Coffman,E.G. , "Markov Chain Analysis of Multiprogramming Computer Systems", Naval Res. Log Quart., 16,2, June 1969, pp. 175-197.

2. Cohen,J.W., The Single Server Queue, North Holland Publishing Co., 1969, pp. 625-629.

3. Fife,D.W., "An Optimization Model for Time Sharing", Proc. AFIPS 66, SJCC, Vol. 28, pp. 97-104.

4. Gaver,D.P., "A Waiting Line with Interrupted Service Including Priorities", Journal Royal St. Soc. (B), June 1962.

5. Adiri,I. and Avi-Itzhak, "A Time-Sharing Queue", Man.Sci., 15,11, 1969, pp. 639-657.

6. Kleinrock, "Analysis of a Time-Shared Processor", Nav.Res.Log. Quart., 2,1 (1964),pp.59-73.

7. Kleinrock and Muntz, "Processor Sharing Queuing Models of Mixed Scheduling Disciplines", JACM July 1972, Vol.19, pp.453-481.

8. Schrage, "The Queue $M|G|1$ with Feedback Priority Queues", Man.Sci., 13 (1967), pp. 466-474.

9. Takacs, Introduction to the Theory of Queues, Oxford U. Press, 1962, pp. 46-80.

10.Takacs, "Priority Queues", Op. Res., Vol.12, 1(1964),pp.63-74.

11.Guimarães,Célio, "Queuing Models with Applications to Scheduling in Operating Systems", Ph.D. Thesis, Technical Report 1127, Computing and Information Sciences Department, Case Western Reserve University, Cleveland, Ohio, May 1973.

TOTAL EXPECTED QUEUE SIZE x QUANTUM SIZE

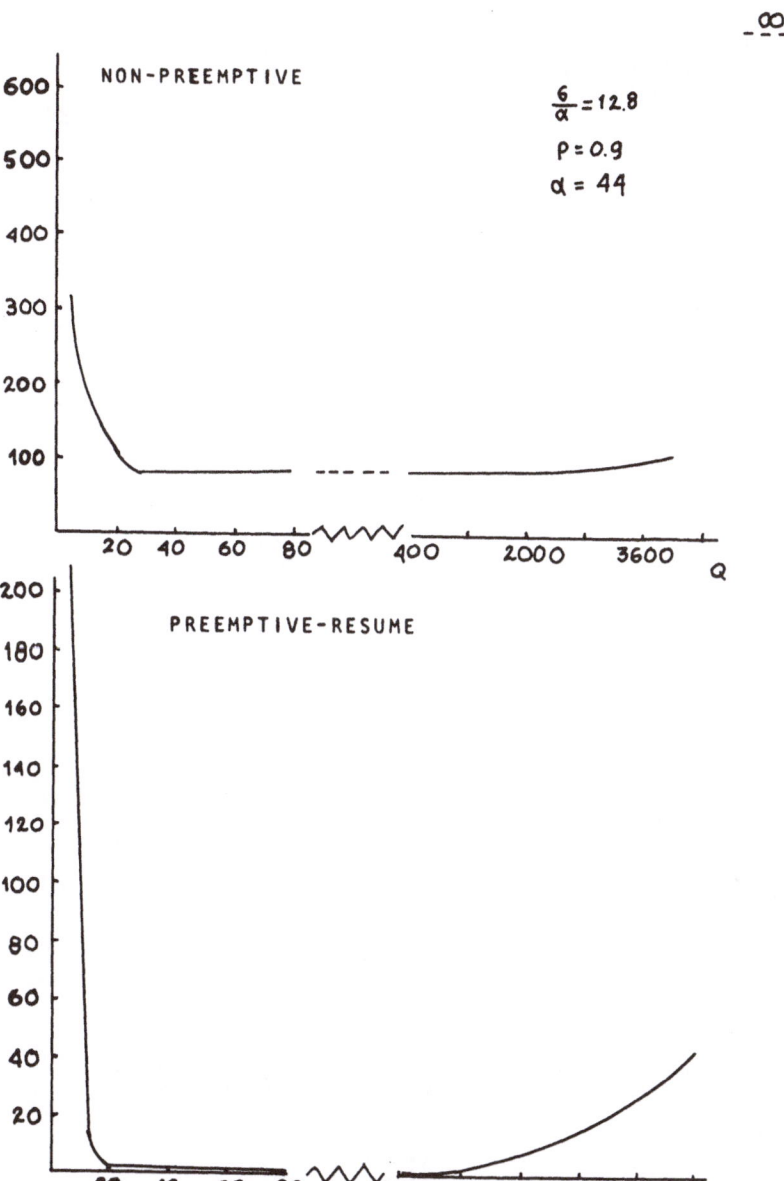

FIG. 2

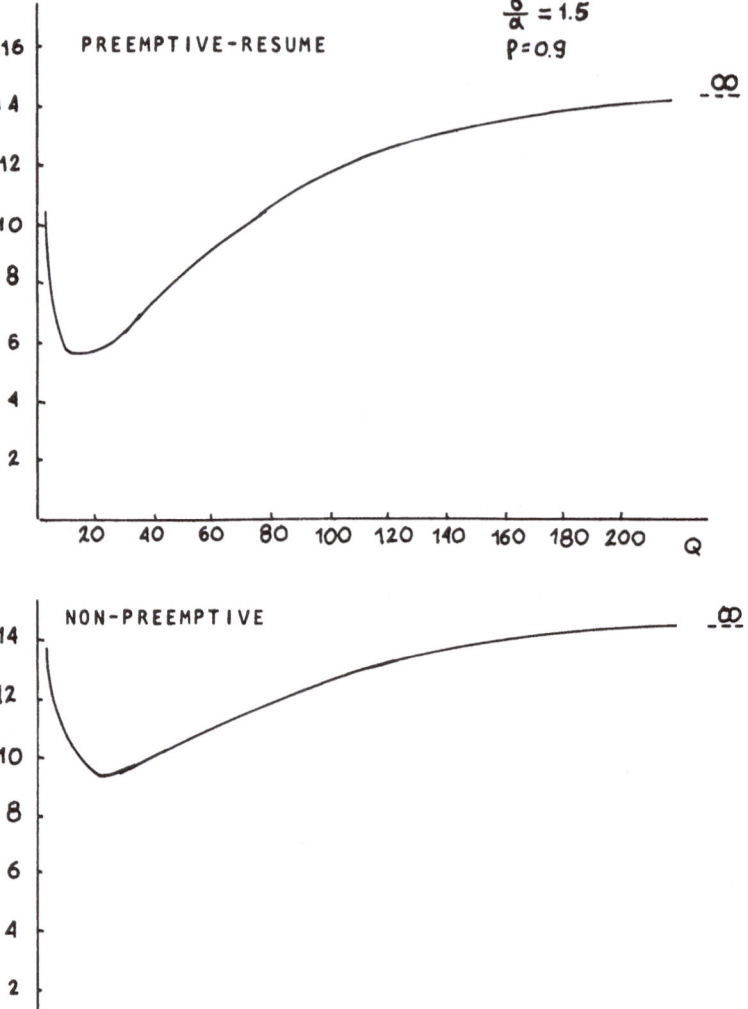

TOTAL EXPECTED QUEUE SIZE x QUANTUM SIZE

FIG. 3

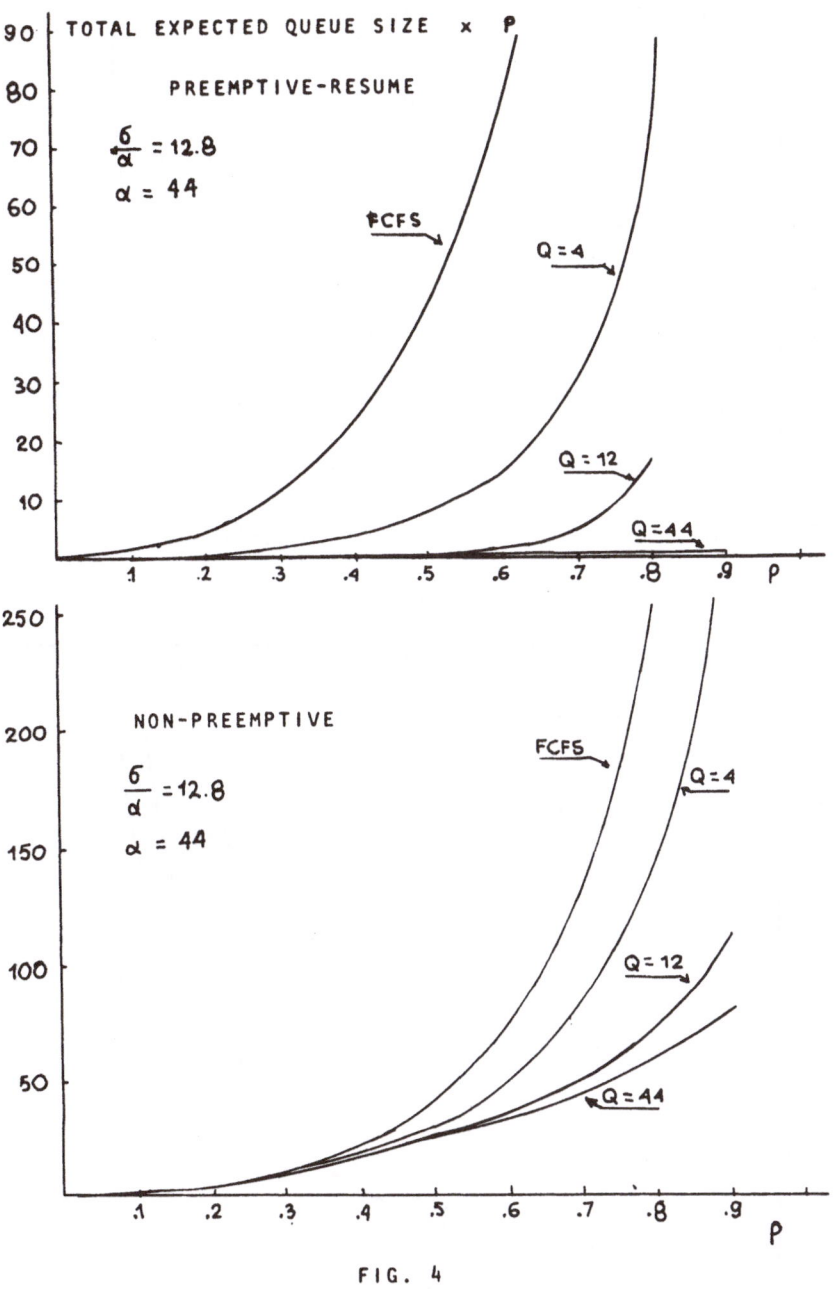

FIG. 4

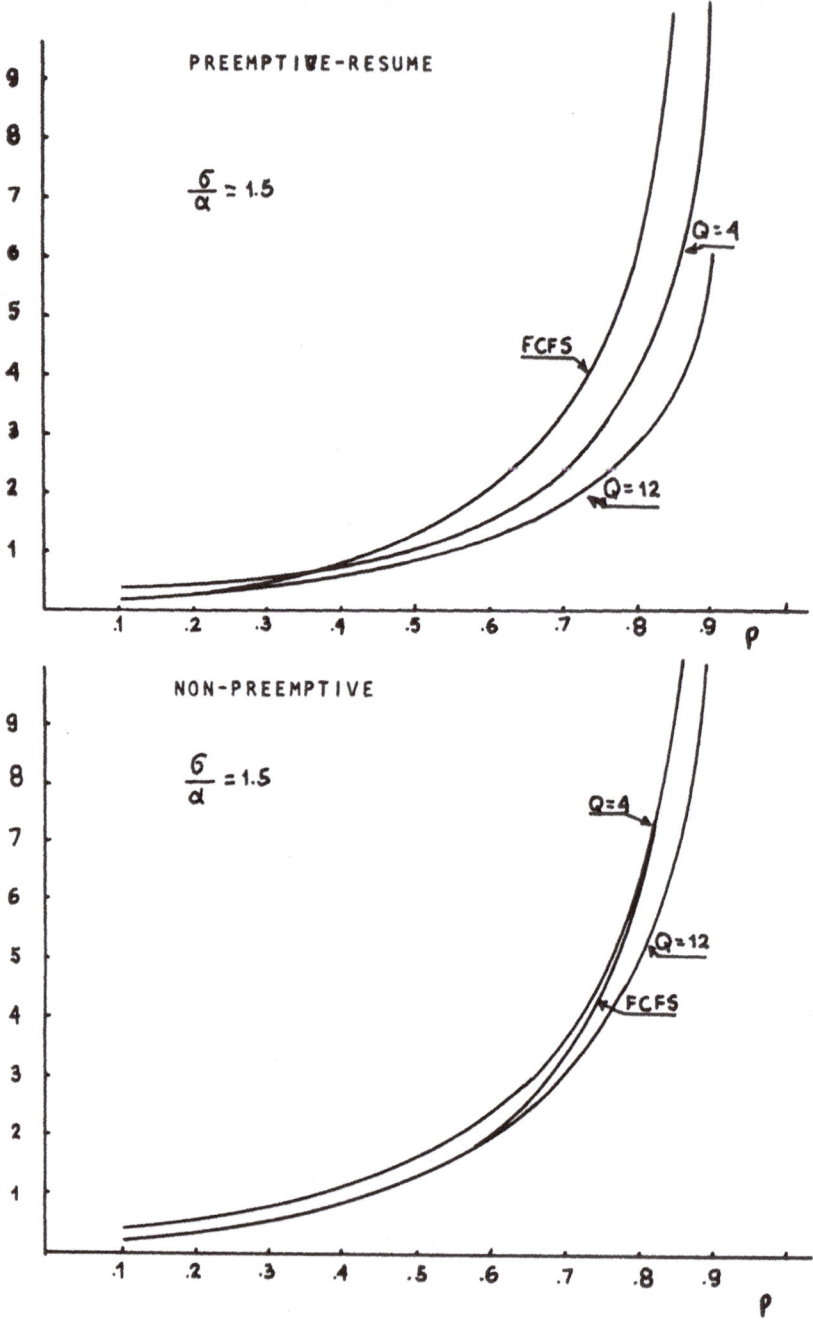

FIG. 5

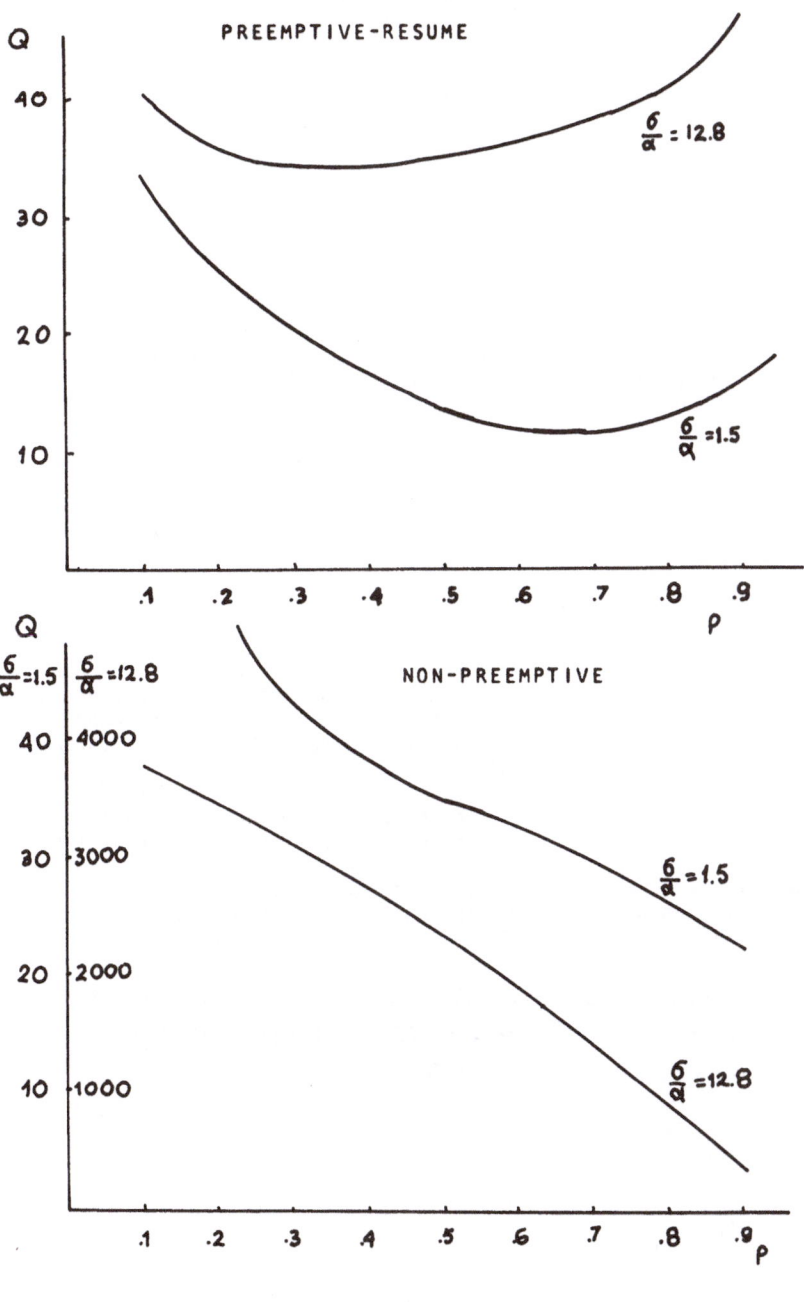

FIG. 6

ESPACE D'ADRESSAGE ET ESPACE D'EXÉCUTION
DU SYSTEME GEMAU

S. Guiboud-Ribaud
Centre Scientifique C.I.I.-Grenoble

J. Briat
ENSIMAG, Grenoble

———

1. INTRODUCTION

GEMAU est un système dont le premier objectif est de procurer une machine "idéale" (noyau) sur laquelle des sous-systèmes très différents puissent cohabiter.

Elle doit offrir par ailleurs une structure allégeant la tâche de conception des sous-systèmes (temps de conception, fiabilité du produit).

Dans ce but, GEMAU doit offrir les possibilités suivantes :

1. l'allocation de ressources dans un sous-système doit se faire au maximum au niveau logique.

   Par exemple, il est commode de ne pas avoir à gérer les ressources nécessaires à la réalisation d'un espace segmenté, mais par contre, on peut désirer allouer des périphériques de communication (bandes, terminaux, etc ..) selon une stratégie propre à chaque sous-système.

2. Le noyau met à la disposition des utilisateurs, c'est-à-dire des réalisateurs de sous-systèmes, un espace de noms qui matérialise les relations de désignation existantes entre les objets du système (programmes, périphériques, fichiers) à un instant donné. Cet espace de noms est le support de mécanismes de protection et de partage les plus généraux nécessaires pour la construction de base de données et de sous-systèmes [7] [13] [15] [16].

Les résultats présentés ici concernent des travaux effectués conjointement par une équipe CII et une équipe IMAG, avec l'aide de la Délégation à l'Informatique.

3. La structure de l'espace de noms doit être telle que :

    . l'implantation des fichiers ou des composants d'un programme
      soit la plus proche possible de leur structure logique

    . il soit possible de considérer un objet comme un simple composant
      dans la réalisation d'un ou plusieurs sous-systèmes. En d'autres
      termes, d'assurer au maximum les caractéristiques de "programming
      generality" [9] qui permettent d'utiliser le travail déjà fait par
      d'autres personnes [6] (MULTICS).

4. Les opérateurs de contrôle proposés (appel de processus, appel de
   procédure) s'appuyant sur la structure de noms doivent favoriser
   la structuration des sous-systèmes et, en particulier, les niveaux
   hiérarchiques de machines [11], ainsi que la modularité des composants d'un sous-système.

Beaucoup de caractéristiques proposées pour la structure de GEMAU ont
existé partiellement dans d'autres systèmes et d'autres machines (MULTICS)
[6] [18], (B 6500) [4] [5], (BASIC MACHINE) [14].

Le but de cet article est de présenter un outil homogène de réalisation
de système, en dégageant clairement les concepts utilisés.

2. PRINCIPES

Nous considérons un système comme un ensemble d'objets (programmes, données, fichiers) et de relations définies sur ces objets. La réalisation d'un sous-système est effectuée sur un noyau qui doit, d'une part, assurer la conservation de ces objets (valeurs) ainsi que leur accessibilité (désignation) et qui doit, d'autre part, permettre de traduire facilement les relations établies entre les objets.

2.1. Désignation

Le noyau gère l'ensemble des noms universels (noté E_{NU}) et l'ensemble des valeurs des objets, V : ces deux ensembles sont en correspondance biunivoque.

Un objet définit une certaine fonction pour laquelle plusieurs algorithmes sont possibles. Nous appelons réalisation particulière d'un objet l'utilisation d'un algorithme. Comme nous voulons pouvoir remplacer une réalisation particulière d'un objet par une autre sans pour cela devoir interrompre ou recompiler les programmes utilisant cet objet, la liaison entre ces programmes et l'objet est maintenue symboliquement pour toute la vie du programme (à la différence du système MULTICS où cette liaison a lieu à des instants précis).

Nous voulons en outre assurer que l'objet désigné par un nom symbolique reste le même pour une action déterminée du système. Cette action peut être l'appel à un opérateur de GEMAU ou à une exécution qui utilise l'objet ; par exemple, le remplacement ("on line") d'une version d'un compilateur par une autre version, ne doit pas détruire les compilations en cours.

Ceci impose donc d'avoir deux moyens distincts pour désigner un objet :

. un nom relatif à un espace d'adressage partagé par tous les utilisateurs,

. un nom local à une exécution de procédure : la création de ce nom local a lieu lors de la substitution paramètre formel - paramètre actuel de la procédure. Il est important de remarquer que la procédure est également repérée par un nom local.

Le noyau gère alors :

. un espace de noms ou espace d'adressage des objets E_{NP}

. un espace de noms locaux ou espace d'exécution E_{NL}

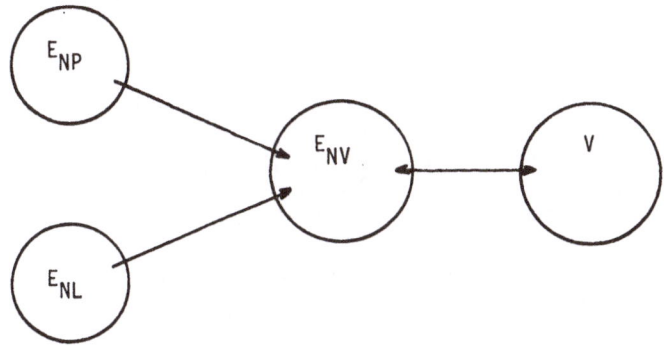

Figure 1

On peut effectuer les opérations sur un objet en le désignant par l'intermédiaire soit de E_{NP} soit de E_{NL}.

Les noms locaux sont nécessaires pour accéder directement la valeur d'un objet (par exemple, lire un mot d'une donnée, l'écrire, ..).

La cohérence d'une action sur un objet est alors garantie indépendamment de tout changement dans la réalisation de celui-ci.

Toute référence à un élément d'un objet est faite relativement à son nom local (type d'adressage : base + déplacement). Dans la suite, le nom local sera noté rb_i.

2.2. Structure

Notre but, comparable à celui de Brinch Hansen [2], est de créer une
structure d'accueil pour la construction de systèmes, puis de sous-systèmes
qui sont capables eux-mêmes de supporter d'autres sous-systèmes.

Il existe donc entre les sous-systèmes (et les objets qui les composent) des
relations de parenté (ou de visibilité) analogues à celles que propose
Brinch Hansen pour les processus. Dans notre cas, il ne s'agit pas uniquement
de processus, mais aussi d'objets composant les sous-systèmes.

Ainsi il n'est pas nécessaire de laisser à une procédure l'accès à tout
l'espace d'adressage (E_{NP}). Il suffit de lui assurer l'accès aux objets

non passés en paramètre lors de son appel et qui lui sont nécessaires
durant son exécution. De même, l'état caractérisant l'activité d'un processus ne concerne que le processus qui l'a créé pour effectuer une tâche
précise.

Ces relations de dépendance et d'indépendance se matérialisent bien sur une
arborescence où nous pouvons en isolant un sous-arbre, parler d'environnement
d'une procédure, d'un sous-système, ou bien de famille de processus (fig. 2).

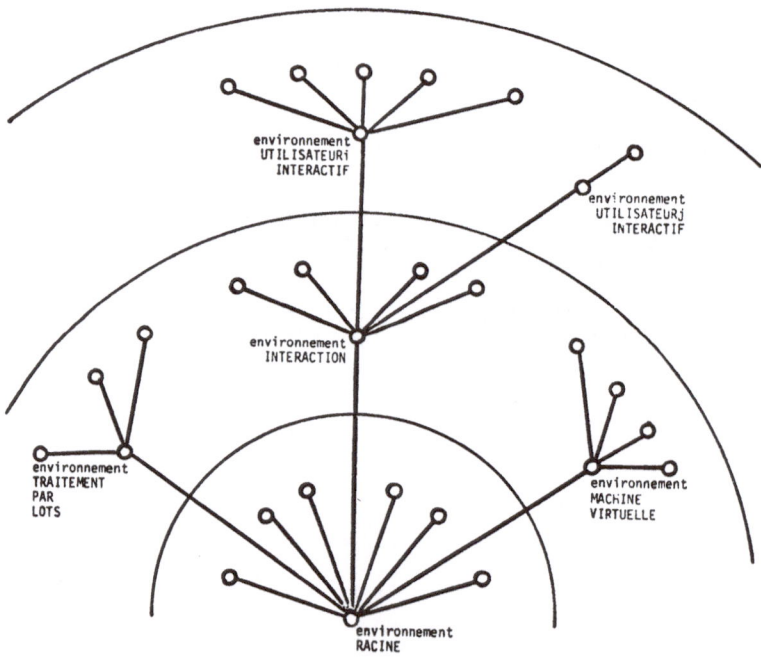

Figure 2 - Hiérarchie de sous-systèmes

2.3. Partage des objets. Protection et synchronisation

L'existence d'une communauté d'utilisateurs hétérogènes impose de garantir la cohérence d'un objet dans le cadre d'utilisations différentes et simultanées.

Nous considérons l'objet comme défini par l'ensemble des opérateurs (par exemple, lire, exécuter, ..) que l'on peut lui appliquer ainsi que par le fait qu'il soit utilisable simultanément ou non par plusieurs utilisateurs (par exemple, objet réentrant, objet à accès exclusif). Ces propriétés sont indépendantes de la manière dont on y accède à partir de E_{NL} ou E_{NP}. Elles lui sont intrinsèques.

Les objets seront donc potentiellement partageables par les utilisateurs pouvant les désigner, la gestion de ce partage étant réalisée au niveau de l'objet lui-même. Par exemple, un programme non réentrant peut être partagé entre plusieurs utilisateurs sans pour cela être utilisé concurremment (accès exclusif).

Cependant, on peut être amené à restreindre dans certains cas la puissance du partage ; par exemple, on peut vouloir qu'un programme ne puisse être modifié que par son propriétaire et non par les utilisateurs de ce programme.

Cette restriction ou protection est liée à la manière dont un utilisateur accède à l'objet [6] , [15] , [16] . Une solution naturelle est de lier cette protection au nom de l'objet.

3. DEFINITION

3.1. Espace d'adressage

Comme suggéré en 2.2., une structure arborescente permet de réaliser
simplement les fonctions de désignation, de partage et de protection [7].

Appelons annuaire les noeuds (objets) non terminaux de l'arborescence.
Un annuaire est le descripteur des objets qui lui sont directement ratta-
chés. Un segment est un objet de type donnée ou programme, et périphérique
un objet de type périphérique ou entrée-sortie.

Un annuaire permet de nommer symboliquement des objets qui peuvent être
des segments, des annuaires ou d'autres types à définir. Un objet possède
donc un nom d'entrée dans un annuaire. Ce nom permet de désigner de façon
unique l'objet de cet annuaire. Appelons nom partiel d'un objet par rapport à un annuaire la liste de tous les noms d'entrée des objets situés
sur le chemin issu de l'annuaire et menant à l'objet. Il existe un annuaire
prédéfini appelé racine.

Chaque objet est défini par un descripteur dans un annuaire (exception
faite de la racine). Ce descripteur contient les caractéristiques dudit
objet. On y trouve notamment :
 . le nom d'entrée,
 . la protection,
 . le type de l'objet : annuaire - segment - périphérique,
 . le nom universel (magnum) de l'objet.

Le contrôle de l'espace d'adressage, et en particulier la définition des
noms partiels connus, est réalisé par le mécanisme d'environnement. La
racine est l'environnement initial. Un environnement est un annuaire
distingué. Une procédure est située dans un environnement donné, si
dans son nom partiel à partir de cet environnement, ne figure pas d'autres
environnements. S'il en existe, ceux-ci sont dits englobés, le premier
étant dit englobant.

Un environnement fournit à une procédure y étant située, un sous-ensemble
de l'espace d'adressage. Tout nom émis par la procédure est résolu comme
un nom partiel à partir de cet environnement ; l'ensemble des objets
nommables à partir d'un environnement définit son espace visible.

133

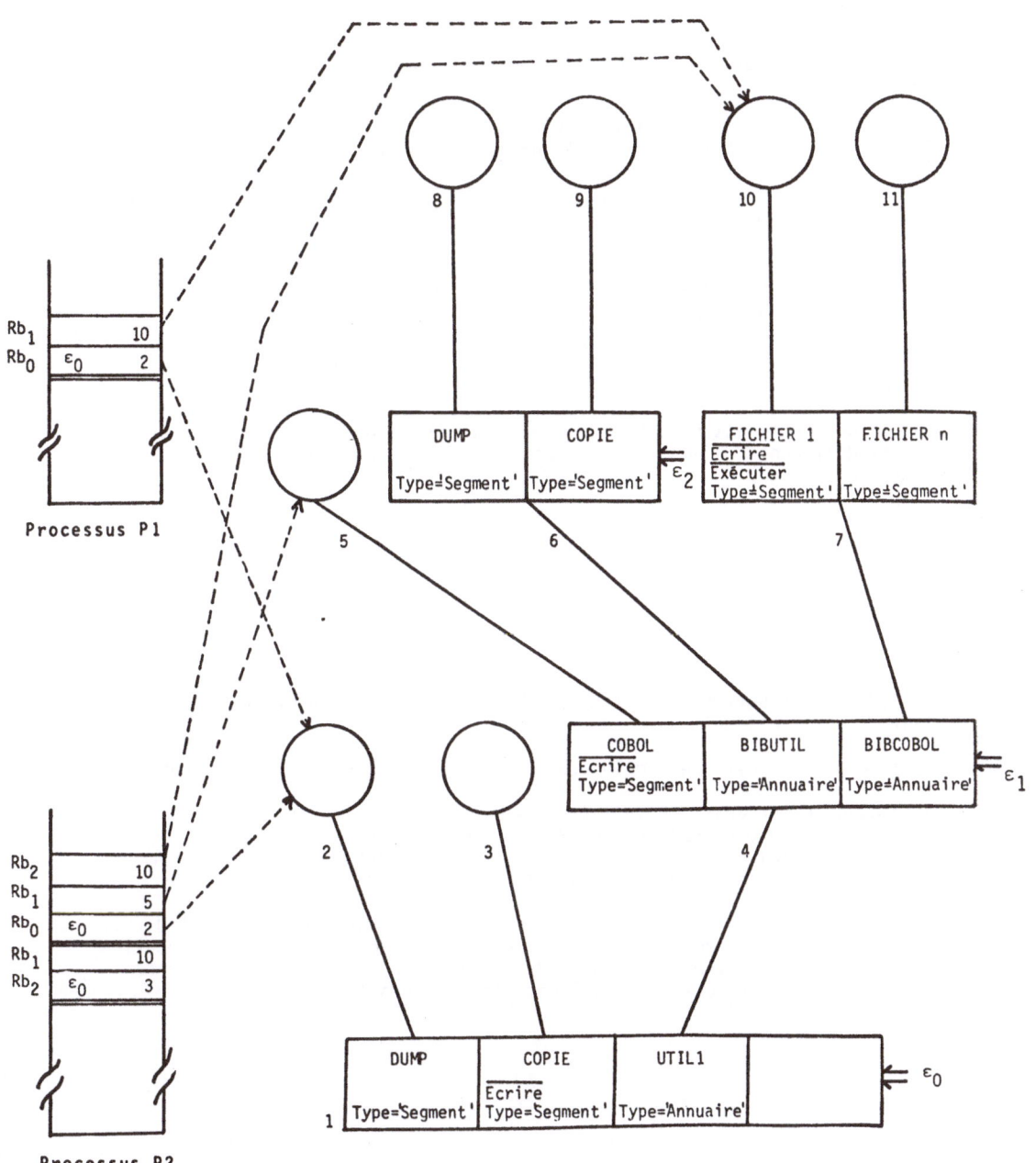

Figure 3 - Espace d'adressage et Espace d'exécution

Exemple de structure de noms

Considérons la figure 3. L'objet 1 est la racine. ε_0, ε_1 et ε_2 sont des environnements.

Les noms partiels de l'objet 8 sont respectivement : UTIL1.BIBUTIL.DUMP, BIBUTIL.DUMP et DUMP dans ces environnements (ε_0, ε_1 et ε_2).

L'objet 5 a pour noms, respectivement UTIL1.COBOL et COBOL dans ε_0 et ε_1, mais n'est pas nommable par une procédure située dans l'environnement ε_2.

Nous avons les ensembles d'objets visibles suivants :

$$E_v (\varepsilon_0) = \{2, 3, 4, 5, 6, 7, 8, 9, 10, 11\}$$
$$E_v (\varepsilon_1) = \{5, 6, 7, 8, 9, 10, 11\}$$
$$E_v (\varepsilon_2) = \{8, 9\}$$

Nous voyons qu'il est possible de nommer les mêmes objets depuis des environnements différents, s'ils sont visibles depuis ces environnements. Ceci permet le partage.

3.2. Espace d'exécution

Une procédure est parfaitement définie par ses noms locaux et son environnement.

Les noms locaux peuvent se référer à des objets provenant éventuellement d'autres environnements.

L'espace visible est l'ensemble des objets manipulables par la procédure.

Une procédure est aussi définie par l'ensemble des primitives de GEMAU qu'elle doit pouvoir appliquer pour s'exécuter. Ce sont ses prérogatives. Il paraît naturel de lier les prérogatives d'une procédure à l'environnement qui définit les objets qu'elle pourra manipuler (niveau de machine).

L'espace d'exécution est structuré en processus. Chaque processus est décrit par une pile dans laquelle chaque élément se compose de l'espace d'exécution (noms locaux) et de l'environnement d'une procédure appelée et non encore terminée. Le sommet de la pile définit l'état courant du processus.

La figure 3 donne un exemple d'espace d'execution. Remarquons dans cet exemple, que l'état courant du processus P2 peut être le résultat de l'exécution dans l'objet 3 de :

    APPELER(DUMP,UTIL1.COBOL,UTIL1.BIBCOBOL.FICHIER1)

ou

    APPELER(DUMP,Rb$_1$,UTIL1.BIBCOBOL.FICHIER1)

La création d'un processus exige la fourniture d'une procédure initiale, de ses arguments et d'un environnement de référence. C'est celui du processus père au moment de l'ordre de création du fils.

L'espace d'exécution du fils est construit à partir de l'environnement courant de son père. Ceci garantit qu'un processus créé n'outrepassera jamais les prérogatives du processus créateur.

La fin d'un processus n'est effective qu'au retour de sa procédure initiale.

Pour des raisons de contrôle de processus, nous privilégions la relation de filiation entre processus : un processus père est responsable de ses fils. Toute autre relation entre processus ne peut alors être définie qu'au moyen des objets de l'espace d'adressage.

Cette structure hiérarchique exige l'existence a priori d'un processus ancêtre prédéfini dont l'environnement initial est la racine de l'espace d'adressage.

Dans la figure 4 nous trouvons le processus ancêtre et son environnement. Il assure la génération du système à partir des programme et périphérique initiaux

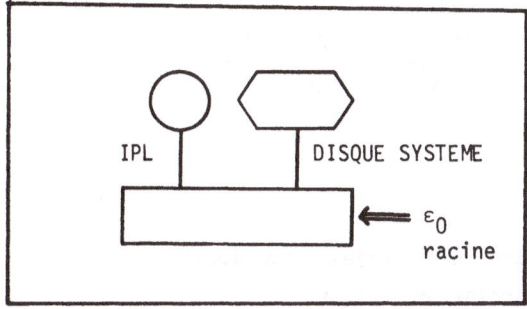

Figure 4 - Environnement initial du processus ancêtre

4. ESPACE D'ADRESSAGE. ENVIRONNEMENTS

4.1. Opérateurs sur les objets

i) Definition

Le système fournit un certain nombre de primitives (ou verbes) permettant de manipuler des objets. Ces primitives seront différentes selon le type de l'objet sur lequel elles s'appliquent.

ii) Modifications de l'espace d'adressage

```
CREER( designation d'annuaire (*)
     , nom d'entrée
     , valeur initiale
     , description )(**)
```

entrer un nouvel objet dans un annuaire et définir en même temps les caractéristiques de cet objet (type, protection, nom, etc ..)

```
DETRUIRE( designation d'annuaire , nom d'entrée )
```

retirer un objet d'un annuaire. Cet objet ne possède plus de nom partiel. Il n'est plus accessible que par l'intermédiaire de noms locaux.

iii) Modification de l'espace d'exécution

```
(Liste de  rb) ← APPELER( designation de segment/peripherique
                    , liste de  designation d'objets )
```

permet d'exécuter une procédure et de fabriquer l'espace d'exécution correspondant. Les noms locaux (rb) correspondant aux paramètres d'appel sont créés, ainsi que celui (rb_0) correspondant à la procédure. Si les désignations d'objet sont des noms partiels alors la résolution est faite relativement à l'environnement de la procédure appelante. L'environnement de la procédure appelée devient l'environnement courant du processus.

(*) designation d'objet ::= nom partiel / nom local
(**)voir § 4.4. pour la description précise.

L'espace d'exécution de la procédure appelante est sauvegardé dans une pile.

La procédure appelée peut éventuellement fournir des résultats (objets) qui seront affectés aux noms locaux (rb_i) indiqués.

```
RETOURNER( liste de  designation d'objets  )
```

termine l'exécution de la procédure courante, les noms locaux correspondants disparaissent (dépilage), l'environnement courant et les noms locaux sont alors ceux de la procédure appelante avec éventuellement création des nouveaux noms locaux spécifiés par RETOURNER et affectation aux paramètres formels indiqués dans APPELER.

```
rb_i ← LIER( designation d'objet )
```

crée un nom local pour un objet (résolution par rapport à l'environnement de la procédure).

```
LIBERER(rb_i)
```

détruit un nom local.

iv) Espace des objets

Tout objet est créé par un ordre (CREER). Il n'est pas détruit par un ordre explicite. Sa destruction est effective lorsqu'il n'est plus adressable, c'est-à-dire qu'il n'a plus de nom d'entrée et qu'aucun nom local ne le désigne.

Cette propriété va permettre de réaliser simplement la création et destruction d'objets temporaires (fichier de travail ..).

Ces objets seront des segments - données/programmes qui n'existeront que par l'intermédiaire de noms locaux.

Ils sont créés par l'opération :

```
rb_i ← LIER
```

et détruits soit explicitement par l'opération LIBERER, soit implicitement à la disparition du dernier nom local le répérant (retour de procédure).

v) Moment de liaison

De tels opérateurs encouragent l'identification de l'utilisation logique
d'un objet à son utilisation physique, mais permettent toutefois de sé-
parer ces utilisations pour garantir la cohérence d'une exécution. En
effet, entre deux moments de liaison, une substitution d'objet est possible. La liaison doit alors être maintenue tant qu'une substitution est
néfaste.

Considérons les deux programmes :

```
Π 1 :                          Π 2 :
        :                              :
        :                              :
        :                              :
                               rb₃ ← LIER(COBOL) ;
    REPETER n fois             REPETER n fois
    (                          (
        .                              .
        .                              .
    APPELER(COBOL) ;               APPELER(rb₃) ;
        .                              .
        .                              .
        .                              .
    )                          )
        .                              .
        .                              .
        .                              .
```

Apparemment ces deux programmes sont identiques et fournissent le même résultat. En fait, c'est ignorer l'existence d'autres processus dans le système.
Si en parallèle un second processus détruit COBOL et crée un nouveau segment
COBOL, le programme Π 1 utilisera au prochain appel APPELER(COBOL) le nouveau
segment, alors que Π 2 utilisera toujours l'ancien, car sa référence est
dans rb_3.

4.2. Protection

Le type d'un objet définit les opérateurs qui lui sont applicables. La
protection d'un objet se réalise simplement par une restriction des opérateurs applicables sur l'objet.

```
restrictions  ::=  restrictions de manipulation / restrictions
                                                    d'utilisation

restrictions de manipulation  ::= CREER/DETRUIRE

restrictions d'utilisation  * ::= (CREER/DETRUIRE)/(LIRE/ECRIRE/EXECUTER)
```

* ces restrictions dépendent naturellement du type de l'objet.

Considérons la figure 3. Indiquons pour chaque entrée les restrictions d'accès à l'objet.
Par exemple, ECRIRE signifie pour l'objet 5 que l'écriture est interdite et
ECRIRE/EXECUTER pour l'objet 10, que l'écriture et l'exécution sont inter-
dites.

Ainsi : APPELER(UTIL1.BIBCOBOL.FICHIER1) est interdit car l'objet 10 est en
lecture seule.

4.3. Partage : accès concurrentiel

La structure de l'espace d'adressage a été conçue de façon à permettre un
partage aisé des objets. Toutefois il est possible qu'un objet fichier ne
puisse être lié   que par un processus et un seul à un instant donné. Il
en est de même pour un objet de type programme non réentrant, ou éventuellement de type périphérique. Comme nous l'avons déjà vu, une telle propriété
est caractéristique de l'objet.

On appelle degré de multiprogrammation associé à un objet, le nombre maximal
de processus différents pouvant lier   ou manipuler cet objet au même
instant.

La synchronisation est effectuée au niveau de l'objet ; il n'est pas possible
de définir des synchronisations plus fines, par exemple sur des enregistrements, si l'objet est un fichier. Dans ce cas, la synchronisation s'effectue-
ra en donnant un degré de multiprogrammation fini au programme de manipulation de ce fichier.

Les processus demandant l'objet seront mis en attente si le nombre de processus l'ayant capturé à cet instant est égal au degré de multiprogrammation. Ils seront débloqués au gré des libérations de l'objet par les processus l'utilisant. Ceci est valable pour tous les opérateurs applicables à l'objet y-compris la destruction.

4.4. Récapitulatif sur les objets et les noms

```
objet annuaire   ::=   descriptif annuaire , {REFERENCE( objet )} (*)
descriptif annuaire  ::= type = 'annuaire',
                          opérateurs ,
                          degré de multiprogrammation ,
                          taille
REFERENCE( objet ) ::=  nom d'entrée ,
                        restriction ,
                        nom universel
opérateurs ::= CREER/DETRUIRE
```

Le descriptif annuaire est la caractéristique intrinsèque d'un annuaire. Sa valeur (REFERENCE) est l'ensemble des descripteurs d'objets du point de vue de l'espace d'adressage (caractéristiques extrinsèques).

```
objet segment   ::= type = 'segment',
                      opérateurs ,
                      degré de multiprogrammation ,
                      taille ,
                      vecteur de mots 10070
opérateurs   ::= CREER/DETRUIRE/LIRE/ECRIRE/EXECUTER
```

(*) les crochets { } indiquent une répétition.

```
objet périphérique  ::= type = 'périphérique',
                        degré de multiprogrammation ,
                        opérateurs ,
                        procédure système
opérateurs  ::= CREER/DETRUIRE/EXECUTER
```

Il est maintenant possible de détailler ce qu'est un nom local

```
nom local  ::=  nom universel ,
                type de l'objet  ,
                restrictions
type de l'objet  ::= 'annuaire'/'périphérique'/'segment'
restrictions ::= défini  par le nom partiel de l'objet
```

Ceci permet de fournir les précisions suivantes sur les paramètres des primitives :

```
désignation d'objet  ::= ( nom partiel / rb_i), restrictions
```

Les restrictions permettent de limiter l'utilisation qui peut être faite des objets passés en paramètre.

4.5. Environnements

i) Définition

Rappelons que l'environnement est l'annuaire de référence pour les noms partiels utilisés par une procédure ; il fixe aussi les pouvoirs ou prérogatives de la procédure.

```
objet environnement  ::=  objet annuaire
                          , attribut  : 'environnement'
                          , prérogatives
```

Les prérogatives sont un sous ensemble des primitives du système.

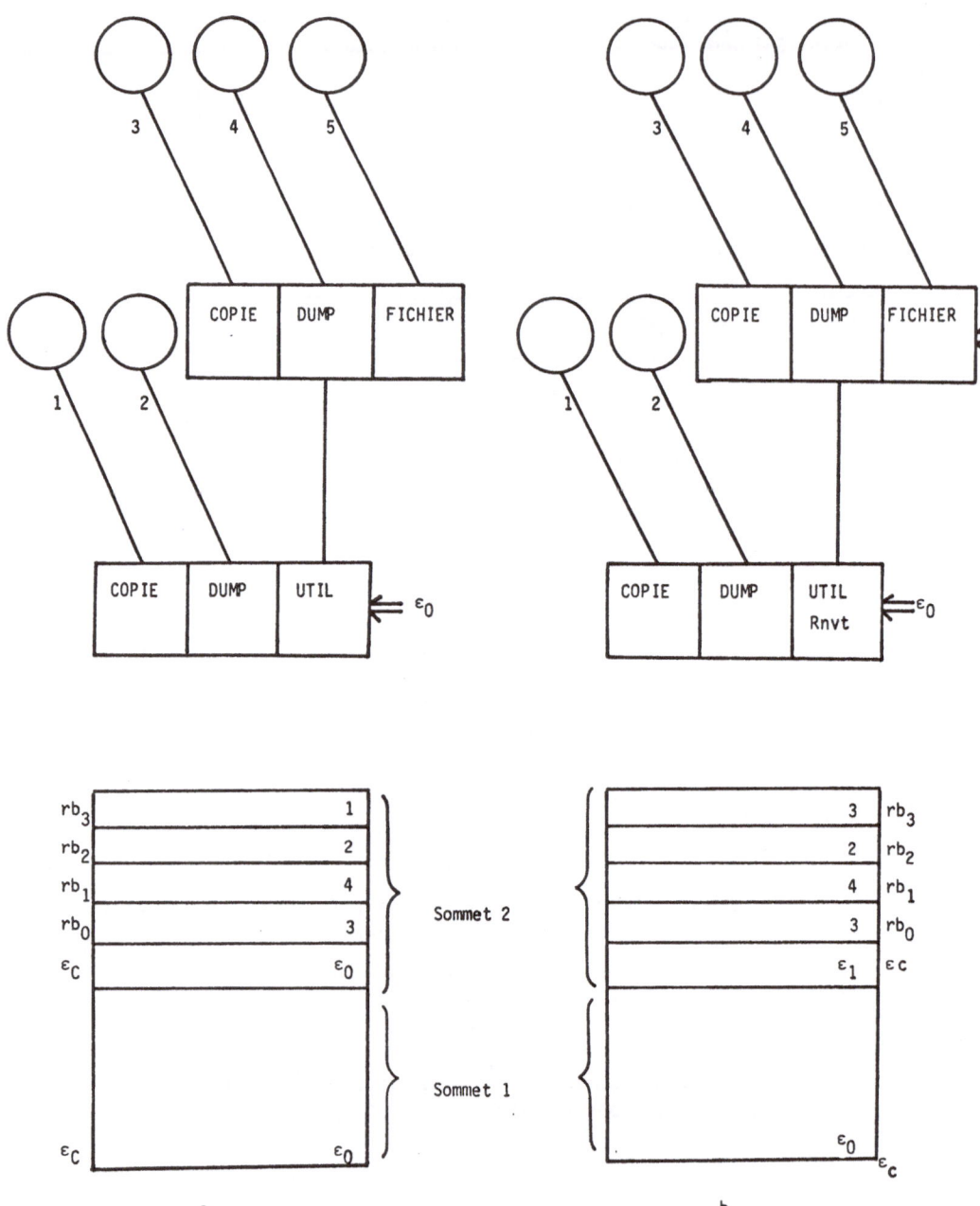

Figure 5 - Mécanismes des environnements

ii) <u>Exemple</u> (figure 5)

Dans le cas 5 b., l'annuaire de nom d'entrée UTIL dans ε_0 possède l'attribut environnement (envt), ce qui n'est pas le cas dans 5 a.

L'état 1 est l'état initial et l'environnement courant (ε_c) associé au processus est ε_0.

Supposons que l'on ait :

    APPELER(UTIL .COPIE,UTIL .DUMP,DUMP)

l'état courant du processus est alors l'état 2. L'environnement courant est soit ε_0 (5 a.), soit ε_1 (5 b.).

Supposons que le programme 3 comporte

    $rb_3 \leftarrow$ LIER(COPIE)

le résultat est respectivement 1 et 3.

Dans le cas 5 b., l'objet 2 qui a été passé en tant que paramètre lors de l'appel n'est utilisable que sous le nom local rb_2, mais n'a pas de dénomination dans l'environnement ε_1.

iii) <u>Prérogatives</u>

Sur la plupart des machines actuelles, il existe deux modes de fonctionnement : maître / esclave.

A chacun de ces modes, des prérogatives différentes sont associées ; c'est le cas des instructions privilégiées.

Les prérogatives d'un processus sont les opérateurs (objets) utilisables par ce processus. Elles sont définies à un instant donné par l'environnement courant qui lui est associé.

A sa création, un environnement est muni d'une liste de primitives. Ce sont les prérogatives de l'environnement. Ces prérogatives sont un sous-ensemble des prérogatives du processus créant l'environnement. Nous imposons de plus aux prérogatives de suivre les règles d'inclusion des espaces visibles.

144

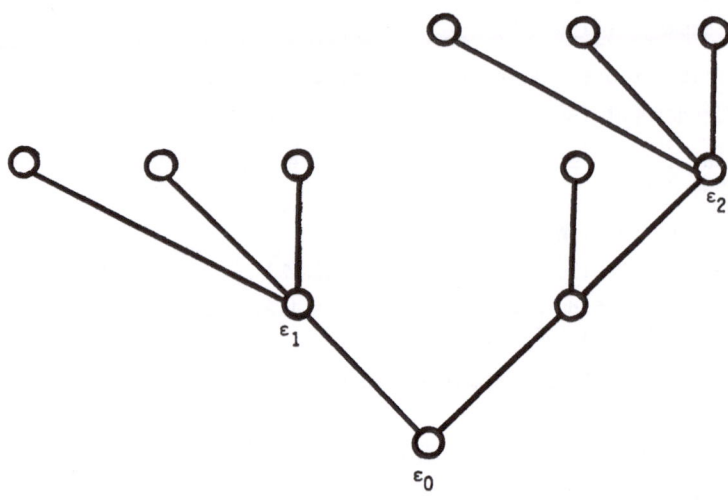

Figure 6 - Inclusion de prérogatives

Par exemple, dans la figure 6, les prérogatives de l'environnement ε_2, ainsi que celles de l'environnement ε_1, sont incluses dans celles de l'environnement ε_0 car l'espace visible de ε_2 comme celui de ε_1 est inclus dans l'espace visible de ε_0.

Ceci signifie que les prérogatives iront en décroissant en descendant une branche de l'espace d'adressage.

iv) Relation prérogative - protection

Les prérogatives sont définies par l'environnement courant du processus. Tout changement d'environnement entraîne un changement des prérogatives du processus.

La protection (ensemble des opérateurs applicables) est spécifique du nom d'un objet. Elle est valide dans un domaine bien défini, c'est-à-dire quand l'objet considéré se trouve dans l'environnement courant. Si cet objet est dans un environnement englobé, la seule protection qui lui est associée est alors celle liée à son type, ou alors une protection définie au niveau de l'appel de procédure (restriction d'accès) ; dans ce cas, la protection est associée au nom local et est relative à l'exécution considérée.

4.6. Liens

i) Motivations

L'environnement permet de définir un cadre local pour la résolution des noms d'objets référencés par les processus et fixer les prérogatives.

Il est indispensable d'introduire un moyen permettant, depuis une branche de l'arborescence, l'accès d'objets situés sur une autre branche. On désire en effet pouvoir accéder un même objet depuis des environnements différents avec des protections différentes, ou bien augmenter localement ses pouvoirs pour un travail déterminé.

C'est notamment le cas de programmes bibliothèque que l'on désire mettre à la disposition des utilisateurs, ou de procédures système d'utilisation courante (SPOOL, gestion de fichier).

Un objet de type lien permet de définir de nouveaux noms partiels pour un objet : un lien est une référence vers un autre objet. La structure de l'espace d'adressage est alors un "graphe orienté".

ii) Exemple (figure 7)

Depuis l'environnement ε_0 on a pu créer quatre liens qui ont pour nom et valeur respectifs :

. UTIL1.INTERP(8) pointe vers SYST.INTERP(7)

. UTIL1.IMP(9) pointe vers SYST.UTILIT.SPOOL(12)

. UTIL1.TTY(10) pointe vers TTYi(5)

. SYST.UTILIT.IMP(11) pointe vers IMP(4)

Un processus s'exécutant dans l'environnement ε_0 aura deux façons de nommer l'objet 4 :

. IMP

. SYST.UTILIT.IMP

On voit donc qu'il peut exister plusieurs noms partiels pour un même objet (non unicité de noms).

L'avantage de la multiplicité des noms réside dans les différentes restrictions d'accès qu'ils permettent d'exprimer. Les protections sont alors associées aux chemins d'accès, l'objet lui-même définissant les opérateurs applicables ; la protection minimum est alors associée au nom d'entrée.

147

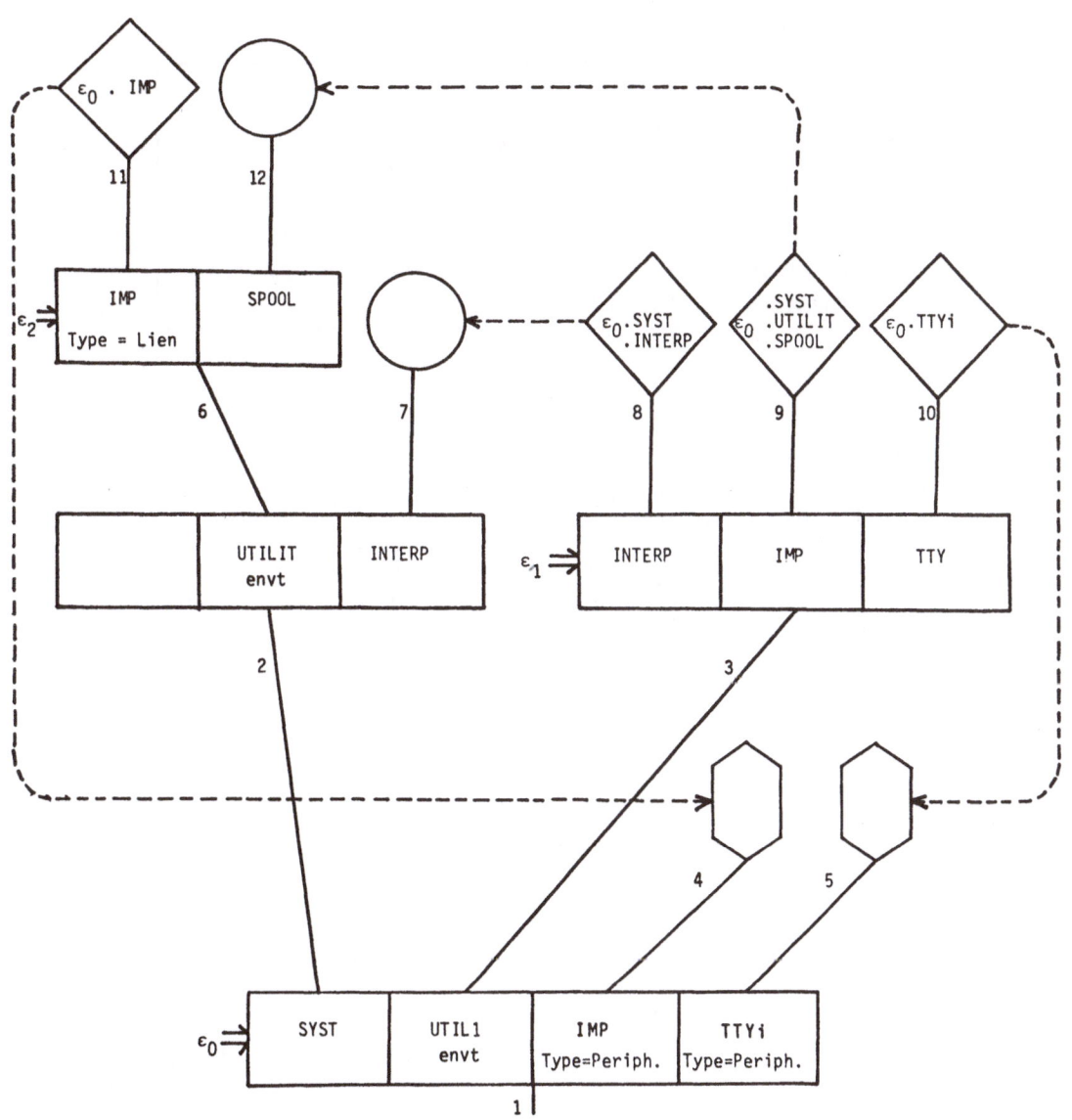

Figure 7 - Liens

iii) Description d'un objet-lien

```
objet lien  ::= type = 'lien',
                opérateurs ,
                nom d'objet référencé ,
                restriction d'accès à l'objet référencé
                      (elles dépendent de l'objet)
nom d'objet référence  ::=  nom universel { nom partiel }
opérateurs  ::= CREER/DETRUIRE
```

iv) Création

Un lien peut désigner un objet de type quelconque. La structure de l'espace d'adressage implique qu'un processus ne peut créer un lien que dans son espace visible. Dans l'exemple de la figure 7, un processus situé dans l'environnement ε_1 connaît les objets INTERP (segment) et TTY (périphérique) avec leurs caractéristiques éventuelles ; il peut ignorer complètement que INTERP n'est pas un segment, mais un lien vers un segment.

5. ESPACE D'EXECUTION - PROCESSUS

L'espace d'exécution est structuré en une hiérarchie de processus. Chaque processus est décrit par la pile des exécutions des procédures (noms locaux, environnements), depuis une procédure initiale. Le contrôle élémentaire d'un processus s'effectue au moyen des transitions procédurales (APPELER, RETOURNER).

Ce mécanisme intéressant du point de vue de la structuration et de la modularité (pas de GOTO), est inadapté dans le cas d'événements invalidant une suite d'exécutions de procédures (erreur arithmétique ou logique, erreur d'adressage) ou signifiant une alternative à l'exécution séquentielle, par exemple une fin de fichier (ENDFILE de PL/1).

5.1. Point de contrôle

Le principe de ce mécanisme de contrôle est d'associer lors d'une exécution, une action de contrôle à tout événement [4], [18].

Cette action sera exécutée si l'événement considéré se produit (généralisation du mécanisme des interruptions).

Si nous considérons l'environnement comme définissant un niveau de machine ou de sous-système [11], il est naturel de définir le domaine d'un point de contrôle comme la suite des procédures de la pile du processus appartenant au même environnement que la procédure ayant créé le point de contrôle (premier élément de la liste).

La destruction d'un point de contrôle est faite soit explicitement (RETIRER) soit à la disparition de la procédure qui l'a créé (RETOURNER).

Dans la figure 8, le domaine du point de contrôle est représenté par les exécutions de procédure P_3 P_4.

Un point de contrôle est armé lorsque l'événement qui le caractérise est arrivé.

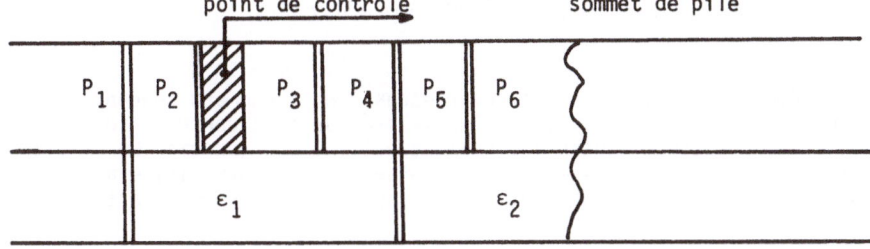

Figure 8

5.2. Evénements synchrones et asynchrones

Nous considérons qu'à toute exécution élémentaire (instruction machine ou opérateur) ou procédurale, est associé l'ensemble des événements possibles.

Par exemple, dans le cas des instructions machine, on peut citer :
. les erreurs arithmétique et logique, les erreurs d'adressage,
et pour les opérateurs GEMAU :
. opérateur illégal, procédure avortée.

Des événements peuvent également être programmés dans une procédure, par exemple un événement FINFICHIER lors de la lecture d'un fichier.

Nous distinguons deux types d'événements :

. les événements synchrones qui, comme les exemples précédents, se produisent durant l'exécution considérée,

. les événements asynchrones qui, bien que liés à une exécution bien définie, peuvent se produire après celle-ci.

Par exemple, si un événement pour débordement de pile se produit de façon synchrone à l'opération d'empilage, un événement associé à une interaction télétype (touche BREAK) se produit de façon asynchrone à l'opération de demande d'interaction. Il en est de même pour un événement caractérisant la fin d'un processus par rapport à l'opération qui a créé ce processus.

5.3. Action de contrôle

C'est le sous-ensemble des primitives du système que l'on peut associer à un point de contrôle et qui seront exécutées lors de l'occurence de :

APPELER(segment procédure , paramètres)

la procédure traite l'événement ; l'occurrence de l'événement force l'appel de cette procédure. A sa fin, l'exécution est normalement reprise dans la procédure courante.

RIEN : aucune action de contrôle n'a lieu (masque)

RETOURNER : la procédure courante effectue un retour forcé. L'exécution est donc reprise en séquence de son appel.

AVORTER : l'exécution de la procédure courante est là aussi terminée, mais parallèlement un événement APPELAVORTE est produit.

Remarque :

Le besoin éventuel de traiter les occurrences d'un événement séquentiellement et non récursivement, impose que la procédure de contrôle soit automatiquement masquée contre l'événement qui lui est associé. En effet, un choix inverse aurait laissé un point interruptible entre l'instant où le segment procédure a été appelé et celui où il se remasque (l'action de contrôle est RIEN).

5.4. Opérateurs de contrôle de processus

Ces opérateurs comprennent les actions de contrôle précédemment décrites :

. La création d'un point de contrôle est réalisée par la primitive :

> SUR(événement)FAIRE(action de contrôle)

L'exécution de procédure courante et son environnement définissent son domaine.

> RETIRER(événement)

détruit le point de contrôle associé à l'événement dans l'environnement courant.

> ETAT(événement)

permet d'obtenir une description caractérisant l'événement et l'exécution l'ayant engendré.
Par exemple, dans le cas d'une erreur arithmétique ou logique, l'instruction en cause et sa localisation, dans le cas d'une entrée-sortie une identification de périphérique et un état de l'opération d'entrée-sortie, ou encore un message conventionnel pour un événement engendré par programme.

> SIGNALER(événement , message)

engendre un événement avec le message comme descripteur.

Tous ces opérateurs font l'objet de prérogatives et peuvent donc être interdits.

5.5. Contrôle synchrone

i) Evénements primitifs

Les événements primitifs sont les événements prédéfinis et liés aux instructions machine ou aux opérateurs de GEMAU ; leur occurrence a lieu dans l'environnement courant ; le point de contrôle est armé ; l'action de contrôle est effectuée immédiatement à la suite de l'exécution élémentaire ayant produit cet événement ; le point de contrôle est alors désarmé.

Par exemple, dans la figure 9, l'occurrence d'un événement (EVi) pendant l'exécution de PROGRAMMECONTROLE se traduit par un appel forcé au segment TRAITEMENTSPECIFIQUEi. Au RETOURNER correspondant, l'exécution de PROGRAMMECONTROLE sera reprise à la suite de l'instruction déroutée.

Si aucun point de contrôle n'a été créé pour l'événement considéré dans l'environnement courant, celui-ci est dépilé avec toutes les exécutions de procédure en cours.

Un événement ENVIRONNEMENTAVORTE est alors engendré. Il est relatif alors
à l'appel de la première procédure de l'environnement avorté.

Si aucun point de contrôle n'existe encore pour cet événement dans le nouvel environnement courant, le procédé est réitéré éventuellement jusqu'à
la fin du processus.

Dans la figure 9, le "système" de mise au point se divise en deux parties :
un ensemble de traitements prédéfinis géré par la procédure INIT. Si ces
traitements échouent ou si un événement non prévu arrive, l'exécution de
PROGRAMMECONTROLE est arrêtée. Après modification (interactive) elle est
relancée. Cette modification peut être aussi bien un simple changement de
valeur d'un élément du segment contrôlé qu'une édition suivie d'une compilation ayant pour but de créer une nouvelle version de ce programme.

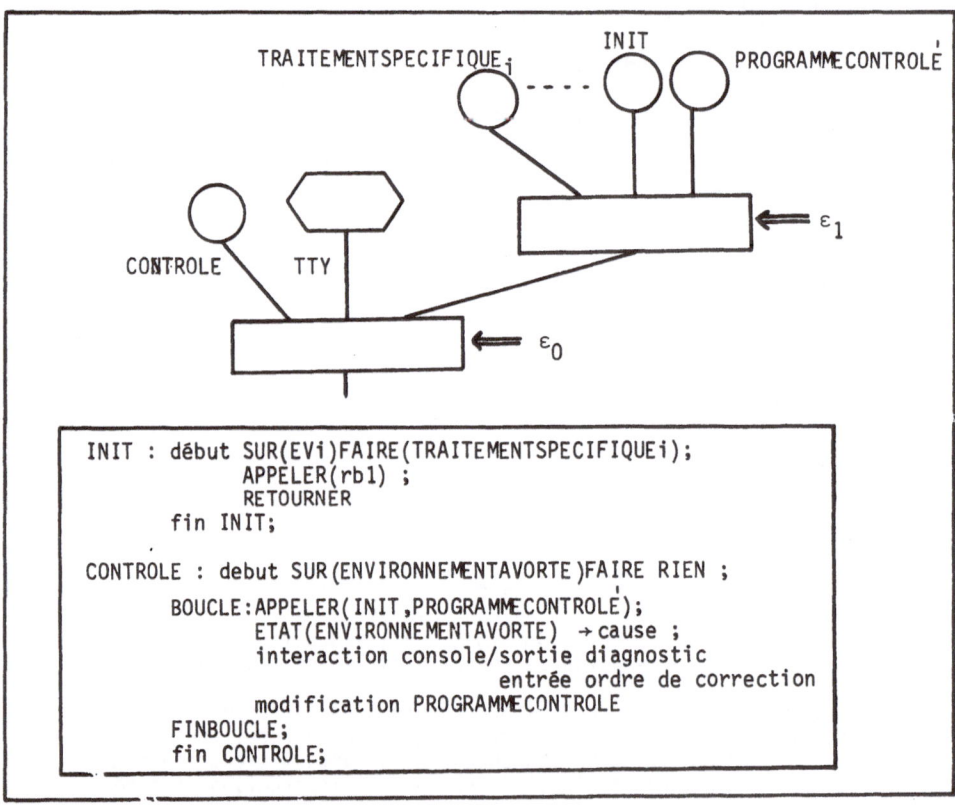

```
INIT : début SUR(EVi)FAIRE(TRAITEMENTSPECIFIQUEi);
            APPELER(rb1) ;
            RETOURNER
     fin INIT;


CONTROLE : debut SUR(ENVIRONNEMENTAVORTE)FAIRE RIEN ;
        BOUCLE:APPELER(INIT,PROGRAMMECONTROLE);
            ETAT(ENVIRONNEMENTAVORTE) → cause ;
            interaction console/sortie diagnostic
                            entrée ordre de correction
            modification PROGRAMMECONTROLE
        FINBOUCLE;
        fin CONTROLE;
```

Figure 9 - Système de mise au point

ii) Evénement_programmé

Le but recherché est de généraliser la notion d'événement associé à un opérateur du système à l'appel d'une procédure (opérateur construit).

L'événement est engendré par l'instruction SIGNALER dans l'environnement associé à la procédure courante, c'est-à-dire qu'il peut être hors du domaine du point de contrôle. Le point de contrôle est alors recherché dans l'environnement précédent de la pile du processus ; il est armé. L'action sera alors différée jusqu'au retour du processus dans le domaine de définition du point de contrôle.

Exemple : la figure 10 présente un programme assurant la recopie d'un fichier séquentiel dans un autre à partir de procédures du système de gestion de fichier.

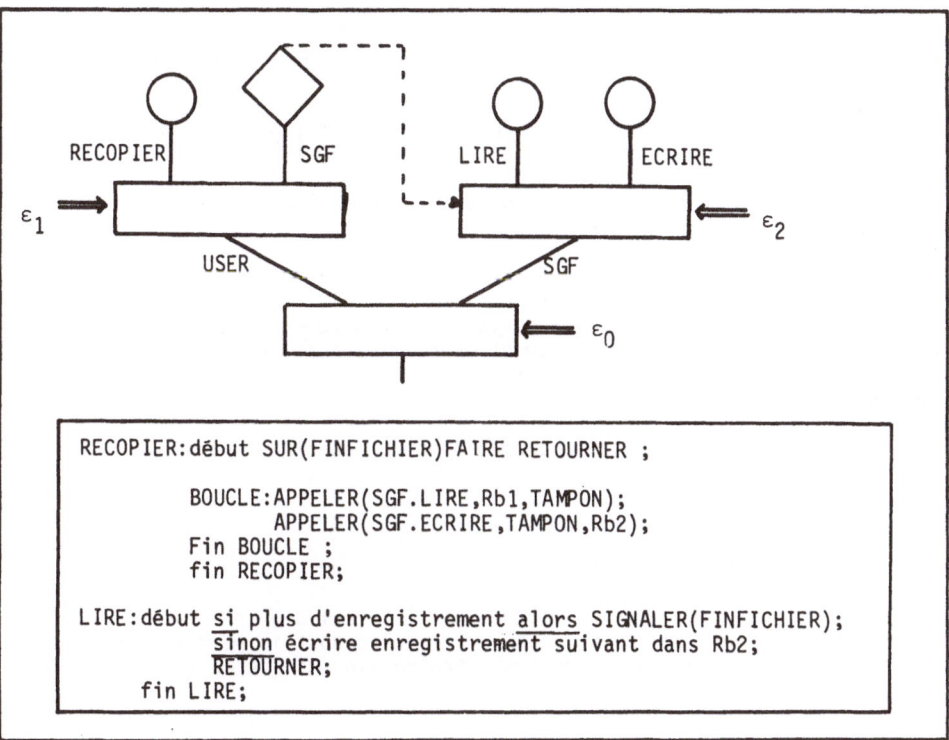

```
RECOPIER:début SUR(FINFICHIER)FAIRE RETOURNER ;

        BOUCLE:APPELER(SGF.LIRE,Rb1,TAMPON);
               APPELER(SGF.ECRIRE,TAMPON,Rb2);
        Fin BOUCLE ;
        fin RECOPIER;

LIRE:début si plus d'enregistrement alors SIGNALER(FINFICHIER);
          sinon écrire enregistrement suivant dans Rb2;
          RETOURNER;
      fin LIRE;
```

Figure 10

5.6. Contrôle asynchrone, asservissement

i) Création et contrôle d'un processus

Un événement asynchrone est, pour un processus, un événement associé à une activité parallèle de l'exécution courante de ce processus, ce qui, compte tenu de la structure hiérarchique choisie pour les processus, impose à ces événements de ne traduire que l'état de l'activité d'un processus fils.

La liaison père - fils se fait en deux parties :

. création d'un point de contrôle (par événement),

. association d'un événement au processus fils par la primitive :

```
LANCER(liste d' événement )APPELER(liste de désignation d'objet )
```

Les relations père - fils ne s'expriment alors qu'à travers le concept d'événement.

Ceci signifie qu'à tout processus est associée au moins une procédure de contrôle chez son père.

Remarque : le premier point de contrôle de LANCER est associé par défaut à la fin du processus fils créé.

La terminaison du fils ou l'exécution par lui d'un SIGNAL arme le point de contrôle correspondant du père.

L'événement peut se produire à un instant où l'environnement courant du père n'est pas dans le domaine du point de contrôle considéré. Dans les mêmes conditions, plusieurs événements peuvent être engendrés par le processus fils. Ces différents événements sont mémorisés. L'action de contrôle est différée jusqu'au retour du père dans l'environnement du point de contrôle.

On note qu'un point de contrôle permet ainsi de contrôler plusieurs processus fils.

iii) Destruction d'un processus

Le dépilage (RETOURNER) ou la destruction (RETIRER) d'un point de contrôle implique la destruction des processus parallèles dont il permet le contrôle. La destruction d'un processus entraîne alors celle de toute sa filiation.

Pour des raisons de fiabilité et de cohérence de l'espace d'adressage, il peut être nécessaire de différer une destruction de processus jusqu'à ce que celui-ci soit sorti d'un sous-système de cet espace d'adressage, par exemple un sous-système de périphériques virtuels ("SPOOL").

Cette destruction n'aura lieu qu'à la condition que le processus se trouve dans l'espace visible de son environnement initial, celui défini par sa procédure initiale (voir figure 11).

iii) Asservissement

Un processus peut désirer s'asservir à un événement lié à un ou plusieurs de ses fils.

Ceci se réalise par l'opérateur :

```
ATTENDRE(  événement  )
```

L'exécution séquentielle de la procédure courante ne sera reprise que sur occurrence d'un des événements de la liste. Toutefois les actions de contrôle peuvent toujours s'exécuter. A leur terminaison, le processus se suspend de nouveau (18).

iv) Exemple

La figure 11 présente un exemple d'initialisation par le processus ancêtre des usagers d'un système conversationnel, les entrées-sorties étant réalisées par un système de SPOOL.

Le processus ancêtre exécute la procédure INIT ; les procédures LOGIN, LOGOUT, IN et OUT sont à accès exclusif.

Chaque usager dispose d'un système personnel et de périphériques virtuels réalisés par le sous-système de SPOOL.

Le segment procédure INIT est exécuté à l'initialisation du système par le processus ancêtre.

Lors de la destruction des processus usagers créés dans les environnements ε_2 (à partir de ε_1), la disjonction de ε_2 et de l'environnement du spool ε_1' garantit que les processus usagers travaillant dans le spool seront détruits seulement quand ils en sortiront. De même, si l'usager à sa console désire interrompre un travail (touche BREAK), cette interruption ne sera effective que si ce processus est dans l'espace visible de l'usager.

156

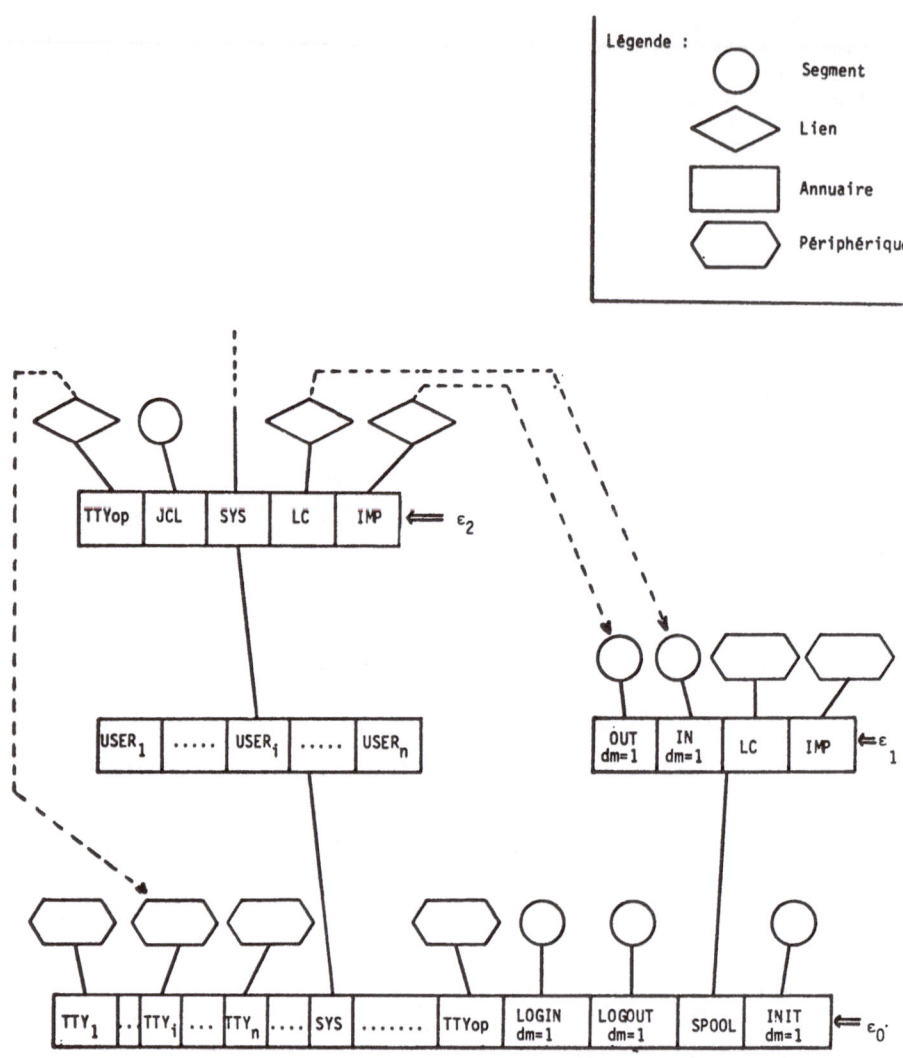

Figure 11.a. - Exemple d'un espace d'adressage pour un système à accès multiple

```
INIT : début initialisation du sous-système de SPOOL
          SUR(BREAK)FAIRE APPELER(LOGIN) ;
          SUR(BREAKOP)FAIRE RIEN ;
          SUR(USEREND)FAIRE APPELER(LOGOUT) ;

          LANCER(BREAK) APPELER(TTY1,tampon1) ;
          LANCER(BREAK) APPELER(TTyn,tamponn) ;
          BOUCLE : LANCER(BREAKOP) APPELER(TTYOP,tamponop) ;
                   ATTENDRE(BREAKOP) ;
                   acquisition du message de l'opérateur
                   si fin de session alors
                       début RETIRER(USEREND) ;
                             EXIT BOUCLE ;
                       fin
                   sinon autres controles ;
          FINBOUCLE ;
          action de contrôle et sauvegarde du système
     RETOURNER ;
   fin INIT ;
```

```
LOGIN : début tty name →ETAT(BREAK)
          acquérir nom d'usager(USERi) et mot de passe
          CREER(type = 'LIEN',SYS.USERi.TTYOP, ttyname)
          LANCER(USEREND) APPELER(SYST.USERi.JCL)
          RETOURNER ;
     fin LOGIN ;
```

```
LOGOUT : début ETAT(USEREND) →username
          détruire le lien vers le télétype et réinitialiser l'attente
          d'interaction
          LANCER(BREAK) APPELER(TTY ,tamponj) ;
          RETOURNER ;
     fin LOGOUT ;
```

Figure 11.b.

6. CONCLUSION

Au moment où nous écrivons cet article, GEMAU est implanté sur 10070
avec comme utilisateur un petit système interactif.

Il faudra attendre les mesures d'utilisation pour en déduire le coût de
l'espace d'adressage présenté.

Cependant, il faut tenir compte dans l'interprétation des mesures, des
faits suivants :

> . la machine hôte est un CII 10070, c'est-à-dire ne possède pas les
> mécanismes cablés de l'IRIS 80 (segmentation plus pagination) ;

> . le but de l'étude est finalement de proposer des mécanismes cablés
> susceptibles d'augmenter l'efficacité générale.

Parallèlement à la réalisation de cet espace d'adressage, la méthode de
structuration exposée peut être utilisée pour augmenter nettement la
localité des programmes. En effet, la structuration proposée implique un
groupement des informations par fonctions (module). Ce groupement fonc-
tionnel est implanté physiquement dans un espace mémoire qui est très
localisé (quelques pages bien déterminées - toutes les mêmes pour une
période de temps égale au traitement logique envisagé).

Par ailleurs, la connaissance a priori des segments qui vont être exécu-
tés au bénéfice d'un processus, peut permettre d'asservir le progrès du
calcul à la disponibilité des ressources physiques nécessaires. On peut
en effet mesurer les "besoins probables" des objets logiques contenus
dans l'espace d'adressage. L'interprétation qui intervient à chaque appel
sur un nouvel objet est mise à profit pour permettre une allocation fondée
sur des mesures statistiques qui ne sont généralement, dans les systèmes
classiques, associées qu'à une seule entité : le processus (ou programme).

Nous laissons au lecteur le soin d'apprécier les avantages suivants
(difficilement chiffrables) :

a) la gestion des ressources dans un sous-système de GEMAU est réduite à
la gestion des ressources logiques (pas de gestion d'espace mémoire
principale ou secondaire, pas de gestion de processeur) ;

b) la hiérarchie de l'espace d'adressage permet d'assurer une protection
mutuelle entre utilisateurs, ainsi que localement contre soi-même.

En effet, la protection entre utilisateurs est assurée d'une part, par
l'arborescence stricte qui permet d'allouer des environnements différents à des utilisateurs différents et d'autre part, par l'ajout des
liens qui permettent de contrôler (restrictions d'accès) l'utilisation
qui est faite par un utilisateur depuis un environnement donné d'un
objet situé dans l'environnement (disjoint) d'un autre utilisateur.
Comme les liens ne peuvent être définis que depuis un environnement
qui permet de nommer origine et extrêmité, la protection entre utilisateurs est définie par le processus ou la procédure qui a créé le
lien.

Par ailleurs, l'emboîtement des environnements sur une même branche de
l'arborescence, permet à un utilisateur, par le choix de l'environnement
d'exécution et l'utilisation de restrictions lors de la liaison, de s'exécuter avec plus ou moins de protection.

c) Les sections critiques sont emboîtées et directement associées aux
objets ;

d) il n'existe pas d'éditeur de liens au sens classique du terme [17] ;

e) le contrôle dans l'ensemble des objets est uniquement procédural,
c'est-à-dire qu'il n'y a pas possibilité, pour un processus, d'aller
s'exécuter dans un environnement disjoint (par l'intermédiaire d'un
lien) sans revenir dans la procédure appelante et a fortiori la procédure initiale (pas de GOTO).

Si la procédure appelée fait partie d'un sous-système et ne fournit
pas de retour (boucle), alors il s'agit d'une erreur dans le sous-
système. Seul un processus ascendant voyant ce sous-système peut alors
détruire sa filiation et réparer l'erreur.

La hiérarchie assure de plus qu'il y a toujours un processus (à la
limite l'ancêtre) pour détruire la filiation.

f) Le contrôle des processus est toujours garanti, car ses seules ressources sont définies à sa création.

Ces avantages devraient permettre d'écrire très rapidement des sous-systèmes "à la carte". Dans notre cas, il a fallu moins de trois hommes/
mois pour écrire et tester un petit système interactif.

Au moment où les problèmes de conception et de fiabilité deviennent pré-
pondérants devant le coût du matériel, il semble qu'une machine offrant
directement les avantages de la structure présentée, puisse avoir des
chances de succès.

160

7. REMERCIEMENTS

Cet article serait incomplet sans remerciements à toute l'équipe qui participe au projet GEMAU et sans laquelle il n'aurait pas été possible d'obtenir de tels résultats.

Monsieur Claude OTRAGE pour sa participation plus qu'active à la définition des structures d'adressage et d'exécution, ainsi qu'à la méthodologie de réalisation.

Monsieur Philippe DARONDEAU pour son aide apportée dans les développements formels à apporter au projet.

Monsieur Roland BALTER qui a réalisé entièrement la structure d'adressage de GEMAU sur 10070.

Messieurs Jacques CHARLET et Pierre LAFORGUE pour leur réalisation d'un système interactif sur GEMAU, qui a permis de tester la structure avancée.

Monsieur Jacques LECOURVOISIER pour l'aide apportée dans la réalisation des mécanismes de synchronisation.

Monsieur Alain INGLESE qui a travaillé pour définir la pagination sur 10070 et qui travaille maintenant à la réalisation d'une machine virtuelle 10070 sur GEMAU.

Monsieur Xavier ROUSSET de PINA pour l'introduction de la gestion prédictive des ressources.

Monsieur Harm SMIT pour la réalisation des mécanismes d'entrées-sorties associés aux utilisateurs.

8. BIBLIOGRAPHIE

[1]   BALZER
        Dataless Programming
        FJCC, 1967

[2]   P. BRINCH HANSEN
        The Nucleus of a Multiprogramming System
        C.ACM, April 1970

[3]   P. BRINCH HANSEN
        Concurrent Programming Concepts
        International Summer School, Munich, 1973

[4]   J.C. CLEARY
        Process Handling on Burroughs B 6500
        4th Australian Computer Conference, Adelaïde, 1969

[5]   CREECH
        Architecture of the B 6500
        COINS 1969, 3rd International Symposium

[6]   DALEY & DENNIS
        Virtual Memory, Processes and Sharing in Multics
        C.ACM, May 1968

[7]   DALEY & NEUMAN
        A General Purpose File System for Secondary Storage
        FJCC, 1965

[8]   Ph. DARONDEAU
        Langage de Spécification Fonctionnelle et Simulation de
        Systèmes
        IMAG, Juillet 1972

[9]   DENNIS
        Programming Generality, Parallelism and Computer Architecture
        MIT, MAC, M409, 1970

[10]   DENNIS & VAN HORN
        Programming Semantic for Multiprogrammed Computation
        C.ACM, March 1966

[11]   E.W. DIJKSTRA
        THE Multiprogramming System
        C.ACM, May 1968

[12]   D. EVANS & J.Y. LECLERC
       Address Mapping and the Control of Access in Interactive
       Computer
       SJCC, 1967

[13]   GRAHAM
       Protection in an Information Process Utility
       C.ACM, 1968

[14]   J.K. ILIFFE
       Basic Machine Principles
       Macdonald Computer Monographs, London 1968

[15]   LAMPSON
       Dynamic Protection Structures
       FJCC, 1969

[16]   J.H. MORRIS Jr
       Protection in Programming Languages
       C.ACM, January 1973

[17]   L. PRESSER & J.R. WHITE
       Linkers and Loaders
       ACM Computing Surveys, 4,3, September 1972

[18]   E.I. ORGANICK
       The Multics System, an Examination of its Structure
       The MIT Press

A NEW APPROACH TO AVOIDANCE
OF SYSTEM DEADLOCKS

A.N. Habermann
Department of Computer Science
Carnegie-Mellon University, Pittsburgh

————

ABSTRACT

A new approach to the avoidance of system deadlocks is based on the notion
of promoting a process to a higher rank when a resource is allocated to it. An
advantage of this method is that it can prevent the occurrence, and therefore
avoid the dynamic safety test, of many unsafe allocation states. Also, an algorithm that tests how many resources can safely be allocated is easily found and
the method makes it possible to attach a cost factor to resource allocation depending on the demand and the allocation test.

INTRODUCTION

This paper deals with the special case of many (non-preemptive) resources of
one kind. Deadlock situations in allocating the resources can be avoided if it
is known in advance how many resources a process ultimately needs in order to
finish. This number is known as its "claim" and it is given when a process
starts competing for the resources with other processes. During the competition
a process will be assigned a "rank" which initially equals its claim and which is
decremented (incremented) by one every time a resource is allocated to it (is released by this process). When the rank has reached the value zero, a process
has all the resources it needs, so it is able to finish and return all the resources in due time.
Given the constraint that a process cannot be forced to release a resource
until it finishes, an allocation state is considered "safe" if it can be shown
that every process can reach rank zero at some time. In this paper a safety
test is cast in terms of promotions. A process is "promoted" to the next higher
rank when a resource is allocated to it. The counter action of promotion is
"demotion" which takes place when a process releases a resource and drops to the
next lower rank. When a process is demoted to its original claim it has released
all the resources allocated to it. At that moment the process is supposed to de-
part from the set of competing processes. We assume in addition that allocation

This research was supported by the National Science Foundation under Contract
No. GJ 32259.

of the first resource is always associated with admission of a process to the set
of competitors. These rules of arrival and departure imply that every contending
process holds at least one resource.

REALIZABLE STATES AND CONVENTIONAL SAFETY TESTS

Let $\{C_1,...,C_m\}$ be the set of processes contending for the set of resources
$\{R_1,...,R_t\}$ all of one kind, where $m \geq 1$ and $t > 1$. Let $claim_i$ represent the
number of resources that process C_i ultimately needs so that it can finish and
let $rank_i$ represent the difference of $claim_i$ and the number of resources currently allocated to process C_i. Thus, $rank_i$ reflects the number of resources that C_i
can still request at a given moment.

An allocation state is completely determined by the number t and the vectors
CLAIM and RANK describing the claims and ranks of all the contending processes.
An allocation state is "realizable" if the following conditions hold for all
$i \in \{1,...,m\}$

(1) $0 \leq rank_i \leq claim_i \leq t$
(2) $\Sigma_i (claim_i - rank_i) \leq t$

The first line states that a process C_i must not request more than it claims and
not claim more than the total number of resources available. The second line
says that the total number of allocated resources cannot be more than the total
number available. We deal throughout this paper only with realizable allocation
states. E.g.: the state

$$t = 4, \quad CLAIM = (2\ 4\ 4), \quad RANK = (1\ 3\ 3), \quad \text{remaining 1 resource}$$

is a realizable state. This state, however, is not safe in the sense as defined
in the introduction, because it results in a deadlock state if, for instance, C_2
and C_3 both request two more resources before releasing any. After allocating
the one remaining resource and the one that is released when C_1 finishes, both
processes are going to wait for another resource, but none will ever become available if C_2 or C_3 does not release any.

Deadlock states can be avoided if the allocation moves from one safe state
to another safe state. It was shown in [1] that a given realizable state or
state transition can be tested for safety by an algorithm that places the processes in line for successive allocation. The processes do not have to be served in
exactly that order, but the allocation state is safe if and only if such a line
can be formed. Although m processes can be placed in line in m! different ways,
it was shown in [1] that the safety test does not need more than $O(m^2)$ steps for
the general case of m processes competing for resources of different types. This
result was refined in [2,3] to an $O(m.T)$ algorithm at the cost of maintaining
some additional information (m is the number of processes, T the number of resource types). Apparently, in the case of one resource type a linear algorithm
depending on the number of competing processes suffices. In [4] it is shown that
in this particular case an $O(\min(m,t))$ algorithm suffices, where t is the total
number of resources. Algorithms based on the results of this paper are proportional to $MAX(claim_i)$ which is less or equal to the total number of resources and
independent of the number of competing processes.

A SAFETY TEST BASED ON PROMOTIONS

A promotion of a process C_i consists of allocating a resource to it and
decrementing $rank_i$ by one. We choose to describe the allocation state S as if it
were the result of an arbitrarily ordered series of promotions starting from a
fictitious initial state S_0 in which no resources are allocated (implying that
$rank_i = claim_i$ for all $i \in \{1,...,m\}$). A process is promoted until its current
rank has been reached.

Let x_k represent the total number of promotions from rank = k to rank = k-1, when the current state S is recreated from the fictitious initial state S_0. The value of x_k depends in actual fact solely on the current state S and not on the fictitious history, because x_k equals the number of processes for which rank $< k \leq$ claim.

In the terminology of rebuilding the current state from the fictitious initial state S_0, it is as if a process for which this relation holds "passed through" rank $= k$. E.g. if the allocation state is given by:

$$t = 4, \quad \text{CLAIM} = (2\ 3\ 4), \quad \text{RANK} = (1\ 1\ 3), \text{ then}$$

$\underline{x} = (0\ 2\ 1\ 1)$, because no process was promoted from rank $= 1$ to rank $= 0$, processes C_1 and C_2 were promoted from rank $= 2$ to rank $= 1$, and before that process C_2 was promoted from rank_3 to rank_2 and finally, process C_3 was promoted from rank_4 to rank_3. Element x_0 is omitted, because its value is constantly zero since no promotions take place from rank $= 0$.

Our real interest is not so much in the numbers x_k, but in an accumulation of some of these numbers. Define $p_k = \sum_{j=k}^{t} x_j$ for $k \in \{1,\ldots,t\}$, i.e. p_k counts the number of promotions that took place from all the ranks in the range k through t. A visual representation is given in Figure 1 for $t = 5$.

rank \ upper bound	5	4	3	2	1	
1	x_1					
2	x_2	x_2				
3	x_3	x_3	x_3			
4	x_4	x_4	x_4	x_4		
5	x_5	x_5	x_5	x_5	x_5	+
	p_1	p_2	p_3	p_4	p_5	

Figure 1. Composition of the promotion vector $\underline{p}$

For the example given earlier on in this section we find

$$\begin{aligned} p_1 &= x_1 + x_2 + x_3 + x_4 = 4 \\ p_2 &= x_2 + x_3 + x_4 = 4 \\ p_3 &= x_3 + x_4 = 2 \\ p_4 &= x_4 = 1 \end{aligned}$$

or, summarizing, $\underline{p} = (4\ 4\ 2\ 1)$.

We find easily enough that for realizable states $\underline{p} \geq \underline{0}$ (i.e. $p_k \geq 0$ for all $k \in \{1,\ldots,t\}$). It turns out that the safe states are precisely characterized by an upperbound of $\underline{p}$. This explains the top line in Figure 1.

Theorem. A realizable allocation state is safe if and only if

$$\underline{p} \leq \underline{t}$$

where $\underline{t} = (t\ t\text{-}1\ t\text{-}2\ \ldots\ 1)$.

Sketch of a Proof. The kth element of $\underline{t}$ is $t_k = t+1-k$. Let k be a given number in the range $1,\ldots,t$. An amount of p_k resources have been allocated so as to promote processes at most up to rank $= k\text{-}1$. This leaves rem $= t-p_k$ resources which can be used for promotions in the ranks ranging from k-1 to t. A process in rank = k-1 may need exactly k-1 promotions in that range. Thus, a process in that rank can definitely finish if and only if rem $\geq$ k-1, or $t-p_k \geq$ k-1, or $p_k \leq$ t+1-k, or $p_k \leq t_k$. The safety test $\underline{p} \leq \underline{t}$ decides that the given example is unsafe, because $\underline{p} = (4\ 4\ 2\ 1) \leq \underline{t} = (4\ 3\ 2\ 1)$ is false.

DEADLOCK AVOIDANCE WITHOUT A SAFETY TEST

Interestingly enough, the theorem has as a result that one-type resource deadlocks can be avoided without an explicit safety test, relying on the coordination of processes only. Though not very practical for large t, it is interesting to know that it can be done.

Represent vector $\underline{t}$ by t different kinds of chips, for instance, distinguishable by color. We have t chips of the first kind, t-1 of the second kind, etc. (see Figure 2).

```
              RED    WHITE   BLUE   YELLOW
              . .    + +     * *      @
  rank \ t = . .     +
     1         .
     2         .     |
     3         .     +       *
     4         .     +       *        @
```

Figure 2. Symbolic representation of promotions for t = 4

Vector $\underline{t}$ shows what is present before the competition for the resources start. The competition follows these rules:

(1) Characteristic for a rank = k is a series of chips one of a type, ranging from type t_1 through type t_k (see Figure 2).

(2) A promotion from rank = k is possible only if the kth characterisitc string of chips can be taken away from the current state; if promotion is not possible, a process waits until it finds the characteristic string after chips have been returned.

(3) When a process demotes itself to rank = k, it returns the kth characteristic string of chips.

In programming terms we can translate a type of chip into a counting semaphore as defined by Dijkstra [5]. The number of chips initially available corresponds to the initial value of the semaphore. Taking a chip away corresponds to a P-operation and returning a chip to a V-operation. The steps taken by a process that claims four resources are:

<u>Comment</u> start at rank = 4;

$P(t_4); P(t_3); P(t_2); P(t_1);$ take resource; <u>comment</u> rank = 3;

$P(t_3); P(t_2); P(t_1);$ take resource; <u>comment</u> rank = 2;

$P(t_2); P(t_1);$ take resource; <u>comment</u> rank = 1;

$P(t_1);$ take resource; <u>comment</u> rank = 0;

$V(t_1);$	release resource; comment rank = 1;
$V(t_1);\ V(t_2);$	release resource; comment rank = 2;
$V(t_1);\ V(t_2);\ V(t_3);$	release resource; comment rank = 3;
$V(t_1);\ V(t_2);\ V(t_3);\ V(t_4);$	release resource; comment rank = 4;

Comment rank back to claim implies departure.

The order of the P, V operations is chosen in this particular way to make sure that interleaved execution of these operations does not cause a deadlock. The P-operations are performed on the semaphores in descending index order so as to avoid the situation that a process must wait on a semaphore t_k while it blocks semaphores with lower index. That is to say, when a process cannot be promoted from rank = k, it should not hinder promotions from ranks k-1 through 1. The proof that this order of P-operations does not cause a deadlock of the semaphore waiting lists is omitted here.

Observe that in this arrangement a process asking for a promotion from rank = k can get permanently blocked [4,6] by processes that claim less than k.

AN ADMISSION TEST

We stated in the introduction that a process enters the set of competitors when the first resource is allocated to it and it leaves as soon as its rank equals its claim. This implies that every competitor holds at least one resource.

Let y_k be the number of processes whose claim = k. Analogous to $p_k = \sum_{j=k}^{t} x_j$ in Section 3, we define $n_k = \sum y_j$ for $k \in \{1,\ldots,t\}$, i.e. n_k represents the total number of processes whose claim is greater than or equal to k.

Since every process in the set of competitors holds at least one resource, at least y_k promotions took place from rank = k. Thus, $y_k \le x_k$, hence $n_k \le p_k$ or $\underline{n} \le \underline{p}$. We conclude that

$$\underline{n} \le \underline{t}$$

is a necessary condition for safety, because $\underline{n} \le \underline{p}$, and $\underline{p} \le \underline{t}$ is a necessary and sufficient condition for safety (theorem, Section 3). E.g. the realizable state

$$t = 4, \quad \text{CLAIM} = (3\ 3\ 4)$$

cannot be safe, because $\underline{y} = (0\ 0\ 2\ 1)$ and $\underline{n} = (3\ 3\ 3\ 1) \le \underline{t} = (4\ 3\ 2\ 1)$ is false (see Figure 3).

claim \ $\underline{t}$ =	4	3	2	1
1	y_1			
2	y_2	y_2		
3	y_3	y_3	$y_3=2$	
4	y_4	y_4	$y_4=1$	y_4 +
	n_1	n_2	n_3	n_4

Figure 3. The number of processes whose claim $\ge$ k is bounded by t_k

This necessary condition limiting the total number of processes whose claim $\ge$ k has some nice properties. The test is not more elaborate than the safety test. However, in contrast to the safety test, vector $\underline{n}$ does not change when resources are allocated or released, because $\underline{n}$ depends entirely on CLAIM and not on RANK. The right moment of applying the test is when a process tries to enter the set of competitors while $\underline{n}$ also must be updated when a process leaves the set.

The test $\underline{n} \leq \underline{t}$ is very useful if applied as admission test; a process should not be admitted to the set of competitors until the test is successful. This way we do not allow an arbitrary set of processes to contend for the resources, but instead a preselected set excluding such combinations of competitors which cannot simultaneously hold resources anyway. E.g. in the situation pictured in Figure 3 it makes no sense to admit, for instance, three processes whose claim = $3(n_3 = 3)$ or two processes whose claim = $4(n_4 = 2)$, because the necessary condition $\underline{n} \leq \underline{t}$ implies that $n_3 + n_4 \leq 2$ and $n_4 \leq 1$ must hold. Table 1 shows the usefulness of the admission test for the case $t = 4$. First all possible ways of allocating four resources are considered, ranging from allocating all four to one process to one to each of four processes. Each situation is tested for safety and admissibility. The last column shows how few allocation states are accepted if no deadlock algorithm is necessary, because, instead, the total claim is required to be less than or equal to the total amount of resources available. The latter policy is the most conservative deadlock prevention strategy.

After having considered all states in which four resources are allocated, the states with respectively three, two and one allocated resource are listed.

Number of allocated resources	Frequency	Safe	Not safe	Caught in admission test	Caught in safety test	Accepted by conservative policy
4	80	38	42	32	10	5
3	34	26	8	7	1	7
2	13	11	1	1	0	7
1	4	4	0	0	0	4
Total	131	79	51	40	11	23

Table 1

Without admission test all 51 unsafe states show up when the safety test is applied and not just once, but probably many times. The admission test eliminates the majority of the unsafe states. Observe that the conservative policy admits only about 30% of the safe allocation states.

MAXIMAL SAFE ALLOCATION

Using the conventional safety tests, it is a matter of trial to determine the maximal number of resources that can be allocated to a particular process without getting into an unsafe state. The problem can constructively be solved using the promotions.

Let process C_i whose $rank_i = k$, where $k \in \{1,\dots,m\}$, inquire how many resources it can maximally get without loss of safety. The answer is found if we determine how many of the characteristic strings we can successively take away (see Section 4).

To be more precise: let $\underline{u}_k$ be the vector consisting of ones in the first k positions and zeros in the remaining (t-k) positions (if any). The vector $\underline{u}_k$ is the characteristic of rank = k. When a process is promoted from rank = k to rank = k-1, the characteristic $\underline{u}_k$ must be added to $\underline{p}$. The new allocation state is, of course, safe if and only if $\underline{p} \leq \underline{t}$ is still true.

The answer to the question of how many resources can safely be allocated to a given process whose rank = k is: find the largest value for variable max in the range $\{0,\dots,k\}$ such that

$$\underline{p} + \sum_{j=k}^{k-max} \underline{u}_j \le \underline{t}$$

This number max can be found by means of a linear scan working from right to left, i.e. from p_k to p_1:

    <u>let</u> max, j = 0

    <u>while</u> max < k <u>and</u> p_{k-max} + k ≤ t <u>do</u> max + 1 <u>od</u>

    j := k-max

    <u>while</u> j > 0 <u>do</u> <u>if</u> p_j + max > t + 1 - j <u>then</u> max := t + 1 - j - p_j <u>fi</u>; j-1 <u>od</u>

The first while statement starts at the kth position and works to the left until it finds the leftmost position for which the incremented max can be added to p_{k-max} without exceeding t_{k-max} (= t + 1 - k + max). If this statement halts with max < k, we must check whether the elements p_1 through p_{k-max} allow addition of max without exceeding the corresponding element in $\underline{t}$. This is what the second while statement tests; it also corrects max to the permissible value.

<u>Example</u>. Given the state $\underline{t}$ = (5 4 3 2 1), $\underline{p}$ = (4 3 1 0 0). Suppose a process whose claim = 4 asks how many resources it can get before trying to enter the set of competitors. The algorithm is started with k = 4. The first while statement halts with max = 2, so it seems that the process can be promoted up to rank = k-max = 2. The second while statement, however, detects that max is too large for p_2 and so it decrements max to one. Element p_1 causes then no problem. The resulting decision is that this process cannot be promoted further than rank = 3, so it can get no more than one resource.

THE COST FACTOR IN RELATION TO THE COMPETITION

The impact a process has on the resource allocation is primarily determined by its claim and the length of time during which it uses resources weighed by the number of resources it uses. It is therefore quite natural to base a cost calculation upon this data. However, it is reasonable from the system's viewpoint to make the cost also dependent on the current load or current competition. We therefore search for a method of measuring the competition for resources.

Let $N_k = \sum_{j=k}^{t} n_j$ and $\underline{N} = (N_1, N_2, \ldots, N_t)$. We argue that $\underline{p} \le \underline{N}$. The number of promotions x_j from a particular rank = j is less or equal to n_j, because only processes with a claim ≥ j pass through rank = j. Hence, $p_j = \sum_{\ell=j}^{t} x_\ell \le \sum_{\ell=j}^{t} n_\ell = N_j$. Since $\underline{p} \le \underline{N}$ and since $\underline{p} \le \underline{t}$ is a sufficient condition for safety, also $\underline{N} \le \underline{t}$ is a sufficient condition for safety. A test involving $\underline{N}$ has the same advantage as a test involving $\underline{n}$, both vectors depend only on CLAIM and do not change when resources are allocated or released. Obviously, $\underline{n} \le \underline{N}$ is true. We therefore might consider to replace the admission test $\underline{n} \le \underline{t}$ by the test $\underline{N} \le \underline{t}$. A safety test would then be completely unnecessary because of $\underline{p} \le \underline{N}$. However, requiring $\underline{N} \le \underline{t}$ turns out to be equivalent to the most conservative policy which requires that the processes together claim not more than the amount of resources available. We saw in Table 1 that such a restrictive policy ignores a large amount of entirely acceptable safe states. Thus, applying $\underline{N} \le \underline{t}$ as admission test is too strong.

Suppose it is known that $N_k \le t_k$. This implies that $p_k \le t_k$, so it is not necessary to test p_k when resources are allocated. We argue that $N_k \le t_k$ implies $N_\ell \le t_\ell$ for k ≤ ℓ ≤ t. This statement is obviously true for k = t. Suppose $N_\ell \le t_\ell$ and k ∈ {1,...,t-1}. If $N_k = 0$, then also $n_{k+1} = 0$, because $N_k = n_k + N_{k+1}$ and none of these numbers is negative. In that case $N_{k+1} \le t_{k+1}$ is true, because $t_{k+1} > 0$.

If $N_k > 0$, then $n_k > 0$, because $n_k \geq n_{k+1} \ldots \geq n_t \geq 0$ (the number of processes with a claim $\geq k$ must be larger than or equal to the number of processes with a claim $\geq k+1$). Thus $n_k \geq 1$ and $N_{k+1} \leq N_k - 1 \leq t_k - 1 = t_{k+1}$. So we proved that in any case $N_{k+1} \leq t_{k+1}$. The proof can obviously be extended for all N_ℓ where $k \leq \ell \leq t$.

Combining the statements $\underline{p} \leq \underline{N}$ and $N_k \leq t_k$ implies $N_\ell \leq t_\ell$ for all $k \leq \ell \leq t$ gives this result: if it is known that $N_k \leq t_k$ for a particular $k \in \{1, \ldots, t\}$, then it is unnecessary to test any of the elements p_ℓ for $k \leq \ell \leq t$, i.e. if $N_k \leq t_k$, we have to test only the relations $p_1 \leq t_1, \ldots, p_{k-1} \leq t_{k-1}$. The admission test can, of course, also be restricted to testing the relations $n_1 \leq t_1, \ldots, n_{k-1} \leq t_{k-1}$.

Let k be the smallest index for which $N_k \leq t_k$. This figure is an adequate parameter for measuring the resource allocation intensity. If k is small, the load is apparently light and the cost unit can be small. The larger k gets, the more difficult allocation is going to be and the higher the cost unit should be.

CONCLUSION

In case of one type of resource the safety regulations cast in terms of promotions have several advantages. One of the most important consequences is the application of an admission test which cuts out many undesirable allocation states. The sufficiency test of the last section points to the direction of a considerable savings in the number of comparisons when resources are allocated. It will be shown in another paper that these savings make it possible to reduce a safety test under normal circumstances to a simple test that neither depends on the number of processes nor on the number of resources.

This paper dealt with the special case of one resource type. A next step in these matters obviously is an investigation of the impact that these results have on the case of more than one resource type. It is expected that an adequate safety test will then be proportional to the number of different resource types.

The motivation for applying a deadlock avoidance strategy is higher resource utilization and improvement of throughput. The results of this paper show that the overhead of applying a safety test can be reduced to reasonable proportions. In future research hard figures should be produced that measure the trade off between overhead and increased throughput and resource utilization.

REFERENCES

[1] Habermann, A. N., Prevention of system deadlocks, CACM 12, July 1969.
[2] Holt, R. C., Some deadlock properties of computer systems, Operating Systems Review 6, June 1972, 64-71.
[3] Russell, R. D., A model for deadlock-free resource allocation (thesis), SLAC Report No. 148, Stanford Linear Acceleration Center, Stanford, Calif., June 1972.
[4] Holt, R. C., On deadlock in computer systems (thesis), Computer Science Department, Cornell University, Ithaca, N. Y., December 1970.
[5] Dykstra, E. W., Cooperating sequential processes, Programming Systems, Genuys ed., Academic Press, London, 1968.
[6] Coffman, E. G., Jr., M. J. Elphick, A. Soshani, System deadlocks, Computing Surveys 3, June 1971, 67.

A PROGRAM STRUCTURE FOR ERROR DETECTION AND RECOVERY

J.J. Horning
University of Toronto, Canada

H.C. Lauer, P.M. Melliar-Smith, B. Randell
University Newcastle upon Tyne, England

———

<u>ABSTRACT</u>

The paper describes a method of structuring programs which aids the design and validation of facilities for the detection of and recovery from software errors. Associated with the method is a mechanism for the automatic preservation of restart information at a level of overhead which is believed to be tolerable.

1.   Introduction

Prior research into reliable computing has concentrated on the reliability of the hardware, on the detection of hardware errors, and on the configuring of systems to allow continuation of service in the presence of hardware errors. But observation of present-day large systems indicates that software faults represent a problem whose significance is at least as great as that of the hardware faults. Whilst conceding the importance of current research on improving the quality of software (e.g. work on program "correctness proofs"), the present paper is based on the view that it is also worth providing error detection and recovery facilities for both hardware and software errors. In what follows we will concentrate on software errors although we believe much of our work is of equal relevance to many types of hardware errors.

This paper describes the recovery block concept, a method of structuring programs which is aimed at aiding the design of error detection and recovery facilities, and the recursive cache, an associated mechanism which provides means for automatic "back-tracking" at a level of overhead which is believed to be tolerable.

2.   Error Detection and Recovery

Reliable operation of a computing system depends on both error detection and error recovery. Several classes of error detection techniques are available, some of which operate automatically on an instruction-by-instruction basis, while others take a broader view of correct operation based on programmed checks and assertions. It is characteristic of error detection that several techniques can readily be used together, and the recovery block concept aims to provide error recovery after any kind of detected error.

Recovery and restart of the program after error detection is a difficult problem. Where instruction-by-instruction error detection is provided, the number of possible errors is too great to provide explicit recovery action for each possible case, while any automatic recovery operation which simply aims to repair the state of the program so as to allow its continuation in a valid manner cannot be expected to achieve correctness rather than mere legality. Alternatively, on detection of an error by a programmed check, the number of possible ways in which the program may have erred is very large and obscure side-effects of the error may have spread into the system. The analysis, with certainty, of such an erroneous program state is in general beyond our capabilities, and therefore repair of the program state cannot be recommended.

For many applications, frequently the applications requiring the highest reliability, error recovery by repetition of whole job steps or other major program units must imply a substantial recovery overhead and a degradation of service. Such applications require a recovery mechanism which can achieve local recovery from an error whenever possible.

It is characteristic of error recovery operations that they are very much more error prone than the main programs, and are very difficult to check. It is an objective of the recovery block concept that the error recovery actions should be testable and that they should be checked with the same rigour as the main program. It is of course obvious that repetition of the operation with the same program will not always achieve recovery from a program error.

The recovery block concept is aimed at the provision of a well-structured context for explicitly considered error recovery operations. These can be constructed at various levels within the program so that if a local recovery operation should fail a more global recovery action can be substituted. Another aim is that the structure should make explicit the nature of the checks which are applied and also the nature of the action to be taken in the event of error, the number of such actions being strictly limited.

3.   Recovery Blocks

A well-structured program is constructed from identifiable operations, many of which are themselves constructed from further smaller operations. The proposed scheme is based on the selection of a set of these operations upon which to base the recovery operations. These will be referred to as Recovery Blocks. Recovery blocks can be nested like Algol blocks, but a recovery block must have a more complex internal structure than an Algol block so as to support error recovery. Each recovery block contains a primary block, an acceptance test, and zero or more alternate blocks.

The primary block corresponds exactly to the block of the Algol-like program, and is entered to perform the desired operation.

The acceptance test is executed on exit from the primary block to confirm that the primary block has performed acceptably.

If the primary block is detected to be in error, the alternate block is entered and is required to perform the desired operation in a different way or to perform some alternative action acceptable to the program as a whole. The acceptance test is then repeated.

The diagram of a recovery block's structure given in Figure 1 is intended to be illustrative, rather than syntactically representative. The double vertical lines define the scopes of recovery block, while the single vertical lines define the scopes of primary and alternate blocks. Figure 2 shows how the primary and alternate blocks can contain, nested within themselves, further recovery blocks.

4.   Acceptance Tests

The acceptance test is a section of program which is invoked on exit from a primary or alternate block. This acceptance test can be regarded as an assertion of the effects of the execution of the recovery block which are required for the correct operation of the surrounding program [1]. The acceptance test provides a binary decision as to whether the assertion is satisfied and thus as to whether the recovery block has been executed in a manner acceptable to the rest of the system. There is no requirement that the test be, in any formal sense, a check on the absolute 'correctness' of the operation – it is for the designer to decide on the appropriate level of rigour of the test. For each recovery block there is a single acceptance test, invoked on exit from the primary and also on exit from the alternate should the alternate be required. Thus in figure 2, the acceptance test BT is invoked on completion of primary block BP, so as to check the acceptability of the results of BP.

The acceptance test does not lie within the primary block, but can be considered to be a part of the next enclosing block. Thus the acceptance test cannot access the local variables of the primary or alternate blocks; indeed there is no reason why the local declarations of these blocks should be the same. The function of the acceptance test is to ensure that the operation performed by the recovery block is to the satisfaction of the program which invoked it. The acceptance test is therefore performed by reference to the variables accessible to that program, rather than to local variables which can have no effect or significance after exit.

The .acceptance test can reference any variable within the current scope immediately enclosing the recovery block. The primary block may modify some of these variables. For convenience and increased rigour, the acceptance test is enabled to access such variables either for their modified value or for their original unmodified value.

5.   Rejection by an Acceptance Test

There are four possible causes for the rejection of a primary or alternate block. These are:

a)   an error within the block, detected explicitly by the acceptance test,

b)   failure to terminate, detected by a timeout,

c)   detection of an error within the block by one of the implicit error detection mechanisms (e.g. protection violation, divide by zero, etc),

d)   explicit or implicit rejection within an inner recovery block which exhausts the recovery capability at that level.

If the primary of a recovery block is rejected then the recursive cache mechanism invokes an alternate. When this alternate terminates, its results are submitted to the same acceptance test, and should the acceptance test be satisfied, the program proceeds using the results generated by the alternate. If the acceptance test is again not satisfied then a further alternate is tried. Thus, in figure 2, if the results of primary block BP are rejected by acceptance test BT, then alternate block BQ is invoked. If the results from BQ are still unacceptable to BT, then BR must be invoked.

Should all the alternate blocks have been obeyed, and all have failed to satisfy the acceptance test, then the entire recovery block must be regarded as having failed. This causes rejection of the enclosing block which invoked the recovery block, and the alternate to that enclosing block must be attempted instead. Thus, in figure 2, if the results from alternate block BR are still unacceptable to acceptance test BT, then recovery block B as a whole, and therefore primary block AP, must be regarded as having failed. The next program to be attempted is alternate block AQ.

If an error occurs during the execution of the program of an acceptance test, this is regarded as an error occurring within the next enclosing recovery block. The alternate invoked is therefore that for the enclosing block rather than that for the block whose acceptability is being tested. Thus if an error is detected whilst executing the program of acceptance test BT, the alternate block AQ must be entered.

6.   Primary and Alternate Blocks

It is an objective of the recovery block concept that primary blocks can be written in exactly the same manner as in a conventional system. There are no restrictions on the operations which are performed by the primary blocks, no restrictions on the calling of procedures or the modification of global variables, no requirements for the explicit preservation of restart information, and no special programming conventions.

175

Similarly the intention is that the alternate blocks can be written in exactly the same manner. The design of an alternate block is not affected by the prior unsuccessful execution of the primary block. The recursive cache mechanism described below ensures that an alternate block is executed as though the primary had never been entered, and as though the alternate had been substituted for the primary in a conventional program structure.

When an alternate block is entered it must therefore be presented with exactly the same environment as was its primary when it was entered. All the operations of the primary must have been undone, all the non-local variables altered by the primary must have been restored to their previous values. It is a requirement on the mechanisation that this recovery be achievable with reasonable efficiency both for assignments, as described below in section 8, and for more complex operations, as described in section 11. The recovery block scheme provides a structuring of programs in time and space so that the recovery information can be retained with greater facility and efficiency than would be possible with, for instance, a core image checkpoint mechanism.

In particular it should be noted that the alternate has no access to the reason why the primary was rejected and no access to any results calculated by the primary. It is important that a record of each rejection is preserved for subsequent investigation, but it is envisaged that the records will lie beyond the scope of the program being run. There may be occasions when it would be convenient for the alternate to know what had gone wrong with the primary, but the number of possible error conditions is very large, and it is not always easy to distinguish one error from another. Since the alternate cannot be expected to categorise and accommodate each cause of error explicitly, it would appear preferable that the alternate should always start again from the entry to the recovery block without any record of previous rejections. Errors which are expected to be sufficiently frequent that special handling would be appropriate can perhaps be regarded as normal program conditions rather than unforeseeable errors.

As mentioned earlier, an alternate block might perform the desired operation in a different way, presumably less efficiently, but perhaps by a simpler and less error-prone algorithm. However the more likely case is for an alternate block to be designed to provide an operation which, though less desirable , is still acceptable to the program as a whole. Thus the recovery block structure might be used as a means of structuring the rather ad hoc error recovery facilities that many existing systems incorporate [2].

7.   Orthogonality of Design

We believe that the recovery block concept should not impose any constraint on the programming or the architecture of the computer, for any design which imposes constraints may preclude, or be precluded by, other techniques intended to facilitate reliable computing.

Each primary and alternate block is programmed in exactly the same manner as a conventional program, written in any desired programming language and with any desired programming style or methodology. Extensions to existing languages are required only to define the recovery block structure, and to permit access to prior values of variables during acceptance tests.

It is natural to equate the recovery blocks with a subset of the blocks of an Algol-like program, but it is not necessary that all the Algol blocks be recovery blocks, or even that the programming language provide an Algol-like block structure. The only requirements are that the recovery blocks should be explicitly defined, that they should be dynamically nested, and that entry to and exit from recovery blocks should be explicit. Clearly, well-structured programming techniques are to be encouraged, but the recursive cache concept does not depend on them. It is as applicable to programming in assembler on a S/360 as to Algol on a B6700. Thus the recovery block concept is substantially orthogonal to programming languages and methodologies.

The recursive cache mechanism, described below, operates entirely with "words" in a single linear virtual address space. The user may program with various sizes of data, may use vectors, heaps, own variables, complex list structures, parameters, or even recursive procedures. It is assumed that the computer architecture will accommodate this variety and, by a display, descriptors, indexing or other mechanisms, will convert all store references into references to words in a linear virtual address space. The address of such a word will be known as a "virtual address". The mechanism operates entirely with these words and their virtual addresses, and the significance of this data to the user program is of no concern to the cache mechanism. The description below is in terms of a classical Algol stack machine, but it is believed that conventional computer architectures can readily be accommodated, and thus the error recovery scheme is orthogonal to the architecture of the computer.

8.   The Recursive Cache Mechanism

The requirement that an alternate block be presented with exactly the same environment as was its primary could be mechanised by appropriate core image check points, (or even by retaining enough information to allow programs to be executed backwards, instruction by instruction [3]), but the associated overheads would defeat the purpose of the concept. Consequently a specialised mechanisation is presented which aims to reduce the overheads to an acceptable level, while remaining invisible to the user.

The heavy overhead of recording a conventional checkpoint on entry to each recovery block is caused by the recording of the entire context of the recovery block, a substantial quantity of information. But in many cases only a few of the non-local variables will be modified by the recovery block, and all that would be needed to restore the environment are the virtual addresses and prior values of those variables which are actually modified [4]. Thus in this mechanisation only on writing into a "word" is the virtual address and previous value of that word recorded, in an additional storage area to be called the cache.

Since only the values of the variables on entry to the recovery block need be preserved, it is appropriate to associate with each word a boolean flag to indicate that the required value has already been preserved in the cache. All these flags are cleared on entry to the recovery block, and each writing operation tests the appropriate flag. If the flag is clear, then the virtual address and current value of the word must be recorded in the cache, and the flag must be set. If it is set, then no special action is required before the write operation.

Because the recovery blocks are nested, the cache can be organised as a stack, as is shown in Figure 3. Stack marks are placed in the cache stack to indicate recovery block entries, and similar stack marks in the main stack facilitate the recognition of variables local to the current primary or alternate block. The marks divide the main stack and cache stack into (possibly empty) regions. Each main stack word contains a value and a boolean flag which (for non-local variables) indicates modification within the current recovery block. Each cache entry contains the virtual address of a word and the value of that word on entry to the recovery block. Note that the set of words flagged in the main stack corresponds exactly to the set of words recorded within in the top region of the cache stack.

The term recursive cache was originally introduced by (inaccurate) analogy to the cache of the IBM 360/85. In fact our usage of cache can be viewed as matching its dictionary meaning of a "hiding-place", since prior values of variables are hidden in the cache in case they might be needed again. In contrast IBM's usage of this term, which they have now abandoned in favour of "buffer-store", was in relation to the high speed store of a demand paged virtual memory system; such a high speed store would contain current values of variables.

9. The Algorithm of the Mechanisation

On entry to a recovery block, stack marks are placed in the main and cache stacks, and all the flags are cleared. The flags will subsequently be reset by examination of the appropriate cache region and the same technique may be used to clear them. For examples see stages (b) or (c) in Figure 4.

Reading any variable (local or global, whether modified or not) is done by fetching the value of the word with the appropriate virtual address, stage (e) in Figure 4. The flag is ignored. Thus no overhead is incurred on reading, an important consideration.

Assignment to a local variable is also performed conventionally, important because many assignments are to local variables, stages (b) or (c) in Figure 4. Local variables do not need to be cached and thus the flag is of no significance.

Assignment to a non-local variable involves testing the flag. If on assignment the flag is found to be clear, then the flag must be set and an entry, comprising the virtual address of the word and its current value, is pushed onto the cache stack. The assignment is then performed, stages (d) or (e) in Figure 4. If the flag is set then the prior value has already been cached and the assignment proceeds conventionally, stage (f) in Figure 4.

The performance of an acceptance test implies exit from the primary or alternate block, and therefore the deletion of all local variables from the main stack. If the acceptance test involves access to prior values of variables, these values may be obtained by searching the top region of the cache stack, though it may be appropriate first to check the flag of the word in the main stack, where the required value will be if it is actually unchanged.

If the acceptance test should reject the block then the environment must be restored to exactly the situation existing on entry. This is done by popping each entry of the top region of the cache stack, and using its value to reset the word at the virtual address cited, the flag also being cleared, stage (h) of Figure 4. Note that this must clear all the flags, the condition established on entry to a recovery block. By removal of stack marks, this operation may be performed repeatedly to obtain recovery at an outer recovery block.

The action if the acceptance test is passed is more complex. The aim is to set up the cache and the stack as though the accepted block had consisted solely of its non-local assignments, some of which might of course be local to the enclosing block, others of which might have been preceded by assignments to the same variables during this enclosing block. First, all the flags are cleared. Then the entries in the top-but-one region of the cache stack are accessed and the flags are set for all the words those entries address. Next the entries of the top region of the cache are processed.

If the word addressed by the cache entry is local to the enclosing recovery block then the cached value may be discarded as caching is not required for local variables. Similarly, if the flag of the word addressed is set then the cached value may be discarded, for the value cached in the lower cache region is the true value of the word on entry to that recovery block.

If the flag is not set, then the cached value is the value that a non-local variable had on entry to the enclosing recovery block. The cache entry must therefore be included in the top-but-one region of the cache stack, and the flag must be set.

While the top region of the cache stack is being processed it may be necessary to enlarge the top-but-one region. It is therefore appropriate to process this top region in the reverse sequence (FIFO rather than LIFO). When the top region has been fully processed and the stack marks removed, processing may resume on the enclosing, now the current, recovery block. Stage (g) of Figure 4 shows a few of the possible circumstances. The main overheads of this implementation are incurred at block entry and block exit time, and will depend linearly on the number of different non-local assignments that have occurred. The scanning of the cache that is involved is comparatively simple, and is in our opinion quite appropriate for hardware implementation. The one instance of a search is that involved in accessing the prior value of a variable that has been changed, which occurs only in acceptance tests. The space needed in the cache will depend on the program structure, but for a given choice of recovery blocks no unnecessary information will be saved, a claim which would be very difficult to make for a system with programmer-specified check-pointing.

10.   Assignments and Procedure Calls within Acceptance Tests

In the basic scheme, an acceptance test is a transparent operation whose sole effect is to provide a binary decision on the acceptability of a recovery block. In practice however an acceptance test may be a quite complex program containing assignments and procedure calls.

Because of notational problems, it would appear to be inappropriate to allow an acceptance test to contain a recovery block. But if the acceptance test is allowed to call procedures which contain recovery blocks, then the required effect is readily achieved. The use of procedures may be very desirable for the proper structuring of complex acceptance tests.

Only minor extensions to the basic recursive cache mechanism are required to accommodate procedure calls within acceptance tests. The most significant extension required is to allow an acceptance test to pass to a procedure, as a parameter, a reference to the previous value of a variable which has been altered within the recovery block. The parameter may be of course a complex data structure, only parts of which have been altered. It would appear necessary to extend the address or reference to the parameter with a recovery block level field, which can be carried over into any subsequently derived address or reference. This level field can be used to ensure recovery of the correct values from the cache.

Modification of these original values within an acceptance test is clearly reprehensible and without any possible justification. The appending of the level number to an address could therefore be used to render the data thus referenced read only.

11. Recoverable Procedures

The programs discussed above generated their results entirely by assignment to storage locations, and were recovered simply by reversal of those assignments. But many programming operations generate results other than by assignments, or need to preserve some results even when the processing of the operation is abandoned and an alternate is attempted. Typical examples are operations which involve file access and input-output interfaces, accounting routines, diagnostic traces, and interactive user interfaces. It is characteristic of such programs that error recovery is more complex than automatic reversal of assignments, and an opportunity must be provided for the program designer to specify the appropriate recovery action.

It is proposed that operations requiring special recovery action should be structured into procedures, to be known as recoverable procedures. A recoverable procedure is not itself a recovery block with an acceptance test and alternates, though its body consists of a recovery block. Such a procedure may declare own variables, whose values are not automatically reset by the recursive cache mechanism in the event of error, but can be restored by program within the recoverable procedure. It may be appropriate to allow several recoverable procedures to be associated and to share a set of own variables. Such a structure would follow naturally from the classes of Simula [5] or the Type mechanism of Campbell and Habermann [6].

Just as the recovery of simple variables involves the saving of a value on first assignment within a recovery block, multiple further assignments without special action, and the restoration of the prior value in the event of error, so the recoverable procedure must provide three entry points, the save, the normal and the reverse entry points as is shown in Figure 5. The save entry point preserves such recovery information as the programmer specifies before performing the required action, and the mechanism will enter here the first time that the procedure is called within a recovery block. Subsequent calls of the procedure within the recovery block will enter at the normal entry point. (The assumption is that the information saved on the occasion of the first call of the procedure suffices to allow the system to be reinstated to the satisfaction of the programmer, even if there are many further calls). It is important to note that the program which calls the recoverable procedure is not aware of the save entry point, which is invoked automatically by the cache mechanism. The reverse entry point is also invoked automatically by the cache mechanism, in the event of an error in the block that invoked the procedure, so as to provide an opportunity to restore the recoverable procedure in accordance with the information saved on entry through the save entry point.

An example of a recoverable procedure might be a file access interface which maintains own variables indicating the current position of each file. The save operation would simply record the values of these variables on entry to each recovery block, while the reverse operation would use the saved values to reposition the files.

12. The Mechanisation of Recoverable Procedures

When the program enters the scope within which the recoverable procedure is declared, a descriptor providing access to the procedure is placed on the main stack, as are the own variables of the procedure. Both the descriptor and the own variables are provided with flags for use by the cache mechanism, just as any other variables on the main stack. An example is shown in Figure 5.

When the recoverable procedure is invoked for the first time, the flag on its descriptor will be found clear, indicating that the procedure has not been used previously within this recovery block. The cache mechanism now sets the flag and records the descriptor and its virtual address in the cache. It then enters the save entry point of the procedure. The recoverable procedure now obtains a further area of the cache stack within which to record its recovery information and enters its internal recovery blocks which perform the saving of recovery information and the function required of the procedure.

Subsequent calls on the recoverable procedure within the same recovery block will find the flag on the descriptor already set. The recoverable procedure will then be entered through the normal entry point with no special action. But should the program enter a further recovery block before again calling the recoverable procedure, then the flag on its descriptor will have been cleared and a further set of recovery information must be recorded in the cache stack to correspond to the new recovery block within which recovery may be required.

On successful exit from a recovery block, the descriptor and its associated save area in the cache stack are treated by the cache mechanism just like any other variable recorded in the cache stack. They are transferred from one cache region to the next, resetting the main stack descriptor flag, until either they become local or the descriptor is already present in that cache region. Within the recovery blocks inside the recoverable procedure, the own variables of the procedure, and the variables within the save area in the cache stack, are regarded as non-local and can be restored just like any other variable in the event of error. But once the acceptance test of the first recovery block of the procedure is satisfied, during the exit from the recovery block these variables are regarded as local within the next recovery block, regardless of their position in the main stack, and their cached prior values are therefore discarded. Thus exit from the recoverable procedure effectively renders permanent any assignments to the own variables, and subsequent recovery can only be through the recovery program contained within the recoverable procedure. However any assignments made by the procedure to non-local variables, either directly or through some parameter mechanism, are treated normally and therefore can be undone by the cache mechanism.

After an error, the top cache stack region is processed in the conventional manner, and when the descriptor for the recoverable procedure is found, the cache mechanism invokes the reverse entry point of the procedure. The reverse entry point may involve a recovery block, further procedure calls and recovery blocks, and any other processing necessary to restore the own variables to appropriate values. (We have yet to consider the need for allowing assignments to other non-local variables from within a reverse operation.)

13. Exercising the Alternates

Within many systems containing error recovery mechanisms, the mechanisms are not tested with sufficient rigour. Adequate validation of a system's ability to cope with errors occurring in the midst of attempts to recovery from an earlier detected error can be particularly difficult. Thus errors remain within the recovery programs and the reliability of the system is adversely affected.

It is proposed that, in the recovery block system, provision should be made for the automatic exercising of the alternates, either all alternates being exercised or only a proportion on a probabilistic basis. Rejections would be recorded for subsequent analysis. This provision can be made either by an explicit mechanism, or else perhaps by appropriate programming of the acceptance tests.

14. Further Research

The recovery block scheme is only in the early stages of development, and its value has yet to be demonstrated. At present, a programmed emulator incorporating a recursive cache mechanism is being implemented for our dual processor PDP11/45, and a variety of application programs, structured into recovery blocks, will be programmed to test the concept for both efficacy and cost. Subsequently we hope to extend the recovery block concept into the code of the operating system.

We have already received encouragement from some brief experiments carried out by a colleague, David Wyeth, which involved interpretive execution of a number of Algol W programs. Even regarding each block as being a recovery block, it was found that the amount of space that would be needed for a cache was in every case considerably smaller than that needed for the stack. It would of course be possible to design a program, and its recovery block structure, so that the cache size greatly exceeded that of the stack. We believe this to be unlikely in practice, but could imagine that a scheme for removing part of the cache to backing storage, which could take advantage of the simplified patterns of access to the cache, might be worthwhile.

The most significant limitation of the recovery blocks described here is that they apply only to a single sequential process in isolation. In fact some useful progress has been made towards the recovery of asynchronous co-operating processes, and investigation continues. We hope to publish some preliminary results in this area shortly.

The recovery block concept is only one aspect of a project at the University of Newcastle upon Tyne to investigate computer system reliability. Another, closely related, aspect of this research is the design of highly structured addressing and protection schemes. A proposed 'recursive virtual machine architecture' has been documented separately [7]; a simplified version of this architecture is also being incorporated in the emulator.

15. Conclusion

Just as existing protection schemes provide error containment firewalls in space, so the recovery block concept can be thought of as providing firewalls in time. It allows programs containing provisions for error detection and recovery to be structured so as to distinguish clearly between the main program, the acceptance tests, and the action to be taken in error conditions. The provision of successive levels of error recovery permits attempts at purely local error recovery with low overheads, while the errors are contained so that the alternative programs can be run within the same environment as was the main program. The recoverable procedure concept provides a means for the extension of the recovery block concept into more complex situations. These structuring techniques are complemented by a hardware mechanism, whose overheads are in our opinion quite tolerable, which ensures that, for a given choice of recovery blocks, no unnecessary information is saved.

16. Acknowledgements

The development of the recovery block scheme, and the present description of it, has been greatly aided by discussions with colleagues working on or associated with the research project at the University of Newcastle upon Tyne on the Design of Highly Reliable Compter Systems. The funds for this project are provided by the Science Research Council.

References

1. Floyd, R.W., Assigning meanings to programs, in Mathematical Aspects of
        Computer Science, ed. Schwartz, J.T., Amer. Math. Soc. 1967.

2. Randell B., Operating Systems : the problems of performance and
        reliability. IFIP Congress 1971, Invited Papers, p. 100.

3. Balzer, R.M., EXDAMS, Extendable Debugging and Monitoring Systems,
        SJCC 1969, p. 567.

4. Prenner, C.J. et al, An Implementation of Backtracking for Programming
        Languages, ACM Annual Conference, 1972, p. 763.

5. Birtwistle, G.M. et al, SIMULA begin,
        Student Litteratur/Auerbach 1973.

6. Campbell, R.H. and Habermann, A.N., The Specification of Process
        Synchronisation by Path Expressions. (Published at this
        conference.

7. Lauer, H.C. and Wyeth D., A Recursive Virtual Machine Architecture,
        TR 54, Computing Laboratory, University of Newcastle upon
        Tyne, (September 1973).

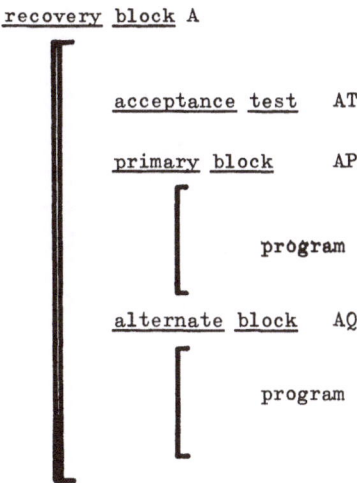

recovery block A

acceptance test   AT

primary block   AP

program

alternate block   AQ

program

Figure 1.

A diagramatic representation of a recovery block structure.

The primary block corresponds exactly to the block of the Algol–like program and is entered to perform the desired operation.

The acceptance test is executed on exit from the primary block to confirm that the primary block has performed acceptably.

If the primary block is detected to be in error, the alternate block is entered and is required to perform the desired operation in a different way. The acceptance test is then repeated.

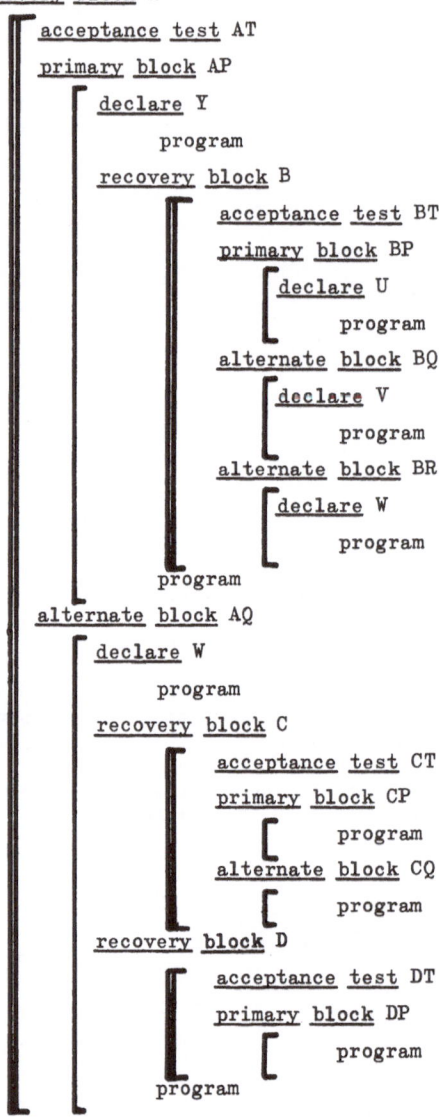

declare X
recovery block A
  acceptance test AT
  primary block AP
      declare Y
        program
      recovery block B
            acceptance test BT
            primary block BP
                declare U
                  program
            alternate block BQ
                declare V
                  program
            alternate block BR
                declare W
                  program
        program
  alternate block AQ
      declare W
        program
      recovery block C
            acceptance test CT
            primary block CP
                  program
            alternate block CQ
                  program
      recovery block D
            acceptance test DT
            primary block DP
                  program
        program

Figure 2.

A more complex recovery block structure, showing how the primary and
alternate blocks can contain, nested within themselves, further recovery blocks.

185

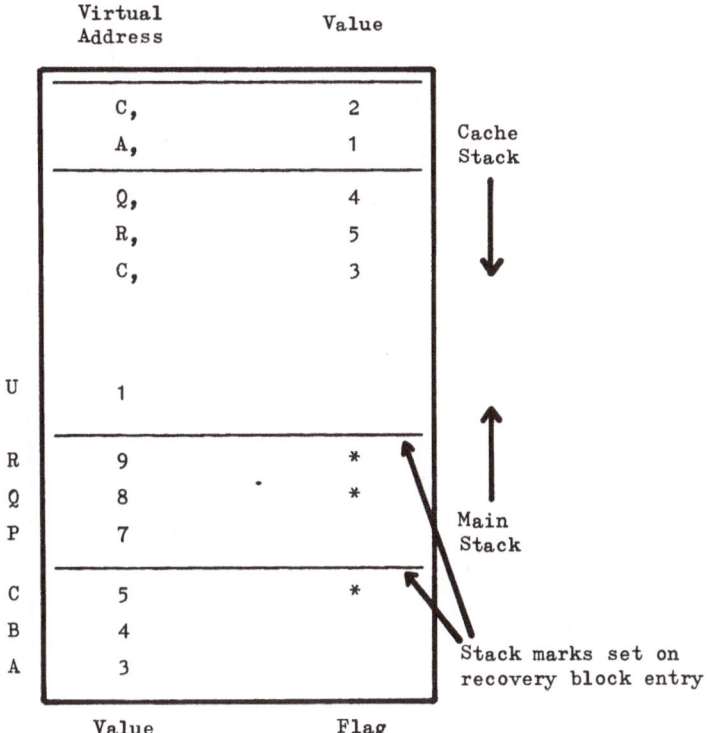

Figure 3.

A diagramatic representation of the main stack and the cache stack.
Assignments to C, Q, R have been made within the current recovery block.
Thus these variables have been flagged and their previous values recorded
in the cache.

186

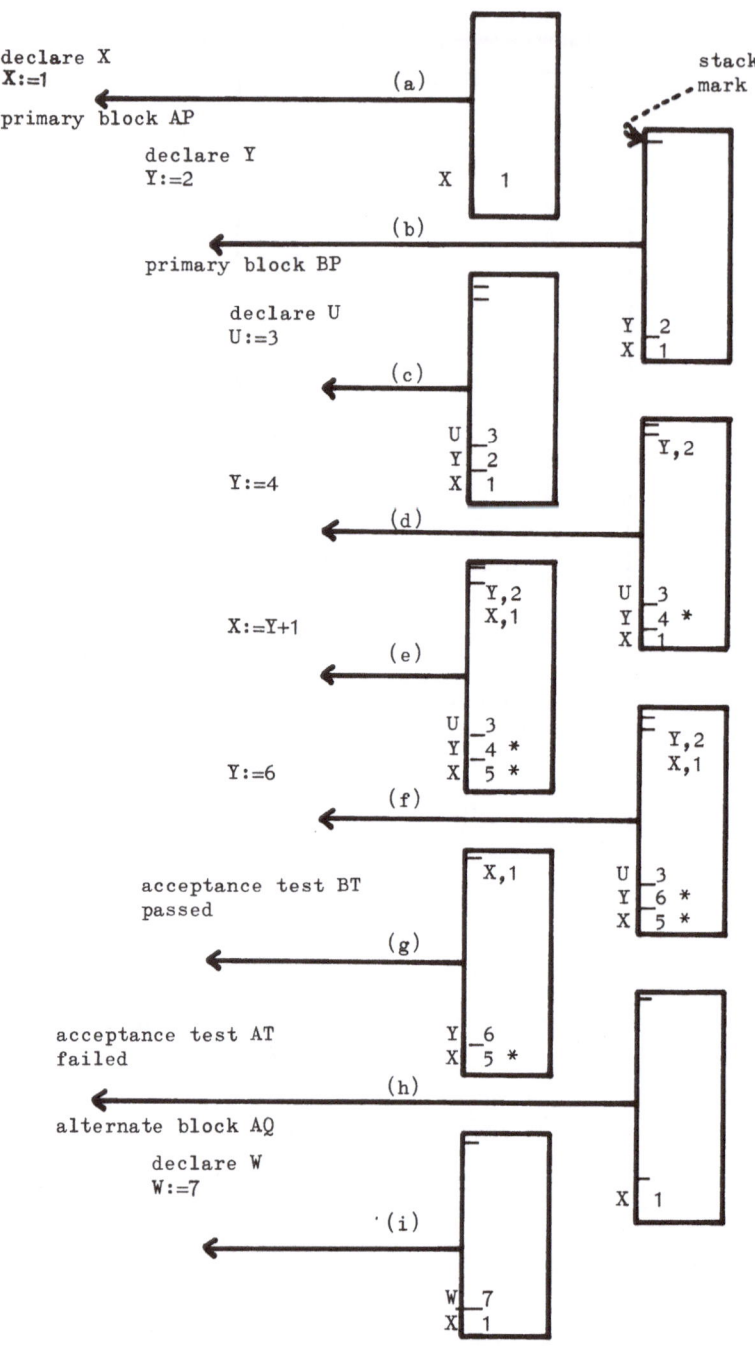

<u>Figure 4</u>

The states of the stack and the cache during the execution of the program of Figure 2. For descriptions of the various operations depicted see the text, Section 9.

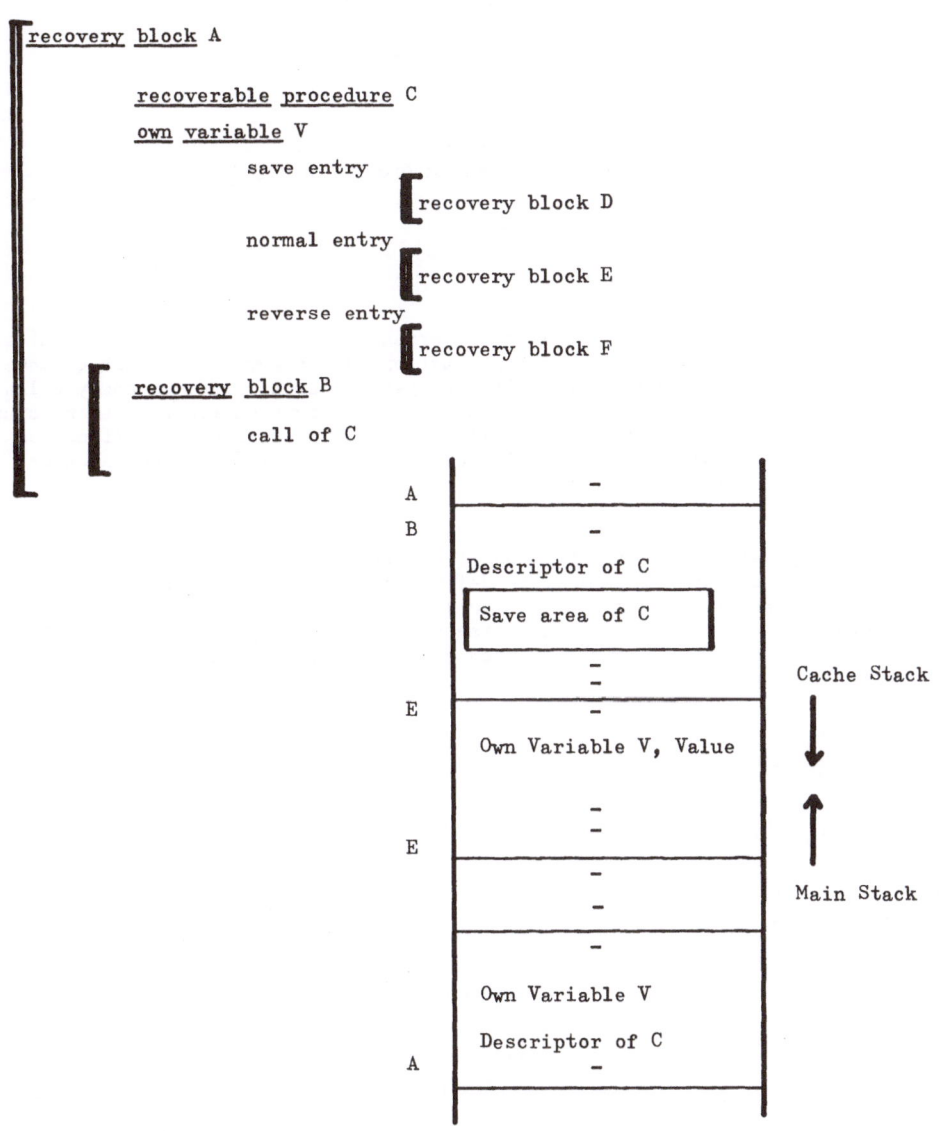

recovery block A

recoverable procedure C
own variable V
save entry
recovery block D
normal entry
recovery block E
reverse entry
recovery block F
recovery block B
call of C

Figure 5.

A program containing a recoverable procedure and a diagramatic
representation of the stacks and their contents.

ANALYSE DE QUELQUES PANNES
D'UN SYSTEME D'EXPLOITATION

C. Kaiser

IRIA-LABORIA

S. Krakowiak

Université de Grenoble I, Laboratoire d'Informatique *

———

Résumé. On s'intéresse dans cet article aux erreurs dans les programmes, et plus particulièrement dans les systèmes d'exploitation. Après avoir introduit quelques définitions touchant la production et la propagation des erreurs, on analyse les symptômes et les causes de trois pannes survenues au cours du fonctionnement d'un système d'exploitation. Cette analyse sert de base à un essai de classification des erreurs dans les systèmes. En conclusion, on tente de tirer de cette expérience quelques enseignements pratiques.

Abstract. This paper deals with the subject of errors in programs, and more specifically in operating systems. Some definitions regarding error production and propagation are introduced. The symptoms and causes of three run-time errors which were observed in the last stages of the development of an operating system are analyzed. This analysis is used as a basis for a tentative classification of systems programming errors. Some practical conclusions are finally proposed.

———

* Ce travail a été réalisé quand cet auteur était à l'IRIA.

"Although "bugs" in programs are often embarrassing to a programmer, if we are to learn from our mistakes we should record them and tell other people about them instead of forgetting them !".

D. E. KNUTH
The Art of Computer Programming, vol I.

"Programmers call their errors "bugs" to preserve their sanity ; that number of "mistakes" would not be psychologically acceptable !".

M. E. HOPKINS
in *Software Engineering Techniques*, 2nd NATO Conference

ANALYSE DE QUELQUES PANNES
D'UN SYSTEME D'EXPLOITATION

1 - INTRODUCTION

1.1 - *Motivations de l'étude*

Une part notable de l'activité des programmeurs est consacrée à la recherche et à la correction d'erreurs dans les programmes. Compte tenu de son importance pratique, il ne semble pas que ce sujet ait reçu toute l'attention qu'il
mérite. Un nombre croissant d'études sont consacrées aux méthodes visant à
réduire la probabilité d'occurrence des erreurs par une meilleure structuration
des programmes et des données. Les techniques de détection et de correction des
erreurs font également l'objet de nombreux travaux. Mais l'étude des erreurs
elles-mêmes, de leur nature, de leurs différents types et des raisons de leur
apparition, semble être un domaine négligé, et la bibliographie que nous avons
pu rassembler sur ce sujet est brève (citons en particulier [4, 10, 11]). Une
raison en est peut-être la difficulté de dépasser en cette matière la simple
description, voire l'anecdote. Une autre source de difficulté pour une présentation logique est que le domaine des "solutions incorrectes" à un problème
est incomparablement plus vaste que celui des solutions correctes. Il nous
a néanmoins paru intéressant d'analyser un certain nombre d'erreurs "vécues",
dans l'espoir de mieux comprendre les causes de leur production et de dégager
des règles permettant d'éviter dans l'avenir des erreurs du même type.

Les erreurs ici décrites sont apparues, parmi de nombreuses autres, au
cours de la construction d'un système d'exploitation [1]. Dans ce type de
programme, les erreurs revêtent une importance particulière.
Il y a à cela plusieurs raisons :
- les programmes de systèmes sont généralement de grande taille,
- le nombre de programmeurs est élevé, ce qui amplifie les problèmes de
documentation et de communication,
- le parallélisme dans l'exécution des programmes introduit de nouvelles
classes d'erreurs, dont les conséquences dépendent du temps et qui sont
difficilement reproductibles.
Il ne semble pas qu'une terminologie reconnue existe dans le domaine
des erreurs de programmation. Nous tenterons donc d'abord de préciser ce
point.

1.2 - *Terminologie*

1.21 - *Production, manifestation et détection des erreurs*

La notion d'action sera considérée ici comme une notion première. Une
action est un phénomène de durée finie se déroulant dans un certain univers
(que l'on appellera le système), dont on sait définir l'état avant et après
l'action (mais non nécessairement pendant son déroulement). L'effet (voulu)
d'une action est de modifier l'état du système. Plus précisément, l'effet
d'une action A qui fait passer le système de l'état $S1$ à l'état $S2$ peut être
spécifié [3] par une assertion initiale $p_A(S1)$ et une assertion finale $q_A(S2)$:
ce sont deux fonctions de l'état du système, à valeur booléenne, telles que
si $p_A(S1) = \underline{vrai}$, on ait $q_A(S2) = \underline{vrai}$. Un programme est la description d'un
ensemble d'actions dans un certain vocabulaire, qui comporte la définition d'un
répertoire d'actions élémentaires et de règles permettant de combiner ces
actions entre elles. Nous supposerons que ces règles interdisent l'exécution si-
multanée d'actions élémentaires ; le phénomène constitué par l'exécution du programme, c'est-à-dire l'exécution de la suite d'actions élémentaires décrites par
le programme, est appelé processus sequentiel, ou simplement processus. Un processus est destiné à provoquer un certain effet et peut lui-même, s'il a une
durée finie, être considéré comme une action. Nous dirons qu'il y a production
d'une erreur si, après l'exécution d'une action d'un processus, l'assertion
finale correspondant à cette action n'est pas vérifiée alors que l'assertion

initiale l'était. Cette erreur peut provenir d'une <u>faute</u> dans le texte d'un programme ou d'une <u>défaillance</u> du matériel.

Une telle définition de l'erreur n'est guère exploitable dans la pratique en raison du grand nombre des actions ; aussi la plupart des assertions finales ne sont en fait ni explicitées lors de la conception d'un programme, ni contrôlées lors de son exécution. Cette situation a deux conséquences. La première est qu'il peut s'exécuter un nombre considérable d'actions entre la production d'une erreur et sa <u>détection</u>, c'est-à-dire la constatation qu'une assertion n'est pas vérifiée. La seconde est qu'une erreur peut échapper à toute détection si elle n'a de conséquences sur aucune assertion effectivement contrôlée ou sur aucune action ultérieure ; mais une modification du programme, par exemple, peut changer cette situation et mettre au jour une erreur sans corrélation apparente avec la modification, et donc très difficile à localiser.

<u>Exemple</u> : L'exécution d'un appel au superviseur (soit Q) a un certain effet, prévu par sa spécification ; supposons qu'elle ait en outre l'effet, non spécifié, de mettre à zéro le registre $R5$. Cette erreur ne sera pas détectée si on ne tente jamais de réutiliser l'ancien contenu de $R5$ après l'appel de Q. Elle ne le sera pas non plus si ce contenu se trouve toujours être zéro avant l'appel de Q. Un changement de la politique d'utilisation des registres risque de faire apparaître l'erreur.

Ces remarques nous conduisent à introduire la terminologie qui suit (figure 1) : nous appellerons <u>manifestation</u> d'une erreur la première non-vérification de l'assertion initiale d'une action ; il s'agit en fait de la première conséquence irréversible de l'erreur (nous ne considérons ici que le cas d'une erreur isolée, laissant de côté les interférences entre erreurs). Entre la production d'une erreur et sa manifestation, nous dirons que l'erreur est <u>latente</u> ; entre sa manifestation et sa détection, nous dirons que l'erreur est <u>propagée</u>.

PRODUCTION

délai de latence   erreur latente

MANIFESTATION

délai de propagation   erreur propagée

DETECTION

erreur détectée

<u>figure 1</u>. Phase d'apparition d'une erreur

Dans notre exemple, l'erreur constituée par la mise à zéro de $R5$ est latente entre le retour de Q et la première utilisation (si elle existe) du contenu de $R5$ supposé non modifié entre temps. Entre cette utilisation et sa conséquence visible (si elle existe), l'erreur est propagée.

La possibilité d'un délai de latence s'explique comme suit : soient A et B deux actions, et p_A, q_A, p_B, q_B les assertions correspondantes. La validité de la construction A ; B nécessite que $q_A \supset p_B$, mais l'identité $q_A \equiv p_B$ n'est pas requise. On peut donc se trouver, après une exécution de A, dans une situation telle que $q_A = \textit{faux}$ (une erreur s'est produite dans A) et $p_B = \textit{vrai}$. Dans ce cas, l'erreur traversera B en restant latente.

Deux remarques doivent maintenant être faites sur l'observabilité du système :

1) - Le découpage en actions est, dans une large mesure, arbitraire ; en particulier, une suite d'actions A_1 ; A_2 ; ... ; A_k est elle-même une action A avec $p_A = p_{A_1}$ et $q_A = q_{A_k}$. Liée à la notion d'action, la notion d'erreur est donc elle-même relative à un niveau d'observation. Ainsi, si on choisit, dans l'exemple de l'appel du superviseur, de considérer l'action Q comme indivisible, la production de l'erreur se situe immédiatement après l'exécution

de Q. Mais si on se place à un niveau d'observation plus fin (l'exécution d'une instruction), on pourra localiser, à l'intérieur de Q, la production puis la manifestation de l'erreur.

2) - L'état d'un système a été défini pour un processus unique. Il est plus difficile de le faire dans le cas de l'exécution parallèle de plusieurs processus ; on doit pour cela introduire des "points observables" où l'état de l'ensemble du système peut être défini, et où les assertions peuvent être formulées.

Nous allons à présent distinguer divers types d'erreurs.

1.22 - *Incidents et pannes*

Considérons la réaction et la détection d'une erreur. Il peut se faire que l'occurrence, en un point donné, d'un certain type d'erreur soit explicitement prévue et qu'en particulier des actions ultérieures dépendent de cette occurrence : nous parlerons alors d'un incident. Dans le cas contraire, où l'erreur est imprévue et empêche généralement le programme d'assurer la fonction pour laquelle il est écrit, nous parlerons d'une panne.

Pour être compatible avec celles du 1.21, la définition d'un incident suppose l'existence, pour toute action, d'un second niveau d'assertion, dans lequel peuvent être décrites les violations du premier niveau. C'est en fait ce qui se passe dans un système d'exploitation bien conçu où une erreur affectant les programmes d'un usager, et qui est pour lui une panne, doit être traitée comme un simple incident par le moniteur pour ne pas dégrader ou interrompre le service rendu aux autres usagers. De même le moniteur doit tenter d'annuler ou de limiter les effets d'un mauvais fonctionnement du matériel. Les programmes de traitement des incidents ont donc une importance particulière dans un système d'exploitation.

1.3 - *Notions nécessaires sur le système Esope*

Les pannes qui sont l'objet de cet article ont été observées sur le système Esope. Nous ne présentons ici de ce système que les éléments nécessaires à une bonne compréhension de notre analyse. Pour une description moins succincte, on se reportera à [1].

1.31 - *Le matériel*

Le matériel utilisé est un CII 10070 monoprocesseur. Il dispose d'une unité d'échanges multiples qui permet de faire fonctionner plusieurs coupleurs de périphériques en même temps que l'unité centrale. Celle-ci commande l'unité d'échange et les divers coupleurs avec des instructions d'entrée-sortie, SIO, AIO, HIO, dont le temps d'exécution n'est pas lié au délai de transfert d'information entre périphérique et mémoire centrale. Les événements significatifs pour le transfert (fin de transfert, erreurs) peuvent être indiqués à l'unité centrale par le biais d'un signal d'interruption qui est commun à tous les coupleurs et que l'unité centrale a la possibilité de masquer.

L'état de fonctionnement de l'unité centrale est conservé dans un mot d'état du programme qui contient, entre autres, un indicateur de mode (maître ou asservi) et un indicateur de type d'adressage (physique ou virtuel). Certaines instructions, en particulier celles d'entrée-sortie ne sont exécutables qu'en mode maître. Le type d'adressage précise si l'instruction en cours fait directement référence à la mémoire centrale - l'adresse est alors un élément de l'espace d'adressage physique - ou si elle indique une adresse virtuelle intermédiaire, élément d'une mémoire virtuelle. Dans ce cas, l'application de la mémoire virtuelle dans l'espace physique est définie par une table conservée dans l'unité centrale et appelée mémoire topographique. En changeant le contenu de cette mémoire topographique, on peut définir autant de mémoires virtuelles que l'on veut ; seul l'espace physique reste unique. Pour simplifier la définition de l'application, l'espace physique est découpé en cases de 512 mots et la mémoire virtuelle en 256 pages, elles aussi de 512 mots ; la mémoire topographique ne comprend ainsi que 256 cellules.

1.32 - *Le moniteur*

Le système Esope gère d'autres objets que ceux introduits par la structure du matériel : nous allons rencontrer des processus, des sémaphores, des usagers, des fichiers et des primitives.

Les processus sont des suites d'exécutions d'instructions - ou suites d'actions - particularisées par le découpage du système. Ils ont en général des progressions indépendantes. Ils se synchronisent entre eux, si besoin est, en agissant par des opérateurs P ou V sur des <u>sémaphores</u> qui leur sont communs.

Les <u>usagers</u> sont des regroupements de processus. A chaque usager **sont** associés une mémoire virtuelle et un <u>processus premier</u> qui est le délégué du moniteur auprès des autres processus de cet usager ; le processus premier arrête la progression des autres processus de l'usager dès qu'il est sollicité. Les processus d'un usager s'exécutent en mode asservi dans leur mémoire virtuelle commune.

Les <u>fichiers</u> sont des suites de pages d'information de 512 mots.

Les <u>primitives</u> du système sont les extensions programmées du code d'opérations de la machine qui sont mises à la disposition des usagers par le biais d'une opération dite "d'appel au superviseur" *(CAL)*. Ce sont par exemple les opérations sur les processus (création, destruction), sur les sémaphores (création, destruction, P, V), sur les fichiers (création, destruction, ouverture, fermeture, catalogage, association, couplage d'une page d'un fichier avec une page de la mémoire virtuelle).

Le <u>moniteur</u> regroupe les primitives du système, un ensemble de processus résidant en mémoire centrale et utilisant l'adressage physique, et l'ensemble des processus premiers de tous les usagers.

2. ANALYSE DE TROIS PANNES

Il paraît important de mentionner que les pannes ici décrites ont été observées dans la phase finale du développement du système : les mécanismes fondamentaux de gestion des processus et d'allocation des ressources fonctionnaient correctement et le système pouvait être utilisé, de façon expérimentale, avec un temps moyen entre pannes de l'ordre de quelques heures. L'expérience semble montrer que les erreurs qui subsistent à cette étape du développement sont celles dont la manifestation est rare et qui ont un long délai de propagation. Une des raisons en est la capacité qu'a un système, au delà d'un certain degré de complexité, de continuer à assurer tout ou partie de ses fonctions en présence d'une erreur. Cette résistance à la dégradation, qui peut être considérée comme une qualité en ce qui concerne l'utilisation du système, contribue en **revanche** à faire disparaître les informations permettant de localiser l'erreur si aucune précaution spéciale n'a été prise pour les conserver.

Le langage utilisé pour la description des algorithmes est inspiré de PASCAL [13].

2.1 - *Une forme imprévue d'interblocage*

La panne que nous présentons ici a eu pour origine une mauvaise programmation des entrées-sorties sur le télétype de l'opérateur.

2.11 - *Explication de l'erreur*

Tout incident dans une primitive du moniteur s'exécutant dans l'espace physique donne lieu à une réaction immédiate : l'impression d'un message sur le télétype du pupitre de la machine, puis l'arrêt du système en attente d'une action de l'opérateur. L'impression du message ne peut pas utiliser les interruptions car elles sont masquées pendant l'exécution d'une telle primitive. On procède alors comme suit :

```
procédure primitive ;                        {programme d'une primitive du système}
begin
masquer les interruptions ;
...
if erreur then
     begin
     bastringue ("erreur système n° j") ; {impression du message d'erreur}
     attente opérateur
     end ;
...
démasquer les interruptions
end ;
```

Si une ligne est en cours d'impression, la procédure *bastringue* en attend la fin ; puis elle envoie l'ordre d'impression du message et attend la fin de cette impression. Un délai anormal d'attente est interprété comme une défaillance du télétype. Dans ce cas, la procédure attire l'attention de l'opérateur avec le dernier moyen qui lui reste : le haut-parleur de la machine.

```
function coupleur libre : boolean ; {coupleur libre ou libéré}
     var n : integer ; cc : boolean ;
     begin
     coupleur libre := false ; n := 0 ;
     repeat
     TIO(cc) ; {test câblé du coupleur. S'il est disponible, cc := true}
     coupleur libre := cc ;
     n := n + 1 ;
     until  (n > limite) ∨ coupleur libre
     {limite correspond au temps maximum d'impression d'une ligne}
     end ;
```

```
procédure siffler ; {utilisation du haut-parleur de la machine}
     repeat forever
          WD (65) ;                          {ordre de sifflement}
```

```
procédure bastringue (message : alfa) ; {impression de message}
     begin
     if ¬ coupleur libre then siffler ;{attente}
     SIO (message) ;                       {ordre câblé d'impression}
     if ¬ coupleur libre then siffler     {attente}
     end ;
```

En dehors des réactions aux incidents, le télétype de l'opérateur sert de communication normale pour la gestion des travaux et des périphériques du centre de calcul. La gestion du télétype est réalisée par un processus *servant* qui utilise le parallélisme entre l'unité centrale et le coupleur.

```
var SIT : semaphore ; {valeur initiale : SIT := 0}
procédure servant ;    {ceci est le programme du processus servant}
     repeat forever
     begin
     ...
     SIO (message) ; {ordre câblé d'impression}
     P(SIT) ;        {attente}
     ...
     end ;
```

interrupt procedure _entrée-sortie_ ; {_cette procédure est appelée par l'inter-_
                                        ruption d'entrée-sortie}

    begin
    AIO ; {_reconnaissance de l'interruption et libération du coupleur_}
    V(SIT)
    end

    Cette solution contient une erreur. En effet, lorsque le servant est
bloqué par _P(SIT)_, un autre processus _p_ reçoit l'unité centrale. Si, avant
l'arrivée de l'interruption d'entrée-sortie, il se produit une erreur dans une
primitive exécutée par _p_, la procédure _bastringue_ est appelée dans d'état :

$$\left\{\begin{array}{l} \text{interruptions masquées} \\ \text{coupleur occupé par le } \textit{servant} \end{array}\right.$$

    On reste indéfiniment dans cet état, car le coupleur ne peut être libéré
par _AIO_ que si les interruptions sont démasquées.
    L'interprétation des opérations câblées en termes de sémaphores met
l'erreur en évidence.
    Par exemple le masquage des interruptions et la prise du coupleur se
traduisent respectivement par des opérations _P_ sur des sémaphores _masque_ et
coupleur de valeur initiale _1_. On a représenté sur la figure 2 le schéma des
divers processus en jeu, en ne conservant que les opérations de synchronisation
entre ces processus :

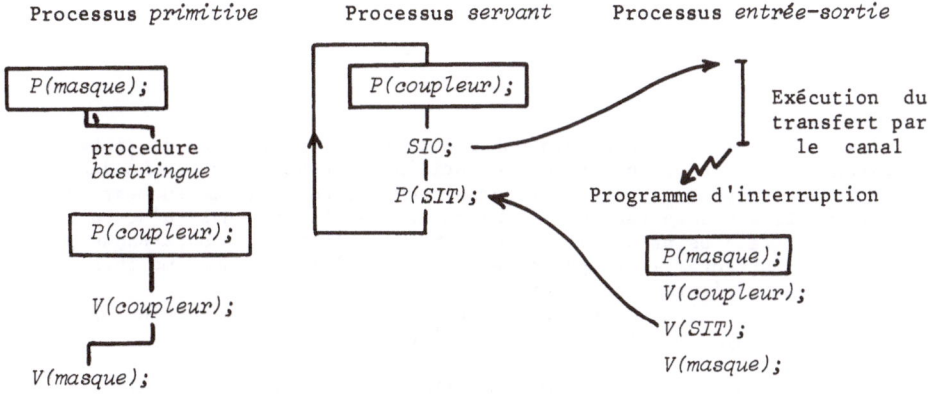

Figure 2. Communication avec le télétype de l'opérateur

N.B. L'ordre _P(masque)_ ; _V(coupleur)_ dans le programme d'interruption est imposé
    par le dispositif câblé qui lance l'exécution de ce programme.

    On retrouve le schéma habituel de l'interblocage, avec ici l'exécution
parallèle des deux séquences :

    a) _P(masque)_ ; _P(coupleur)_ par les procédures _primitive_ et _bastringue_

    b) _P(coupleur)_ ; _P(masque)_ par les procédures _servant_ et _entrée-sortie_.

    La détection de cette erreur est immédiate : ses délais de latence et de
propagation sont nuls.

2.12 - *Correction de l'erreur*

Les corrections de cette erreur sont celles de l'interblocage.

a) *Utilisation des sémaphores dans le même ordre.*

Cette sorte de remède ne convient pas. En effet, imposer la séquence *P(coupleur) ; P(masque)* revient à réserver le télétype avant toute entrée dans une primitive du système, ce qui n'est pas réaliste; et adopter la deuxième solution *P(masque) ; P(coupleur)* empêche l'utilisation des interruptions et du parallélisme par le *servant* qui doit alors être programmé comme l'est *bastringue*.

b) *Réquisition d'une des ressources.*

La réquisition peut porter sur l'une des deux ressources, le masque d'interruption ou le télétype, selon qu'on veut favoriser le processus en cours ou le processus *servant*.

La réquisition du masque d'interruption revient à favoriser le *servant*.

```
procedure primitive ;          {remède possible}
begin
P(masque) ;

...

if erreur then
      begin
      V(masque) ;             {démasque les interruptions}
      bastringue ("erreur système n° j") ;
      P(masque) ;             {rétablit le masquage des interruptions}
      attente opérateur ;
      ...
      end ;
...
V(masque)
end
```

Cette façon de faire a l'inconvénient d'autoriser l'impression de toute une chaîne de messages quand le processus *servant* utilise le chaînage de commandes pour accélérer ses entrées-sorties. Sur notre machine, comme le masque est unique pour tous les matériels d'entrée-sortie, cette méthode libère aussi d'autre processus qui peuvent être plus prioritaires que *servant*. L'action de *bastringue* peut être retardée et l'erreur a le temps de se propager. L'état du système lors de la manifestation de l'erreur est alors perdu.

La solution finalement adoptée est la réquisition du coupleur par la procédure *bastringue* ; cela revient à écrire :

```
procedure bastringue (message : alfa) ; {remède utilisé}
begin
HIO ; {arrêt de l'entrée-sortie en cours et libération du coupleur}
SIO (message) ;
if ¬ coupleur libre then siffler
end ;
```

La réquisition est tellement brutale que même le message en cours d'impression est interrompu.

2.13 - *Commentaires*

a) L'utilisation de deux méthodes distinctes de synchronisation : interruptions et sémaphores a masqué la faute de programmation. Dans l'exemple donné, et plus généralement dans le traitement des entrées-sorties, il n'a pas été possible de se ramener à un mécanisme unique comme dans le reste du système.

b) L'utilisation d'un télétype unique pour les messages à l'opérateur a introduit une liaison imprévue entre deux états indépendants de fonctionnement du système.

2.2 - *Une forme cachée du* goto

2.21 - *Mécanisme de traitement des incidents*

Nous avons décrit en 2.1 le mécanisme permettant au moniteur de réagir à la détection d'une erreur dans un de ses propres processus. Nous considérons maintenant la réaction à un incident survenant dans un processus d'un usager. Le fonctionnement du dispositif de traitement d'incidents a été marqué par une série de pannes que nous allons analyser en détail, car elles nous paraissent illustrer plusieurs erreurs de conception caractéristiques.

Les incidents peuvent apparaître dans un processus d'un usager pendant l'exécution d'une instruction de la machine (en mode asservi) ou d'une primitive. Dans le premier cas, ils sont détectés par le dispositif câblé de déroutement et dans le second, par un contrôle programmé ; dans ces deux cas, l'incident se traduit par l'appel d'une procédure unique de traitement dont l'effet dépend du processus appelant, de l'état final détecté et non du chemin suivi pour arriver à cet état. Cette politique permet d'utiliser une procédure très simple pour le traitement des incidents :

- si l'incident se produit dans le moniteur, l'opérateur en est averti, (cf. 2.1),
- si l'incident apparaît dans un processus d'un usager u, on force le blocage de ce processus derrière un sémaphore *erreur(u)* réservé à cet effet et le processus premier de l'usager u est activé pour corriger l'erreur ou dialoguer avec l'utilisateur conversationnel concerné,
- si l'incident affecte le processus premier lui-même, un indicateur d'erreur est mis en place et ce processus se poursuit : la réaction à l'incident est laissée à sa charge et doit avoir été prévue dans la procédure qu'il exécute.

Ceci se traduit par :

```
procedure traitement incident ;
    begin                        {p est le processus élu}
    if p ∈ moniteur then
        bastringue ("erreur système n° j")
    else {p ∈ usager u}
        begin
        {passage du contrôle au processus premier de l'usager u}
        if p ≠ premier(u) then
            begin
            placer p dans la file du sémaphore erreur(u) ;
            activer processus premier(u)
            end
        else
            begin
            placer indicateur d'erreur ;
            retour            {sortie de primitive ou de déroutement}
            end
        end
    end ;
```

Une description plus détaillée de ce schéma figure dans [6].

Cette méthode de traitement des incidents fut à l'origine de diverses pannes dont la manifestation commune était un blocage progressif des processus des divers usagers du système.

2.22 - Manifestation et explication des erreurs

1) *Première erreur.* Le schéma décrit en 2.21 est trop simple car il ne tient pas compte du chemin suivi par un processus avant l'incident. Cette lacune s'est révélée dans l'utilisation des primitives du système. En raison des problèmes d'accès aux données, ces primitives ont deux formes, une forme simple et une complexe. Une primitive simple n'utilise que des données résidentes et s'exécute donc en adressage physique. Une primitive complexe utilise en outre des données du moniteur accessibles dans la mémoire virtuelle de l'usager appelant ; son exécution comporte l'appel d'une procédure réentrante exécutable en mode asservi dans la mémoire virtuelle et comprend des sections critiques correspondant à l'accès en exclusion mutuelle aux données du moniteur. Une primitive complexe peut appeler une ou plusieurs primitives simples, mais l'inverse n'est pas possible.

L'appel de la procédure *traitement incident* peut alors se produire à l'issue de l'un des chemins suivants (figure 3) :

1 : déroutement dans un processus d'un usager
2 : incident dans une primitive simple appelée par l'usager
3 : incident dans une primitive complexe appelée par l'usager
4 : incident dans une primitive simple appelée par une primitive complexe
5 : déroutement dans une primitive complexe.

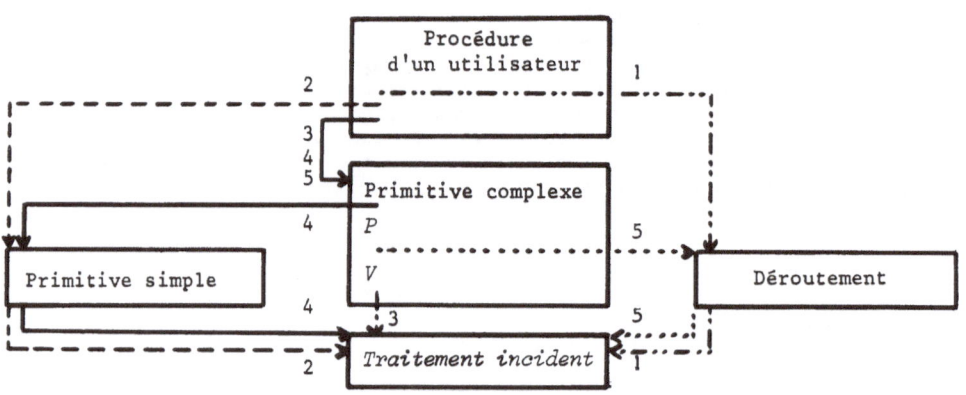

Figure 3. Chemins menant à la procédure *Traitement incident*

L'ignorance du chemin suivi devient catastrophique lorsque l'incident se produit dans une primitive complexe pendant qu'elle exécute une section critique. En effet, le processus de l'usager est alors bloqué dans cette section critique et le processus premier activé ne peut pas avoir accès aux données en exclusion mutuelle. Si cette exclusion concerne seulement les processus de l'usager, la panne se limite à celui-ci ; mais,si les données sont en exclusion mutuelle pour tous les usagers, la panne touche l'ensemble du système.

Une autre panne, due au mauvais rétablissement du mot d'état du programme s'est produite à l'issue d'un incident dans une primitive complexe. Supposons que le processus premier modifie l'adresse de l'instruction courante du processus bloqué par *traitement incident,* puis le réactive par l'exécution de la primitive *V(erreur(u)).* Ces opérations sont licites et interviennent fréquemment pour la mise au point de programmes. Elles peuvent conduire à réactiver le processus en dehors de la primitive complexe avec les pouvoirs qu'il a obtenus pour l'exécution de celle-ci seulement,et à lui permettre par exemple de modifier les données du moniteur en exécutant le programme d'un utilisateur quelconque.

2) *Problème posé par le parallélisme des processus d'un usager.* Pendant le déroulement de sa procédure réentrante, exécutable dans la mémoire virtuelle, la primitive complexe est interruptible. Puisque tous les processus d'un usager partagent la même mémoire virtuelle, il n'y a pas de protection entre eux à ce niveau : dès qu'un processus exécute une primitive complexe, les autres processus actifs de l'usager ont également accès aux données du moniteur. Cette situation doit être proscrite. En l'absence d'un mécanisme de protection permettant d'attacher à chaque processus des droits d'accès distincts à la mémoire virtuelle, ce problème est résolu de façon brutale en interdisant toute exécution parallèle de processus de l'usager appelant u pendant la phase interruptible d'une primitive complexe. L'arrêt du parallélisme est imposé en plaçant derrière un sémaphore *arrêt(u)* tous les processus actifs de l'usager u à l'exception du processus appelant lui-même. A la fin de la partie interruptible, tous les processus bloqués derrière *arrêt(u)* sont réactivés.

Les procédures suivantes sont utilisées :

procedure arrêt du parallélisme (u : usager) ;
    begin   {u est l'usager appelant}
    placer tous les processus actifs de u, à l'exception du processus appelant
    dans la file du sémaphore arrêt (u) ;
    end ;

procedure reprise du parallélisme (u : usager);
    begin   {u est l'usager appelant}
    activer tous les processus
    bloqués derrière arrêt(u) ;
    end ;

La première erreur constatée a également eu des répercussions sur ce schéma. En effet lorsque la phase interruptible d'une primitive complexe contient un appel à une primitive simple, un incident dans cette dernière primitive provoque l'appel de la procédure *traitement incident* et l'activation du processus premier (chemin numéro 4 de la figure 3). Mais les autres processus de l'usager appelant, u, restent bloqués derrière *arrêt(u)* et ne seront jamais réactivés. La même situation se produit en cas de déroutement dans la phase interruptible d'une primitive complexe. Cette panne n'affecte en général que les processus d'un seul usager. Mais il peut arriver qu'une partie virtuelle de primitive comporte une section critique globale assurant la protection de données communes (telles que les catalogues de fichiers) entre processus d'usagers différents. Si l'incident se produit dans une telle section critique, la panne qui en résulte atteint l'ensemble du système.

3) *Corrections de la première erreur.* Pour pallier les effets de cette forme peu apparente du *goto* (appel sans retour de la procédure *traitement incident*), les modifications suivantes furent apportées pour rétablir des conditions normales de sortie de primitive :
    a) - énumération des causes potentielles d'incident (incident dans un appel simple, déroutement pour page non couplée, adresse inexistante...) à l'intérieur d'une section critique globale, et élimination de ces causes par un contrôle des paramètres avant l'entrée en section critique.

    b) - inclusion, dans la procédure *traitement incident,* d'un appel de *reprise du parallélisme.* Cette décision était justifiée par le raisonnement suivant : si l'appel de *traitement incident* a lieu dans une section où le parallélisme est arrêté, on rétablit la situation antérieure à l'appel complexe de la primitive ; sinon, on exécute une action vide.

4) *Seconde erreur*. La procédure *traitement incident* a deux réactions selon que le processus fautif est ou non un processus premier. Les modifications apportées à cette procédure s'appliquaient indifféremment aux deux cas. Ceci n'a pas de conséquences tant que le processus premier d'un usager est en exclusion mutuelle avec les autres processus de l'usager. Si cette assertion est vérifiée, on réalise à la fois la protection des données du moniteur et l'exclusion mutuelle à ces données. A cause de cette exclusion mutuelle, l'arrêt et la reprise du parallélisme sont des actions vides dans un processus premier. Lorsque fut réalisé le traitement des entrées-sorties, on voulut mettre en jeu plusieurs processus parallèles ayant accès aux catalogues du système. On leur donna alors le même statut qu'un processus premier. Il en résulta l'erreur suivante dans le cas des deux processus *imp1* et *imp2* gérant les deux imprimantes de l'installation : le processus *imp1* bloque *imp2* par *arrêt du parallélisme* à l'entrée d'une primitive complexe, et subit un incident dans la partie virtuelle de cette primitive. Le traitement de l'incident libère *imp2*, qui peut donc à son tour s'engager dans la partie virtuelle dont *imp1* n'est pas sorti, puisque *traitement incident* le considère comme un processus premier (figure 4).

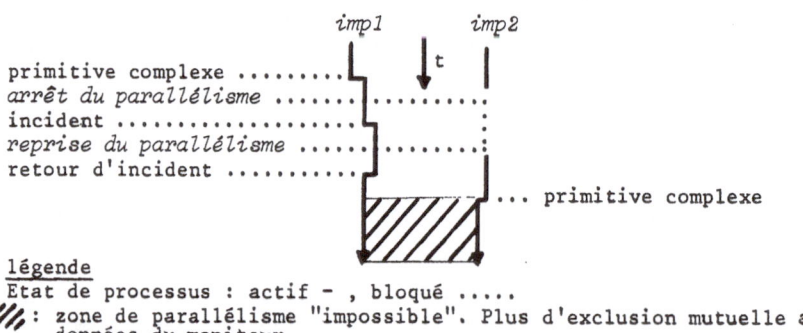

légende
Etat de processus : actif - , bloqué .....
%%% : zone de parallélisme "impossible". Plus d'exclusion mutuelle aux données du moniteur.

Figure 4. Violation d'une assertion après une modification.

Cette erreur ne peut se manifester que si *imp1* et *imp2* exécutent chacun une primitive complexe à des instants très voisins. La probabilité de cet événement étant très faible, l'erreur passa longtemps inaperçue.

On pourrait ici objecter que l'erreur initiale consiste à laisser un incident se produire dans un processus du moniteur tel que *imp1*. L'incident consistait en fait en une tentative d'ouverture d'un fichier déjà ouvert, ce qui, dans le cas particulier, provoquait le passage par *traitement incident* et la reprise du parallélisme alors que cette tentative ne devait pas être considérée, ici, comme une action interdite.

5) *Troisième erreur*. L'élimination des erreurs dans les primitives fut encore compliquée par la circonstance suivante : une analyse superficielle ayant semblé montrer que les sémaphores *arrêt* et *erreur* étaient, pour un même usager, utilisés dans des cas disjoints, il fut décidé, pour des raisons d'économie, de n'utiliser qu'un sémaphore par usager pour ces deux fonctions. Il s'ensuivit une série de pannes dont l'explication, qui fut longue à obtenir, est la suivante :

a) - un incident survient au cours de l'exécution d'un processus q de l'usager u. Le processus q est donc placé derrière *erreur(u)*.

b) - le processus premier de l'usager u est activé. Il exécute un programme de mise au point pour déterminer la cause de l'incident. Ce programme comprend en particulier l'appel d'une primitive complexe.

c) - à la sortie de la partie virtuelle de cette primitive complexe, tous les processus bloqués derrière *erreur(u)* sont activés, et en particulier le processus q.

d) - le processus premier étant toujours actif, une assertion du système est maintenant violée, à savoir l'exclusion mutuelle entre le processus premier et les autres processus d'un usager : il y a donc une erreur latente.

e) - l'erreur a ici encore une probabilité faible de se manifester : en effet, la conséquence de l'incident initial est souvent la destruction du processus q par le processus premier. Mais si q exécute une primitive complexe, il peut maintenant y provoquer un incident non prévu (puisque le système est dans un état "impossible"). Si cet incident survient dans une section critique globale, il y a panne du système.

2.23 - *Critique du mécanisme*

La description des algorithmes a été idéalisée pour rendre plus claire l'explication des pannes ; elle ne rend compte qu'imparfaitement de la complexité des mécanismes mis en jeu et de la difficulté de détection de ces pannes. L'analyse précédente a néanmoins permis de dégager les dangers potentiels suivants.

1) - *Changement intempestif d'environnement.*

Le terme d'environnement est pris ici dans le sens suivant : ensemble des objets (variables, procédures, ...) accessibles à un processus en un point donné de son exécution et des droits spécifiant cet accès. Dans le cas simple d'un processus unique constitué par l'exécution d'un programme ALGOL (par exemple), l'environnement est l'ensemble des objets désignés par les identificateurs connus à une étape donnée de l'exécution. L'environnement est donc modifié à chaque entrée ou sortie d'un bloc ou d'une procédure. La sortie peut se faire soit par la voie normale (fin du bloc ou de la procédure) soit par un *goto*. Les inconvénients de cette dernière construction dans les programmes destinés à une exécution séquentielle ont été souvent dénoncés depuis [2]. Mais dans un système, où coexistent des processus parallèles, la notion de variable accessible doit être remplacée par celle plus large de vecteur d'état, et les mécanismes de changement d'environnement sont nombreux. Même si les interruptions sont traduites, selon la suggestion de [12], par des opérations sur des sémaphores et sont donc intégrées dans un schéma plus général de gestion des processus, il reste que les mécanismes tels que l'appel au superviseur, les instructions de chargement ou de modification explicite du "mot d'état de programme" (représentation câblée d'une partie de l'environnement), et enfin les déroutements, ont des effets apparentés à ceux d'un *goto* et doivent donc être manipulés avec la même prudence. Ces mécanismes sont d'autant plus dangereux qu'ils prennent souvent,pour le programmeur,la forme rassurante d'un appel de procédure ou, dans le cas du déroutement, sont totalement invisibles. Il semble qu'une bonne précaution consisterait, pour le programmeur de systèmes, à se limiter autant que possible, pour toute construction de ce type, à des schémas réellement équivalents à un appel de procédure, c'est-à-dire comportant la sauvegarde et la restauration de l'environnement initial.

2) - *Traitement des incidents.*

Il est significatif que toutes les pannes analysées en 2.22 aient eu pour origine le traitement d'un incident. Cette opération provoque toujours un changement d'environnement ; mais, ici, on ne peut rétablir sans précautions l'environnement antérieur à l'incident, puisque, par définition, l'exécution du processus fautif ne peut s'y poursuivre.

On peut conclure cette analyse en disant que le schéma du 2.21 souffre de deux fautes de conception : une centralisation excessive, due à une sous-estimation des problèmes de changement d'environnement, et une analyse insuffisante des causes d'incidents. La démarche consistant à éliminer par énumération les causes d'incidents s'est révélée inadéquate (cas de l'erreur "impossible"). Il aurait mieux valu admettre qu'un incident se produise et y réagir correctement. Enfin, l'établissement de liaisons parasites entre processus indépendants (par l'arrêt du parallélisme et la confusion *arrêt-erreur*) a encore aggravé la situation.

2.3 - *Une défaillance du matériel*

La panne que nous présentons maintenant provient d'une défaillance d'un mécanisme câblé de protection. L'erreur fut d'autant plus difficile à cerner qu'elle fut la première, et la seule, concernant ce matériel auquel nous accordions jusque là une confiance absolue - ce qui fut notre faute de conception - et qu'elle se propageait de façon aléatoire sur l'ensemble des usagers du système.

2.31 - *Fonctionnement normal du système en page à la demande*

Pour éviter la surcharge du système, les usagers qui demandent de la mémoire sont répartis en deux classes : les usagers courants, dont les demandes sont satisfaites dans la limite des cases disponibles et les usagers prêts, auxquels aucune case n'est allouée.

Les usagers prêts sont admis à l'état courant suivant le nombre de cases disponibles et les prévisions de demandes. Pour garantir à l'ensemble des usagers un service suffisant, aucun usager ne peut rester à l'état courant pendant plus d'un délai fixe, appelé temps de résidence ; au bout de ce délai, il repasse à l'état prêt et toutes les cases qu'il possède sont restituées à la réserve commune.

Les cases de mémoire sont allouées les unes après les autres aux usagers courants au fur et à mesure des accès de ces usagers à de nouvelles pages virtuelles : c'est la méthode dite de la page à la demande. Pendant le transfert en mémoire d'une nouvelle page demandée par un usager, l'unité centrale lui est retirée au profit d'un autre usager et il passe dans l'état suspendu. A l'arrivée de la page, l'usager est de nouveau candidat à l'emploi de l'unité centrale et devient éligible ; l'unité centrale est successivement allouée aux usagers éligibles pour un temps au plus égal à un quantum fixé. L'usager qui possède, à un instant donné, l'unité centrale est dit élu.

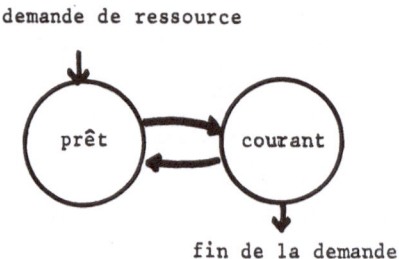

a) service de l'allocateur

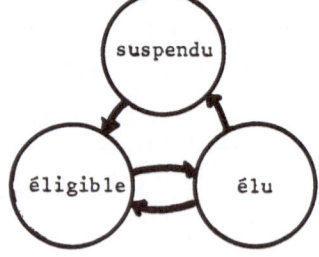

b) détail de l'état courant

Figure 5. Etats d'un usager pour l'allocateur de ressource

Le choix de la case de mémoire centrale à associer à une page virtuelle demandée et l'application pages-cases sont réalisés par le moniteur. Les usagers sont protégés les uns des autres car ils n'ont pas directement accès aux cases.

La mémoire virtuelle d'un usager u est représentée dans le moniteur par une Table de Pages Virtuelles $TPV(u,V)$ qui contient, pour chaque page V, le numéro $CASE(V)$ de la case qui lui est associée et un bit $I(V)$ d'interdiction d'accès à cette case (0 : accès autorisé, 1 : accès interdit). Lorsque l'usager reçoit l'unité centrale, le contenu de sa TPV est recopié dans la mémoire topographique pour être utilisé par le mécanisme câblé qui assure, lors de chaque référence à la mémoire, le contrôle d'accès et la substitution d'une case à une page. Une page donnée peut se trouver ainsi dans n'importe quelle case. Pour indiquer l'absence d'une page virtuelle V en mémoire centrale, il suffit d'y interdire l'accès $(I(V) = 1)$. Toute référence à cette page cause alors un déroutement qui est interprété par le moniteur comme un signal de demande de case.

Soit par exemple l'instruction MTW,A B ; son effet peut se décrire par :

type accroissement = -8..7 ;
entier = $-2^{31}..(2^{31}-1)$;
procedure MTW(A : accroissement ; B : entier) ;
begin B := B+A _end_ ;

Si l'accès à la page qui contient B est interdit, l'instruction n'est pas exécutée (c'est-à-dire que ni B, ni le compteur ordinal de la machine ne sont modifiés) et il se produit un déroutement pour défaut de case.

2.32 - _Description de la défaillance_

A la suite de travaux sur le matériel de l'IRIA pour modifier la configuration de l'installation, l'opération MTW, et elle seule, fut le siège d'une défaillance du système de déroutement qui se manifestait de la manière suivante (fig. 6) : soit V la page virtuelle qui contient le mot d'adresse B . Si $I(V)=1$ (l'accès à V est interdit), il se produit bien un déroutement pour défaut de case et le compteur ordinal ne progresse pas (ce qui correspond au fonctionnement normal), mais l'opération est néanmoins exécutée dans la case qui se trouve à cet instant associée à V dans la mémoire topographique.

Deux cas peuvent alors se présenter :

1) Si la page V est en mémoire centrale, l'accès y est autorisé $(I(V)=0)$, il n'y a pas de déroutement, et l'instruction MTW fonctionne correctement.

2) Si la page V est absente de la mémoire, l'accès y est interdit $(I(V)=1)$. La valeur de $CASE(V)$ est le numéro d'une certaine case Q car on n'a pas le moyen de représenter dans la mémoire topographique la valeur indéterminée (on dispose de 256 valeurs pour 256 cases). C'est donc cette case Q qui est modifiée (figure 6a). Après le déroutement, une case P est allouée à l'usager, la page V y est chargée $(CASE(V)=P, I(P)=0)$ et l'exécution de MTW modifie normalement la case P lorsque l'usager redevient élu (figure 6b).

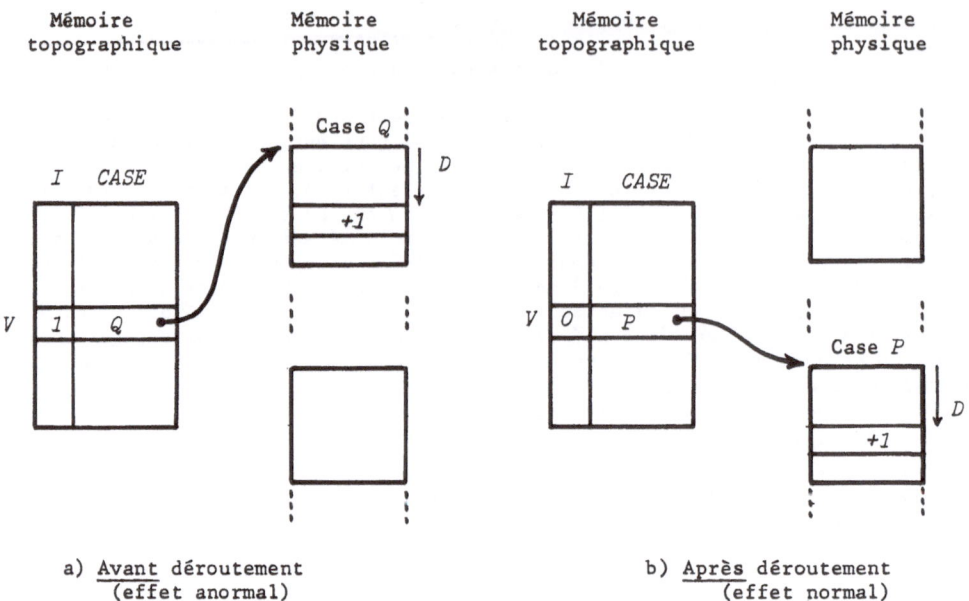

Mémoire topographique   Mémoire physique   Mémoire topographique   Mémoire physique

a) Avant déroutement
   (effet anormal)

b) Après déroutement
   (effet normal)

Figure 6. Fonctionnement défaillant de l'instruction $MTW,1\ B$ $B = 512 * V + D$

La case Q qui a été modifiée par erreur contient une page quelconque, et l'erreur peut donc se produire chez un usager autre que l'usager élu. Cette erreur restera latente tant que cet usager n'utilisera pas le mot modifié, s'il le fait jamais. La manifestation de l'erreur peut donc varier d'une exécution à une autre car elle dépend du fonctionnement de l'allocateur de mémoire centrale, donc du nombre et de l'activité des usagers à tout instant depuis le démarrage du système. La défaillance se manifestait ainsi tout à fait comme une erreur aléatoire qui resta longtemps invisible du fait de la robustesse du système.

2.33 – *Détection de la défaillance*

Le fonctionnement de l'allocateur dans un de ses cas particuliers a permis de trouver la source de l'erreur. Toutes les cases d'un usager qui sort de l'état courant reçoivent une interdiction d'accès. S'il a encore besoin de l'unité centrale, l'usager passe à l'état prêt et fait la queue pour repasser à l'état courant. S'il y revient assez vite, certaines cases contiennent encore des pages de sa mémoire virtuelle qui n'ont pas été vidées sur disque. L'allocateur en garde trace et au moment de la demande de case pour une telle page, il récupère la case déjà prête. Cette récupération devient systématique quand le système n'a qu'un seul utilisateur dont le programme tient entièrement dans les cases disponibles. Le cycle courant-prêt est maintenu, même dans ce cas, car il permet d'entretenir la liste des dernières pages demandées par l'usager.

Lorsqu'il y a récupération, l'erreur devient franche et se manifeste toujours chez l'usager élu, où $MTW,A\ B$ réalise $B := B + 2A$ au lieu de $B := B + A$. En effet, $B := B + A$ est réalisé au moment du déroutement, puis à nouveau après la récupération (la case P est identique à la case Q dans le schéma de la figure 6). C'est ainsi que la défaillance a été révélée par un programme, mis au point avant la modification de l'installation (le chargeur) ; ce programme met initialement à zéro une variable C et exécute N fois $MTW,1\ C$; ces N opérations sont réparties sur toute l'exécution qui est assez longue pour qu'il y ait récupération. Le programme se terminait alors en imprimant une valeur de C supérieure à N connu par ailleurs

2.34 - *Correction de l'erreur et commentaire*

Cette panne n'a pris une telle ampleur que parce que nous avons fait la faute de conception d'accorder une trop grande confiance au mécanisme de protection et de croire qu'il suffisait de mettre à 1 le bit d'interdiction d'accès pour indiquer l'absence d'une page en mémoire. Il faut aussi introduire une valeur de case indéterminée. Bien que la machine ne contienne pas cette valeur, il est possible de simuler partiellement son effet en utilisant l'adresse d'une case protégée en écriture par un système de clé et de verrous. La défectuosité du déroutement pour défaut de case est alors immédiatement détectée si le contrôle par clé et verrous fonctionne correctement.

3. CONCLUSION : ESSAI DE CLASSIFICATION DES ERREURS DANS LES SYSTEMES

Nous cherchons essentiellement ici à mettre en évidence quelques types d'erreurs caractéristiques des systèmes d'exploitation. Ce recensement, qui ne prétend pas être complet, laisse de côté le domaine plus vaste des erreurs de programmation, pour lequel quelques éléments sont donnés dans [11]. Une telle analyse permet de distinguer dans les systèmes deux types d'erreurs : les erreurs de synchronisation et les erreurs d'environnement.

3.1 - *Erreurs de synchronisation*

1) - *Erreurs d'exclusion mutuelle*

L'exclusion mutuelle est une contrainte qui se présente dès qu'il y a coexistence de processus parallèles. Elle peut donner lieu à plusieurs sortes d'erreurs
- sections critiques imbriquées : si l'ordre d'imbrication n'est pas toujours le même, il y a risque d'interblocage. Ce risque est d'autant moins apparent que les mécanismes utilisés dans un même système pour réaliser l'exclusion mutuelle sont nombreux (masquage d'interruptions, sémaphores,...)

- sorties multiples de section critique : il faut bien prendre garde de lever l'exclusion mutuelle à chaque point de sortie. Le risque d'erreur est augmenté si la multiplicité des points de sortie est peu apparente (appels de procédure, déroutements,... à l'intérieur d'une section critique).

D'une façon générale, l'indication qu'un processus se trouve dans une section critique doit être considérée comme une partie de son environnement, avec les conséquences que cela implique (sauvegarde, possibilité de contrôle,...).

2) - *Erreurs de commutativité*

Un mécanisme de synchronisation n'est pas commutatif lorsque sa validité dépend d'une hypothèse (explicite ou non) sur les vitesses relatives des divers processus en jeu. La validité d'un tel schéma est en général beaucoup plus difficile à établir que celle d'un schéma commutatif, et sa mise en oeuvre est plus délicate. Les mécanismes du type "événement non mémorisé" ne sont pas commutatifs et sont donc des sources potentielles d'erreurs ; ils doivent être, dans la mesure du possible, éliminés ou remplacés par des mécanismes commutatifs. C'est en ce sens, en particulier, que la traduction des interruptions par des opérations V sur des sémaphores [12] permet de mieux maîtriser leur utilisation. Dans l'exemple du 2.2, la procédure *reprise du parallélisme* rendait non commutatif le mécanisme de synchronisation.

3.2 - *Erreurs d'environnement*

Parmi les aspects d'un processus qui font directement intervenir son environnement, deux sont particulièrement sujets aux erreurs : le traitement des incidents et l'accès à l'information.

1) - *Erreurs liées au traitement des incidents*

La spécification du traitement des incidents au cours de l'exécution d'un processus comporte l'analyse des cas d'incidents et la définition de la réaction aux incidents. Si l'analyse laisse échapper les incidents d'un certain type, la détection d'un tel incident risque de n'avoir lieu qu'après une propagation plus ou moins longue et sa cause initiale ne sera pas toujours facile à rétablir.

D'un point de vue logique, il semble préférable de traiter un incident dans l'environnement même où il s'est produit. Il y a à cela deux raisons :

a) - c'est dans cet environnement que l'on dispose des informations nécessaires,

b) - un changement d'environnement sans retour risque d'avoir des conséquences catastrophiques.

C'est une solution de ce type qui est proposée dans [8] dans l'hypothèse d'une structure en "niveaux" : tout incident est détecté par un dispositif analogue au déroutement, et retransmis au niveau qui a déclenché ce déroutement (qui peut lui-même le renvoyer à un niveau supérieur). Dans tous les cas, on doit tenir compte du fait que le traitement d'un incident peut donner temporairement au processus fautif un pouvoir plus étendu que son pouvoir initial. On doit aussi veiller à ce qu'un traitement d'incident ne laisse pas le système dans un état "impossible", c'est-à-dire non prévu par les spécifications et pouvant donc lui-même engendrer de nouvelles erreurs. Toutes ces considérations mettent en évidence l'importance de l'analyse des incidents et donc la nécessité de ne pas limiter les spécifications aux cas de fonctionnement "normal".

2) - *Erreurs liées à l'accès à l'information*

Une faute fréquente consiste à laisser un processus accéder à des informations qui devraient lui être inaccessibles, ou bien à lui donner accès à des informations autorisées, mais avec un mode d'accès interdit. L'erreur peut provenir soit d'une mauvaise spécification de l'environnement soit d'un mauvais contrôle à l'exécution. Il nous paraît utile d'insister ici sur deux points souvent négligés :

a) - Lorsqu'un objet a une durée de vie plus brève que celle des processus qui y ont accès, il faut s'assurer qu'il devient effectivement inaccessible à la fin de sa durée de vie. Si le mécanisme d'adressage ne permet pas d'interdire l'accès à des emplacements ayant contenu un objet disparu, il faut donner au contenu de ces emplacements un état "neutre". Cette précaution est souvent négligée en vertu de raisonnements fondés sur l'"impossibilité" de certains états du système ; de tels raisonnements peuvent être mis en défaut à la suite d'un incident, ou simplement d'une modification des programmes.

b) - pour des raisons d'efficacité et de sécurité, l'information contenue dans un système présente en général une grande redondance. C'est ainsi que l'accès à un même objet peut se faire par différentes voies. On a intérêt, dans ce cas, à prévoir une voie d'accès standard ; si on ne le fait pas, on doit prouver dans tous les cas (y compris les cas d'incident) l'équivalence des diverses voies d'accès et s'assurer que cette équivalence est respectée après toute modification du système.

Remerciements. Les auteurs tiennent à remercier les autres membres de l'équipe qui a conçu et réalisé le système Esope : C. BETOURNE, J. FERRIE et J. MOSSIERE, pour leur importante contribution au travail ici présenté.

REFERENCES

[1] - BETOURNE C., BOULENGER J., FERRIE J., KAISER C., KRAKOWIAK S., MOSSIERE J.
Le système ESOPE, *Congrès AFCET*, Paris (1970).

[2] - DIJKSTRA E.W.
Goto statements considered harmful, letter to the Editor,
CACM 11,3 (1968)

[3] - FLOYD R.W.
Assigning meanings to programs,
Proc. Symp. Appl. Math.,Amer. Math. Soc., Vol.19 (1967)

[4] - HENDERSON P., SNOWDON R.,
An experiment in structured programming, *BIT* 12, 1 (1972)

[5] - HOARE C.A.R.
Towards a theory of parallel programming, in *Operating Systems Techniques*, (Hoare & Perrott, editors), Academic Press (1972)

[6] - KAISER C.
Conception et réalisation de systèmes à accès multiples : gestion du parallélisme.
Thèse d'Etat, Paris (1973)

[7] - NEEDHAM R.M.
Handling difficult faults in operating systems,
Third ACM Symposium on Operating Systems Principles, Stanford (1971)

[8] - PARNAS D. L.
Response to detected errors in well-structured programs,
Carnegie-Mellon University (1972)

[9] - PARNAS D. L.
A technique for software module specification with examples,
CACM 15,5 (1972)

[10] - PYLE I.C., Mc LATCHIE R.C.F., GRANDAGE B.
A second-order bug with delayed effect,
Software-Practice & Experience 1,3 (1972)

[11] - SCHWARTZ J.T.
An overview of bugs, in *Debugging techniques in large systems*
(R. Rustin, editor), *Prentice-Hall* (1971)

[12] - WIRTH N.
On multiprogramming, machine coding, and computer organization,
CACM 12,9 (1969)

[13] - WIRTH N.
Systematic programming, an introduction,
Prentice Hall (1973)

[14] - WULF W., SHAW M.
Global variables considered harmful,
ACM SIGPLAN Notices (feb. 1973)

AN OPEN OPERATING SYSTEM FOR A
SINGLE-USER MACHINE

B.W. Lampson
Xerox Palo Alto Research Center, U.S.A.

———

Abstract

The file system, memory management and program linking facilities of a single-user operating system are described. The main points of interest are the openness of the system, which establishes no sharp boundary between itself and the user's programs, and the techniques used to make the system robust.

1. Introduction

In the last few years a certain way of thinking about operating systems has come to be widely accepted. According to this view, the function of an operating system is to provide a kind of womb (or, if you like, a virtual machine) within which the user or his program can live and develop, safely insulated from the harsh realities of the outside world [2, 5, 10]. The author, in fact, was an early advocate of such "closed" systems [9]. They have a number of attractive features:

when, as is often the case, the hardware is too dreadful for ordinary mortals to look upon, it is a kindness, if not a necessity, to conceal it;

useful and popular facilities can be made available in a uniform manner, with the name binding and storage allocation required to implement them kept out of the way;

the system can protect itself from the users without having to make any assumptions about what they do (aside from those implicit in the definition of the virtual machine);

a more robust facility can perhaps be provided if all of the underlying structure is concealed.

On the other hand, a good deal may be lost by putting too much distance between the user and the hardware [4], especially if he needs to deal with unconventional input-output devices. Furthermore, a lot of flexibility is given up by the flat, all-or-nothing style of these systems, and it is extremely difficult for a user to extend or modify the system because of the sharp line which is drawn between the system and the user.

In this paper we explore a different, more "open" approach: the system is thought of as offering a variety of facilities, any of which the user may reject, accept, modify or extend. In many cases a facility may become a component out of which other facilities are built up: for example, files are built out of disk pages. When this happens, we try as far as possible to make the small components accessible to the user as well as the large ones. The success of such a design depends on the extent to which we can exploit the flexibility of the small components without destroying the larger ones. In particular, we must pay a great deal of attention to the robustness of the system, i.e. recovery from crashes and resistance to misuse.

In a multi-user system, of course, there must be compulsory protection mechanisms which ensure equitable and safe sharing of the hardware resources, and this consideration sets limits to the openness which can be achieved. Within these limits, however, much can be done, and indeed the facilities discussed below can be provided in a protected way without any great changes, although this paper avoids an explicit analysis of the problem by confining itself to a single-user system.

To describe an entire system in this way would be a substantial undertaking. We will confine ourselves here to the disk file system, and the storage allocation and program management facilities.

2. Background

The operating system from which the examples in this paper are drawn was written for a small computer which has a 16 bit processor, 48k or 64k words of 800 ns memory, and a moving-head disk drive which can store 2.5 megabytes on a removable pack and can transfer 64k words in about one second. The processor executes an instruction set similar to that of the Data General Nova, except that there are special instructions to support procedure calls and returns.

The system is written entirely in Bcpl [11], and in fact this language is considered to be the standard way of programming the machine. The compiler generates ordinary machine instructions, and uses no runtime support routines except for a storage allocator which is invoked when the hardware procedure call has exhausted its supply of procedure activation frames.

Only one user at a time is supported, and peripheral equipment other than the disk is infrequently used, so the current version of the system has only two processes, one of which puts keyboard input characters into a buffer, while the other does all the interesting work. The keyboard process is interrupt driven and has no critical sections, so there are no synchronization primitives and no scheduler. As a result, the system does not control processor allocation, and in fact gets control only when some system facility is called by a user program.

The system does control storage allocation to some extent, both in main memory and on the disk, in order to make it possible for the user's programs to coexist and to call each other. Some care has been taken, however, to make this control as inoffensive as possible, by providing the user with subsets of each storage device which have properties very similar to those of the entire device.

Thus the system can reasonably be viewed as a collection of procedures which implement various potentially useful abstract objects. There is no significant difference between these system procedures and a set of procedures which the user might write to implement his own abstract objects.

There are four main kinds of abstract object: input-output streams, files, program modules and storage beads. All of these objects are implemented in such a way that they can be values of ordinary variables; since Bcpl is a typeless language this means that each object can be represented by a 16 bit machine word. In many cases, of course, this word will be a pointer to something bigger.

The streams are copied wholesale from Stoy and Strachey's OS6 system [13], as are many aspects of the file system. We give a summary description here for completeness. A stream is an object which can produce or consume items, which can be arbitrary Bcpl objects: bytes, words, vectors, other streams etc. There is a standard set of operations defined on every stream:

Get an item from the stream;
Put an item into the stream (normally only one of these is defined);
Reset;
Test for end of input;

and a few others. These operations are invoked by ordinary Bcpl procedure calls.

A stream is thus something like a Simula class [6]. It differs from a class in that the procedures which implement the operations are not the same for all streams, and indeed can change from time to time, even for a particular stream. A stream is represented by a record (actually a Bcpl vector) whose first few components contain procedures which provide that stream's implementation of the standard operations. The rest of the record holds state information, which may vary from stream to stream.

3. Pages and files

The system organizes long-term storage (on disk) into *files*, each of which is a sequence of fixed-size *pages*; every page is represented by a single disk sector. Although a file is sufficient unto itself, one normally wants to be able to attach a string name to it, and for this purpose an auxiliary *directory* facility is provided. Since the integrity of long-term storage is of paramount importance to the user, a *rebuilding* procedure is provided to reconstruct the state of the file system from whatever fragmented state it may have fallen into. The requirements of this procedure govern much of the system design. The remainder of this section expands on the outline just given.

3.1 *Pages*

The simplest object which can be used for long-term storage is a page. It consists of:
    an *address* - one word which uniquely specifies a physical disk location (H);
    a *label*, which consists of:
        F: a file identifier - two words (A);
        V: a version number - one word (A);
        PN: a page number - one word (A);
        NL: a next link - one word (H);
        PL: a previous link - one word(H);
    a *value* - 256 data words (A).

The information which makes up a page is of two kinds, *absolutes* (A) and *hints* (H). The page is completely defined by the absolutes. The hints, therefore, are present solely to improve the efficiency of the implementation. Whenever a hint is used, it is checked against some absolute to confirm its continued validity. Furthermore, there is a recovery operation which reconstructs all the hints from the absolutes.

Thus a page has a unique *absolute name*, which is the file identifier, version number and page number (represented by (FV,n), where n is the page number and FV is the file identifier and version), and it has a *hint name*, which is the address. The *full name* of a page is the pair (absolute name, hint name). The links of the page (FV,n) are the addresses of the pages whose absolute names are (FV,n-1) and (FV,n+1), or NIL if no such pages exist. The basic operations on a page are to read and write the data, and to read the links, given the full name. Note that it is easy to go from the full name of a p⁼qe to the full names of the next and previous pages.

3.2 *Files*

A file is a set of pages with absolute names (FV,0),(FV,1),...,FV,n). The name of page (FV,0) is also the name of the file. The basic operations on files are
    create a new, empty file,
    add a page to the end of a file,
    delete a page from the end,
    delete the entire file.

Thus, if page (FV,n) exists, pages (FV,i) exist for all i between 0 and n. Hence, if the address of one page of a file is known, every page can be accessed by following the links.

3.3 *Representation of pages*

The physical representation of a page on the disc is called a *sector*, and consists of three parts:
    a *header*, which contains the disk pack number and the disk address;
    a label, which contains the 6 words specified above;
    a value, which contains the 256 data words.

A single disk operation can perform read, check or write actions independently on each of these parts, with the restriction that once a write is begun, it must continue through the rest of the sector. A check action compares data on the disk with corresponding data taken from memory, word by word, and aborts the entire operation if they don't match. If a memory word is 0, however, it is replaced by the corresponding disk word, so that a check action is a simple kind of pattern match.

The system uses these facilities to make the disk a rather robust storage medium. Disk pages are always accessed by their full names. The label of a sector is always checked before it is written, and is only written on two occasions:

    when the page is freed - its full name must be given, and the check is that the
        label is the right one. Then zeros are written into label and value;

    the first time the page is written after it has been allocated - the check is that
        the page is free. Then the proper label for the page is written.

This scheme costs a disk revolution each time a page is allocated or freed, but it makes accidental overwriting of a page quite unlikely. On any other write the label is checked, at no cost in time. The reason for distinguishing the check action from a read is to permit the operation to be aborted before anything is written, without taking an extra revolution. The label is also checked on reads, of course. These checks ensure that the hints (addresses) used to access disk pages actually lead to the page specified by the absolute part of the full name. As we shall see below, it is also possible to find a page from the absolute name alone (though not very efficiently) and to reconstruct all the hint names from the absolute names.

3.4 *Directories*

So far we have constructed a data storage facility based on pages, and an allocation facility based on files. Allocation is not provided at the page level because losing track of pages is too easy, which in turn is because a page, being of fixed size, cannot be a logical unit of storage. A file, on the other hand, can be of arbitrary size and hence is a suitable receptacle for a collection of data which the user views as a unit, as long as it isn't too small. Since a file is a logical unit, moreover, it should have a logical name, i.e. a string name, as well as its unique file identifier, and the name should be interpreted in some context, so that names can be assigned independently without fear of conflict.

This is the familiar line of reasoning which leads to a tree-structured directory hierarchy [5]. Our system takes a somewhat different tack (following OS6) because of our desire to treat files as independent objects in their own right. We take the view that any operation on a file can be performed with a knowledge of its full name (which is the full name of its first page), and that a separate mechanism exists for associating names with files. This is done by a file called a *directory*, which contains a set of pairs (string, full name). A file may appear in any number of directories. Since there is nothing special about a directory from the point of view of the file system, it is possible to have a tree, or indeed an arbitrary directed graph, of directories. We do need to be able to identify all the directories for the rebuilding procedure described below, and to this end we reserve a subset of the file identifiers for directory files.

Our insistence on independent existence implies that a file should carry with it any status information which belongs to it: in our system, its protection and dates of creation and last access. This information is stored in a *leader* page whose absolute name is (FV,-1), along with the address of page (FV,0).

A further implication (and here we part company with OS6) is that it must be possible to recover some logical name from the file itself, so that the file can survive even if the directory entries for it are lost or scrambled. To this end we also keep in the leader page a string name for the file, a full name for its *guardian* directory, and a full name for its *owner*'s directory; the significance of the guardian and the owner will appear from the roles they play in the rebuilding procedure discussed in the next section.. This information is considered to be absolute, since these are names by which the file can be located even if all the directory entries for it are destroyed. Directory entries, by contrast, are taken less seriously, although they are not entirely redundant and hence cannot be treated as pure hints. If a directory is destroyed, we don't lose any files, but we do lose some information, namely the information that a certain set of files was referenced from that directory by a certain set of names.

3.5 *Rebuilding*

By reading all the labels on the disk, we can check that all the links are correct (reconstructing any that prove faulty), obtain full names for all existing files, and produce a list of free pages. To do this, all we have to do is create a list of all the non-zero labels (in a special reserved section of the disk for simplicity) and sort it by absolute name. If there is enough main memory to hold a table with 32 bits per sector, a suitable choice of data structure will allow this processing to be done without any auxiliary storage.

We can then read all the directories and verify that each entry points to page 0 of an existing file, fixing up the address if necessary and detecting entries which point elsewhere. If any files remain unaccounted for by directory entries, we can make new entries for them from the names in the leader:
    in the guardian directory if it exists;
    failing that, in the owner's directory;
    failing that, in a system directory of orphaned files.

This is the sole function of the names in the leader page.

This entire process is called rebuilding. It takes about 30 seconds, and is done whenever the system is started. When it is complete, all hints have been recomputed from absolutes, and any inconsistencies (incomplete files, null directory entries, nameless files etc) have been detected. The question of what to do with the inconsistencies is beyond the scope of this paper.

As we have noted, rebuilding cannot fully reconstruct lost directories. This could be accomplished by writing a journal of all changed to directories and taking an occasional snapshot of all the directories. By applying the changes in the journal to the snapshot we would get back the current state. This is of course a standard technique by which the integrity of any data base may be safeguarded. For the reasons already mentioned, we do not consider our directories important enough to warrant such attentions. If the user disagrees, he is free to modify the system-provided procedures for managing directories, or to write his own.

3.6 *Partitioning the disk*

The file system as described so far isolates the user from the physical structure of the collection of sectors on the disk, i.e. the existence of cylinders and packs. To correct this deficiency, we define *partitions*, which are sets of tracks defined by expressions of the form: surfaces 0-1, tracks 20-40. A file is constrained to be entirely contained in a single partition, and the partition from which space for a file is allocated can be specified when the file is created. There is an operation which copies all the non-free blocks in a partition into another partition (which may be contained in the first), and one which copies a file from one partition to another. With these primitives the user can split his files between packs, or allocate a group of cylinders in the center of the disk to use as a swapping area. He can also make room for a *consecutive file* which is exactly like an ordinary file except that its pages are represented by consecutive sectors in a partition, so that their addresses can be computed and don't have to be stored.

When leader pages are moved, the hint names of files become invalid (the same is true for pages, but the moving operations fix up the links). They can be refreshed by a rebuilding operation, but that is rather expensive. Instead, we have extended the idea of hints a little to allow incremental refreshing. We add a *file number* to the hint name of a file, and keep a table FLA whose ith entry is the leader address for the file with file number i. When trying to access the leader page of file (FV,n,a), we first read the page at address a. If its label contains the absolute name (FV,-1), all is well. Otherwise we fix up a from FLA[n] and try again.

4. Main Memory Allocation

In allocating main memory for a typeless machine, we felt it extremely important not to impose any constraints on the program's use of storage which would not be present on the bare machine. On the other hand, we wanted to take advantage of the fact that a great deal of the data which takes up memory space is used in highly stylized ways. Finally, we wished to cater for large programs, and it was therefore necessary to face the problem of integrating the disk with the main memory into a one-level system.

In dealing with a system in which the physical store is as big as the natural 16-bit address space, the standard paging techniques for creating a one-level store are not much help, because management of the address space is a more severe problem than squeezing the most out of the physical storage. Furthermore, in the typeless environment imposed by Bcpl, it is not possible to do any encoding of the addresses used to reference ordinary data, since the language permits, and indeed encourages, arbitrary arithmetic on addresses. We therefore divide storage into two classes: *fixed* and *floating*. All ordinary variables and vectors are allocated in fixed storage, using a standard dynamic storage allocator [8] with a slight modification which is discussed below. Code, on the other hand, is kept in floating storage, since references to code can be controlled strictly enough that we have a great deal of freedom in moving it around.

4.1 Floating storage and segments

The inhabitants of floating storage are called *segments*. The most important kind of segment is called *direct*. Each direct segment has a segment number, and an address in a segment is a pair (segment number, word within segment). Such a pair is called a segmented address [1]. The segment number is an index into a segment table, which contains the physical address of word 0 of the segment, or an **absent** indicator. Success and happiness depends on referencing data in segments only through segmented addresses, and recomputing the physical address from the segment table entry on each reference, unless there is a guarantee that the segment has not been moved since the last time this computation was done.

Two kinds of segmented address are used for code segments. The first, called an *entry*, packs the segment number and word number into a single machine word. This arrangement is forced by the semantics of Bcpl. which demands that a procedure entry be represented as an ordinary variable The alternative would be another level of indirection through a multi-word "procedure descriptor", which would cause serious problems when code is swapped out of memory. The packing allows for 256 segments with 128 entry points each, which is ample even for very grandiose computations.

This scheme won't do for return links, which are the other kind of reference to code permitted in Bcpl, because 128 return points is an unacceptable restriction. Fortunately, however, return links are not ordinary variables, and hence can be represented in two words. The microcoded procedure call and return operations are the only ones which have to deal with segmented addresses, and they take care of interpreting both kinds of address, and of constructing the return link. While a particular segment is being executed, its base address is kept in a register and the program counter is kept in absolute form. This is perfectly safe, since rearrangement of the floating storage can only happen as a result of a procedure call to a system routine, and the call will convert the program counter into a segmented return link.

The above description is actually an oversimplification. Programs can also use floating storage for data, by providing with each floating data segment a *fixup procedure* which will take care of relocating the segment. In the simplest case the program might use a floating vector which is always accessed through a single variable, and the procedure would simply adjust the value of that variable appropriately. Direct segments are another simple case, in which the procedure has only to adjust the segment table entry.

4.2 Fixed storage and beads

Fixed storage is allocated in contiguous units called *beads*. Since beads cannot be moved around, they don't offer much scope for ingenuity. It is still important to be able to remove fixed storage from memory, however, and this is provided for by grouping the beads into larger contiguous regions called *zones* [12]. At any given time allocation is done out of a single zone, and a zone can be written out onto the disk and read back in later without difficulty, subject to two constraints:

  there must be no references to the zone while it is out, since there is no way to
      detect such references;
  the same physical storage (actually the same part of the address space, but it
      comes to the same thing) must be available when the time comes to recover
      the zone.

A simple way to satisfy these constraints is to allocate one zone for all the storage used by a single node in a conventional, tree structured overlay scheme [7].

In order to accomodate parallel processes, coroutines and other non-hierarchical global control structures [3, 6], we do not allocate frames for procedures from a stack, but instead get them from the general fixed storage allocator. In order to obtain acceptable efficiency, this allocator keeps a vector of lists of beads of various popular sizes. When a bead of size n is required, the nth list is consulted first. If it is non-empty, the allocation is very fast, in fact almost as fast as allocation from a stack if an overflow check is included. To keep the vector small and avoid excessive fragmentation, frame sizes are quantized geometrically, so that each size is a few percent larger than the next smaller one.

5. Program linking

The problem addressed by this part of the system is the conversion of symbolic external references in programs into addresses which can be interpreted by the hardware. The goal is to allow the user to perform this binding at the point which is most convenient for him, while still leaving the final disk representation of a code segment independent of actual machine locations. A collection of code segments can thus be linked up before hand, but still left free to run in whatever space is available at the time they are invoked for execution. This kind of flexibility is essential if we want it to be possible for any program to call any other. It is necessary to be quite careful about the disk representation because code segments may still be swapped out, and we don't want to have to make another disk copy in order to get acceptable efficiency when a segment is swapped back in.

The basic object with which we deal is a *module*. Loosely, a module is a collection of data with some external references which must be filled in, and some definitions of names which can be used to fill in external references in other modules. The destiny of a module is to be loaded into core and referenced as part of a computation. Most modules are of two kinds:

code modules, normally generated by the compiler. The code is self-relocating. These modules are loaded into floating segments, and references to them from other modules take the form of one-word segmented addresses at execution time (except for return links);

static data modules, normally generated during linking. The user specifies a set of code modules, called a *unit*, which are to share a static module. During linking, static definitions in the code modules are copied into the static module and replaced by external references. The necessary space is allocated in the static module and filled in with any initial values which may be provided by the definitions in the code module. From then on, the static module contains the definitions for those names. These modules are loaded into fixed beads, and references to them from other modules are absolute machine addresses at execution time.

The grand strategy is to replace an individual symbolic reference to a location L (an SR below) with a symbolic reference to the module M which contains L, together with the relative address of L in M (an RR below); this is called *resolving* the reference. The motivation for this transformation is to reduce the amount of name lookup which has to be done at the last minute, when storage is actually allocated.

A module consists of:

a *length* L;

a block of L words called the *contents*;

a list of *definitions* (DEFs), each of which is a pair:
  name - a string;
  binding - an address in the segment;

a list of *symbolic references* (SRs), each of which contains
  name - a string;
  source - an address in the module which is making the reference;

    type – specifies whether a segmented address, an absolute address, or a
       value should be stored in the source;
    value – NIL or a block of words. If the latter, this is a static definition;

a list of *resolved references* (RRs), each of which is like a SR execpt that the
name has been replaced by a local segmented address (LSA), which is a pair:
local segment number (LSN);
displacement (D);

a list of *referenced modules* (RMs), each of which contains:
name;
local segment number;
displacement within the named module (in case one LSN isn't enough for a
    module because of limited displacement size in a LSA).

We provide three basic operations on modules:

resolve – convert SRs to RRs by looking up the names in the DEFs of other
modules (or entering them, for static definitions). This may involve adding
modules to the RM list. A module can be resolved several times; each time
some SRs are converted into RRs. When all are converted, it is only
necessary to provide absolute addresses or segment numbers for all the RMs,
and do the fixups specified by the RRs, to make the module ready to run.

link – attach, i.e. find addresses or absolute SNs for, all the RMs, and then
complete all the RRs. Any remaining SRs are replaced by traps. Note that the
addresses of all the static RMs are fixed by this step.

load – get the module into core, creating a segment for it if it is floating and
doesn't already have one. Set up the segment table to reflect the presence
of the module. Usually linking and loading are done at the same time, in order
to avoid making a disk copy of the linked module.

With this machinery, the user can construct almost any discipline for linking and loading
which he wants.

6. Conclusion

We have described the design of three major parts of a small operating system. In
each case considerable trouble has been taken to make all the facilities accessible to
users, in the sense that they can build up their own macro-operations from the primitives
in the system if the macro-operations provided by the system prove unsatisfactory. In
the treatment of files we emphasized the methods used to minimize the probability that
data will be destroyed, and to permit full automatic recovery after a crash. Our
discussion of memory allocation concentrated on techniques for getting the most out of
a 16-bit address. Finally, we showed how programs written in a typeless language can
be flexibly packaged into modules so that most of the symbolic linkage can be done
without making any commitment to the storage locations which the program will finally
occupy.

Acknowledgements

Many of the facilities described above have been implemented by Gene McDaniel.

References

1.   Bensoussan, A. et al, The Multics Virtual Memory, *Comm. ACM* **15**, 5 (May 1972)

2.   Bobrow, D. G. et al, Tenex, a Paged Time Sharing System for the PDP-10, *Comm. ACM* **15**, 3 (March 1972)

3.   Bobrow, D. G. and B. Wegbreit, A Model and Stack Implementation of Multiple Environments, *Comm. ACM* **16**, 10 (Oct 1973)

4.   Brinch Hansen, P., *Operating Systems Principles*, Prentice-Hall, New York, 1973

5.   Corbato, F. J. et al, An introduction and overview of the Multics system, *Proc AFIPS Conf.* **27** (1965 FJCC)

6.   Dahl, O-J. and C. A. R. Hoare, Hierarchical Program Structures, in *Structured Programming*, Academic Press, New York, 1972

7.   Hoare, C. A. R. and R. M. McKeag, A Survey of Store Management Techniques, in *Operating Systems Techniques*, Academic Press, New York, 1972

8.   Knuth, D. E. *The Art of Computer Programming*, vol 1, Addison-Wesley, Reading, Mass., 1968.

9.   Lampson, B. W. et al, A User Machine in a Time-sharing System, *Proc IEEE* **54**, 12 (Dec 1966)

10. Meyer, P. A. and L. H. Seawright, A Virtual Machine Time-Sharing System, *IBM Systems Journal* **9**, 3 (July 1970)

11. Richards, M., BCPL: a tool for compiler writing and system programming, *Proc. AFIPS Conf.* **35** (1969 SJCC)

12. Ross, D. T., The AED Free Storage Package, *Comm. ACM* **10**, 8 (Aug 1967)

13. Stoy, J. E. and C. Strachey, OS6 - An experimental operating system for a small computer, *Computer Journal* **15**, 2 and 3

**EVALUATION SUR DES MODELES DE COMPORTEMENT
DE PROGRAMME DE LA TAILLE D'UN ENSEMBLE DE TRAVAIL**

J. Lenfant
Université de Rennes

_____

1 - Introduction

Dans un calculateur à mémoire paginée, la plupart des programmes
s'exécutent dans une zone de mémoire physique qui ne peut contenir qu'une frac-
tion de leur espace virtuel. Cette situation se traduit par des échanges de
pages entre la mémoire principale et la mémoire secondaire : souvent il n'en
résulte pas pour autant une dégradation notable du temps de réponse ou du taux
horaire de traitement du système. Ceci est dû à une propriété intrinsèque du
comportement de beaucoup de programmes. Même si un programme référence un grand
nombre de pages différentes au cours de son exécution, dans tout intervalle de
temps "raisonnable" les adresses auxquelles il accède ne sont pas éparpillées
sur tout l'espace virtuel : elles en constituent au contraire un sous-ensemble
strict qui est la "localité" dans laquelle s'exécute le programme à l'instant
donné.

L'existence de ces localités a plusieurs causes. D'une part, l'attention du programmeur se porte successivement sur des fractions de l'algorithme
qu'il met en oeuvre, certaines structures de données favorisant aussi cette
concentration.

D'autre part, un programme comporte de nombreuses boucles qui, étant
exécutées un grand nombre de fois, ont pour effet de circonscrire momentanément
la partie utilisée de l'espace virtuel.

La connaissance et l'utilisation de cette propriété des programmes
peuvent être utiles pour assurer une gestion efficace de l'ensemble des ressour-

ces physiques et logiques d'un système, et pas seulement de la mémoire centrale.
De nombreuses expériences ont mis en évidence l'influence de ce phénomène sur
l'intensité du trafic entre mémoire principale et mémoire secondaire et sur les
performances des systèmes ; elles ont montré sa sensibilité au style de programmation et au choix des structures de données [1] [2].

Pour formaliser cette notion floue de "localité", P. Denning [3] a
introduit le concept d'ensemble de travail (en anglais : Working set). Pour une
exécution donnée d'un programme, l'ensemble de travail (E.T.) de fenêtre T est,
à l'instant t, l'ensemble noté W(t,T) des adresses qui ont été référencées dans
l'intervalle de temps $]t-T,t]$. Sur un modèle de programme assez général, Denning
et Schwartz [4] ont calculé l'espérance mathématique de la taille de cet ensemble
de travail en fonction de la distribution de l'intervalle entre deux références
successives à une même adresse. Toutefois, la seule connaissance de cette espérance mathématique est insuffisante pour qui veut analyser des politiques d'allo-
tion de ressources : dans ce cas l'efficacité du système dépend autant de la dis-
persion autour de la valeur moyenne que de cette valeur moyenne elle-même. Il
est donc nécessaire de connaître la distribution de la taille w (t,T) de l'E.T.
ou, au moins, ses deux premiers moments. C'est ainsi que pour comparer l'efficacité d'une partition dynamique et d'une partition statique de la mémoire principale, Coffman et Ryan [5] ont admis que la distribution de la variable aléatoire
w (t,T) est presque normale. Cette approximation, bien que suggérée par plusieurs
auteurs, n'a jamais été justifiée de manière convaincante.

L'objet de cette note est le calcul de la distribution de la taille de
l'E.T. sur deux modèles de comportement de programme : le modèle à références
indépendantes et le modèle à liste LRU. Ces deux modèles, dont nous rappellerons
la définition au paragraphe 2, ont déjà été utilisés pour évaluer analytiquement
les performances d'algorithmes de remplacement de pages [6] [7] [8]. Ils permettent également de représenter le comportement des programmes pour des études
en simulation [9].

2 - Modélisation des programmes

Pour que des mesures soient possibles et exploitables, il est souhaita-
ble de regrouper les adresses par pages. Nous appellerons donc espace virtuel du
programme étudié l'ensemble N de ses n pages :

$N = \{1,2,\ldots,n\}$

La suite des adresses auxquelles le programme accède au cours d'une
exécution est considérée comme une réalisation d'un processus stochastique à
temps discret $(R_t)_{t \in N}$; la valeur de la variable aléatoire R_t est le numéro de
la page virtuelle référencée à l'instant t : c'est un élément de N. Remarquons

qu'une réalisation de ce processus stochastique est une suite infinie alors qu'un programme ne peut évidemment exécuter qu'un nombre fini de références : cette différence n'a pas de conséquence fâcheuse pour les études de comportement. Avec ce formalisme, définir un modèle de comportement de programme c'est énoncer un ensemble d'hypothèses sur le processus (R_t).

Avant de particulariser le modèle nous allons définir de manière plus précise l'ensemble de travail.

Définition 1

Soient t et T deux entiers positifs tels que $T \leq t$. Pour une réalisation :

$$r_o\ r_1\ r_2 \ldots \ldots r_t \ldots$$

du processus (R_t) l'ensemble de travail de fenêtre T est, à l'instant t

$$W(t,T) = \{i \in N \mid (\exists u \in \mathbb{N})\ (t-T+1 \leq u \leq t) : r_u = i\}$$

La taille de $W(t,T)$ (notée $w(t,T)$) est son nombre d'éléments.

Définition 2

Le taux d'absence de page $m(t,T)$ est la probabilité que la page référencée à l'instant t+1 n'appartienne pas à l'E.T. $W(t,T)$

$$m(t,T) = \Pr\left[r_{t+1} \notin W(t,T)\right]$$
$$= \Pr\left[w(t+1, T+1) - w(t,T) = 1\right]$$

2.1. Le modèle de comportement de programme de Denning et Schwartz

Pour toutes pages i et j et tous entiers strictement positifs t et x, nous désignerons par $g_{ij}(t,x)$ la probabilité que la première référence à la page j après l'instant t ait lieu à l'instant t+x, sachant que la page i est référencée à l'instant t :

$$g_{ij}(t,x) = \Pr\left[r_{t+1} \neq j\ ;\ldots ;\ r_{t+x-1} \neq j\ ;\ r_{t+x} = j \mid r_t = i\right]$$

Le modèle de Denning et Schwartz est caractérisé par les hypothèses suivantes :

DS 1   Pour tout i appartenant à N, $g_{ii}(t,x)$ ne dépend pas de t. Nous noterons

$$g_{ii}(t,x) = f_i(x)$$

DS 2   Pour tout i, $\sum_{x \geq 1} f_i(x) = 1$

DS 3   Pour tout i, la durée moyenne de l'intervalle X_i entre deux références successives à la page i est finie :

$$\bar{X}_i = \sum_{x \geq 1} x\, f_i(x) < + \infty$$

<u>DS 4</u>   Il existe un instant t_{asym} tel que toute page de N est référencée avant t_{asym} .

Rappelons le théorème démontré par Denning et Schwartz.

La probabilité absolue qu'une référence concerne la page i est égale à $\dfrac{1}{\bar{X}_i}$. Posons :

$$f = \sum_i \frac{1}{\bar{X}_i}\, f_i$$

et désignons par F la fonction cumulative associée à f :

$$F(y) = \sum_{x=1}^{y} f(x)$$

<u>Théorème 1</u>

Soit un programme dont le comportement obéit aux hypothèses DS1 à DS4. Pour tout entier $t \geq t_{asym}$ et tout entier positif $T \leq t$:

$$\overline{w(t,T)} = \sum_{y=0}^{T-1} (1-F(y))$$

$$m(t,T) = 1 - F(T)$$

On remarque que la taille moyenne de l'E.T. et le taux d'absence de page ne dépendent pas de t. En outre

$$m(T) = \bar{w}\,(T+1) - \bar{w}\,(T)$$

2.2. Le modèle de comportement de programme à références indépendantes

Définition

Le modèle de comportement de programme est dit à "références indépendantes" si le processus stochastique (R_t) satisfait aux trois conditions suivantes :

<u>RI1</u> Pour toute famille finie t_1, t_2,...,t_p d'entiers positifs deux à deux distincts, les variables aléatoires R_{t_1}, R_{t_2} ...... R_{t_p} sont indépendantes.

<u>RI2</u> Toutes les variables aléatoires R_t ont la même distribution. Pour toute page i et tout entier positif t, nous noterons :

$$\text{Pr}\, [R_t = i] = \alpha_i$$

<u>RI3</u> Pour tout i, α_i est différent de 0.

Remarquons que ce modèle ne prend pas en compte les propriétés de localité des programmes. En revanche, il traduit l'importance relative-en durée d'exécution - des différents parties du programme. Statistiquement la probabilité α_i peut être interprétée comme le pourcentage des références qui, au cours d'une longue période, concernent la page i.

Ce modèle de comportement est un cas particulier de celui qui est défini au paragraphe 2.1.. En effet, l'intervalle entre deux références successives à la page i a une densité de distribution indépendante de t :

$$f_i(x) = (1-\alpha_i)^{x-1} \alpha_i \qquad (x \geq 1)$$

qui vérifie en outre :

$$\sum_{x \geq 1} f_i(x) = \alpha_i \sum_{x \geq 1} (1-\alpha_i)^{x-1} = \frac{\alpha_i}{\alpha_i} = 1$$

et

$$\sum_{x \geq 1} x \, f_i(x) = \alpha_i \sum_{x \geq 1} x(1-\alpha_i)^{x-1} = \alpha_i < +\infty$$

Comme, pour tout i, la probabilité que la page i ne soit pas référencée entre 0 et t tend vers 0 lorsque t tend vers l'infini, l'hypothèse DS4 est également vérifiée.

2.3. Le modèle de comportement de programme à liste LRU

Pour ce modèle, la probabilité qu'une page soit référencée dépend de sa position instantanée dans la liste LRU, c'est-à-dire dans la liste des pages classées par ordre d'ancienneté croissante de la dernière référence.

Soit $\mathscr{S}$ l'ensemble des permutations de N. Nous désignerons par $\sigma = (a_1, a_2, \ldots, a_k, \ldots, a_n)$ un élément de $\mathscr{S}$. Nous dirons que la page a_k est à la distance k dans σ. $\mathscr{S}$ est l'ensemble des états du programme, l'état initial étant désigné par σ_0. Au cours de l'exécution le programme passe par une suite d'états:

$$\sigma_0, \sigma_1, \sigma_2, \ldots, \sigma_t, \ldots$$

telle que pour $t \geq 0$, si l'on note

$$\sigma_t = (a_1, a_2, \ldots, a_n)$$

il existe un entier $1 \leq d_t \leq n$ tel que

$$\sigma_{t+1} = (a_{d_t}, a_1, a_2, \ldots, a_{d_t -1}, a_{d_t +1} \cdots a_n)$$

Le nombre d_t sera considéré comme la réalisation d'une variable aléatoire D_t. Il est essentiel de remarquer que pour un état initial σ_0 donné, la connaissance du processus stochastique $(R_t)_{t \in \mathbb{N}}$ équivaut à celle de $(D_t)_{t \in \mathbb{N}}$ puisque pour tout t : $a_{d_t} = r_t$.

Définition

Le modèle de comportement de programme est à liste LRU si le processus stochastique $(D_t)_{t \in \mathbb{N}}$ satisfait aux trois conditions suivantes :

LRU1   Pour toute famille t_1, t_2,..., t_p, d'entiers positifs deux à deux distincts, les variables aléatoires D_{t_1}, D_{t_2},..., D_{t_p} sont indépendantes.

LRU2   Toutes les variables aléatoires D_t ont la même distribution.

Pour tout $1 \leq i \leq n$ nous noterons

$$\Pr[D_t = i] = \beta_i$$

LRU3   Pour tout i, β_i est différent de 0.

Ce modèle, inspiré par les bonnes performances de l'algorithme de remplacement de pages LRU, tient compte de la propriété de localité des programmes. Mais sur une longue période, toutes les pages sont référencées avec la même fréquence relative. Nous ne considérons que le comportement stationnaire d'un programme à modèle LRU : le choix de l'état initial σ_o n'a aucune influence sur ce comportement. Remarquons enfin que ce modèle est également un cas particulier du modèle de Denning et Schwartz.

3 - Taille de l'E.T. d'un programme conforme au modèle à liste LRU.

Pour un tel modèle de comportement, l'E.T. W(t,T) a exactement k éléments si et seulement si la chaîne

$$D_{t-T+1} \quad D_{t-T+2} \quad ....D_t$$

des distances associées aux références exécutées entre t-T+1 et t est de la forme

(1) $\delta_1(1)^{r_1} \quad \delta_2(1,2)^{r_2} \quad \delta_3(1,2,3)^{r_3} \quad .... \quad \delta_k(1,2,...,k)^{r_k}$

où

δ_i est une distance supérieure ou égale à i, les r_i sont des entiers positifs ou nuls dont la somme est T-k

$(1,2,...,1)^r$ désigne une suite de r distances toutes non supérieures à 1.

Par suite de l'indépendance des variables aléatoires (D_t), la probabilité d'un E.T. de taille k ($1 \leq k \leq \min (n,T)$) est donc

(2) $\Pr\left[W(t,T) = k\right] = \Pr\left[D \geq 1\right] \times \Pr\left[D \geq 2\right] \times \ldots \times \Pr\left[D \geq k\right] \times$

$$\sum_{\substack{r_i \geq 0}} \beta_1^{r_1} \left(\beta_1 + \beta_2\right)^{r_2} \ldots \left(\beta_1 + \beta_2 + \ldots + \beta_k\right)^{r_k}$$

$r_1 + \ldots + r_k = T-k$

Désignons par $P(\beta_1, \beta_2, \ldots, \beta_k)$ la sommation figurant dans le membre de droite et posons $S_i = \sum_{j=1}^{i} \beta_j$. Puisque $\Pr\left[D \geq i\right] = 1 - S_{i-1}$ $(1 \leq i \leq n)$, l'égalité (2) équivaut à :

(3) $\Pr\left[W(t,T) = k\right] = (1-S_1)(1-S_2) \ldots (1-S_{k-1}) P(\beta_1, \beta_2, \ldots, \beta_k)$

Pour simplifier l'expression de $P(\beta_1, \beta_2, \ldots, \beta_k)$ remarquons que ce nombre est le $(T-k)^e$ coefficient du développement en série entière de la fonction rationnelle :

$$Q_{(z)} = \frac{1}{(1-S_1 z)(1-S_2 z) \ldots \ldots \ldots (1-S_k z)}$$

Puisque tous les pôles de Q sont simples (hypothèse LRU 3) sa décomposition en éléments simples est :

$$Q(z) = \sum_{i=1}^{k} \frac{S_i^{k-1}}{\prod_{\substack{1 \leq j \leq k \\ j \neq i}} (S_i - S_j)} \times \frac{1}{(1 - S_i z)}$$

En utilisant cette expression de Q pour calculer les coefficients de son développement en série entière, nous obtenons :

(4) $$P(\beta_1, \beta_2, \ldots, \beta_k) = \sum_{i=1}^{k} \frac{S_i^{T-1}}{\prod_{\substack{1 \leq j \leq k \\ j \neq i}} (S_i - S_j)}$$

Enonçons ce résultat :

Théorème 2

La distribution de la taille de l'E.T. d'un programme se comportant suivant le modèle LRU est déterminée pour tout entier k positif et au plus égal à min (n,T) par :

$$\Pr\left[w\,(t,T)=k\right] =(1-S_1)\,(1-S_2)\,\ldots\,(1-S_{k-1})\sum_{i=1}^{k}\frac{S_i^{T-1}}{\prod_{\substack{1\le t\le k\\ j\ne i}}(S_i-S_j)}$$

Cette formule permet de faire rapidement le calcul effectif de la distribution de w(t,T) ainsi que de la valeur moyenne $\overline{W}$ (t,T) et du taux d'absence de page m(t,T). Remarquons en particulier que :

$$m(t,T) = \sum_{k=1}^{\min(n,T)} (1-S_k)\ \Pr\left[w(t,T) = k\right]$$

4 - Taille de l'E.T. d'un programme conforme au modèle à références indépendantes

Pour un programme ayant un comportement à références indépendantes, la probabilité que la chaîne des pages référencées entre t - T + 1 et t soit :

$$\gamma = i_1\ i_2\ \ldots\ldots\ i_T$$

est égale à :

$$\pi(\gamma) = \Pr\left[R_{t-T+1} = i_1\right] \times \Pr\left[R_{t-T+2} = i_2\right] \times\ldots\times \Pr\left[R_t = i_T\right]$$

$$= \alpha_{i_1} \times \alpha_{i_2} \times \ldots \times \alpha_{i_T}$$

Par suite la probabilité que l'E.T. W(t,T) ait pour taille k $(1 \le k \le \min\,(n,T))$ est :

(5) $\qquad \Pr\left[w(t,T) = k\right] = \sum_{*} \pi(\gamma)$

la sommation $\sum_{*}$ étant étendue à toutes les chaînes de T éléments de N comportant exactement k éléments distincts. Pour évaluer (5) nous allons utiliser une méthode analogue à celle qui est utilisée pour démontrer le théorème d'inversion de Möbius [10] .

Nous dirons qu'une chaîne γ de N^T a la propriété P(i) si elle ne contient pas l'élément i ; i_1, i_2,..., i_q étant q éléments de N, nous désignerons par $N_{i_1\,i_2\ldots i_q}$ l'ensemble des chaînes de N^T ayant à la fois les propriétés $P(i_1)$, $P(i_2)$,..., et $P(i_q)$ (et éventuellement d'autres propriétés)et par $\pi_{i_1 i_2\,\ldots\,i_q}$ la probabilité de cet ensemble. Il est clair que :

(6) $\quad \pi_{i_1 i_2 \ldots i_q} = \text{Pr} \left[N_{i_1 i_2} \ldots i_q \right] = \sum_{\gamma \in N_{i_1 i_2 \ldots i_q}} \pi(\gamma)$

$$= (1 - \alpha_{i_1} - \alpha_{i_2} - \ldots - \alpha_{i_q})^T$$

Nous allons démontrer que, pour tout $1 \le k \le \min (n,T)$:

(7) $\quad \text{Pr} \left[w(t,T) = k \right] = \sum_{r=n-k}^{n} (-1)^{r-n+k} \, C_r^{n-k} \sum_{i_1 < i_2 \ldots < i_r} \pi_{i_1 i_2 \ldots i_r}$

(La sommation $\sum_{i_1 < i_2 < \ldots i_r}$ est une sommation sur toutes les combinaisons de r

entiers choisis dans N).

En effet, soit γ une chaîne de T références. Trois éventualités sont à considérer.

a) Si γ contient strictement plus de k termes différents, elle a strictement moins de (n-k) propriétés du type P(i) : elle ne figure donc dans aucun des ensembles $N_{i_1 i_2 \ldots i_q}$ dont les probabilités sont prises en compte dans le membre de droite de l'égalité (7).

b) Si γ contient exactement k termes différents, c'est-à-dire si elle possède les propriétés $P(j_1)$, $P(j_2)$ ... $P(j_{n-k})$ à l'exclusion de toute autre, sa probabilité $\pi(\gamma)$ contribue à $\pi_{j_1 j_2 \ldots j_{n-k}}$ (qui est affecté du coefficient $C_{n-k}^{n-k} = 1$) et seulement à ce terme.

c) Si γ a exactement s propriétés du type P(i) (s > n-k) sa contribution à

$$(-1)^{r-n+k} \, C_r^{n-k} \sum_{i_1 < i_2 \ldots < i_r} \pi_{i_1 i_2 \ldots i_r} \qquad (n-k \le r \le s)$$

est égale à :

$$(-1)^{r-n+k} \, C_r^{n-k} \, C_s^r \, \pi(\gamma)$$

La contribution totale d'une telle chaîne au membre de droite de l'égalité (7) est donc :

(8) $\quad (-1)^{k-n} \, \pi(\gamma) \sum_{r=n-k}^{s} (-1)^r \, C_s^r \, C_r^{n-k}$

En dérivant (n-k) fois l'identité binomiale :

$$(1+x)^s = \sum_{r=0}^{s} C_s^r \ x^r$$

en divisant par (n-k) ! l'identité ainsi obtenue et en posant x = -1, il vient :

$$\sum_{r=n-k}^{s} (-1)^r \ C_s^r \ C_r^{n-k} = \frac{1}{(n-k)!} \left. \frac{d^{(n-k)}}{dx^{(n-k)}} (1+x)^s \right|_{x=-1}$$

quantité qui est nulle puisque s > n-k. La contribution de la chaîne γ au membre de droite de (7) est donc nulle également dans ce cas.

Il résulte de cette étude que le membre de droite de (7) est la somme des probabilités des chaînes de N^T qui contiennent exactement k éléments distincts : cette somme est égale à Pr $\left[w(t,T) = \bar{k} \right]$ d'après l'égalité (5). D'où le théorème :

Théorème 3

La distribution de la taille de l'E.T. d'un programme se comportant suivant le modèle à références indépendantes est déterminée pour tout entier k positif et au plus égal à min (n,T) par :

$$(9) \ . \quad Pr \left[w(t,T) = k \right] = \sum_{r=n-k}^{n} (-1)^{r-n-k} \ C_r^{n-k} \ U_r$$

où l'on a posé :

$$U_r = \sum_{i_1 < i_2 \ldots < i_r} (1 - \alpha_{i_1} - \alpha_{i_2} \ldots - \alpha_{i_r})^T$$

et $\quad U_0 = 1$

Corollaire :

Pour un programme ayant un comportement à références indépendantes la moyenne et la variance de la taille d'un E.T. sont respectivement égales à :

$(10) \quad \overline{w}(T) = n - U_1$

et

$(11) \quad \sigma^2(T) = - U_1^2 + (2n-1) \ U_1 + 2 \ U_2$

Pour démontrer ces deux formules, utilisons l'égalité (9)

$$Pr \left[w(T) = n \right] = C_0^o \ U_0 - C_1^o \ U_1 + C_2^o \ U_2 - C_3^o \ U_3 + C_4^o \ U_4 - \ldots + (-1)^n \ C_n^o \ U_n$$

$$Pr\ [w(T)=n-1] = \quad C_1^1\ U_1 - C_2^1\ U_2 + C_3^1\ U_3 - C_4^1\ U_4 + \ldots + (-1)^{n-1}\ C_n^1\ U_n$$

$$Pr\ [w(T)=n-2] = \quad C_2^2\ U_2 - C_3^2\ U_3 + C_4^2\ U_4 + \ldots + (-1)^{n-2}\ C_n^2\ U_n$$

$$\ldots\ldots\ldots\ldots\ldots\ldots\ldots\ldots\ldots\ldots\ldots\ldots\ldots\ldots\ldots\ldots\ldots\ldots$$

$$Pr\ [w(T)=n-1] = \quad C_1^1\ U_1 - C_{1+1}^1\ U_{1+1} + \ldots + (-1)^{n-1}\ C_n^1\ U_n$$

$$\ldots\ldots\ldots\ldots\ldots\ldots\ldots\ldots\ldots\ldots\ldots\ldots\ldots\ldots\ldots\ldots\ldots\ldots$$

$$Pr\ [w(T)=1] = \quad C_{n-1}^{n-1}\ U_{n-1} - C_n^{n-1}\ U_n$$

$$Pr\ [w(T)=0] = \quad C_n^n\ U_n$$

En évaluant "par colonnes" la somme $\sum_{r=0}^{n} r\ Pr\ [w(T) = r]$ on obtient :

$$\overline{w}(T) = \sum_{k=0}^{n} \sum_{1=0}^{k} (n-1)\ (-1)^{k+1}\ C_k^1\ U_k$$

(12)

$$= \sum_{k=0}^{n} (-1)^k\ U_k \sum_{1=0}^{k} (n-1)\ (-1)^{1}\ C_k^1$$

La sommation la plus à droite peut se scinder en deux :

— $n \sum_{1=0}^{k} (-1)^{1}\ C_k^1$ est égal à n si k=o, sinon à $n(1-1)^k = 0$

— $\sum_{1=0}^{k} 1(-1)^{1-1}\ C_k^1$ est la valeur pour x = -1 de la dérivée de $(1+x)^k$

cette somme est donc nulle sauf si k=1, auquel cas elle vaut 1.

Finalement, l'égalité (12) implique :

$$\overline{w}(T) = n\ U_0 - U_1 = n - U_1$$

ce qui est le résultat cherché.

Un calcul analogue nous permet de trouver le second moment de la distribution de w(T). En effet :

(13)

$$E(w^2(T)) = \sum_{k=0}^{n} (-1)^k\ U_k \sum_{1=0}^{k} (n^2 - 21 + 1^2)\ (-1)^{1}\ C_k^1$$

Compte tenu de ce que $\sum_{1=0}^{k} 1^2\ C_k^1\ (-1)^{1}$ est la valeur au point x=-1 de $-\frac{d}{dx}\ [x\ \frac{d}{dx}\ (1+x)^k]$, l'égalité (13) conduit à :

$$E(w(T)^2) = n^2\ U_0 - U_1 + 2U_2$$

La variance de la taille de l'E.T. est donc :

$$\sigma^2(T) = E(w(T)^2) - E(w(T))^2 = - U_1^2 + (2n-1)\, U_1 + 2U_2$$

Notons enfin que l'égalité (10) a déjà été établie par Denning et Schwartz comme conséquence du théorème 1.

Remarque sur une autre approche possible

Il est possible de calculer cette distribution de $w(t,T)$ par une méthode analogue à celle qui a été employée pour les programmes suivants un modèle de
comportement à liste LRU. Calculons la probabilité que $w(t,T)$ soit égal à
$k(1 < k < \min(n,T))$. L'ensemble de travail $W(t,T)$ est égal à $\{1,2,\ldots,k\}$ si la
chaîne des T références exécutées entre l'instant $t-T+1$ et l'instant t est :

- soit une chaîne de la forme

$$(14) \qquad 1(1)^{r_1}\, 2(1,2)^{r_2}\, 3(1,2,3)^{r_3}\, \ldots\, k(1,2,3,\ldots,k)^{r_k}$$

où les r_i sont des entiers positifs ou nuls de somme $T-k$ et où $(1,2,\ldots,l)^r$
désigne une suite de r références à des pages du sous-ensemble $\{1,2,\ldots,l\}$

- soit une chaîne déduite d'une chaîne du type précédent par une
permutation sur $\{1,2,\ldots,k\}$

La probabilité qu'une suite de T références générées par le programme
soit de la forme décrite en (14) est égale à

$$\alpha_1 \alpha_2 \cdots \alpha_k \sum_{\substack{r_i \geq 0 \\ r_1+\ldots+r_k=T-k}} \alpha_1^{r_1}\, (\alpha_1 + \alpha_2)^{r_2}\, \ldots\, (\alpha_1 + \alpha_2 + \ldots \alpha_k)^{r_k}$$

c'est-à-dire à :

$$\alpha_1\, \alpha_2 \cdots \alpha_k\, P(\alpha_1,\alpha_2,\ldots,\alpha_k)$$

où P désigne la même fonction qu'au paragraphe 3.

Par additivité, il en résulte :

$$\Pr[W(t,T) = \{1,2,\ldots,k\}] = \alpha_1\, \alpha_2 \cdots \alpha_k \sum_{*} P(\alpha_{\sigma(1)},\alpha_{\sigma(2)} \cdots \alpha_{\sigma(k)})$$

la sommation $\sum_{*}$ étant étendue à toutes les permutations σ de $\{1,2,\ldots,k\}$; de
même

$$\Pr[w(t,T) = k] = \sum_{**} \alpha_{i(1)}\, \alpha_{i(2)} \cdots \alpha_{i(k)}\, P(\alpha_{i(1)}\, \alpha_{i(2)},\ldots\, \alpha_{i(k)})$$

la sommation $\sum_{**}$ étant étendue à l'ensemble I_k des arrangements i des n premiers

entiers positifs choisis k ã k, c'est-à-dire à l'ensemble des injections i de
{1,2,...,k} dans {1,2,...,n} . Du calcul de P qui a été fait au paragraphe 3 on
tire donc l'expression suivante pour la distribution de w(t,T) :

$$(15) \qquad \Pr\,[w(t,T) = k] = \sum_{i \in I_k} \alpha_{i(1)}\ \alpha_{i(2)}\ \cdots\ \alpha_{i(k)}\ \sum_{r=1}^{k} \frac{S_{r,i}^{T-1}}{\displaystyle\prod_{\substack{1 \le s < k \\ s \ne r}} (S_{r,i} - S_{s,i})}$$

où $S_{1,i} = \alpha_{i(1)} + \alpha_{i(2)} + \ldots + \alpha_{i(1)}$

En raison du nombre élevé d'arrangements $(|I_k| = \frac{n!}{(n-k)!})$ la formule
(9) est préférable pour le calcul effectif de la distribution de w(t,T).

5 - Résultats numériques

Sur les figures 1 et 2 est rapportée la taille de l'E.T. de deux comportements de programme : le premier de ces comportements est à références indépendantes, le second à liste LRU. La valeur de $\Pr\,[w(T) = k]$ $(1 \le k \le n)$ y est
comparée à son approximation gaussienne :

$$\Pi_k = \Phi\left(\frac{k+1/2 - \bar{w}(T)}{\sigma}\right) - \Phi\left(\frac{k - \frac{1}{2} - \bar{w}(T)}{\sigma}\right)$$

où l'on désigne par σ l'écart-type de w(T) et par Φ la fonction de répartition
de la distribution normale réduite :

$$\Phi(x) = \frac{1}{\sqrt{2\pi}} \int_{\infty}^{x} e^{-\frac{t^2}{2}}\ dt$$

Sur ces figures, ainsi que sur les quelques centaines d'autres résultats de ce type que nous avons obtenus, l'accord entre $\Pr\,[w(T) = k]$ et Π_k est
très bon ; il est d'autant meilleur que n est plus grand. Toutefois lorsque T
est très supérieur à n (par exemple : T=480 sur la figure 2) la différence entre
$\Pr\,[w(T) = k]$ et Π_k peut être sensible : ceci n'est pas surprenant car on appro-
xime alors par une distribution continue une distribution discrète dont seules
quelques valeurs ont une probabilité non négligeable.

Les figures 3 et 4 représentent la variation en fonction de T de la
moyenne et de l'écart-type de la taille de l'E.T. du programme déjà considéré
sur la figure 2.

BIBLIOGRAPHIE

[1] B.S. BRAWN et F.G. GUSTAVSON
Program behavior in a paging environment.
Proc. of A.F.I.P.S. F.J.C.C., 1968.-

[2] D. SAYRE
Is automatic folding of programs efficient enough to displace manual ?
C.A.C.M., décembre 1969.-

[3] P.J. DENNING
The working set model for program behavior.
C.A.C.M., mai 1968.-

[4] P.J. DENNING et S.C. SCHWARTZ
Properties of the working set model
C.A.C.M., mars 1972.-

[5] E.G. COFFMAN Jr et T.A. RYAN Jr
A study of storage partitioning using a mathematical model of locality.
C.A.C.M. mars 1972.-

[6] A.V. AHO et P.J. DENNING et J.D. ULLMAN
Principles of optimal page replacement
J.A.C.M., janvier 1971.-

[7] W.F. KING III
Analysis of demand paging algorithms
Proc. of the I.F.I.P. Congress 1971, North-Holland Publishing Company.-

[8] E. GELENBE
A unified approach to the evaluation of a class of replacement algo-
rithms
I.E.E.E. Trans. on computers, juin 1973.-

[9] C. BETOURNE et S. KRAKOWIAK
Simulation de l'allocation de ressources dans un système à mémoire
virtuelle paginée
Congrès A.F.C.E.T., novembre 1972

[10] M. HALL Jr
Combinatorial theory
Blaisdell Publishing Company, 1967.-

CARACTERISTIQUES DU PROGRAMME

Nombre de pages : n = 15

Modèles à références indépendantes

$\alpha_i = C(16-i)$

(C est la constante de normalisation)

T = 15

k	1	2	3	4	5	6	7	8
Pr [w(T) = k]	0,000	0,000	0,000	0,000	0,002	0,024	0,112	0,260
Approximation gaussienne	0,000	0,000	0,000	0,000	0,003	0,027	0,114	0,257

k	9	10	11	12	13	14	15
Pr [w(T) = k]	0,316	0,204	0,068	0,011	0,001	0,000	0,000
Approximation gaussienne	0,311	0,202	0,071	0,013	0,001	0,000	0,000

T = 125

k	1	2	3	4	5	6	7	8
Pr [w(T) = k]	0,000	0,000	0,000	0,000	0,000	0,000	0,000	0,000
Approximation gaussienne	0,000	0,000	0,000	0,000	0,000	0,000	0,000	0,000

k	9	10	11	12	13	14	15	16
Pr [w(T) = k]	0,000	0,000	0,000	0,003	0,064	0,402	0,532	
Approximation gaussienne	0,000	0,000	0,000	0,001	0,062	0,462	0,427	0,048

FIGURE 1

CARACTERISTIQUES DU PROGRAMME

Nombre de pages n = 40

Modèle à liste LRU

$\beta_i = C \times 20$ si $1 \leqslant i \leqslant 8$

$\beta_i = C \times 10$ si $9 \leqslant i \leqslant 20$

$\beta_i = C \times 7$ si $21 \leqslant i \leqslant 23$

$\beta_i = C \times 6$ si $24 \leqslant i \leqslant 26$

$\beta_i = C \times 5$ si $27 \leqslant i \leqslant 29$

$\beta_i = C \times 4$ si $30 \leqslant i \leqslant 32$

$\beta_i = C \times 3$ si $33 \leqslant i \leqslant 35$

$\beta_i = C \times 2$ si $36 \leqslant i \leqslant 38$

$\beta_i = C \times 1$ si $39 \leqslant i \leqslant 40$

(C est la constante de normalisation)

T = 20

k	6	7	8	9	10	11	12	13	14
$\Pr[w(T) = k]$	0,000	0,000	0,002	0,013	0,051	0,128	0,216	0,248	0,194
Approximation gaussienne	0,000	0,000	0,003	0,014	0,051	0,127	0,215	0,246	0,192

k	15	16	17	18	19	20
$\Pr[w(T) = k]$	0,102	0,036	0,008	0,001	0,000	0,000
Approximation gaussienne	0,102	0,037	0,009	0,002	0,000	0,000

FIGURE 2

T = 80

k	19	20	21	22	23	24	25	26	27
Pr [w(T) = k]	0,000	0,001	0,004	0,016	0,047	0,100	0,162	0,203	0,193
Approximation gaussienne	0,000	0,001	0,005	0,017	0,047	0,100	0,161	0,201	0,193

k	28	29	30	31	32	33
Pr [w(T) = k]	0,142	0,081	0,034	0,011	0,003	0,000
Approximation gaussienne	0,142	0,081	0,035	0,012	0,003	0,001

T = 480

k	32	33	34	35	36	37	38	39	40
Pr [w(T) = k]	0,000	0,000	0,001	0,011	0,062	0,211	0,396	0,255	0,065
Approximation gaussienne	0,000	0,000	0,000	0,007	0,065	0,238	0,369	0,244	0,068

k	41	42
Pr [w(T) = k]		
Approximation gaussienne	0,008	0,000

FIGURE 2 (SUITE)

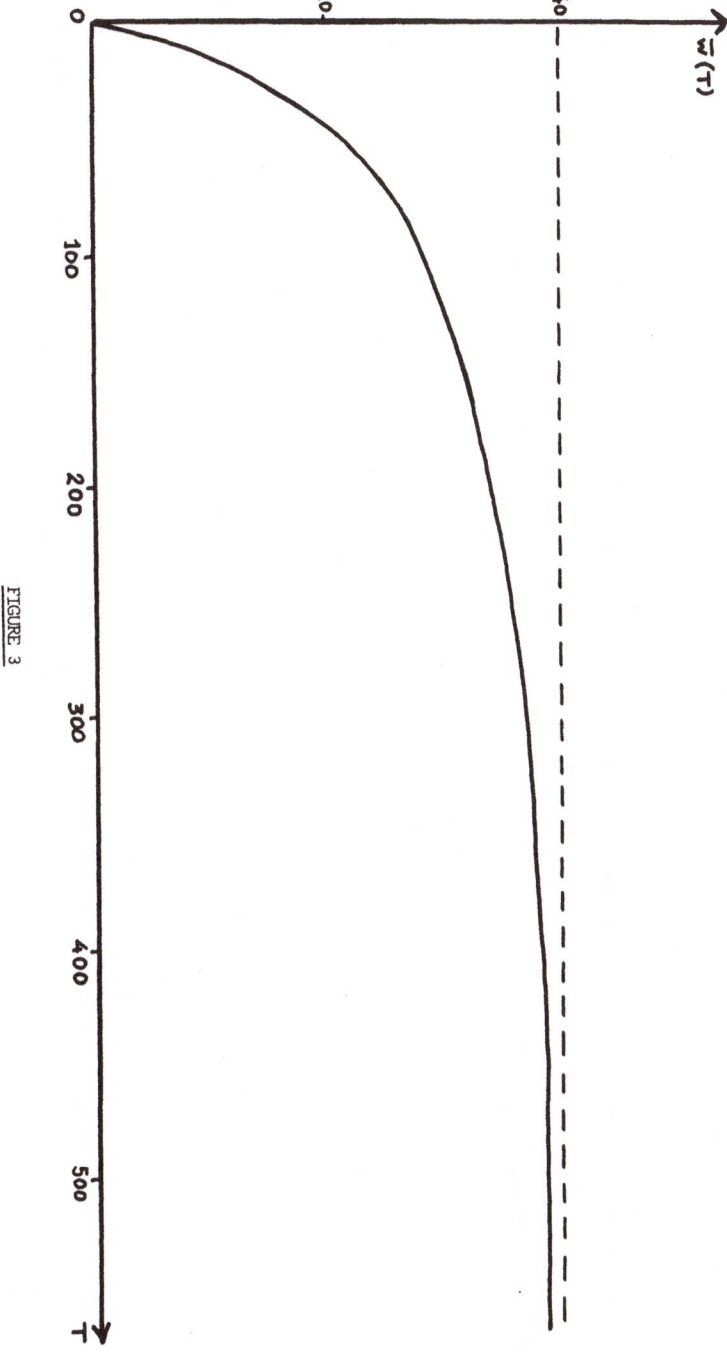

FIGURE 3

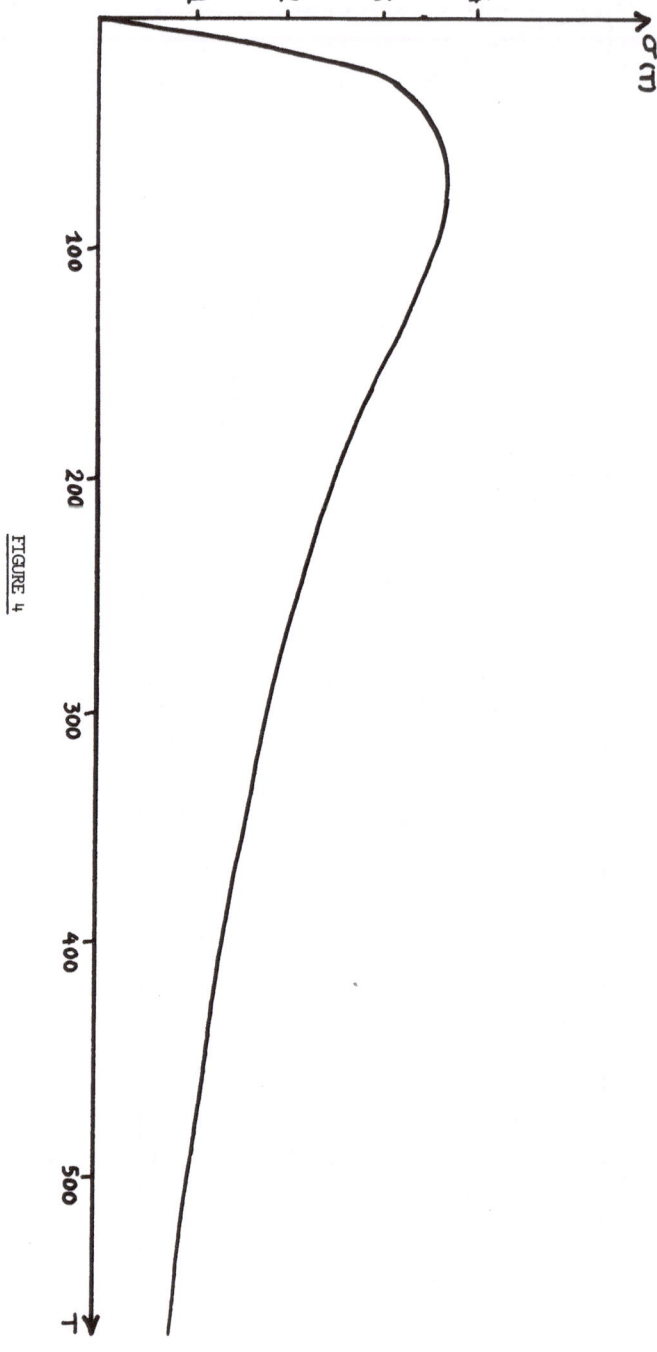

FIGURE 4

SCHEDULERS AS ENFORCES IN SYNCHRONIZATION PROCESSES

R.J. Lipton
Yale University New Haven

———

Abstract

A formal model of the process concept is presented. This model can represent
many sets of processes such as PV and its many generalizations. In this model
the concepts of process and scheduler are separated. This separation allows one
to make explicit many statements that otherwise would be implicit. In particular,
this separation is used to study how schedulers enforce "fairness", i.e., how
schedulers can force certain actions to execute infinitely often.

1. Introduction

In the study of sequential processes we can usually afford to be informal, for
the concept of a sequential process is well understood. On the other hand, in
the study of parallel or concurrent processes we must be precise, for the concepts here are not yet well understood. A large number of phenomena concerning
concurrent processes is subtle; hence, the justification for studying formal
models. This paper is part of an attempt to construct formal models, not for
their own sake, but in order to understand the complex behavior of concurrent
processes.

The particular issue we address ourselves to is how can we enforce "fairness"
among processes, i.e., how can we enforce that certain "delays" are always finite
or that certain actions execute infinitely often. The current attempts to
formalize the concept of process cannot adequately answer these questions. For
one, they cannot formally define the concepts "scheduler", "blocking", "PV
release mechanism", and "fair". However, these concepts must be central to any
theory of synchronization of processes. For instance, these concepts are fundamental to an understanding of the second reader-writer problem as presented in
Courtois, Heymans, Parnas [1]. A part of this problem states that "writers only
wait for a bounded time while readers execute". Indeed, the controversy between
Brinch Hansen [2] and Courtois, Heymans, Parnas [3] can be traced to their
inability to formally define the concepts of schedulers and fairness.

A formal model of the process concept (Lipton [4]) will be presented, and then this model will be used to study the scheduler concept. This model can represent many important classes of processes such as PV (Dijkstra [5]). In this model the concept of scheduler is separated from the concept of processes. This separation allows us to study the same processes with respect to several schedulers. For example, this separation allows a precise statement of the theorem of Habermann [6] concerning PV processes: in our model this theorem is a property of PV processes and a particular scheduler. The main application of this model is the study of "fairness". The concept of fairness is used, for example, to understand the controversy between Brinch Hansen and Courtois, Heymans, Parnas. In particular, it shows that in Brinch Hansen's solution "writers can wait forever" while in Courtois, Heymans, Parnas's solution "writers cannot wait forever".

2. Preliminaries

We will model systems of processes as a collection of <u>actions</u> and a set of <u>states</u>. Each state is assumed to be of the form

$$(L_1,\ldots,L_n,G).$$

The $L_1,\ldots,L_n$ represent the program counters of the system, while G represents both the program variables and the semaphores of the system. There is no loss of generality in assuming that G contains both program variables and semaphores, for we have made, as yet, no assumptions about the structure of G. The number of processes in the system is n; each process uses its own program counter. Actions are functions that map states to states. They correspond to what is often called an "indivisible step"; hence, the vague concept of "indivisible step" is replaced by the precise concept of function. In addition, each action f is assumed to be defined as follows: (assume n = 2)

$$f(L_1, L_2, G) = \begin{cases} (b(G), L_2, t(G)), & \text{if } L_1=a \text{ and } p(G); \\ \\ (L_1, L_2, G), & \text{otherwise.} \end{cases}$$

Thus, $f(L_1, L_2, G)$ can "execute" if and only if its program counter $L_1 = a$ and the predicate $p(G)$ is true. When $f(L_1, L_2, G)$ can execute it changes L_1 to $b(G)$ and G to $t(G)$. In general we do not allow arbitrary states and actions; indeed, we can model important classes of systems of processes by placing restrictions on the states and actions.

Our notational conventions are: lower case greek letters denote finite or infinite sequences, $\wedge$ is the empty sequence, juxtaposition denotes concatenation, sequences are indexed from 1 to n, and α_i is the ith element in the sequence α. $\overset{\infty}{\forall}kR(k)$ means that $R(k)$ is true for an infinite number of integers k.

It is convenient to have the following notation for functions. Let D be a set of the form $D_1 x \ldots x D_k$, and let $(x_1,\ldots,x_k)$ be a typical element of D. The notation

$$\underline{when} \ B(x_1,\ldots,x_k) \ \underline{do} \ x_1 \leftarrow f_1(x_1,\ldots,x_k);\ldots;x_k \leftarrow f_k(x_1,\ldots,x_k)$$

where B is a predicate and each f_i is a function, denotes the function g, from D to D, defined by if $B(Y_1,\ldots,Y_k)$, then $g(Y_1,\ldots,Y_k) = (f_1(Y_1,\ldots,Y_k),\ldots,f_k(Y_1,\ldots,Y_k))$;

otherwise, $g(Y_1,\ldots,Y_k) = (Y_1,\ldots,Y_k)$.

For example, let $``(x_1,x_2,x_3)"$ be a typical element in $\{1,2,3\} \times \{1,2,3\} \times \{1,2,3\}$, and let

$$f = \underline{\text{when}}\ x_1 < x_2\ \underline{\text{do}}\ x_1 \leftarrow x_2;\ x_2 \leftarrow 2;\ x_3 \leftarrow x_3.$$

Then $f(2,3,1) = (3,2,1)$. Also "assignments" of the form $`x \leftarrow x'$ are deleted. Therefore,

$$f = \underline{\text{when}}\ x_1 < x_2\ \underline{\text{do}}\ x_1 \leftarrow x_2;\ x_2 \leftarrow 2.$$

Finally, if $y = (Y_1,\ldots,Y_k)$ is in D, then $\underline{x_i[y]}$ denotes Y_i.

<u>Definition</u> $P = \langle A,D,w \rangle$ is a <u>system of processes</u> provided there are functions <u>address</u> and <u>program counter</u> with domains A such that

(1) $w \in D$. Each element of D is a <u>state</u>; w is the <u>initial state</u>.

(2) Each element of A is an <u>action</u>. An action f is a function from D to D of the form

$$\underline{\text{when}}\ L_k = \text{address}(f) \wedge p(G)\ \underline{\text{do}}\ L_k \leftarrow b(G);\ G \leftarrow t(G)$$

where $k = $ program-counter(f); $``(L_1,\ldots,L_n,G)"$ is a typical state of D; and for all x in D, $b(G[x]) \neq \text{address}(f)$.

(3) If address$(f) = $ address(g) and program-counter$(f) = $ program-counter(g) for actions f and g, then $f = g$.

Informally, $L_1,\ldots,L_n$ are "program counters" while G includes both the "program variables" and the "semaphore variables". In view of condition (3) of the definition of a system of processes, each program counter L_i contains the address of at most one action. Thus, a system of processes cannot contain the pair of actions.

$$\underline{\text{when}}\ L_1 = 1 \wedge S = 0\ \underline{\text{do}}\ L_1 \leftarrow 2$$

$$\underline{\text{when}}\ L_1 = 1 \wedge S > 0\ \underline{\text{do}}\ L_1 \leftarrow 3.$$

<u>Definition</u> A <u>timing</u> for the system of processes P is a finite or infinite sequence of actions of the system of processes P.

<u>Definition</u> Suppose that $P = \langle A,D,w \rangle$ is a system of processes. The function value_p is defined as follows:

(1) $\text{value}_p (\wedge) = w$;

(2) if α is a finite timing and f is an action, then $\text{value}_p (\alpha f) = f(\text{value}_p (\alpha))$. When there can be no confusion, the subscript $`P'$ will be deleted.

The function value maps finite timings to D; for example, value(fg) = g(f(w)). This model includes "parallelism" or "asynchronous" behavior, for the order actions get "executed" in is arbitrary.

Definition Suppose that $P = <A,D,w>$ is a system of processes, and let $\langle\!\langle (L_1,\ldots,L_n,(G,S_1,\ldots,S_m))\rangle\!\rangle$ be a typical element of D where $D = D_1 x \ldots x D_n x E x \mathbb{Z}^m$ and $\mathbb{Z}$ is the set of integers. Then P is a <u>PV system of processes</u> provided each action of P is in one of the following forms:

(1) <u>when</u> $L_i = a \wedge S_j > 0$ <u>do</u> $L_i \leftarrow a'$; $S_j \leftarrow S_j - 1$

(2) <u>when</u> $L_i = a$ <u>do</u> $L_i \leftarrow a'$; $S_j \leftarrow S_j + 1$

(3) <u>when</u> $L_i = a$ <u>do</u> $L_i \leftarrow b(G)$; $G \leftarrow t(G)$.

An action of the form (1) is called a $P(S_j)$; an action of the form (2) is called a $V(S_j)$. Each S_j is called a <u>semaphore</u>. The definition of a PV system of processes is essentially due to Dijkstra [5].

Many sets of processes used in the synchronization literature can be considered as systems of processes. They include: PVchunk (Vantilborgh and van Lamsweerde [7]), PVmultiple (Patil [8] and Dijkstra [9]), up/down (Wodon [10]), and block-wakeup (Saltzer [11]).

Definition Suppose that $P = <A,D,w>$ is a system of processes, and let $\langle\!\langle (L_1,\ldots,L_n,G)\rangle\!\rangle$ be a typical element of D.

(1) For actions f and g, <u>process</u>$_P$ (f,g) iff program-counter(f) = program-counter(g).

(2) An action f is in <u>ready-set</u>$_P$ (α) where α is a finite timing iff f(value(α)) $\neq$ value (α).

(3) An action f is in <u>pointer-set</u>(α) where α is a finite timing iff L_k[value(α)] = address(f) where k = program-counter(f).

In each of these notions the subscript P is dropped when this will cause no confusion.

For example, consider the system of processes EX1. A formal representation is in figure 1; an informal representation is in figure 2. The "execution" of the timing 1234 is informally: ("(L_1,L_2,L_3,S)" is a typical state of EX1)

1 this action changes L_1 to 2 and S to 0, i.e., value(1) = (2,1,0);

2 this action changes L_1 to 1 and S to 1, i.e., value(12) = (1,1,1);

3 this action changes L_2 to 2 and S to 0, i.e., value(123) = (1,2,0);

4 this action changes L_2 to 1 and S to 1, i.e., value(1234) = (1,1,1).

Also note that ready-set(123) = { 4}; hence, 4 is the only action that can change the state that results from executing 123.

The notions process, ready-set, and pointer-set are sufficient to express the basic concepts of the synchronization area. For instance, these notions can express the concept of "safe" and "deadlock free" as defined by Dijkstra [5]; this is demonstrated in Lipton [12].

Theorem 1. Suppose that P is a system of processes and α is a finite timing. Then

(I)   ready-set$(\alpha) \subseteq$ pointer-set(α);

(II) if process(f,g) and f and g are both in pointer-set(α), then $f=g$;

(III) if not process(f,g), then $f\epsilon$pointer-set(α) iff $f\epsilon$pointer-set(αg).

Proof. Let "$(L_1,\ldots,L_n,G)$" be a typical element of D where $P = \langle A,D,w \rangle$.

(I)   Suppose that f is in ready-set(α). Then by the definition of a system of processes,

$$f = \underline{\text{when}}\ L_i = \text{address}(f) \wedge p(G)\ \underline{\text{do}}\ L_i \leftarrow b(G);\ G \leftarrow t(G)$$

where $i = $ program-counter(f). Also by the definition of ready-set, $f(\text{value}(\alpha)) \neq$ value(α). Thus, by the definition of $\underline{\text{when}}\ \underline{\text{do}}$ notation, $L_i[\text{value}(\alpha)]=\text{address}(f)$; hence, f is in pointer-set(α).

(II) Suppose that f and g are both in pointer-set(α) and process(f,g). Since f and g are actions, we can assume that

$$f = \underline{\text{when}}\ L_i = \text{address}(f) \wedge p(G)\ \underline{\text{do}}\ L_i \leftarrow b(G);\ G \leftarrow t(G)$$

$$g = \underline{\text{when}}\ L_i = \text{address}(g) \wedge p'(G)\ \underline{\text{do}}\ L_i \leftarrow b'(G);\ G \leftarrow t'(G).$$

Since f and g are both in pointer-set(α), $L_i[\text{value}(\alpha)] = \text{address}(f)$ and $L_i[\text{value}(\alpha)] = \text{address}(g)$. Therefore, by condition (3) of the definition of a system of a process, $f=g$.

(III) Suppose that not process(f,g). The definition of a system of processes implies that $L_i[\text{value}(\alpha)] = L_i[\text{value}(\alpha g)]$ where $i = $ program-counter(f). By the definition of pointer-set, (III) is seen to be true. $\square$

These properties will be referenced by their respective roman numerals. Property II states: each program counter points to at most one action. Property III states: program counters cannot be changed by actions from another process, i.e., by actions that use another program counter.

3. Schedulers

In this section the concept of scheduler is defined. This concept is used to state the theorem of Habermann [6]. More importantly, the concept of scheduler is central to an understanding of "fairness".

Definition Suppose that P is a system of processes. Then T is a scheduler for P provided T is a predicate on the timings of P.

A scheduler can select timings according to a number of criterion. First, the scheduler might "enforce a priority" among the actions. For example, the actions that control a hardware device may be given priority over the actions of a user's program. Second, the scheduler might enforce "fairness" among the actions. For instance, consider a disk queuer that uses the "least arm movement criterion" to select the next request. Often the scheduler is designed so that requests for a distance part of the disk do not wait forever. Third, the scheduler might "enforce the release mechanism of PV" (Dijkstra [13]).

The separation of the notion of scheduler from the notion of process allows a great deal of freedom. It is possible to study the same system of processes with respect to a variety of schedulers. No one scheduler is presented as the "correct one"; instead, several schedulers are studied.

Definition A timing α in P a system of processes is semi-active provided for $1 \leq i \leq \text{length}(\alpha)$, $\alpha_i \epsilon \text{pointer-set}(\alpha_1 \ldots \alpha_{i-1})$.

Theorem 2. Suppose that P is a system of processes, and suppose that $P_1, \ldots, P_m$ are the equivalence classes of process$_P$. Also suppose that $N_1, \ldots, N_k$ are in the set $\{1, \ldots, m\}$. Then there is at most one semi-active timing α such that for all $1 \leq i \leq k$, $\alpha_i \epsilon P_{N_i}$.

Proof. Immediate from property II. □

Theorem 2 is implicitly used in other theories of processes. They usually consider timings as sequences of "process names" instead of as sequences of actions. The key observation is: for semi-active timings, it is immaterial whether timings are considered as sequences of process names or as sequences of actions.

3.1 Blocking and the PV release scheduler

It is instructive to consider the timing 13521 of the system of processes EX1. This timing is semi-active. The "execution" of this timing is informally:

    1 this action changes L_1 to 2 and a to 0;

    3 this action does not change the state - it is now "blocked";

    5 this action does not change the state - it is now "blocked";

    2 this action changes L_1 to 1 and a to 1;

    1 this action changes L_1 to 2 and a to 0.

The usual definition of PV (e.g., Dijkstra [13]) rules out this timing. The informal reason that the timing 13521 is not allowed is: "P's that are blocked, i.e., 3 and 5, must be given priority over P's that are not blocked, i.e., 1". The way our model handles this restriction is that there is a scheduler T such that

        if a timing satisfies T, then the timing "gives blocked P's
        priority over other P's".

In particular, 13521 does not satisfy T.

Definition Suppose that α is a finite timing. Then define blocked-set(α) inductively as follows:

    (1) blocked-set($\wedge$) is the empty set;

    (2) if $\alpha_k \notin$ ready-set($\alpha_1 \ldots \alpha_{k-1}$), then

        blocked-set($\alpha_1 \ldots \alpha_k$) = blocked-set($\alpha_1 \ldots \alpha_{k-1}$)$\cup \{\alpha_k\}$;

    (3) if $\alpha_k \in$ ready-set($\alpha_1 \ldots \alpha_{k-1}$), then

        blocked-set($\alpha_1 \ldots \alpha_k$) = blocked-set($\alpha_1 \ldots \alpha_{k-1}$)$- \{\alpha_k\}$.

Note, $\cup$ is set union and $-$ is set difference.

Informally, the action α_k is "added" to blocked-set($\alpha_1 \ldots \alpha_{k-1}$) if α_k cannot "run"; the action α_k is "removed" from blocked-set($\alpha_1 \ldots \alpha_{k-1}$) if α_k can "run". For example, consider again the timing 13521 of the system of processes EX1. Then blocked-set(13521) = $\{3,5\}$; this formalizes the intuitive statement made earlier.

In order for an action to be in blocked-set($\alpha_1 \ldots \alpha_k$), it must have been "tried". More exactly, blocked-set($\alpha_1 \ldots \alpha_k$) $\subseteq \{\alpha_1 \ldots \alpha_k\}$. For instance, consider the timing 13 in the system of processes EX1. Clearly, blocked-set(13) = $\{3\}$. Note, action 5 is not in ready-set(13). However, action 5 is not in blocked-set(13); for it has not been tried.

For timings that are not semi-active, blocked-set(α) can behave in strange ways. For instance, (in EX1) action 2 is not in ready-set($\wedge$); hence, blocked-set(2)=$\{2\}$. However, it is definitely "pathological" to have a V(a) inserted into blocked-set. This "pathology" can be avoided by only considering blocked-set(α) for semi-active timings α. In fact suppose that P is a PV system of processes. Then

      if f $\in$ blocked-set(α) and α is semi-active, then f is a P(S), for some S.

Theorem 3. Suppose that P is a system of processes and α is a finite semi-active timing. Then blocked-set(α) $\subseteq$ pointer-set(α).

Proof. This an immediate consequence of property III and the definitions of blocked-set and semi-active. $\square$

Definition A timing α is a _release_ timing in a system of processes provided for $1 \le i \le$ length(α),

    if blocked-set($\alpha_1 \ldots \alpha_{i-1}$)$\cap$ ready-set($\alpha_1 \ldots \alpha_{i-1}$) is non-empty, then

    $\alpha_i \in$ blocked-set($\alpha_1 \ldots \alpha_{i-1}$)$\cap$ ready-set($\alpha_1 \ldots \alpha_{i-1}$)

Suppose that αf is a semi-active timing in a system of processes. Informally, the set of actions in the set blocked-set(α)$\cap$ ready-set(α) is the set of actions that satisfy

    (1) they can "run",

(2)   they were at "one time blocked",

(3)   they have never been "unblocked".

The release restriction is: if this set is nonempty, then f must be in this set.
A release timing "enforces a kind of priority rule": the actions in blocked-set
(α) $\cap$ ready-set(α) have a "priority" over all other actions. However, there is
no priority among the actions in blocked-set(α) $\cap$ ready-set(α). The definition
of release is essentially due to Dijkstra [13].

Consider once again the timing 13521 of EX1. The objection stated informally
earlier is: 13521 is not a release timing. Both 13523 and 13525 are release
timings. The release restriction enforces no priority based on "the order an
action is added to blocked-set".

Most discussions of PV systems of processes implicitly assume that schedulers
always select release timings. An example of this assumption in the theorem
found in Habermann [6]. This theorem is a property of PV systems of processes
and the release scheduler. Some folklore in the synchronization area states
that there are two kinds of PV. In our model there is one kind of PV system of
processes; however, PV systems of processes behave differently for different
schedulers.

Suppose that P is a PV system of processes and that S is a semaphore. Also
suppose that α is a semi-active release timing. In order to state Habermann's
theorem, define three functions as follows.

(1)   ns(i) = the number of k with $1 \leq k \leq i$ such that

$\alpha_k \in$ ready-set($\alpha_1...\alpha_{k-1}$) and α_k is a V(S).

(2)   np(i) = the number of k with $1 \leq k \leq i$ such that

$\alpha_k \in$ ready-set($\alpha_1...\alpha_{k-1}$) and α_k is a P(S).

(3)   nw(i) = the number of k with $1 \leq k \leq i$ such that

$\alpha_k \notin$ blocked-set($\alpha_1...\alpha_{k-1}$) and α_k is a P(S).

The functions ns, np, and nw indicate respectively:

ns: how many times V(S) was executed;

np: how many times P(S) was executed;

nw: how many times P(S) was tried.

Say the integer i performs a release iff α_i is a V(S) and blocked-set($\alpha_1...\alpha_{i-1}$)
contains a P(S). Then Habermann's theorem is:

(4)   if i does not perform a release, then

$$np(i) = MIN(nw(i), ns(i) + S_o)$$

where S_o is the initial value of S.

Habermann's theorem can be rephrased into a more intuitive form. First, nw(i) -
np(i) is the cardinality of the set blocked-set($\alpha_1...\alpha_i$)$\cap$ {f|f is a P(S)}.

Second, $ns(i) + S_o - np(i)$ is equal to $S[value(\alpha_1...\alpha_i)]$. Thus, (4) is equivalent to

(5) if i does not perform a release, then either

(a) blocked-set$(\alpha_1...\alpha_i)$ contains no P(S), or

(b) $S[value(\alpha_1...\alpha_i)] = 0$.

Informally, if i does not perform a release, then either there are no "blocked P(S)'s" or the "semaphore S is 0".

For example, let P = EX1 and let α = 13523. The values of the functions ns, np, nw are displayed in figure 3. Since 5 does not perform a release,

$$np(5) = MIN(nw(5), ns(5) + 1).$$

Note, $np(4) \neq MIN(nw(4), ns(4) + 1)$: this is true since 4 does perform a release. The relation $np(i) = MIN(nw(i), ns(i) + 1)$ does not hold "when a release is in progress"; it does hold at all other places.

3.2 "Fairness"

The intuitive concept of "fairness" is not expressed by the release scheduler. For example, consider the timing 12... (12 repeated forever) in EX1. This timing is a semi-active release timing; however, intuitively it is not "fair".

Definition The timing α is pointer-bounded provided if f is in pointer-set $(\alpha_1...\alpha_k)$ and f is not in pointer-set$(\alpha_1...\alpha_{k-1})$, then for some m > k, α_m=f.

Note, if k=0, then by convention: pointer-set(α_{-1}) is the empty set. Thus, if α is pointer-bounded and f is in pointer-set($\wedge$), then for some m $\geq$ 0, α_m=f.

Informally, a timing is pointer-bounded if no action "waits forever for a chance to be tried". For instance, the timing 12... (12 repeated forever) in EX1 is not pointer-bounded.

The rest of this section explores the ramifications of the assumptions semi-active, release, and pointer-bounded. It is claimed that timings that satisfy these three restrictions express the concept of "fairness". Caution, the timing 135231413... (231413 repeated forever) is a semi-active release pointer-bounded timing in EX1. In this timing

"one of the processes of EX1 never executes".

Thus, while the notions semi-active release pointer-bounded enforce a notion of fairness, it is a weak one. Clearly, it is possible to define stronger notions of "fairness".

Theorem 4. Suppose that α is an infinite semi-active pointer-bounded timings. Then

$$\forall i \geq m[f \in \text{pointer-set}(\alpha_1...\alpha_i)] \text{ implies } \bigvee^{\infty} j[f \in \text{blocked-set}(\alpha_1...\alpha_j)].$$

<u>Proof</u>. Suppose that $f \in$ pointer-set$(\alpha_1 \ldots \alpha_i)$, for all $i \geq m$. Without loss of generality, also suppose that $f \notin$ pointer-set$(\alpha_1 \ldots \alpha_{m-1})$. Then

(*) if $\alpha_i = f$ and $i \geq m$, then $\alpha_i \notin$ ready-set$(\alpha_1 \ldots \alpha_{i-1})$.

For conversely suppose that $\alpha_i = f$ and $i \geq m$ and $\alpha_i \in$ ready-set$(\alpha_1 \ldots \alpha_{i-1})$. Then by the definition of a system of processes[+], $\alpha_i \notin$ pointer-set$(\alpha_1 \ldots \alpha_i)$. Since $\alpha_i = f$ this is a contradiction; hence, (*) is true. By the definition of pointer-bounded, there is a $j \geq m$ such that $\alpha_j = f$. Finally, by the definition of blocked-set and (*), for all $k \geq j+1$, $f \in$ blocked-set$(\alpha_1 \ldots \alpha_k)$. $\square$

<u>Definition</u> The system of processes P <u>never halts</u> provided for any finite timing α, ready-set(α) is nonempty.

<u>Theorem 5.</u> Suppose that P never halts and α is an infinite semi-active pointer-bounded release timing in P. Then

$$\forall^{\infty} k[\alpha_k \in \text{ready-set}(\alpha_1 \ldots \alpha_{k-1})].$$

<u>Proof.</u> Suppose there is a m such that for all $k \geq m$, $\alpha_k \notin$ ready-set$(\alpha_1 \ldots \alpha_{k-1})$. Since P never halts, there is an action f such that $f \in$ ready-set$(\alpha_1 \ldots \alpha_k)$, for all $k \geq m$. By theorem 4 and property I, $f \in$ blocked-set$(\alpha_1 \ldots \alpha_k)$, for some $k \geq m$. It then follows, by release, that

$$\alpha_{k+1} \in \text{blocked-set}(\alpha_1 \ldots \alpha_k) \cap \text{ready-set}(\alpha_1 \ldots \alpha_k).$$

This is a contradiction. $\square$

Theorems 4 and 5 are basic tools for analyzing semi-active release pointer-bounded timings. Theorem 4 states that "actions that are always in the pointer-set are eventually placed into blocked-set". Theorem 5 states that "a system of processes that never halts must make an infinite number of state changes".

Next a series of four examples will be presented. These examples should demonstrate the "power" of the notion of "fairness" enforced by the scheduler T:

T(α) iff α is a semi-active release pointer-bounded timing.

This scheduler is important since most interesting schedulers T' are stronger than T, i.e., T'(α) implies T(α).

<u>Example 1.</u>

Consider the system of processes EX1. Suppose that α is an infinite semi-active release pointer-bounded timing. Then at least <u>two</u> of the following assertions are true:

[+]In a system of processes, $g \notin$ pointer-set(βg).

(1) $\forall^\infty k[\alpha_k \in \text{ready-set}(\alpha_1 \ldots \alpha_{k-1})$ and $\alpha_k \in \{1,2\}]$

(2) $\forall^\infty k[\alpha_k \in \text{ready-set}(\alpha_1 \ldots \alpha_{k-1})$ and $\alpha_k \in \{3,4\}]$

(3) $\forall^\infty k[\alpha_k \in \text{ready-set}(\alpha_1 \ldots \alpha_{k-1})$ and $\alpha_k \in \{5,6\}]$

Informally, at least two "processes execute infinitely often". Conversely suppose that only (1) is true; the other cases are handled in a similar manner. By theorem 4, there is a k such that for $i \geq k$, 3 and 5 are both in blocked-set $(\alpha_1 \ldots \alpha_i)$. It is easy to see that EX1 never halts; hence, by theorem 5, there is a $j \geq k$ such that $\alpha_j = 2$ and 2 is in ready-set$(\alpha_1 \ldots \alpha_{j-1})$. Clearly, 1 is not in pointer-set$(\alpha_1 \ldots \alpha_{j-1})$; thus, by theorem 3, 1 is not in blocked-set$(\alpha_1 \ldots \alpha_{j-1})$. Finally, by release, α_{j+1} is equal to 3 or 5. This is a contradiction; hence, at least two of the assertions (1), (2), and (3) are true.

Example 2.

Consider now the system of processes EX2. A formal representation of EX2 is contained in figure 4; an informal representation is in figure 5. Suppose that α is an infinite semi-active pointer-bounded timing. Then all three of the following assertions are true:

(1) $\forall^\infty k[\alpha_k \in \text{ready-set}(\alpha_1 \ldots \alpha_{k-1})$ and $\alpha_k \in \{1,2,3,4\}]$

(2) $\forall^\infty k[\alpha_k \in \text{ready-set}(\alpha_1 \ldots \alpha_{k-1})$ and $\alpha_k \in \{5,6,7,8\}]$

(3) $\forall^\infty k[\alpha_k \in \text{ready-set}(\alpha_1 \ldots \alpha_{k-1})$ and $\alpha_k \in \{9,10,11,12\}]$.

Informally, all three "processes execute infinitely often". The proof used in example 1 can be modified to prove that (1), (2), and (3) are true. The key observation is: blocked-set(α) contains at most one P(a) (respectively P(b), P(c)).

Example 3.

Next consider the system of processes H. A formal representation of H is in figure 6; an informal representation is in figure 7. H is obtained from the system of processes used by Brinch Hansen [14] to "solve" the second reader-writer problem of Courtois, Heymans, Parnas [1]. (Note, the footnote correction suggested by Brinch Hansen has been included in the construction of H.) Essentially H is obtained by deleting actions extraneous to this discussion.

Define α to be the timing

1 2 3 4 13 14 15 16 7 5 19 [8 17 6 8 9 17 10

1 2 11 18 2 3 11 4 13 5 14 12 14 15 5 16 7]...

(repeated the bracketed part forever). Note, α_i is underlined if $\alpha_i \notin$ ready-set $(\alpha_1 \ldots \alpha_{i-1})$. The timing α is a semi-active release pointer-bounded timing; moreover, for $k \geq 12$, α_k is not in WRITER. Therefore, in the system of processes H, it is possible for "READER'S to stream by forever", i.e.,

not $\forall^\infty k[\alpha_k \in \text{ready-set}(\alpha_1 \ldots \alpha_{k-1})$ and $\alpha_k \in \text{WRITER}]$.

This is the reason Courtois, Heymans, Parnas [3] claimed that Brinch Hansen did not "solve" the second reader-writer problem.

Example 4.

Finally consider the system of processes CHP2. A formal representation of CHP2 is in figure 8; an informal representation is in figure 9. CHP2 is the system of processes used by Courtois, Heymans, Parnas [1] to "solve" the second reader-writer problem.

Suppose that α is an infinite semi-active release pointer-bounded timing. Then

(1) $\forall^{\infty}k[\alpha_k \in$ ready-set$(\alpha_1 \ldots \alpha_{k-1})$ and $\alpha_k \in$ WRITER-i, for some i].

Informally, in CHP2, it is not possible "for READER-i's to stream by while the WRITER-j's wait forever". Conversely suppose that for $i \geq m$, α_i is not in WRITER-j, for any j. Let f^i be the action in WRITER-i such that

$$f^i \in \text{pointer-set}(\alpha_1 \ldots \alpha_k), \text{ for all } k \geq m.$$

By theorem 4, $f^i \in$ blocked-set$(\alpha_1 \ldots \alpha_k)$, for all $k \geq m'$. Clearly, f^i is either (1,i), (4,i), (6,i), or (9,i). Now all the f^i's cannot be (1,i) and (9,i). Otherwise, m2 is 1 which is a contradiction. Thus, without loss generality, either f^i is (4,1) or (6,1).

Case f^i is (6,1). Let k be the maximum interger such that $\alpha_k=(4,1)$ and $\alpha_k \in$ ready-set$(\alpha_1 \ldots \alpha_{k-1})$. Clearly, a[value$(\alpha_1 \ldots \alpha_{k-1})$]=0; hence, for $i \geq k$, a[value $(\alpha_1 \ldots \alpha_i)$]=0. CHP2 never halts (for a detailed proof of this fact see Lipton [15]). Therefore, theorem 5 implies that for some $i \geq k$ and some n, $\alpha_i=(21,n)$. Thus, a[value$(\alpha_1 \ldots \alpha_i)$] > 0; and this is a contradiction.

Case f^i is (4,1). Again by theorem 5, for some $i > m'$ and some n, $\alpha_i=(21,n)$ and $\alpha_i \in$ ready-set$(\alpha_1 \ldots \alpha_{i-1})$. An easy argument based on the semaphore m3 shows that (15,n') $\notin$ pointer-set$(\alpha_1 \ldots \alpha_{i-1})$, for $n \neq n'$. Thus, by theorem 3, (15,n') $\notin$ blocked-set$(\alpha_1 \ldots \alpha_{i-1})$, for $n \neq n'$; therefore, blocked-set$(\alpha_1 \ldots \alpha_{i-1})$ contains no P(a) from a READER-j. However, by the release restriction, α_i is a (4,j); this is a contradiction.

Hence, statement (1) is true.

4. Conclusions

The concepts of process and scheduler have been developed as separate but related concepts. This separation makes explicit many statements which otherwise would be implicit. These statements include: a formal definition of the PV release scheduler, a statement of Habermann's theorem, and a series of examples demonstrating how schedulers can enforce fairness. While our model demonstrates how separating the concepts of process and scheduler leads to valuable insight, there are many questions that remain. Indeed, our contribution is in supplying a sound definitional framework for future research.

References

1. P. J. Courtois, F. Heymans, D. L. Parnas. Concurrent control with "readers" and "writers". CACM 14(10):667-668.

2. P. Brinch Hansen. A reply on comments on "A comparison of two synchronizing concepts", Acta Informatica 2:189-190.

3. P. J. Courtois, F. Heymans, D. L. Parnas. Comments on "A comparison of two synchronizing concepts by P. Brinch Hansen". Acta Informatica 1:375-376.

4. R. J. Lipton. Limitations of synchronization primitives with conditional branching and global variables. To appear in Sixth Annual ACM Symposium on Theory of Computing, April 1974.

5. E. W. Dijkstra. Cooperating Sequential Processes, Programming Languages, edited by F. Genuys. 43-112.

6. A. N. Habermann. Synchronization of Communicating Processes. CACM 15(3): 171-176.

7. H. Vantilborgh and A. van Lamsweerde. On an extension of Dijkstra's semaphore primitives. Information processing letters. 1:181-186.

8. S. S. Patil. Limitations and capabilities of Dijkstra's semaphore primitives for coordination among processes. Project MAC Computational Structures Group Memo 57.

9. E. W. Dijkstra. Unpublished manuscript.

10. P. Wodon. Still another tool for controlling cooperating algorithms. Carnegie-Mellon University Report.

11. J. H. Saltzer. Traffic Control in a Multiplexed Computer Systems, PhD thesis, MIT (Project MAC).

12. R. J. Lipton. On Synchronization Primitive Systems, Yale University Research Report #22.

13. E. W. Dijkstra. The Structure of the "THE" Multiprogramming System. CACM 11(5):341-347.

14. P. Brinch Hansen. A comparison of two synchronizing concepts. Acta Informatica 1:190-199.

15. R. J. Lipton. Reduction: A New Method of Proving Properties of Systems of Processes. In preparation.

<u>program counter</u> L_1, L_2, L_3; (initially 1)

<u>semaphore</u> S; (initially 1)

PROCESS-1

  (1)   <u>when</u> $L_1=1 \wedge S>0$ <u>do</u> $L_1 \leftarrow 2$; $S \leftarrow S-1$

  (2)   <u>when</u> $L_1=2$ <u>do</u> $L_1 \leftarrow 1$, $S \leftarrow S+1$

PROCESS-2

  (3)   <u>when</u> $L_2=1 \wedge S>0$ <u>do</u> $L_2 \leftarrow 2$; $S \leftarrow S-1$

  (4)   <u>when</u> $L_2=2$ <u>do</u> $L_2 \leftarrow 1$; $S \leftarrow S+1$

PROCESS-3

  (5)   <u>when</u> $L_3=1 \wedge S>0$ <u>do</u> $L_3 \leftarrow 2$; $S \leftarrow S-1$

  (6)   <u>when</u> $L_3=2$ <u>do</u> $L_3 \leftarrow 1$; $S \leftarrow S+1$

    Figure 1.[+]   System of Processes EX1:   formal representation

<u>semaphore</u> S; (initially 1)

PROCESS-1

  (1)   P(S);

  (2)   V(S);

PROCESS-2

  (3)   P(S);

  (4)   V(S);

PROCESS-3

  (5)   P(S);

  (6)   V(S);

    Figure 2.   System of Processes EX1:   informal representation

---

[+]This figure and subsequent ones employ several notational conventions. However, translation to precisely defined systems of processes should be clear.

integer i	ns(i)	np(i)	nw(i)
1	0	1	1
2	0	1	2
3	0	1	3
4	1	1	3
5	1	2	3

Figure 3. The functions ns, np, nw for the timing 13523 in EX1.

program counter L_1, L_2, L_3; (initially 1)

semaphore a, b, c; (initially 1)

PROCESS-1

    (1) when $L_1=1 \wedge a>0$ do $L_1 \leftarrow 2$; $a \leftarrow a-1$

    (2) when $L_1=2 \wedge b>0$ do $L_1 \leftarrow 3$; $b \leftarrow b-1$

    (3) when $L_1=3$ do $L_1 \leftarrow 4$; $a \leftarrow a+1$

    (4) when $L_1=4$ do $L_1 \leftarrow 1$; $b \leftarrow b+1$

PROCESS-2

    (5) when $L_2=1 \wedge a>0$ do $L_2 \leftarrow 2$; $a \leftarrow a-1$

    (6) when $L_2=2 \wedge c>0$ do $L_2 \leftarrow 3$; $c \leftarrow c-1$

    (7) when $L_2=3$ do $L_2 \leftarrow 4$; $a \leftarrow a+1$

    (8) when $L_2=4$ do $L_2 \leftarrow 1$; $c \leftarrow c+1$

PROCESS-3

    (9) when $L_3=1 \wedge b>0$ do $L_3 \leftarrow 2$; $b \leftarrow b-1$

    (10) when $L_3=2 \wedge c>0$ do $L_3 \leftarrow 3$; $c \leftarrow c-1$

    (11) when $L_3=3$ do $L_3 \leftarrow 4$; $b \leftarrow b+1$

    (12) when $L_3=4$ do $L_3 \leftarrow 1$; $c \leftarrow c+1$

Figure 4. System of Processes EX2: formal representation

<u>semaphore</u> a, b, c; (initially 1)

PROCESS-1

    (1) P(a);

    (2) P(b);

    (3) V(a);

    (4) V(b);

PROCESS-2

    (5) P(a);

    (6) P(c);

    (7) V(a);

    (8) V(c);

PROCESS-3

    (9) P(b);

   (10) P(c);

   (11) V(b);

   (12) V(c);

Figure 5. System of Processes EX2: informal representation

<u>program counter</u> L_1, L_2, L_3, L_4; (initially 1)

<u>semaphore</u> a, b; (initially 1)

READER-1

    (1) <u>when</u> $L_1 = 1 \wedge b > 0$ <u>do</u> $L_1 \leftarrow 2$; $b \leftarrow b-1$

    (2) <u>when</u> $L_1 = 2 \wedge a > 0$ <u>do</u> $L_1 \leftarrow 3$; $a \leftarrow a-1$

    (3) <u>when</u> $L_1 = 3$ <u>do</u> $L_1 \leftarrow 4$; $a \leftarrow a+1$

    (4) <u>when</u> $L_1 = 4$ <u>do</u> $L_1 \leftarrow 5$; $b \leftarrow b+1$

    (5) <u>when</u> $L_1 = 5 \wedge a > 0$ <u>do</u> $L_1 \leftarrow 6$; $a \leftarrow a-1$

    (6) <u>when</u> $L_1 = 6$ <u>do</u> $L_1 \leftarrow 1$; $a \leftarrow a+1$

READER-2

    (7) <u>when</u> $L_2 = 1 \wedge b > 0$ <u>do</u> $L_2 \leftarrow 2$; $b \leftarrow b-1$

    (8) <u>when</u> $L_2 = 2 \wedge a > 0$ <u>do</u> $L_2 \leftarrow 3$; $a \leftarrow a-1$

(9) <u>when</u> $L_2=3$ <u>do</u> $L_2 \leftarrow 4$; $a \leftarrow a+1$

(10) <u>when</u> $L_2=4$ <u>do</u> $L_2 \leftarrow 5$; $b \leftarrow b+1$

(11) <u>when</u> $L_2=5 \wedge a>0$ <u>do</u> $L_2 \leftarrow 6$; $a \leftarrow a-1$

(12) <u>when</u> $L_2=6$ <u>do</u> $L_2 \leftarrow 1$; $a \leftarrow a+1$

READER-3

(13) <u>when</u> $L_3=1 \wedge b>0$ <u>do</u> $L_3 \leftarrow 2$; $b \leftarrow b-1$

(14) <u>when</u> $L_3=2 \wedge a>0$ <u>do</u> $L_3 \leftarrow 3$; $a \leftarrow a-1$

(15) <u>when</u> $L_3=3$ <u>do</u> $L_3 \leftarrow 4$; $a \leftarrow a+1$

(16) <u>when</u> $L_3=4$ <u>do</u> $L_3 \leftarrow 5$; $b \leftarrow b+1$

(17) <u>when</u> $L_3=5 \wedge a>0$ <u>do</u> $L_3 \leftarrow 6$; $a \leftarrow a-1$

(18) <u>when</u> $L_3=6$ <u>do</u> $L_3 \leftarrow 1$; $a \leftarrow a+1$

WRITER

(19) <u>when</u> $L_4=1 \wedge a>0$ <u>do</u> $L_4 \leftarrow 2$; $a \leftarrow a-1$

Figure 6.   System of Processes H: formal representation

<u>semaphore</u> a, b; (initially 1)

READER-1

    (1)   P(b);

    (2)   P(a);

    (3)   V(a);

    (4)   V(b);

    (5)   P(a);

    (6)   V(a);

READER-2

    (7)   P(b);

    (8)   P(a);

    (9)   V(a);

  (10)   V(b);

  (11)   P(a);

  (12)   V(a);

READER-3

    (13) P(b);

    (14) P(a);

    (15) V(a);

    (16) V(b);

    (17) P(a);

    (18) V(a);

WRITER

    (19) P(a);

Figure 7. System of Processes H: informal representation

program counter $L_1, \ldots, L_{max}, K_1, \ldots, K_{max}$; (initially 1)

integer r,w; (initially 0)

semaphore m1,m2,m3,a,b; (initially 1)

WRITER-i (1≤i≤max)

(1)	when $K_i = 1 \wedge m2 \geq 1$	do	$K_i \leftarrow 2$; $m2 \leftarrow m2-1$
(2)	when $K_i = 2$	do	$K_i \leftarrow 3$; $w \leftarrow w+1$
(3)	when $K_i = 3$	do	$K_i \leftarrow$ if $w=1$ then 4 else 5
(4)	when $K_i = 4 \wedge a \geq 1$	do	$K_i \leftarrow 5$; $a \leftarrow a-1$
(5)	when $K_i = 5$	do	$K_i \leftarrow 6$; $m2 \leftarrow m2+1$
(6)	when $K_i = 6 \wedge b \geq 1$	do	$K_i \leftarrow 7$; $b \leftarrow b-1$
(7)	when $K_i = 7$	do	$K_i \leftarrow 8$
(8)	when $K_i = 8$	do	$K_i \leftarrow 9$; $b \leftarrow b+1$
(9)	when $K_i = 9 \wedge m2 \geq 1$	do	$K_i \leftarrow 10$; $m2 \leftarrow m2-1$
(10)	when $K_i = 10$	do	$K_i \leftarrow 11$; $w \leftarrow w-1$
(11)	when $K_i = 11$	do	$K_i \leftarrow$ if $w=0$ then 12 else 13
(12)	when $K_i = 12$	do	$K_i \leftarrow 13$; $a \leftarrow a+1$
(13)	when $K_i = 13$	do	$K_i \leftarrow 1$; $m2 \leftarrow m2+1$

READER-i (1≤i≤max)

(14) <u>when</u> $L_i=1 \wedge m3 \geq 1$ <u>do</u> $L_i \leftarrow 2$; $m3 \leftarrow m3-1$

(15) <u>when</u> $L_i=2 \wedge a \geq 1$ <u>do</u> $L_i \leftarrow 3$; $a \leftarrow a-1$

(16) <u>when</u> $L_i=3 \wedge m1 \geq 1$ <u>do</u> $L_i \leftarrow 4$; $m1 \leftarrow m1-1$

(17) <u>when</u> $L_i=4$ <u>do</u> $L_i \leftarrow 5$; $r \leftarrow r+1$

(18) <u>when</u> $L_i=5$ <u>do</u> $L_i \leftarrow$ <u>if</u> r=1 <u>then</u> 6 <u>else</u> 7

(19) <u>when</u> $L_i=6 \wedge b \geq 1$ <u>do</u> $L_i \leftarrow 7$; $b \leftarrow b-1$

(20) <u>when</u> $L_i=7$ <u>do</u> $L_i \leftarrow 8$; $m1 \leftarrow m1+1$

(21) <u>when</u> $L_i=8$ <u>do</u> $L_i \leftarrow 9$; $a \leftarrow a+1$

(22) <u>when</u> $L_i=9$ <u>do</u> $L_i \leftarrow 10$; $m3 \leftarrow m3+1$

(23) <u>when</u> $L_i=10$ <u>do</u> $L_i \leftarrow 11$

(24) <u>when</u> $L_i=11 \wedge m1 \geq 1$ <u>do</u> $L_i \leftarrow 12$; $m1 \leftarrow m1-1$

(25) <u>when</u> $L_i=12$ <u>do</u> $L_i \leftarrow 13$; $r \leftarrow r-1$

(26) <u>when</u> $L_i=13$ <u>do</u> $L_i \leftarrow$ <u>if</u> r=0 <u>then</u> 14 <u>else</u> 15

(27) <u>when</u> $L_i=14$ <u>do</u> $L_i \leftarrow 15$; $b \leftarrow b+1$

(28) <u>when</u> $L_i=15$ <u>do</u> $L_i \leftarrow 1$; $m1 \leftarrow m1+1$

Figure 8. System of Processes CHP2: formal representation

<u>integer</u> r,w; (initially 0)

<u>semaphore</u> m1,m2,m3,a,b; (initially 1)

WRITER-i (1≤i≤max)	READER-i (1≤i≤max)
(1,i) P(m2);	(14,i) P(m3);
(2,i) w←w+1	(15,i) P(a);
(3,i) <u>if</u> w=1 <u>then</u>	(16,i) P(m1);
(4,i) P(a);	(17,i) r←r+1;
(5,i) V(m2);	(18,i) <u>if</u> r=1 <u>then</u>
(6,i) P(b);	(19,i) P(b);
(7,i) writing is performed;	(20,i) V(m1);
(8,i) V(b);	(21,i) V(a);
(9,i) P(m2);	(22,i) V(m3);

(10,i) w←w-1   (23,i) reading is performed;

(11,i) <u>if</u> w=0 <u>then</u>   (24,i) P(m1)

(12,i)   V(a);   (25,i) r←r-1;

(13,i) V(m2)   (26,i) <u>if</u> r=0 <u>then</u>

                                   (27,i)   V(b);

                                   (28,i) V(m1);

Figure 9. CHP2: informal representation

CARACTÉRISATION FONCTIONNELLE
DES SYSTEMES DE FICHIERS

Christine Parent

Institut de Programmation - Université Paris VI

---

1 - INTRODUCTION

Pour les systèmes hardware, l'existence d'études extrêmement importantes comme celles de Bell et Newell [11] et Iverson [10] , qui présentent des méthodes standard pour les décrire, comparer, classer ou évaluer, a montré et prouvé l'intérêt de savoir établir des descriptions purement fonctionnelles. Celles-ci expriment uniquement le service rendu à l'utilisateur par opposition aux descriptions de structure interne qui décrivent le fonctionnement des mécanismes mis en jeu pour réaliser ce service.

Par contre, pour les systèmes d'exploitation, les publications de résultats d'études basées sur des définitions fonctionnelles sont encore rares. Il en est de même pour les systèmes de fichiers, partie importante des systèmes d'exploitation, qui font l'objet de cet article.

Le concept de système de fichiers est employé ici au sens d'un ensemble de programmes permettant à l'utilisateur de créer/détruire, ouvrir/fermer, lire/écrire des fichiers qui sont des récipients d'informations identifiés par un nom, dotés d'une organisation interne et de méthodes d'acces. Parmi les systèmes de fichiers comparés dans cette étude se trouvent,entre autres, ceux de SIRIS.2, EXEC.8, SCOPE.3, OS/360, CTSS ...

Pour les systèmes de fichiers, les articles parus portent généralement sur la description d'un système particulier, ou proposent un modèle d'architecture [1,3] , ou encore, présentent des comparaisons de systèmes par des tableaux contenant diverses caractéristiques hétérogènes [9] .

Cet article présente une méthode pour obtenir la définition fonctionnelle de tout système de fichiers et pour caractériser leurs fonctions par deux mesures, puis les résultats de cette méthode appliquée à un jeu de systèmes de fichiers.

Au chapitre 2, un questionnaire arborescent détaille progressivement les fonctions de base des systèmes de fichiers et engendre une <u>liste de questions</u> portant chacune sur l'existence d'une fonction élémentaire. La liste des réponses d'un système au questionnaire, qui consistent à déterminer pour chaque question si le système possède ou ne possède pas cette fonction élémentaire, constitue sa <u>définition fonctionnelle</u>. Les définitions fonctionnelles de 11 systèmes de fichiers sont ainsi obtenues.

Le chapitre 3 définit deux classes distinctes de systèmes de fichiers et établit un système de pondération de deux qualités des fonctions élémentaires : leur capacité et leur orientation. Ces deux qualités sont mesurées pour chaque question par un poids : <u>poids de capacité</u>, pour mesurer l'importance du service que cette fonction élémentaire rend aux utilisateurs, et <u>poids d'orientation</u>,pour mesurer si elle est plus ou moins caractéristique de l'une des deux classes de systèmes. Tout système de fichiers est ainsi caractérisé par deux mesures, sa capacité fonctionnelle (ou mesure de la puissance du service rendu par l'ensemble de ses fonctions) et son orientation fonctionnelle (ou mesure globale,pour l'ensemble de ses fonctions, de leur caractère spécifique de l'une des deux classes) ; ces deux mesures sont calculées comme étant les sommes respectives des poids de capacité et d'orientation des fonctions élémentaires que le système possède.

Le dernier chapitre présente les résultats de cette étude, à savoir, les valeurs de la capacité et de l'orientation fonctionnelles pour les systèmes étudiés, et leur représentation sur un diagramme qui permet de constater l'existence des deux classes et d'un système singulier qui n'appartient à aucune des deux. Ce diagramme montre aussi que, pour les deux classes,l'orientation et la capacité fonctionnelles des systèmes sont liées : plus grande est la capacité fonctionnelle d'un système, plus grande est son orientation fonctionnelle ; ce qui se traduit par exemple pour le système de fichiers de l'OS/360, de grande capacité, par une orientation "gestion" très forte.

---

2 - QUESTIONNAIRE DE DEFINITION FONCTIONNELLE DES SYSTEMES DE FICHIERS

Ce chapitre est consacré à la présentation de l'outil permettant d'établir la définition fonctionnelle de tout système de fichiers, à savoir le question-naire (cf. fig. 1).

2.1 - Structure du questionnaire :

Une définition fonctionnelle doit rassembler toutes les informations décrivant les services rendus par le système, et uniquement celles-là. Toutes les autres caractéristiques des systèmes (structure interne, taille du système, langage de programmation, classes de machines pour lesquelles le système est construit, performances ...) n'en font pas partie.

Le degré de précision qu'il faut donner à une définition fonctionnelle dépend de son utilisation ultérieure. La définition la plus précise est une traduction exacte de l'interface utilisateur (ce que devraient être les manuels d'utilisation des systèmes). Toutefois, elle ne peut être employée comme base de comparaison, parce que justement trop précise. C'est donc une définition fonctionnelle simplifiée, contenant la liste de toutes les fonctions offertes par le système et leurs caractéristiques principales, qui est établie dans cette étude.

Le questionnaire permettant d'obtenir ces définitions fonctionnelles simplifiées comporte 40 questions booléennes, chacune testant l'absence ou la présence d'une fonction élémentaire, pourvu que celle-ci soit assez importante du point de vue des utilisateurs pour figurer dans le questionnaire et qu'elle ne soit pas offerte par tous les systèmes de fichiers, car alors elle n'introduirait aucune information dans la défintion fonctionnelle des systèmes de fichiers.

La liste des questions a été obtenue par une analyse progressive des fonctions de base des systèmes de fichiers, ce qui a engendré un questionnaire arborescent, dont le dernier niveau est celui des questions.

Cette analyse a été effectuée à partir de l'étude d'une dizaine de systèmes de fichiers choisis parmi les systèmes actuels les plus significatifs et constituant un éventail complet des différentes tendances. Ces systèmes ont été étudiés au moyen de la seule définition fonctionnelle existante, leur manuel d'utilisation.

2.2 - Analyse fonctionnelle des systèmes de fichiers

Dans un système de fichiers, il est possible de distinguer quatre
fonctions de base. Deux d'entre elles sont liées à la définition
même de fichier : l'identification du fichier et plus généralement
tout ce qui a trait à la création du fichier (choix d'un nom et
définition des protections associées au fichier) et l'organisation du
fichier et les méthodes d'accès associées ; ces deux fonctions, visibles
au programmeur, sont regroupées sous la rubrique "programmation".

Les deux autres fonctions de base, regroupées sous la rubrique
"opération", tiennent de l'exploitation des fichiers sur ordinateurs.
La première permet de définir l'implantation du fichier sur les
mémoires secondaires et la deuxième étudie le contrôle des fichiers
(contrôle des générations de fichiers et contrôle de la connexion des
fichiers aux programmes qui les exploitent).

Le questionnaire est engendré en détaillant progressivement ces quatre
fonctions de base dans les paragraphes suivants.

2.2.1 - Création : Cette première fonction de base regroupe les deux sous-fonctions essentielles d'identification et de protection contre les accès non autorisés des fichiers permanents.

L'identification d'un fichier permanent,c'est à dire le choix de son
nom, dépend de l'existence et de la structure de catalogue. En effet,
les systèmes les plus simples n'ont pas de catalogue et c'est à
l'utilisateur de se souvenir sur quels supports sont implantés ses
fichiers ; les systèmes de capacité intermédiaire cataloguent
uniquement les fichiers implantés sur supports inamovibles ; les
systèmes de plus grande capacité cataloguent, quelque soit leur
support, soit tous les fichiers automatiquement, soit uniquement
ceux précisés par l'utilisateur.

La structure du catalogue peut être simple ou hiérarchisée. Dans ce
dernier cas, certains systèmes, pour assouplir le classement des
fichiers introduit par la hiérarchie, permettent d'établir des
"liens de synonymie" d'un sous-catalogue à un autre : c'est-à-dire,
de référencer depuis un sous-catalogue un fichier d'un autre sous-
catalogue (ou un autre sous-catalogue) par un synonyme.

La protection des fichiers permanents contre les accès non aurorisés
[7, 8] dépend : 1°) de l'existence de mécanismes de protection et
2°) de la finesse ce ces mécanismes. Les systèmes en offrent soit
aucun, soit pour un sous-ensemble des fichiers, soit pour tous les
fichiers. Ces mécanismes sont extrêmement variés et chaque système
en offre un ou plusieurs. La protection est globalement définie
comme étant "fine" si leur nombre est supérieur à deux.

La liste des mécanismes que peut offrir un système de fichiers est la suivante :

- fichier de type "privé" qui n'est accessible que par les travaux ayant le même identificateur que celui qui a créé le fichier.

- fichier de type "lecture seule" ou "écriture seule" qui n'est accessible qu'en lecture ou écriture.

- listes d'utilisateurs par fichier, associées à un ou plusieurs droits (lecture, écriture, ajout d'informations, exécution du fichier...)

- mots de passe par fichier, associés à un ou plusieurs droits, comme dans le cas précédent.

- procédure de contrôle, exécutée lors de chaque requête d'ouverture du fichier et dont le rôle est de tester la validité de la requête.

2.2.2 - Organisations et accès :

Cette fonction, qui a souvent fait l'objet d'études [4, 5, 6], regroupe deux sous-fonctions :

1°) l'organisation de base du fichier qui définit essentiellement s'il est constitué d'enregistrements logiques ou non, et 2°) son organisation d'accès (séquentielle, directe, séquentielle indexée, aléatoire ou partitionnée) et les méthodes d'accès associées.

L'organisation de base d'un fichier comprend : 1°) La définition de son élément générique (unité de base dont est constitué le fichier) qui peut être soit le même que celui de la mémoire centrale (le mot ou l'octet) : c'est alors un "fichier-plat" - véritable extension de la mémoire centrale - soit l'enregistrement logique (appelé aussi article) et 2°) dans ce cas, la définition du blocage (fait de regrouper les enregistrements logiques pour les transférer sur mémoire secondaire) effectué par le système.

L'organisation et les méthodes d'accès est une sous-fonction pour laquelle les systèmes proposent des solutions très diverses, sauf pour l'organisation séquentielle qui est offerte par tous les systèmes et qui donc ne figure pas dans le questionnaire.

Elle comprend trois volets :

- l'organisation directe, qui permet d'accéder aux éléments du fichier en fournissant leur adresse au système ; cette organisation existe pour les fichiers-plat et pour les fichiers à enregistrements logiques.

- l'organisation séquentielle indexée pour les fichiers à enregistrements logiques offre de nombreuses variantes : elle permet d'accéder aux enregistrements logiques soit séquentiellement, soit en fournissant leur clé (ou identificateur) au système. L'accès séquentiel peut suivre soit l'ordre physique de rangement des enregistrements dans le fichier ("séquentiel physique"), soit l'ordre lexicographique des clés. L'index qui réalise l'association clé-adresse peut être à plusieurs niveaux permettant de gérer ainsi des fichiers à très grand nombre d'enregistrements logiques : enfin, certains systèmes offrent la possibilité d'indexer un même fichier sur plusieurs clés différentes.

- d'autres organisations moins fréquemment utilisées sont offertes par les systèmes de plus grande capacité pour les fichiers à enregistrements logiques ; ce sont l'"organisation aléatoire" où chaque enregistrement logique est identifié par une clé et l'association clé-adresse est effectuée via une formule (technique de randomisation), et l'"organisation partitionnée" où le fichier est constitué d'un ensemble indexé de sous-fichiers séquentiels.

2.2.3 - Implantation des fichiers sur mémoire secondaire :

Cette fonction de base comprend 1°) le choix du support sur lequel implanter le fichier et 2°) l'allocation d'espace dans le cas de support à accès direct.

Le choix du support est caractérisé par :

- les types de supports proposés : les systèmes se répartissent globalement en deux groupes, ceux qui possèdent des disques inamovibles et ceux qui possèdent des disques amovibles ;
- la part prise par le système dans le choix : celle-ci peut être nulle (choix entièrement à la charge du préparateur / programmeur), partielle (le préparateur / programmeur peut n'indiquer que le type de support voulu) ou totale (choix entièrement effectué par le système).

L'allocation des mémoires secondaires à accès direct est caractérisée par :

1°) Le type d'allocation offert par le système et par, 2°) la part prise par le système dans le choix de l'emplacement des zones à allouer. Les types d'allocation sont au nombre de trois : l'allocation statique permet de définir un volume fixe pour le fichier, l'allocation statique avec incrément permet de définir un volume fixe et un volume d'incrément qui est alloué une ou plusieurs fois au besoin quand la taille du fichier vient à dépasser le volume prévu, tandis que l'allocation dynamique s'effectue au fur et à mesure des écritures dans le fichier. Le choix de l'emplacement des zones à allouer est effectué dans le cas des système les plus simples par le préparateur, sinon soit au choix par le préparateur ou le système soit toujours par le système.

2.2.4 - Contrôle des fichiers :

Cette fonction de base regroupe les deux fonctions de contrôle des générations de fichiers et de contrôle de la connexion des fichiers aux programmes qui les exploitent.

Les <u>générations</u> d'un fichier permanent sont des copies de ce fichier prises pour en faire l'archivage soit dans un but de protection contre toute perte accidentelle du fichier soit de réutilisation ultérieure. La fonction de contrôle des générations est caractérisée par 1°) l'automatisme de prise des copies, et par 2°) le nombre maximum de générations que peut cataloguer le système. En effet, les systèmes prennent soit automatiquement des copies de tout fichier modifié ou créé, soit ne créent une nouvelle génération que sur ordre explicite de l'utilisateur ; d'autre part, le nombre de générations maximum que peut cataloguer un système de fichiers traduit la puissance de la fonction.

<u>Connexion fichier-programme</u> : Pour qu'un travail puisse exploiter un fichier, il faut que le système établisse une connexion entre le fichier défini par le programme et le fichier réel qui est implanté sur mémoire secondaire. Cette connexion peut être effectuée de deux façons totalement différentes selon les systèmes : soit le système requiert l'emploi d'un ordre-JCL, soit dans le cas contraire, le système permet d'ouvrir (ou de créer) dynamiquement tout fichier. Dans le premier cas, suivant leurs possibilités, les ordres-JCL permettent de rendre les programmes indépendants totalement ou partiellement de la définition des fichiers qu'ils exploitent : en général, ils gèrent l'association nom interne - nom externe de fichier ; certains gèrent aussi le facteur de blocage et le format de l'article.

2.3 - <u>Etablissement des réponses des systèmes de fichiers au questionnaire</u> :

Pour obtenir la définition fonctionnelle d'un système de fichiers, il suffit qu'une personne connaissant bien l'utilisation de ce système réponde au questionnaire. La liste des réponses du système de fichiers constitue sa définition fonctionnelle.

Les réponses des 11 systèmes de fichiers étudiés sont données dans le tableau 1.

Par exemple, la liste des réponses positives (c'est-à-dire la liste des fonctions élémentaires) du système de fichiers de l'OS/360 est la suivante :

- catalogue à la demande
- catalogue hiérarchisé
- protection pour tous les fichiers
- un ou deux mécanismes de protection
- l'élément générique est l'enregistrement logique
- blocage des enregistrements logiques
- organisation directe sur fichier à enregistrements logiques
- organisation séquentielle indexée
- (organisation séquentielle indexée) avec index à plusieurs niveaux.
- autre organisation non séquentielle
- disques amovibles
- le préparateur choisit au moins l'unité (pour le support)
- allocation statique avec incrément
- l' adresse mémoire secondaire est choisie par le préparateur ou le système.
- les générations sont créées sur ordre du préparateur
- plus de 20 générations cataloguées au maximum

- JCL avec nom interne/externe de fichier
- JCL avec gestion du facteur de blocage
- JCL avec gestion du format de l'article.

Cette liste est un très bon résumé des fonctions du système de fichiers de l'OS/360.

---

3 - CAPACITE FONCTIONNELLE ET ORIENTATION FONCTIONNELLE DES SYSTEMES DE FICHIERS

Ce chapitre présente la méthode employée pour évaluer tout système de fichiers par deux mesures : sa capacité et son orientation fonctionnelles.

3.1. Méthode des poids.

Les définitions fonctionnelles établies à partir du questionnaire permettent de comparer les deux systèmes de fichiers en étudiant leurs différences question par question. Cette méthode est évidemment fort peu aisée pour des études comparatives d'un ensemble de systèmes ; notamment une synthèse est difficile à dégager dans ces conditions.

Pour répondre à ces besoins la méthode proposée est d'abord d'attribuer à chacune des fonctions du questionnaire un "poids de capacité", qui mesure l'importance du service qu'elle rend aux utilisateurs.
La capacité fonctionnelle (ou puissance d'un système de fichiers) est alors mesurée comme étant la somme des poids de capacité de ses fonctions. Une méthode semblable a déjà permis une évaluation des langages de programmation [12].

D'autre part, l'étude des systèmes de fichiers actuels montre que ceux-ci se répartissent globalement en deux classes de systèmes qui offrent des jeux de fonctions différents correspondant à deux populations d'utilisateurs aux besoins différents; il est donc intéressant de mesurer par la même méthode le degré d'appartenance de tout système de fichiers à l'une ou l'autre des deux classes. Ce degré d'appartenance, appelé orientation fonctionnelle du système de fichiers est calculé de la même façon à partir des poids d'orientation de ses fonctions. Le poids d'orientation d'une fonction est défini comme mesure de sa spécificité de l'une ou l'autre classe; les fonctions offertes indifféremment par les systèmes de fichiers des deux classes ont un poids d'orientation nul.

Pour définir les poids de capacité et d'orientation de chacune des questions, la structure arborescente du questionnaire est utilisée.

Un poids de capacité globale de valeur 100 est donné au niveau 0 du questionnaire; c'est la valeur maximum de la capacité fonctionnelle des systèmes de fichiers. Ce poids est réparti de niveau en niveau en descendant dans le questionnaire, en partant du principe que deux fonctions de même niveau ont même importance. Les répartitions sont donc homogènes, sauf dans quelques cas (au nombre de 2) bien définis et justifiés en 3.3. Au dernier niveau, pour les questions qui traduisent des variantes exclusives d'une même sous-fonction, le poids de cette sous-fonction est réparti proportionnellement au service rendu.

De la même manière un poids d'orientation global est défini au niveau 0 de valeur (-50 , + 50), - 50 étant la valeur de l'orientation fonctionnelle maximum pour un système de fichiers de classe 2, + 50 pour un système de classe 1. Le même principe de répartition homogène est suivi pour les niveaux 1 à 3, sauf dans deux cas qui sont justifiés en 3.3.

La répartition entre les sous-fonctions est expliquée en 3.2.

Pour chaque niveau du questionnaire, les valeurs des poids de capacité et d'orientation des fonctions sont données sur la figure 1.

3.2. Systèmes de fichiers de classe 1 et systèmes de fichiers de classe 2.

Ce paragraphe définit pour chaque classe les besoins spécifiques de leurs utilisateurs et leurs caractéristiques fonctionnelles. Les définitions de ces classes recouvrent ce qu'il est usuel d'appeler respectivement des systèmes de fichiers "gestion" et "accès on line", cependant ces deux termes n'ont pas été retenus du fait que leur acceptation n'est pas comprise de manière uniforme.

3.2.1. Systèmes de fichiers de classe 1.

Les utilisateurs de ces systèmes sont en général des programmeurs. Les fichiers sont structurés en enregistrements logiques qui correspondent bien à l'unité de traitement de leurs programmes. Le nombre d'enregistrements logiques d'un fichier peut être très important (des millions), et l'accès se fait soit séquentiellement, soit sélectivement d'après leur clé. Les mises à jour sont volumineuses et fréquentes, nécessitant des organisations de fichiers appropriées. Les supports employés comprennent essentiellement des volumes amovibles (dispacks) sur lesquels chaque utilisateur ou groupe d'utilisateurs rassemble ses fichiers.

Les systèmes de classe 1 pour répondre aux besoins de leurs utilisateurs, qui peuvent être très différents d'une exploitation à l'autre, offrent le maximum de possibilités pour chaque fonction et donnent le maximum de liberté et de responsabilités à leurs utilisateurs: quand une fonction peut être réalisée automatiquement par le système, ou par le système sur demande explicite de l'utilisateur, la système de classe 1 choisit cette dernière solution de préférence à la première.

Les fonctions caractéristiques des systèmes de classe 1 sont donc :

- Identification des fichiers :
                    Tous les systèmes, qu'ils soient de classe 1 ou de classe 2 peuvent offrir un catalogue, hiérarchisé ou non, mais demander à l'utilisateur de préciser pour chaque fichier s'il veut ou non le cataloguer est une caractéristique des systèmes de classe 1.

- Protection contre les accès non autorisés :
                    Comme le catalogue, l'existence de mécanismes de protection est une fonction utile aux deux types de systèmes, mais les systèmes de classe 2 qui gèrent souvent un plus grand nombre d'utilisateurs doivent offrir une protection plus fine. Le nombre de mécanismes protection différencie donc les deux classes de systèmes.

- Organisation de base :
                    Fichiers à enregistrements logiques, bloqués pour gagner de l'espace mémoire secondaire du fait que les fichiers sont volumineux.

- Organisations et méthodes d'accès :

Grand choix d'organisations comprenant
nécessairement des organisations avec accès sélectif sur clé, rapide
même si le nombre d'enregistrements logiques est important, et permettant
d'effectuer des mises à jour; l'organisation type qui répond à ces critè-
res est l'organisation séquentielle indexée avec index à plusieurs niveaux et éventuellement indexation sur plusieurs clés.

- Supports :

Essentiellement des disques amovibles, avec possibilité pour
l'utilisateur de choisir les volumes sur lesquels doivent être implantés
ses fichiers.

- Allocation des mémoires secondaires à accès direct :

Nécessité pour l'uti-
lisateur de prévoir quelle sera la taille de son fichier, mais aussi
possibilité de choisir ses adresses d'implantation.

- Contrôle des générations :

Nécessité pour l'utilisateur de définir au
système quand il doit créer une nouvelle copie d'un fichier.

- Contrôle de la connexion programme-fichier :

Connexion effectuée sur ordre-JCL

3.2.2. Systèmes de fichiers de classe 2.

Les utilisateurs de ces systèmes ne sont pas forcément des programmeurs;
ils attendent du système qu'il leur simplifie la tâche en ne leur laissant
voir du système que ce qu'il leur est indispensable de connaître.
Leurs fichiers sont en général des fichiers-plat (accessibles en séquentiel et en direct), qu'ils emploient comme des extensions de la mémoire
centrale. Pour les supports, la tendance est de laisser le système déci-
der de l'implantation des fichiers en fonction de leur taux d'accès, ou
bien les utilisateurs choisissent uniquement le type de support et le
système le(s) volume(s) exact(s).
Les systèmes de classe 2, contrairement à ceux de classe 1, simplifient
donc leur interface utilisateur, offrent peu de choix et remplissent souvent des fonctions automatiquement; d'autre part ils essaient d'offrir le
maximum de souplesse à leurs utilisateurs qui ne sont pas toujours habi-
tués aux contraintes qu'impliquent l'emploi d'un système. Enfin, ils ont
tendance à réduire au maximum les interventions opérateur en salle machine
(ce qui permet par exemple au système MULTICS [2] au MIT de tourner seul
pendant le week-end).

Les fonctions types d'un système de classe 2 sont :

- Identification des fichiers :

L'utilisation d'un catalogue hiérarchisé
avec liens de synonymie est spécifique des systèmes de classe 2 (pour
lesquels la souplesse est un facteur important).

- Protection contre les accès non autorisés :

Protection plus fine que celle
offerte généralement par les systèmes de classe 1 (cf. systèmes de
classe 1).

- Organisation de base :
> Fichiers-plat essentiellement.

- Organisations et méthodes d'accès :
> Organisation séquentielle et directe, peu ou pas d'organisations sélectives (qui n'existent que pour des fichiers à enregistrements logiques), du moins pas d'organisation sélective très complexe comme celles offertes par les systèmes de classe 1.

- Support :
> Des disques inamovibles qui ne nécessitent pas d'interventions opérateur. Le choix du support pour l'implantation des fichiers est fait soit totalement soit partiellement par le système.

- Allocation des mémoires secondaires à accès direct :
> Allocation dynamique (avec choix des adresses d'implantation effectué par le système). Toute cette fonction est ainsi invisible au programmeur.

- Contrôle des générations :
> Prise de copie effectuée automatiquement par le système pour tout fichier récemment créé ou modifié.

- Contrôle de la connexion programme-fichier :
> Les systèmes de classe 2 n'emploient généralement pas de cartes contrôles et offrent ainsi la possibilité de créer et d'ouvrir dynamiquement des fichiers.

3.3. Justification des singularités dans la répartition des poids.

Ce paragraphe explique les quelques cas où le principe de répartition homogène des poids en descendant les niveaux du questionnaire n'a pas été respecté.

3.3.1. Poids de capacité.

Les singularités de répartition pour les poids de capacité sont au nombre de deux :

- la fonction de base "organisations et accès" de poids 25 comprend les deux sous-fonctions "organisation de base" de poids 8 et "organisation et méthodes d'accès" de poids 17: pour le programmeur, la largeur de l'éventail des organisations d'accès qu'offre un système est une des caractéristiques principales de sa capacité, tandis que l'organisation de base (fichier à enregistrements logiques ou fichier-plat) est essentiellement une caractéristique d'orientation.

- la sous-fonction "organisation et méthodes d'accès" de poids 17 comprend trois volets : "organisation directe " de poids 4, "organisation séquentielle indexée" de poids 9 et "organisation autre" de poids 4 : l'organisation séquentielle indexée est en effet celle qui peut offrir de très loin le plus de services aux utilisateurs dans ses versions les plus sophistiquées (index à plusieurs niveaux, indexation sur plusieurs clés).

3.3.2. Poids d'orientation.

Les singularités de répartition pour les poids d'orientation sont aussi au nombre de deux :

- la rubrique "programmation" de poids (-25 , + 25) comprend les deux fonctions de base "création" de poids (-10 , + 10) et "organisation et accès" de poids (-15 , + 15) : la création des fichiers comporte les fonctions d'identification et de protection qui ne sont spécifiques d'aucune des deux classes de systèmes et sur lesquelles les deux types de systèmes se différencient peu; les organisations de fichiers dépendent par contre très étroitement du type de système.

- la fonction de base "organisation et accès" de poids (-15, + 15) comporte les deux fonctions "organisation de base" de poids (-5 , + 5) et "organisation de base" de poids (-5 , + 5) et "organisations et méthodes d'accès" de poids (-10 , + 10) : en effet les organisations de fichiers telle que l'organisation séquentielle indexée avec index à plusieurs niveaux est une des premières caractéristiques des systèmes da classe 1, tandis que l'organisation directe sur fichier plat l'est pour les systèmes de classe 2.

> **4 - RESULTATS, CRITIQUE ET CONCLUSION**

4.1. Résultats.

Grâce aux pondérations introduites dans le questionnaire arborescent, les valeurs de la capacité et de l'orientation fonctionnelles des systèmes de fichiers peuvent être facilement calculées à un niveau quelconque, permettant ainsi de comparer des systèmes sur une fonction élémentaire ou globalement sur une fonction de base.

Le plus haut niveau fournit une évaluation synthétique de la capacité et de l'orientation de l'ensemble des fonctions offertes par un système. Pour les systèmes de fichiers étudiés, les valeurs suivantes sont obtenues :

Système	Capacité fonctionnelle	Orientation fonctionnelle
IBM OS/360	74	+ 48
IBM DOS/360	22	+ 25
CII SIRIS.2	53	+ 32
CII SIRIS.7	68	+ 42
UNIVAC EXEC.8	58	+ 9
CTSS.1 (1)	52	- 27
CTSS.2 (1)	66	- 47
CDC SCOPE 3.1	33	- 14
CDC SCOPE 3.4	48	- 13
HIPSIS (2)	65	- 36
H.B. G.58	18	+ 24

(1) première et deuxième versions d'un système implanté sur un IBM 7094 au MIT.

(2) Système de fichiers implanté sur un CDC 6000 pour la météorologie nationale en France.

Ces mesures permettent de représenter l'ensemble des systèmes de fichiers par un diagramme (cf. figure 2) où chaque système est un point dans un espace à deux dimensions (capacité et orientation).

Sur ce diagramme apparaissent les deux classes distinctes définies en 3.2. La classe 1 comprend pour les systèmes de fichiers étudiés ceux du G.58 , DOS/360 , SIRIS.2 , SIRIS.7 et OS/360, pour lesquels l'orientation et la capacité croissent simultanément. Il en est de même pour la classe 2 qui comprend les systèmes de fichiers des deux versions de SCOPE.3 , CTSS1, HIPSIS et CTSS2. C'est ainsi que les systèmes de fichiers les plus puissants des deux classes (OS/360 et CTSS2) sont aussi les plus caractéristiques de leur classe.

Seul le système de fichiers d'EXEC.8 n'appartient à aucune des deux classes de systèmes. En effet, ce système, contrairement à ceux des deux classes, a une capacité forte (58) et une orientation faible (+9) . Il offre effectivement des fonctions caractéristiques des deux classes, comme, par exemple, pour l'allocation des mémoires secondaires un mécanisme d'allocation statique et dynamique. Son orientation faible, qui est la somme de 17 points d'orientation positive et de 8 points d'orientation négative, traduit son ambivalence.

Parmi les autres systèmes; il en est de même pour ceux dont l'orientation ne croît pas aussi vite que la capacité (essentiellement SCOPE 3.4) : ces systèmes, bien qu'appartenant à une classe présentent quelques caractéristiques fonctionnelles de l'autre classe.

En résumé, les systèmes de fichiers, sauf pour de rares exceptions, se répartissent en deux classes distinctes de systèmes pour lesquels l'orientation est une fonction croissante de la capacité.

4.2. Critique des résultats.

Si la liste des fonctions offertes par les systèmes de fichiers et leur décomposition en fonctions élémentaires parce qu'étant le résultat d'une étude approfondie d'une dizaine de systèmes de fichiers, est peu sujette à la critique, il n'en n'est pas de même pour l'évaluation des poids de capacité et d'orientation.

En effet, bien que la méthode de répartition par descente de l'arborescence du questionnaire limite la part de subjectivité dans le choix des poids, ceux-ci reflètent naturellement l'opinion personnelle de l'auteur. Mais la seule solution pour fixer les pondérations serait d'effectuer une enquête auprès d'utilisateurs de systèmes de fichiers, solution qui n'était pas envisageable dans le cadre de cette étude.

Les réponses aux questions des systèmes de fichiers étudiés bénéficient de l'avantage d'avoir été établies par une même personne et ont donc une bonne probabilité d'exactitude.

Par contre, une critique peut être faite à l'encontre de la synthèse
(qui établit une loi sur les deux classes), celle d'avoir été effectuée
à partir d'un nombre restreint de systèmes. Effectivement, cette conclusion
nécessiterait l'étude d'autres systèmes de fichiers, ce qui demande beaucoup de temps... mais le résultat, peut-être légèrement anticipé, méri-
tait d'être présenté.

4.3. Conclusion.

Cette étude des systèmes de fichiers comprend cinq points d'intérêt
principaux :

- elle présente une analyse fonctionnelle complète des systèmes de
  fichiers.

- elle propose une terminologie des fonctions qui a l'avantage de couvrir
  tout l'ensemble des fonctions, contrairement aux diverses terminologies
  usuelles qui se limitent aux fonctions offertes par un type donné de
  systèmes.

- elle permet d'établir la définition fonctionnelle homogène de tout
  système de fichiers, ce qui a comme utilisation immédiate la comparaison
  de deux systèmes.

- elle introduit une caractérisation fonctionnelle des systèmes de fichiers
  en permettant de mesurer deux qualités des fonctions qu'ils offrent :
  leur capacité fonctionnelle (ou mesure de l'intérêt des services qu'ils
  rendent à leurs utilisateurs) et leur orientation fonctionnelle (ou mesure du degré d'appartenance du système à l'une ou l'autre de deux classes qui ont été définies auparavant).

- elle permet d'effectuer une synthèse de l'ensemble des systèmes de fichiers par une représentation graphique dans un espace à deux dimensions
  qui montre que pour les deux classes l'orientation d'un système est
  une fonction croissante de sa capacité.

Pour ces raisons, cette étude intéresse aussi bien les utilisateurs que
les concepteurs de systèmes et la méthode employée pour étudier les systèmes de fichiers pourrait être généralisée de façon à s'adapter, par
exemple, au domaine des systèmes d'exploitation.

REFERENCES
=.=.=.=.=.=.=.=.=.=.=

Etudes d'architecture des systèmes de fichiers.

[1] - R.C. DALEY - P.G. NEUMANN.

"A general-purpose file system for secondary storage"
Proceedings Fall Joint Computer Conference, 1965.

[2] - F.J. CORBATO - V.A. VYSSOTSKY

"Introduction and overview of the MULTICS system"
Proceedings Fall Joint Computer Conference, 1965.

[3] - S.E. MADNICK

" Design strategies for file systems : a working model"
File 68. International Seminar on File Organization. 1.1968
Helsingor (Denmark).

Etudes de fonctions particulières des systèmes de fichiers.

Sur les organisations de fichiers :

[4] - N. CHAPIN

"Common file organization techniques compared"
Proceedings Fall Joint Computer Conference, 1969

[5] - N. CHAPIN

"A comparison of file organization techniques"
Proceding ACM 24th National Conference 1969.

[6] - C. BACHMAN

"The evolution of standard structures"
Communications of the ACM July 1972.

Sur la protection des fichiers :

[7] - T.D. FRIEDMAN

"The authorization problem in shared files"
IBM Systems Journal - Vol. 9 - N° 4 - 1970.

[8] - G.S. GRAHAM - P.J. DENNING.

    "Protection - principles and practice"
    Proceedings Spring Joint Computer Conference 1972.

Etudes comparatives

[9]- C. BYRNES - D. STEIG.

    "File Management systems : a current summary"
    Datamation Nov. 1969 et Oct. 1972.

[10]- A.D. FALKOFF - K.E. IVERSON - E.H. SUSSENGUTH.

    "A formal description of SYSTEM/360"
    IBM Systems Journal - Vol. 3. N° 3 - 1964.

[11] - C.G. BELL - A. NEWELL

    "Computer structures : readings and examples"
    Mc Graw-Hill Book Co, New York, 1971.

[12]- J.E. SAMMET.

    "Problems in, and a pragmatic approach to, programming language
    measurement".
    Proceedings Fall Joint Computer Conference 1971.

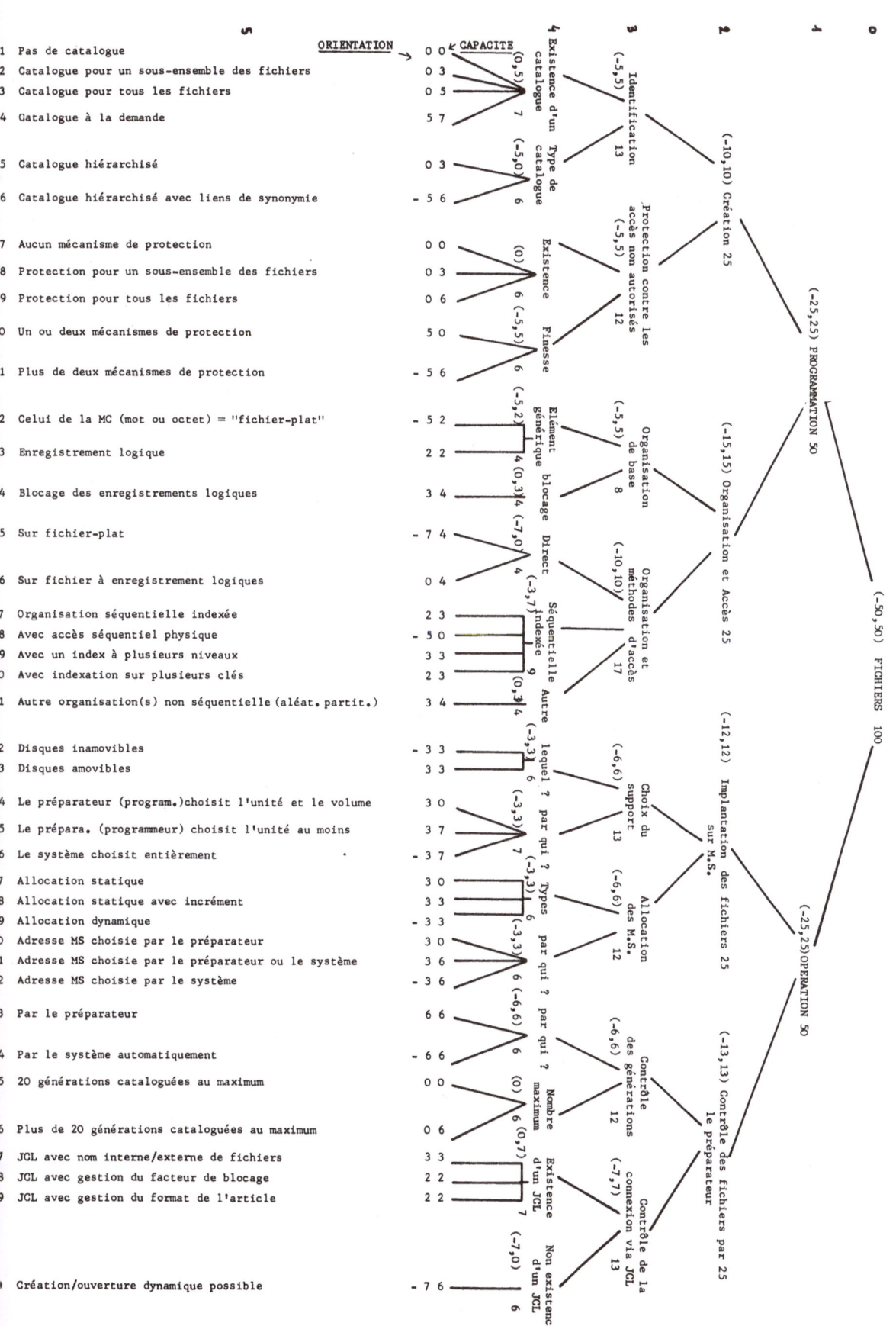

Figure 1 - <u>Questionnaire de définition fonctionnelle et poids de capacité et d'orientation</u>

Pour les niveaux 0 à 4, le graphisme suivant a été adopté :
(poids d'orientation). nom de la fonction . poids de capacité

Pour les branches du niveau 4 au niveau 5 le graphisme suivant a été adopté :

⋀ : fonctions élémentaires exclusives

⊓ : fonctions élémentaires non exclusives

Abréviations utilisées : MC = mémoire centrale   MS = mémoire secondaire

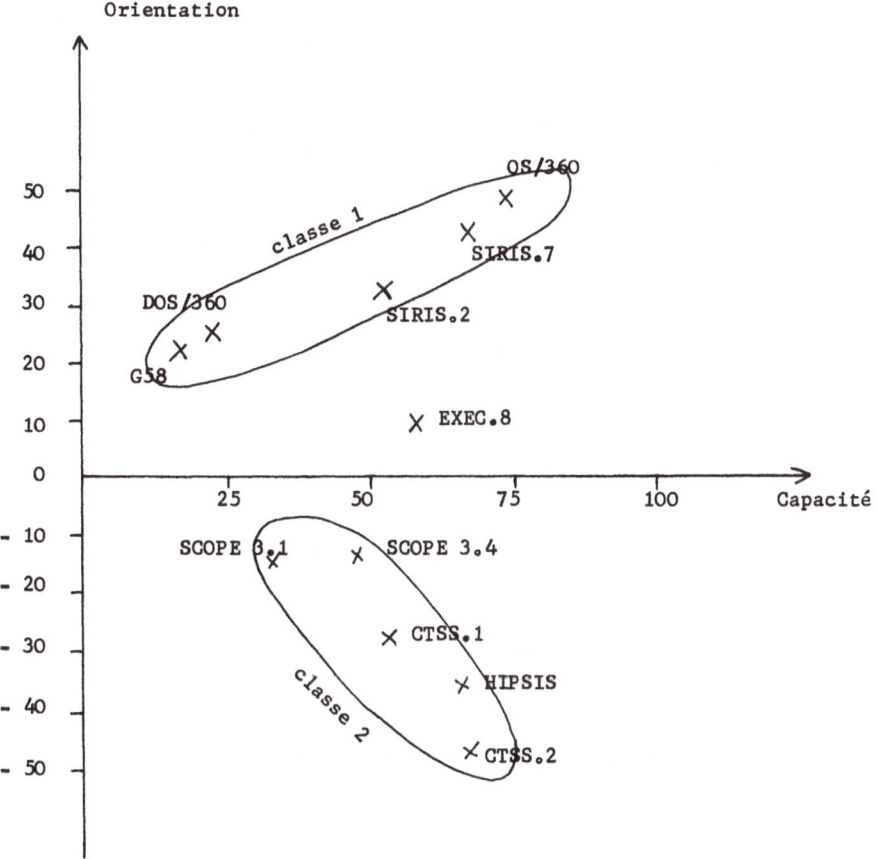

Figure 2 - Diagramme de la capacité et de l'orientation
fonctionnelles des systèmes de fichiers.

question	OS/360	DOS/360	SIRIS.2	SIRIS.7	EXEC.8	CTSS.1	CTSS.2	SCOPE 3.1	SCOPE 3.4	HIPSIS	G58
1	0	1	1	0	0	0	0	0	0	0	1
2	0	0	0	0	0	0	1	1	1	0	0
3	0	0	0	0	1	1	1	0	0	1	0
4	1	0	0	1	0	0	0	0	0	0	0
5	1	0	0	1	1	1	1	0	0	1	0
6	0	0	0	0	0	0	0	0	0	0	0
7	0	0	0	0	1	1	0	0	0	0	0
8	0	0	0	0	0	0	1	0	0	1	0
9	1	0	1	1	1	0	0	0	0	0	0
10	1	0	1	1	1	1	1	0	0	1	0
11	0	0	0	0	0	1	0	0	1	0	0
12	0	0	0	0	1	0	1	0	0	1	1
13	1	1	1	1	1	1	1	0	1	0	0
14	1	1	1	0	0	0	1	0	1	1	1
15	0	1	0	1	1	1	0	0	0	0	0
16	1	1	1	1	1	1	1	0	0	0	0
17	1	1	1	1	0	0	0	1	1	0	1
18	0	0	0	1	0	0	0	1	1	1	0
19	1	1	1	1	0	0	0	0	0	0	1
20	1	1	0	1	0	0	0	0	0	0	0
21	1	1	1	1	0	1	0	0	1	0	1
22	0	0	0	0	0	0	0	1	0	1	0
23	1	1	1	1	1	1	1	0	1	0	0
24	0	1	0	0	1	0	0	0	0	0	1
25	1	0	1	1	1	0	1	1	1	0	1
26	0	0	0	0	0	0	0	0	0	0	0
27	0	0	1	0	1	0	0	1	1	1	0
28	1	1	1	1	1	1	1	0	0	0	1
29	0	0	0	0	0	1	1	1	1	1	0
30	0	1	0	0	0	0	0	0	0	0	-
31	1	0	1	1	1	1	1	1	1	1	0
32	0	0	1	1	1	0	0	0	0	0	0
33	1	0	0	0	0	1	1	0	1	0	1
34	0	0	0	1	1	0	0	1	1	1	0
35	0	0	1	0	1	1	1	0	0	0	0
36	1	1	1	1	0	1	1	1	1	1	0
37	1	1	1	1	1	0	0	0	0	0	0
38	1	0	0	0	0	0	1	0	1	0	0
39	1	1	1	1	0	1	0	1	0	0	0
40	0	0	0	0	0	1	1	1	1	1	0

Tableau 1 - Réponses des systèmes de fichiers au questionnaire

1 = réponse positive
0 = réponse négative

PRESENTATION OF THE CONTROL GRAPH MODELS

Michel Parent
IRIA

———

I-INTRODUCTION

Since the advent of large scale computer systems, the need for a methodology
for the design of such systems has been clearly expressed but up to this point, a
more or less formal procedure is still lacking and the writing of an operating
system is still an art requiring many years of experience.

Although the modularization of both the harware and the software has allowed
the simulation and the optimization of some components, the simulation of an
entire system becomes close in complexity to the system modelled itself. This
complexity in turn, prevents the designer from having a good understanding of the
system and to localize its deficiencies. Futhermore, it is usually of extreme
difficulty to reprogram any change made to the system besides the usual "tuning"
of parameters. All this explains why the usual simulation technique is indeed a
poor design tool when we deal with large systems.

With the Logos project, Case Western Reserve University is undertaking the
task of building a computerized design tool for the development of new large
scale systems and which would meet the following three objectives :

- allow the designer to enter the description of his system or to bring modifications to it in the most convenient way;

- prove the correctness of the operations to be performed by the system and
evaluate their performances (validation);

- bring a better understanding of the system to the designer.

The whole project consists mainly of two parts which can be linked together but which can also be used separately : one function is to prove the "well-formedness" of the structure in terms of computability and the other is to look into the performances and the resource utilisation of the system. The first function based upon the Parallel Program Schemata of R. Karp and R. Miller is being implemented on the university's PDP-10 time-sharing system. The second function is now under research by the author who is presenting the formalization of his technique in this paper.

The technique called   Control Graph Modelling (from the control graph of a parallel program schema),   has been developed with the idea of its future use for a general purpose simulator oriented mainly towards the simulation of operating systems. The simulator is to be implemented on a large scale computer system in the near future and, as in the case of the first function of the Logos project, visual displays will be used by the designers to describe the systems they wish to simulate. This visual technique will also allow them to work on the design "from the outside inwards", describing first the whole system at a very crude level and by successively replacing unknown functions by more and more detailed subsystems as the design progresses.

The main idea behind the Control Graph Models   is to describe a system by concentrating exclusively on four aspects :

- the time needed to execute certain functions without being concerned about the purpose of the function or its interpretation (as example a computing time, a user response time, a disk arm positioning, a data transfert,...);

- the sequencing of these functions (linear sequences, alternatives, parallelism,...);

- the synchronization of several functions;

- the utilisation of resources to perform these functions.

These functions are to be performed by a number of "processes" or tasks which circulate in a kind of flow chart (the graph of the model) indicating the function performed, the sequencing of functions, the synchronization needed and the resources needed to perform the functions.

The formalization of the Control Graph Models   being extremely general, it is possible to describe very different systems by this technique and obtain either analytically or by simulation, results concerning the performance without being concerned about the function of the system itself. In fact, this modelling technique can describe systems which have nothing in common with computer systems but where sequences of operations needing various resources have to be performed in order to get a task or a set of tasks done. Such systems can be for example simple or complex queuing networks but can also involve decision functions, synchronization procedures and any kind of resource requirement.

Anyone familiar with queuing theory knows how difficult it is to obtain analytical results with complex systems but the main objective of the Control Graph Modelling technique is to give to the designers a standard and unified method to describe any system which behaves in a stochastic or deterministic fashion in terms of timing. This will already allow the designer to have a better understanding of the system and often detect inconsistencies just by the drawing of the corresponding Control Graph Model. If a simulator based on this representation is available, it is hoped that the convenience of the description will permit extremely efficient interaction between man and the machine for the design of complex systems whose performances will be known before their realisation.

III-DESCRIPTION OF THE CONTROL GRAPH MODELS

A Control Graph Model (or CGM in short) representing or not a real system is formed by a directed graph on a set of nodes $\Pi = \{N_1, N_2, \ldots, N_n\}$, by the attributes of each node and by a set of resources $\Omega = \{R_1, R_2, \ldots, R_r\}$.

The graph can be descibed either by defining a set of arcs $\Delta = \{A_1, A_2, \ldots, A_m\}$ and a mapping function Ψ between Δ and $\Pi \times \Pi$ or by defining for each node N_i its predecessor nodes $P(N_i)$ and its successor nodes $S(N_i)$. Both definitions are equivalent and there is no problem in going from one to the other.

1- The set of resources

Resources are collections of entities (or units), all identical for a same resource R_i, which can be acquired or released by the processes.

The set Ω of resources is divided into two disjoint subsets Ω_{RT} and Ω_{CS} of returnable and consumable resources. For each returnable resource R_i is defined an integer number $\overline{R_i}^t$ representing the number of units of resource R_i available at time t. For each returnable resource R_i, $\overline{R_i}^0 = \overline{R_i}$ is called the total number of units of the resource.

For each consumable resource R_j is kept a list of integer numbers $\overline{R_j(X)}^t$, each one representing the number of units of the resource released by a process X and not yet consumed at time t $(\overline{R_j(X)}^0 = 0$ for every X).

2- The set of nodes

Each node belongs to one of seven classes of nodes and depending on its class its attributes, its interpretation and its number of predecessors and successors will vary :

Input nodes Π_I

These nodes have no predecessor and only one successor. Their function is to generate the processes. At an input node N_i, the interdeparture times ξ_i^k

between the k-th process and the k+1-st process are random variables whose distributions $F_i^k(X)$ are the attributes of the node N_i.

Output nodes Π_O

The output nodes have only one predecessor and no successor and they can be viewed as the sinks of the graph. The processes reaching these nodes disappear. They have no attributes.

Time nodes Π_T

In these nodes, the processes will be delayed for a random active time τ whose distribution is the attribute of the node. A time node has one predecessor and one successor.

Acquiring nodes Π_A

To each acquiring node N_i is attached a resource $R(N_i) = R_j$ among the set of resources $\Omega = \{R_1, R_2, \ldots, R_r\}$ and an integer number $\overline{N_i}$ representing the number of units of the resource R_j which are requested by a process arriving at the node N_i.

For any acquiring node N_i, we also define the priority $p_i(X,S)$ which may depend upon the arriving process X and the state S of the system at the time of the request.

Releasing nodes Π_R

This is the reverse function from the previous one and every process arriving at one of these nodes N_i will release $\overline{N_i}$ units of resource $R(N_i)$. But since units of returnable resources can be acquired with different priorities depending on the process and the acquiring node, there must be an acquiring node coupled with every releasing node each time the resource involved is returnable :

$$\forall N_i \in \Pi_R \text{ such that } R(N_i) \in \Omega_{RT}$$

we define the coupled acquiring node :

$$A(N_i) = N_j \text{ such that } N_j \in \Pi_A \text{ and } R(N_j) = R(N_i).$$

Note : $\overline{N_i}$ may be different from $\overline{N_j}$.

Branching nodes Π_B

These nodes have one or several predecessors and one or several successors. Depending on the number of predecessors and successors of the node, one or more processes arriving at the node will give birth to one or more processes in the output arcs.

This branching function can be executed in two different ways : one is the conjunctive (AND node), the other is the disjunctive (OR node) way. The set of the branching nodes is hence divided into two subsets :

OR nodes : Π_{B+}

For these nodes, any process arriving from any of the input arcs of the node will be routed to one and only one of the output arcs, each arc having a given probability of being selected. These probabilities which are the same for all the processes, are the attributes of the node :

$$\forall\, N_i \in \Pi_{B+} \quad p_{ij} = \text{Prob(transition from } N_i \text{ to } N_j) \quad N_j \in S(N_i)$$
$$\sum_j p_{ij} = 1$$

AND nodes : Π_{B*}

These nodes have no attribute. We will see in the section dealing with the circulation of the processes how the simultaneous presence of co-processes in all the input arcs of the node gives birth to new co-processes in all the output arcs of the node.

Decision nodes Π_D

All the decision nodes have one predecessor and two successors. A process arriving at one of these nodes will fork to one of the two output arcs depending on the value of the decision function attached to the node :

$$\forall\, N_i \in \Pi_D \quad D_i(X,S) = \begin{cases} N_j \\ N_k \end{cases} \quad S(N_i) = (N_j, N_k)$$

The decision function D_i of node N_i is equal to one of the two successor nodes N_j and N_k depending upon the process X and the state S of the system at the time when X enters the node.

The graphical representation of all the nodes is shown in figure 1.

3- The processes

Processes are entities which are generated by the input nodes of the graph according to given random laws or which can be issued from other processes at AND nodes (co-processes).

Each process generated has a position in the graph which is one of the nodes of the graph and this position can change with time until the process disappears (at an output node or at an AND node). During its "life", a process can acquire and release resources according to its path which is the set of all its successive positions in the graph during its life.

The resource requirements of each process are the numbers of units of each returnable resource which have been requested by the process at the acquiring nodes of its path until the current time t and which have not yet been returned through the corresponding releasing nodes. Whenever a process is active or waiting for a co-process, its resource requirement is met. This is not so in the other cases.

Since when a process is waiting for a co-process in an AND node its position is not sufficient to tell us from what predecessor it comes from, we will add to each AND node n subnodes, n being the number of predecessors of the node (we do not consider the case when n=1 since there is no waiting for co-processes). To each predecessor corresponds one input subnode and the processes will be waiting in these input subnodes until the last co-process arrives. We will denote by $I(N_i)$ the set of the input subnodes of N_i.

Co-processes

We say that two or more processes are co-processes if they are issued from a same parent process. For example when a process arrives at an AND node with a single predecessor (AND forking node), one new process is sent to each successor of the node. The arriving process (parent process) and all the new processes are co-processes. Now if at a time t we have co-processes in all the input subnodes of an AND node, new co-processes are also sent to each successor of the node. This notion of co-processes persists even after a chain of branchings as in figure 2 where all identified processes are co-processes.

4- Structure and identification of co-processes

Due to the problems of synchronization of processes (AND nodes), it is of first importance to be able to tell when a set of processes are issued from a same parent process, that is, if they are co-processes. Furthermore for problems of resource allocation, the parent-infant structure obtained through the AND nodes must also be kept. This can be done by a record keeping scheme using the notion of level of descendance and by decomposing any complex AND node (with several predecessors and several successors) into the equivalent combination of two AND nodes : one having a single successor and the next one having a single predecessor. Using this decomposition, AND nodes can be of two types : forking (one predecessor) and joining (one successor). Now processes generated at an AND forking node are one generation down from the issuing process while the process issued at an AND joining node has the same generation number as the lowest generation issuing co-process. We can further simplify this record keeping by addopting the following rule : when all the infants of a same parent are rejoined, they regenerate the parent process. By simply numbering all the new processes within their generation and by keeping the identification of their immediate parent, it is then simple to keep track of the relationships between all the existing processes at any time. Figure 3 shows such a numbering scheme as it can evolve through time (indices are replaced by generation numbers).

5- Resource requirement and release for co-processes

Whenever a process X gives birth to several new co-processes at an AND node, the requirements of each of these co-processes are the same as the requirements for X at the time of the branching, although the resources are then shared by all the infant processes. This means that if one of the resources in the requirements of X is preempted from X, then all its infants become preempted. Unless one or several infants (but not all) have released the preempted resource.

On the other hand if an infant process acquires new units of a resource, these units are attached only to it (and later to all its infant processes).

The same thing happens if several co-processes are joined to generate a new process. The requirement of this new process is equal to the sum of the requirements of each co-process (but without duplicating common possible requirements).

In order to keep track of all the units of consumable resources which have been allocated and the processes which may share them and their priorities, we must manage one "stack of allocated units" $S_A(R_i)$ per returnable resource R_i. In this stack are kept entries of the form (X_i, N_j) which represent $\overline{(X_i, N_j)}$ units of resource R_i (not necessarily equal to $\overline{N_j}$) acquired by X_i at the node N_j (and hence with priority $p_j(X_i, S)$). If X_i has any infant processes, there must also be a linked list of all these infants with their corresponding requirement for the node N_j (necessarily less than or equal to $\overline{(X_i, N_j)}$).

For all the resources (consumable or returnable) we must also keep track of all the requests which cannot be granted at the present time. For this we have one "stack of requesting processes" $S_R(R_i)$ per resource R_i and the entries have the same form as before : (X_i, N_j) represents $\overline{(X_i, N_j)}$ units of resource R_i requested by X_i through node N_j with priority $p_j(X_i, S)$. The requests can be first time requests (process X_i is in node N_j) or requests after preemption if the resource is returnable (consumable resources are not preemptable). In this case and if the preempted process has given birth to infant processes, the list of all the infants and their requirement for the corresponding acquisition must be attached to the entry as it was previously in the stack of allocated units (the entry is transfered from one stack to the other at the time of the preemption).

6- Circulation of processes through the graph

We have seen that processes are generated at the input nodes of the graph and disappear at the output nodes if they do not circulate in the graph forever. We will extent these notions of generation and vanishing to the infant processes through all the AND nodes : the incoming processes vanish and the new outgoing processes are generated.

We will call the life of a process the time interval between its generation and its vanishing (a process may have several lives since the infants can regenerate their parent). A process which is alive can be in one of the following nodes and in one of the following states :

- in a time node
  . active
  . preempted (from a returnable resource)

- in an AND joining node

 . waiting for a co-process

- in an acquiring node

 . waiting for a resource

Processes cannot be in other nodes which are transient and indicate actions
performed in a null time (but AND joining nodes and acquiring nodes can also be
transient for some processes).

Whenever a process is generated, it is going to reach a non-transient node
(a time node , an AND joining node or an acquiring node) or it will reach instant-
ly a node where it will vanish (output node or AND node where all the necessary
co-processes are present), through a succession of transient nodes forming a path
in the graph and called the "instant path" of the process.

The same thing happens when a process changes position in the graph either
because its delay time in a time node has come to its end or because the resource
it is waiting for has become available.

The instant path is obtained in a simple way which can easily be formalized
(see [13] or [14]) :

 - an instant path is a path of the graph,

 - no time node belongs to the instant path,

 - all the resources acquired through the acquiring nodes of the instant path
must have been available,

 - the successors of the decision nodes have been selected by the decision
function,

 - the successors of the OR forking nodes have been selected by random trials
according to the attached probabilities.

If several processes are generated or change position at a same time t, it
is of premium importance that their instant paths are computed one after the other
if we want to avoid conflicting situation when resources are allocated. It is
hence necessary to define an ordering among the processes and compute their next
position according to this ordering if the behavior of the system is to be well
defined.

7- Management of the resources

We say that a returnable resource R is available to a process X at an acqui-
ring node N at time t if $\overline{R}^t \geq \overline{N}$ or if X can preempt enough units allocated to
other processes which are not parents of X. This is done by comparing the priority
of the request $p(X,S)$ to the acquisition priorities of the entries in the stack
of allocated units of the resource R. If enough processes can be preempted to
satisfy the request, the preempted entries are transfered to the stack of requesting processes (the minimum and the "oldest" subset of processes is selected if

the request can be granted by several different sets of preemptable processes).

If the resource is available, then the attached units counts $(\overline{X_i, N_j})$ of all the preempted entries (if any) are added to the available units counter $\overline{R}$ and $\overline{N}$ is subtracted from $\overline{R}$. The entry (X,N) is added to the stack of allocated units with $(\overline{X,N}) = \overline{N}$.

For a consumable resource R, a function $X_i(X,S)$ defining the set of "sending processes" is attached to each acquiring node N_i. The resource is said to be available for a process X at the acquiring node N_i if :

$$\overline{N_i} \leq \sum_{X_j \in X_i(X,S)} \overline{R(X_j)}$$

where S is the state of the system at request time and $\overline{R(X_j)}$ indicates the number of units of R produced by X_j and not yet consumed.

Here also an ordering among the processes must exist to define from which processes units may be consumed if there are several subsets $\{X_j\}$ satisfying the inequality.

Whenever a releasing node is on the instant path of a process, we must examine if the release of units makes the resource available to some processes. For this, the requesting stack is scanned starting with the highest priority entries and if a process has its request granted, its instant path and its next position are computed. The necessary changes are also made in the requesting stacks and in the available unit counters or vector.

Here again we must point to the importance of the ordering of all these operations, different orderings being very likely to produce different allocation sequences if several resources are released at a same time for example. We must define not only in what order the instant paths are computed but also in what order the resources are examined when several have been released and finally how to sequence these two different operations (shall we compute all the instant paths before examining the resources?).

III-CONCLUSION

Figure 4 shows an example of modelling of a time-sharing system at a crude level where two functions : the processing and the roll-in or roll-out routines have been expanded into subgraphs.

In his models the author has chosen to put the emphasis on the parallelism of tasks, the synchronization of processes and the influence of resource sharing and his graphical representation was designed to express these features in the most convenient way.

The description presented in this article was intended to show the main difficulties of an actual implementation of the simulator on a computer system and anyone whishing to go into the details of the formalization should refer to [13] or [14].

Although this model was developped with the idea of a computer implemented simulator, the author has shown (see [13], [15], [16], [17]) that the Control Graph Models are also very useful as analytical tools for the evaluation of systems. In particular synchronization problems and resource deadlocks can be probed and some performance evaluation can be obtained quite easily in some cases.

It is hoped that further research will extend these capabilities so that new and better designed systems will be produced because their Control Graph Models were carefully constructed and thoroughly analysed and understood.

BIBLIOGRAPHY

1. Aslanian R. and Benett M., "Computer Assisted Operating System Design using evolutive Modelling", Third Symposium on Operating Systems Principles, Oct. 1971.

2. Bradshaw F.T. "Structure and Representation of Digital Computer Systems", Ph. D. thesis, Case Western Reserve University, Cleveland, Ohio, Jan. 1971.

3. Coffman E.G., "Stochastic Models of Multiple and Time shared Computer Operations", Ph. D. thesis, UCLA, Los Angeles, California, June 1966.

4. Dennis J.B. and Van HORN E.C., "Programming Semantics for Multi-programmed Computations", Comm. of ACM vol 9, n°3, March 1966.

5. Dijkstra E.W., "Co-operating Sequential Processes", Programming Languages F. Genuys Ed., New-York, Academic 1968.

6. Dijkstra E.W., "Structure of the "THE" Multiprogramming System", Comm. of ACM, Vol. 11, n°5, May 1968.

7. Glaser E.L., "Introduction and Overview of the Logos Project", CWRU, Cleveland Ohio, Report, Oct. 1971.

8. Grangeon P.L., "The Design and Implementation of a Multi-Level File System", Ph. D. thesis, CWRU, Cleveland, Ohio, Jan. 1974.

9. Hamlet R.G., "Efficient Multiprogramming Resource Allocation and Accounting", Comm. of ACM, Vol. 16, N°6, June 1973.

10. Holt R.C., "On Deadlocks in Computer Systems", Ph. D. thesis, University of Toronto, Canada, Jan. 1971.

11. Karp R.M. and Miller R.E., "Parallel Program Schemata", Journal of Computer and Systems Sciences N°3, 1969.

12. Martin D.F. and Estrin G., "Models of Computation and Systems : Evaluation of the Vertex Probabilities", Journal of ACM, Vol. 14, n°2, April 1967.

13. Parent M.R., "The control Graph Models : a Unified Approach to Performance Evaluation", Ph. D. thesis, CWRU, Cleveland, Ohio, March 1974.

14. Parent M.R., "Formalization of the Control Graph Models", CWRU, Cleveland, Ohio, Report, March 1974.

15. Parent M.R., "Relevance and Consistence of Control Graph Models", CWRU, Cleveland Ohio, Report, March 1974.

16. Parent M.R., "Stochastic Analysis of Control Graph Models", CWRU, Cleveland, Ohio, Report, March 1974.

17. Parent M.R., "An Introduction to the Study of Permanent Blockings", CWRU, Cleveland, Ohio, Report, March 1974.

18. Petri C.A., "Communication with Automata", Translation, Suppl. 1 to Tech. Report RAD C-TR-65-337, Vol. 1, Griffiss Air Force Base, New-York, N.Y., 1966.

19. Ricart J., "Process Structure and Synchronization in CHI-OS Operating System", CWRU, Cleveland, Ohio, Report, June 1973.

20. De Rivet P.H.,"Data Traffic Models for the Performance of Modular Computer Systems", Ph.D. thesis, CWRU, Cleveland, Ohio, June 1971.

21. Rose C.W., "A System of Representation for General Purpose Digital Computer System", Ph.D. thesis, CWRU, Cleveland, Ohio, Sept. 1970.

22. Slutz D.R., "The Flow Graph Schemata Model of Parallel Computation", Ph.D. Thesis, MIT, Cambridge, Mass., Sept. 1968.

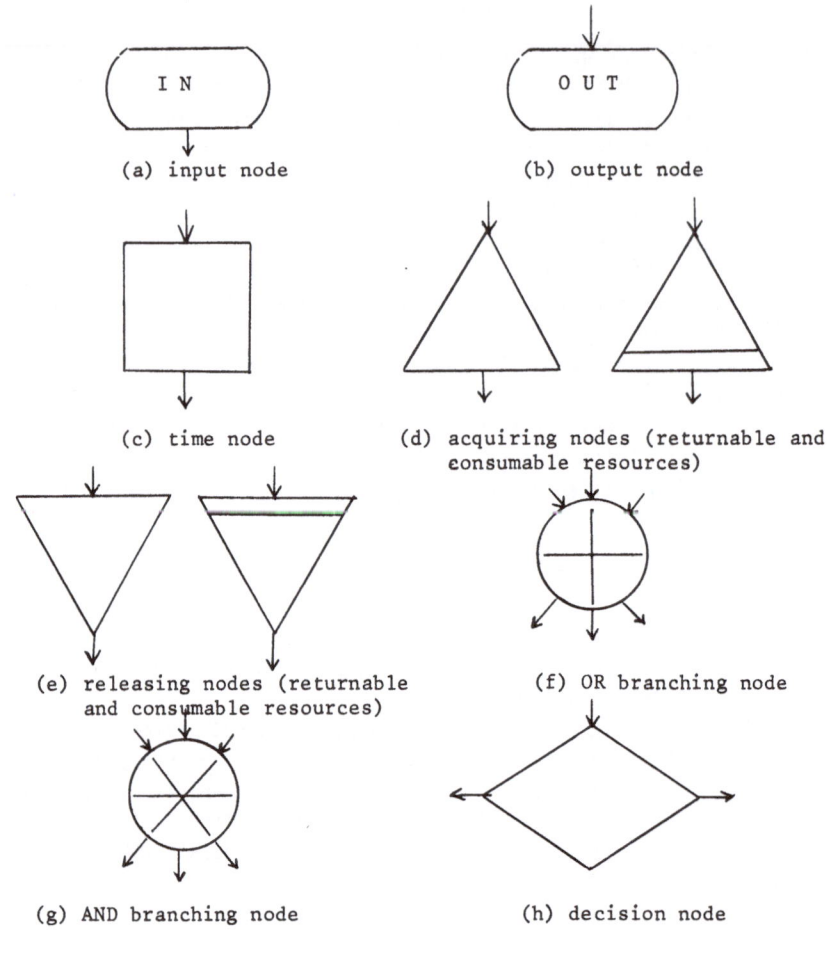

(a) input node

(b) output node

(c) time node

(d) acquiring nodes (returnable and consumable resources)

(e) releasing nodes (returnable and consumable resources)

(f) OR branching node

(g) AND branching node

(h) decision node

Figure 1   Graphical Representation of the Nodes

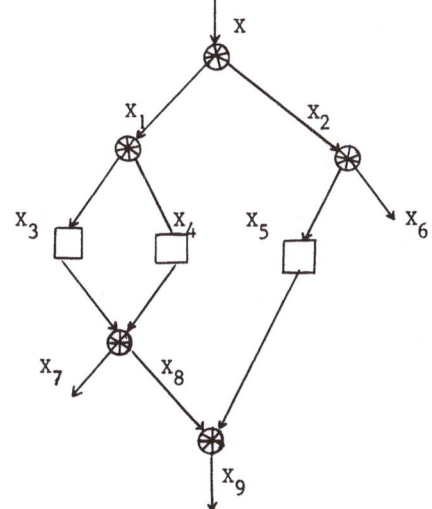

Figure 2   Example of co-processes

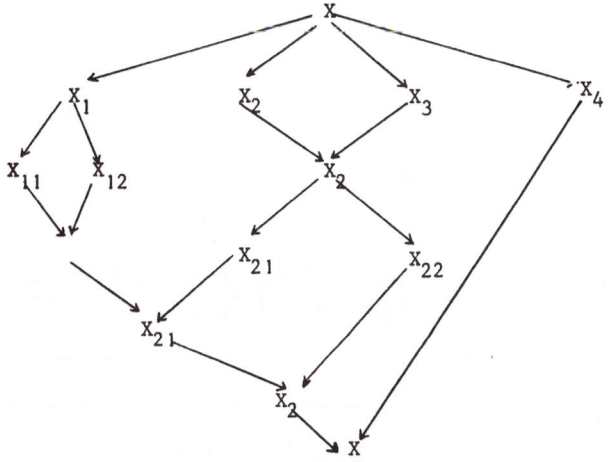

Figure 3   Parent-infant structure of co-processes

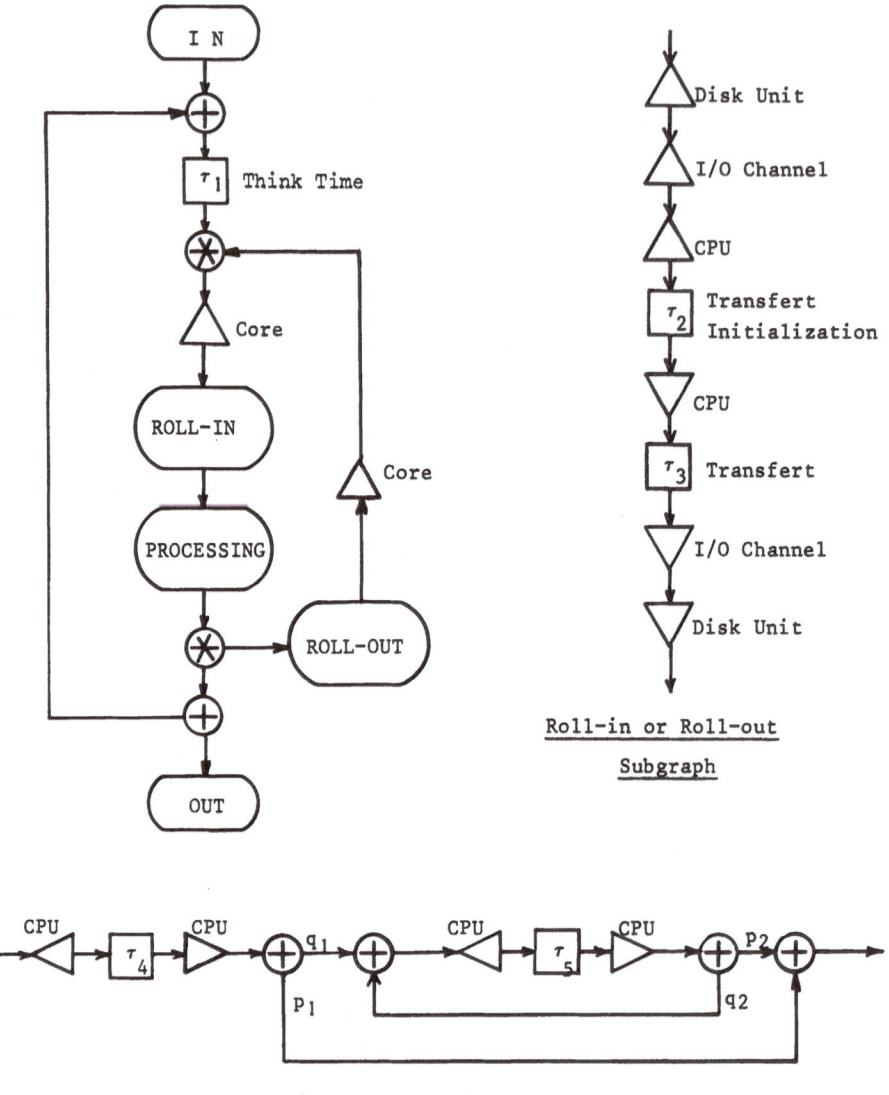

Roll-in or Roll-out
Subgraph

Processing Subgraph (Foreground-Background)

Figure 4 : Example of modelling of a time-sharing system

THE EDINBURGH MULTI-ACCESS SYSTEM SCHEDULING AND ALLOCATION PROCEDURES IN THE RESIDENT SUPERVISOR

N.H. Shelness
Department of Computer Science
Edinburgh University

P.D. Stephens
Edinburgh Regional Computing Centre

H. Whitfield
Mathematisch Instituut
Rijskuniversiteit te Groningen

INTRODUCTION

The Edinburgh Multi-Access System is a large, multi-user, interactive, paged, virtual memory operating system, developed in Edinburgh over the last nine years. An initial design was formulated between 1964 and 1966 (w1). Following this an attempt at implementation was undertaken by a large University/manufacturer team: The Edinburgh Multi-Access Project. This effort commenced in 1967 and came to an end in the summer of 1970, having failed to implement a satisfactory system. The reasons for this will not be discussed here.

The system that existed at the end of the initial project was not robust enough for even such simple system development tasks as editing and compilation. There was, though, a nucleus of code on which a small team, varying in size from 3 to 7, was able, over the next year, to build a system·robust enough for general release. The results of this effort, along with the performance characteristics of the system in the summer of 1972 are presented in a paper written at that time (w2). Since then a new team including some who were associated with this earlier effort, have rewritten a large part of the resident supervisor, with a view to generality, and portability. A number of scheduling and allocation procedures have also been changed as a result of performance monitoring and new design insights. These have resulted in a considerable performance improvement over that reported in (w2). It is the purpose of this paper to discuss the current scheduling and allocation policies, and the motivation for them.

PHYSICAL SYSTEM STRUCTURE

The hardware (ICL 4/75) corresponds to that of many large European third generation machines, being based on an (RCA SPECTRA 70) which is itself based on an (IBM S/360), to which an address translation facility (paging) was added as an afterthought. It possesses four types of memory the first three of which (tape, diskfile and drum) are connected to the last (core) by conventional selector channels. On the initial 1 megabyte configuration in Edinburgh (figure 1), there are 4 nine track tape units on two channels, 2 three hundred and fifty megabyte diskfiles on one channel, 3 six megabyte disk packs on one channel, and 3 two megabyte drums, also on a single channel. The diskfiles have 32 tracks per cylinder, with 2 1/2 pages per track, and 1023 cylinders each. The mean seek time is 100 milliseconds and the maximum transfer rate is 50 pages a second. The drums have 4 pages per track, a rotational time of 20 milliseconds, and a maximum transfer rate accordingly of 200 pages per second. None of the rotating memory devices possess a rotational sensing mechanism. They are not synchronized, nor may more than one device on a channel be transferring at a time. The strategies used by the device handlers to surmount these difficulties (f1) will be discussed later: however, it is true to say that the system possesses less utilizable transfer capacity than one has been led to believe necessary in systems of this type (1T).

LOGICAL SYSTEM STRUCTURE

The system implements a four level storage hierarchy consisting of archive storage (tape), immediate storage (diskfile), active storage (drum) and main storage (core). The unit of allocation in archive store is the file (1-4096 pages), in immediate storage the segment (a set of 1-16 contiguous pages), and in active and main store the page (4096 8 bit bytes). The sole unit of information transfer between levels is the page.

The three fastest levels of the storage hierarchy are managed as a whole by a resident supervisor on the behalf of up to 63 dynamically created virtual processors. Each virtual processor has a linear virtual address space of 16 megabytes. Segments of each virtual address space are associated with segments of immediate memory in one of a number of access modes: private read, private write, shared read and shared write. This is accomplished by placing an entry in the appropriate slot of the virtual processor's master page. Hence, as in MULTICS (c1), there is no file I/O in the conventional sense, all access to files being performed through the virtual memory mechanism.

Each virtual processor contains two virtual processes: a director process and a user process. The director process runs a paged supervisor (r1), the code and global tables of which are shared between all director processes. The segments of virtual memory in which this shared material resides, as well as segments private to each paged supervisor are shaded, and hence inaccessible to the user process. The director process maintains the master page of the virtual processor, both for itself and the user process. Director sub-processes perform console interaction and other external functions through communicating with system processes that perform these tasks. In addition a critical section of the paged supervisor maintains file systems on the entire system, on immediate storage. The director process of each virtual processor creates an environment in which the associated user process is aware only of named sequences of bytes called files which are connected into its unshaded virtual memory at specified segments, and of virtual addresses.

The user processes run one of a number of sub-systems (ml). There are two
types of user processes: executive processes and normal processes. The subsystems of executive processes perform specific system functions that are not as
time dependent as those performed in the resident supervisor. These functions
include: the handling of unit record device I/O, the demons executive: the
transfer of files to and from archive storage, the volumes executive: the
testing of online peripherals, the engineers executive: and systems maintenance
functions, the manager executive. The first two executives run in background
mode without an interactive console, while the last two run in foreground mode,
and are initiated from an interactive console. Director and executive processes
have the same level of software privilege as processes in the resident supervisor
that is the ability to communicate with any process, either resident or virtual.
Normal user processes, having a lower level of software privilege, may
communicate only with their own director processes. The functions provided by a
normal process' sub-system (b3) are those often thought to be part of a system:
loading, command interpretation, compiling, editing etc. In EMAS the programmes
that perform all of these functions have an idential status with programmes
provided by the user, and in fact, a user may easily add to the standard subsystem or provide his own, should he so desire.

The structure of processes in both the virtual processors and the resident
supervisor is provided implicitly by the structure of the IMP high level
programming language (s2) (b4), in which the entire system is written. In order
to allow functions to be serviced by processes in either the resident supervisor
or a virtual processor, all inter-process communication and synchronization is
performed through a single message switching mechanism, provided by the most
basic software level - the kernel. The message switching mechanism is described
in detail in (w2).

There are three levels of hierarchy in the resident supervisor, in
addition to those already described in the virtual processors. A chart of the
system hierarchy is presented in figure 2.

MAIN MEMORY MANAGEMENT

In all of the large and fully implemented paged systems known to the
authors (b1) (c1) (g1) (13), there are at least three distinct supervisory
processes which control the processing of user tasks, or as we chose to call
them virtual computations. These are a process scheduler, a global paging
manager and a CPU scheduler. We will not concern ourselves in this paper
with access control functions that are performed by a segment manager or its
equivalent.
The process scheduler selects a virtual processor from among those desiring
to perform a virtual computation, and inserts it into the multi programming set
MPS. The process scheduler is initiated by the page manager when space is
available in the MPS. It will usually take into account, in making its choice,
the cpu and main storage requirements of previous computations performed in each
virtual processor. In so doing it determines the systems response to various
classes of computation. It will assign to the virtual processor it selects an
amount of CPU time that the virtual computation may use before being removed from
the MPS and rescheduled - a cpu allocation. The process scheduler will not
assign any limit to the number of pages the processor may acquire in main store -
a main store allocation. The decision as to which pages will be resident in
main store at any instant, the resident page set RPS, will be made by the global
paging manager over the entire MPS. In EMAS this is not the case.

The EMAS process scheduler assigns to the selected virtual processor both a cpu and a main storage allocation. Having done this, there is no longer any need for a global paging manager. It can be replaced by a number of local paging managers provided on a one to one basis for each virtual processor in the MPS. By replacing the global paging manager, which requires to operate over the domain (s1) of the entire paging system, by local paging managers, each operating over the domain of a single virtual processor, we immediately reduce complexity and increase systems reliability. A critical failure that occurs, be it hardware or software induced, while in a local paging manager, need only effect a single virtual processor, not the entire system. A second benefit of the EMAS approach is that we eliminate two of the major problems, and greatest sources of programming complexity, encountered by a global paging manager: preventing thrashing, and preventing throughput degradation across the entire system as a result of having a virtual computation in the MPS which displays unstable paging behaviour. In order to see why this is the case, it is necessary to examine how a global paging manager manages the RPS.

Control of the RPS is maintained through a mechanism of page replacement. When a page fault occurs, a choice is made, by the paging manager, of a page currently in the RPS to be replaced by the newly required page. In practice there is usually a buffer pool of pages not included in the RPS, so that the newly required page may be fetched immediately, rather than having to wait for the replaced page to be written back to secondary storage if necessary.

There are basically two algorithms used by a global paging manager for making its replacement choice: least recently used LRU and working set WS (d1). In the first algorithm the least recently used page in the RPS is replaced. In the second algorithm a free page is replaced. A page is free if it is not in the union of the working sets of any virtual processor in the MPS.

The elimination of thrashing in an LRU driven page replacement scheme is difficult, but not impossible. The majority of systems being considered by the authors use an LRU algorithm and don't thrash. This is achieved, at the expense of greater complexity in the CPU scheduler, through altering the size of the active MPS by varying the CPU priority of virtual processors in the MPS.

In simple terms, the processing speed of a virtual processor is increased as it uses its CPU allocation. This guarantees that, as it approaches the end of its residency period, it uses its pages more often, reducing the likelyhood of them being prematurely replaced, than virtual processors that have just started their residency period.

It should be noted that while this approach eliminates thrashing, it increases the vulnerability of the system to high priority virtual processors whose computations vary the size of their working sets radically, as this will force the pages of low priority virtual processors in and out of main store, and hence degrade the speed at which their computations are processed through the system. The same is true of a page replacement scheme driven by the working set algorithm. Thrashing cannot occur, but the system is vulnerable to computations that display wild fluctuations in the size of their working sets, as such behaviour can result in the elimination of free pages in the RPS to be replaced. In such a case, a virtual processor much be removed from the MPS, either temporarily, until the number of free pages grows larger than its working set, or by being rescheduled. In either case, unless it is the misbehaving virtual processor that is rescheduled, all other virtual computations in the system will suffer by taking longer to complete. In EMAS a local paging manager will automatically remove from the MPS any virtual processor whose working set attempts to grow larger than its allocation. The virtual processor will then be rescheduled to run next time with a larger main store allocation. In this way only the throughput of a misbehaving computation will be retarded, not the throughput of the entire system.

It still remains to be shown that the EMAS approach to main store allocation uses the store as effectively as other approaches.

THE PROCESS SCHEDULER

The initial process scheduler is described in detail in (w2) and there is an excellent short description by Wilkes (w3). There are a number of categories, currently 20. Associated with each category is a priority, a main storage allocation, a CPU allocation, and a number of possible category transitions. In addition there are other category parameters, some of which will be discussed later (figure3). All virtual processors, be they already in the MPS, waiting on a priority queue to enter the MPS, or asleep - waiting for an external event , are in one and only one category.

When a virtual processor wakes up - the external event it was waiting for, such as console input occurs, it is placed on a queue associated with its current priority. It will eventually be chosen from that queue, and when certain global constraints are satisfied, inserted into the MPS. The local constraints on its behaviour: its main store, active store and CPU allocations will be those associated with its category. The virtual processor will remain in the MPS until one of two events occur: it attempts to exceed one of its local constraints, or it goes to sleep. At this point it is removed from the MPS, and its next category determined. There are four possible category transitions. The four cases that determine which of the four transitions is to be made are:

1). The virtual processor's working set attempts to grow larger than its main store allocation.
2). The virtual computation overruns its CPU allocation with a working set that would fit in a smaller category.
3). The virtual computation overruns its CPU allocation with a working set that fits into the current category.
4). The virtual processor goes to sleep.

If the virtual processor is still awake, it is immediately placed on the priority queue associated with its new priority. In this way a virtual processor follows a path through the category table towards an entry that matches its current behaviour. If that behaviour is for the most part stable, then we can expect many of the transitions to be back into the same category, and this is in fact the case (figure 4).

The means by which a virtual processor is selected from a priority queue, the choice algorithm, is exceedingly simple. A circular table is cycled through one by one. Each entry contains the identity of the next priority queue to be chosen. In the initial choice algorithm described in (w2), once a priority queue was selected, and if there was a virtual processor on it, it was allowed to enter the MPS only when the amount of unallocated main store was greater than the selected virtual processor's main store allocation. If the priority queue was empty, or after the selected virtual processor had entered the MPS, the choice algorithm was re-enabled to select another priority queue.

The decision to use the number of unallocated main store pages as the global constraint on a virtual processor's entering the MPS was our first choice, on which we intended to improve if monitoring justified it. We have now done this monitoring and it has allowed us to ascertain that with the original global constraint, the main store was not used as effectively as it might have been. There are three identifiable reasons why:

The first is that the measure of unallocated main store excludes pages that are free due to sharing. This occurs because a page that is shared among two or more virtual processors is included in the allocations of each of the virtual processors using it, yet there is only one copy in main store.

The second is that a virtual processor's working set is by definition always less than or equal to is allocation. There is thus the likelyhood that a number of allocated main store pages remain free.

The third relates directly to the performance characteristics of the drums and diskfiles. It is a result of the difference in wait time of a page that is fetched on demand against the wait time of those that are prepaged (figure 5). Prepaged pages arrive three times faster than demand pages. The reasons for this will be discussed later. This difference means that allocated pages that are free while a virtual processor with a large main store allocation demand pages up to its working set, could have been usefully utilized by a prepaging virtual processor that had a small main storage and cpu allocation, as such a virtual processor could have come and gone while the other was still demand paging.

To overcome these deficiencies in the initial global constraint, two changes were made. Monitoring indicated that sharing within a single mix of resident virtual processors was relatively stable, and tended to change only when a new virtual processor entered, or an old virtual processor left the MPS. In light of this evidence the choice algorithm was trivially modified to take account of sharing. A virtual processor is now allowed to enter the MPS if its allocation is less than the unallocated store plus the amount of shared store. A virtual processor may also enter the MPS and prepage up to the unallocated plus shared limit, even if this is less than its full allocation. It is then allowed to run, subject to the constraint that a minimal number of free pages remain, and it is a short computation. Otherwise the computation is suspended until more main store can be allocated to it. We refer to this process as partial prepaging.

Recently the installation of a second machine with switchable peripherals, especially drums, has allowed us to experiment further, with the effects upon main store utilization of various sizes of active and main storage. One result we have arrived at is that the performance of the system in an interactive environment seemed to be limited by the amount, rather than the transfer capacity, of active storage, as we had previously believed. In fact a 3/4 megabyte machine with four drums, seems to result in smaller queues, and hence faster response than a one megabyte machine with three drums. This is an extremely recent result, and we are not yet completely sure of its validity.

INTERACTIVE RESPONSE

In the discussion so far we have ignored the choice algorithm itself, concentrating instead on paging behaviour. Here again problems arose that had not been originally foreseen. These occurred if a priority queue was empty, especially if it was a high priority queue on which small interactive computations are held. For this allowed the store to fill up with virtual processors chosen from lower priority queues - virtual processors with large store and cpu allocations.

The problem that arises is, that once these virtual processors enter the MPS, they block the entry into the MPS of virtual processors that arrive on higher priority queues in the interim. If three or four large virtual processors, with a cpu allocation of ten seconds, are resident together, it could be as long as thirty to forty seconds, in the worst case, before another processor can enter the MPS. This problem has been overcome by limiting the multi-programming level among virtual processors chosen from low priority queues. This guarantees that a certain amount of main store will always be free for allocation to high priority virtual processors. Doing this does not radically affect the cpu utilization of the system, as a single low priority virtual processor is capable of saturating the cpu when its working set is fully resident.

The second change to the choice algorithm was motivated by a political decision; EMAS was to be first and foremost an interactive, rather than a remote batch, system. Thus another simple amendment was made.

If a virtual processor remains active for more than a certain period of elapsed time, currently 6 minutes, or if it was initiated by the batch scheduler, it is considered to be penalized with respect to more interactive virtual processors - those that go to sleep from time to time. If a virtual processor is penalized its paging behaviour remains the same as if it were not. Its store and cpu allocations, category and priority are determined normally. The difference is that three out of every four times it is selected, it is returned to the back of the priority queue from which it was selected, rather than being allowed to enter the MPS. Thus penalized virtual processors enter the MPS less often, unless there are no unpenalized virtual processors on the same queue, in which case they enter the MPS normally.

THE CPU SCHEDULER

Another area where some improvement has been achieved is that of cpu scheduling. This area has been of little interest to us, and we believe that while it may still be possible to effect major improvements in system performance, through improved cpu scheduling, it is unlikely. The goal of cpu scheduling in EMAS is one of satisfying a number of simple constraints. Context changes of a virtual processor are expensive and should be minimized. Demand paging virtual processors should get the cpu as soon after satisfying a page fault as possible, and small computations should be processed in as short an elapsed time as possible, so as to free main store for the next small computation.

In the system described in (w2) a simple queue of virtual processors able to take the cpu (the run queue) was maintained, and we restricted ourselves to experiments with various durations of CPU time slice. What we discovered is that the throughput of small interactive computations increased as we reduced the time slice, though of course at an increased cost in context switching overhead. At that time we settled on a time slice of thiry milliseconds, and worked on improving other areas of the system where we felt our efforts would yield greater results. We have now though managed to satisfy our design constraints more fully.

To do this we introduced a system of three run queues of differing absolute priority. On the first we placed virtual processors that had not completed their previous time slice before page faulting, on the second we placed those virtual processors that had completed a time slice, and were not on the third and lowest priority queue on which we put penalized virtual processors. By doing this we were able to increase the time slice to 100 milliseconds and still improve the throughput of small virtual computations.

ACTIVE MEMORY MANAGEMENT

It is the area of drum handling that we have made our most important improvements, which have in turn impacted back into the scheduling of other resources.

The most important change came as the direct result of the discovery that the drums were only performing one fifth as fast as we thought they were. That the system had been capable of the performance reported in (w2) with drums transferring pages at a rate slower than some disk subsystems has a message in it somewhere. The cause of this performance degradation will be obvious to anyone familiar with the early history of drums. The electronic switching between tracks was taking longer than the inter-record gap. For once this was not a case of the software being unable to keep up, but of a failure of the drum control unit itself to keep up. Luckily there was enough room left over on a track to interpose three dummy records between each page frame. The page frames then occupying records 0,2,4, and 6 rather than 0,1,2, and 3 as before. It is a testimony to the flexibility of the system software as it currently exists, that the change required modification of one table in the rotating memory handler and another in the drum formatting programme. A changeover was achieved successfully in the first systems development slot after the discovery.

The other changes to the rotating memory handler came as a result of experimentation. We have concluded that systems efficiency is improved by prepaging, and by ordering transfer requests in each of the selector queues by type. We place demand page reads first, then prepage reads, and finally pageout writes. This prevents the blocking of demand pages by other forms of transfer, and of reads by writes. It is our understanding that others have reached a similar conclusion (12). It is a little frightening to think that drum controllers have been built that do not impose this sort of discipline, especially as they have been constructed after a great deal of modelling and simulation.

With respect to prepaging, it is obvious that the amount one does is tied to the characteristics of one's backing store. If an immediate access medium such as bulk store is used, then of course it makes no sense to do any prepaging. In our configuration, the following seems to occur. The average number of virtual processors in the MPS is six, of which one is on the cpu, one is in a run queue, and four are waiting for the arrival of one or more pages. If we operated a pure demand page strategy, even with shortest latency time first SLTF ordering of transfers on each drum, we would not achieve much better throughput than that produced by a first in first out FIFO ordering. For there would be little more than a single transfer queueing on each drum. By prepaging we increase the number of transfer requests pending on each drum, and hence in each sector queue. We thus gain the benefits of a SLTF ordering on transfers. Approximately 80% of all pages entering the RPS are prepaged. Of the prepaged pages 20% are never used. While this figure seems high: it should be remembered that a high proportion of prepaged pages (well over half) are transferred in sector windows that would not otherwise be used, and hence to a certain extent are transferred at no cost.

Because of the performance mis-match between the diskfiles and drums, a mis-match that grows considerably worse as the queue of transfers pending on each device grows, it is imperative that the majority of transfer requests be for pages, copies of which are held on the drum. Back of envelope calculations indicated that we should aim for a transfer ratio of 20 drum transfers to 1 diskfile transfer, as this would create a balanced load on each device. Because of the shortage of page frames in active memory it is necessary to optimize the set of pages held in active memory, with respect to their expected future use. It seemed reasonable given our success with a page allocation strategy for main storage, that we should employ a similar strategy for active store. This is especially true if one takes into account the consistency rule for information in immediate storage. This rule states: that every time a page belonging to a virtual processor is updated in immediate storage every page belonging to that virtual processor in immediate storage should also be updated. This guarantees that a virtual processor's image in immediate storage is always self consistent, and that the immediate storage image always represents an instantaneous image of the virtual processor, though rarely the real time image. This rule yields a form of automatic checkpointing.

The observant reader may have noticed a flaw in this argument. What does one do with write shared pages? When these are updated in immediate storage, parts of the images of other virtual processors are also updated. There is in EMAS no attempt to propogate the consistency rule from virtual processor to virtual processor, through the write shared material. As file indexes are connected into multiple virtual memories in write shared mode, it would require the updating of all immediate storage images any time a single virtual processor's immediate storage image was updated. Hence automatic checkpointing in the sense it was initially intended does not exist, though the continued application of the rule does minimize the chance of inconsistencv in a user's files as the result of a system failure. One effect of adhering to the consistency rule is that it is impossible to operate a global allocation policy in active storage.

The method of allocation employed is briefly as follows. A virtual processor is allowed to build up pages in active storage, until one of four events occur. It disassociates a file from its virtual address space (disconnection) it overflows its active storage allocation, it remains asleep for two minutes, or a certain number of residency periods have passed without its active storage working set having been recomputed.

The pages that a processor uses during each period in the MPS are noted, and a cyclic record of page use during the last four periods is kept on its master page. It is from this record that the active storage working set of the virtual processor is calculated. There are three progressively stiffer algorithms that are applied depending upon global active storage saturation.

WS = The union of the four periods.
WS = The union of the intersection of the three oldest periods and the most recent period.
WS = The null set.

All updated pages belonging to that virtual processor are then updated in immediate storage, and those pages in active storage no longer in the virtual processor's working set are deleted. Here as in main store, a virtual processor cannot acquire more than its fair share of a system resource.

PSEUDO MEMORY

There is one other change to the system that needs to be mentioned, and this is the introduction of a pseudo drum as a memory level extension. The concept of allocatable memory extension is exceedingly simple and general.

It is a well known allocation problem, that one needs to keep a certain amount of allocatable resource in hand to avoid deadlocks, or in our case, the need to remove a virtual processor from a memory level prematurely - a form of thrashing. It is thus impossible to utilize all of a memory level, unless one somehow extends the allocatable memory at that level, so as to use all of the real memory. This extension is effected through the use of pseudo memory.

Pseudo memory can be used at any memory level that has an address continuity with the next. Examples are: main memory - mass memory, mass memory-drum memory and drum memory - disk memory. The main memory - drum memory boundary does not display this characteristic of address continuity, as one is addressed in bytes, and the other in pages. We are thus able to use a pseudo drum, which is part of a small disk pack, the rest of which is used as a collection pool for event monitoring records, but not pseudo main memory. With this extension the active storage allocation algorithm can endeavour to allocate all of the real drum pages, secure in the knowledge that if it overflows the real drum, there are pseudo drum pages in which to put the information. We are thus able to achieve full drum utilization.

Needless to say pages are moved from the pseudo drum onto real drum when space becomes available on the latter.

It should be obvious from this discussion about utilizing drum storage that we do not fully utilize main storage. Figure 6 shows main store utilization during a 24 hour period. It is for others to decide how we fare in relation to other techniques.

SYSTEMS PERFORMANCE

The system currently supports a maximum of 55 simultaneous users, with the elbow (the point at which the first critical resource becomes overloaded) in the response curve appearing at somewhere between 45 and 50 users, depending upon the mix. Under this type of loading, the drum channel transfers about 65 pages a second, and the diskfile channel about 6, of which less than 1 - 2 are demand reads. Approximately 90% of the cpu is utilized with this number of users, the remaining 10% being free, due to an instantaneous lack of a compute bound virtual processors. In general 50% of the processor is given to the virtual processors, while the remaining 40% is spent in the resident supervisor. Over 75% of this time is spent in only two resident processes: The drum handler; and the working set calculator. This time would be radically reduced, with the addition of appropriate hardware mechanisms in each case: hardware drum scheduling, and access and usage information on the segment and page tables, rather than the store. There are in fact 8 keys which have to be read out and reset on each page, at every strobe period. Given the current hardware configuration we see no way of improving these figures while running interactively with many users, and fast response.

While running batch work overnight with 6 batch streams, the system achieves effectively 100% cpu utilization, 85% of the time being spent in virtual processors.

The meantime between crashes due to hardware malfunction is currently 25 hours, and we encounter approximately two failures a month, due to software malfunction. This while the supervisor is still under development, and being changed about twice a week. When running proven supervisors, we have found that it is possible to achieve an essentially zero software error rate. Both the hardware and software error rates are lower than they might be due to extensive checking, graceful degradation features, and the vetting of all incoming messages by system processes.

ACKNOWLEDGEMENT

There have been too many people involved in the development of EMAS to mention them all individually. Specific thanks though are due to Professor S.Michaelson for creating the environment in which this work could be undertaken, and to Dr. J.G.Burns, who provided moral support, when few external to the project believed it would be successful. Special thanks are due also to Professor B. Galler of the University of Michigan, without whose encouragement this paper would not have been written.

BIBLIOGRAPHY

b1). Bobrow, G.D.,et.al.,'TENEX,A Paged Time Sharing System for the PDP 10',
      CACM, March, 1972, pp, 135 - 143.

b2). Bobrow, G.D., personal communication.

b3). Burns, J.G. et al, The EMAS User Manual, Edinburgh Regional Computing
      Centre, 1972.

b4). Barritt, M.M.,et.al., the IMP language manual, Edinburgh Regional Computing
      Centre, 1970.

c1). Corbato, F.J. and Vyssotsky, V.A., 'Introduction and Overview of the
      MULTICS System', Proc. AFIPS 1965 FJCC Vol. 27, Part 1, pp. 185-196.

d1). Denning, P.J., 'The Working Set Model for Program Behaviour',
      CACM, May 1968, pp. 323-333

d2). Denning, P.J., 'Virtual Memory', Computing Surveys, Vol 2, No. 3,
      September 1970.

f1). Fuller, S., 'Performance Characteristics of an I/O Channel With Multiple
      Paging Drums', technical report * 27, Stanford Electronics Laboratory,
      August 1972.

g1). Galler, B. personal communication.

1I). Lauer, H.C. 'Bulk Core in a 360/67 Time-Sharing System', Proc. AFIPS
      1967 FJCC, Vol 31, pp.601-609.

12). Lynch, W.C., personal communication

13). Lett, A.S. and Konigsford, W.L., 'TSS 360: A Time Shared Operating System',
      Proc. AFIPS 1968 FJCC, Vol 33, Prt 1, pp.15-28.

m1). Millard, G., 'The Standard EMAS Sub-System', Accepted for publication in
      The Computer Journal

o1). Organick, E.I., The MULTICS System, An Examination of its Structure,
      MIT Press, Cambridge, Mass., 1972

r1). Rees D.J., 'The EMAS Director', Accepted for publication in The Computer
      Journal.

s1). Spier, M.J., 'A Model Implementation for Protective Domains',
      International Journal of Computer and Information Science, Vol 2 No. 3,
      September 1973, pp 201-228

s2). Stephens, P.D., 'The IMP Programming Language', Accepted for
      publication in The Computer Journal

w1). Whitfield H., 'The Organization of the University of Edinburgh Time
      Sharing System', International Seminar on Advanced Programming Systems,
      vol.ii, No. v, Jerusalem, 1968

w2). Whitfield H. and Wight, A.S., 'EMAS, The Edinburgh Multi-Access System',
      The Computer Journal, Vol 16 No.4, November 1973.

w3). Wilkes, M.V., 'The Dynamics of Paging', The Computer Journal, Vol 16 No 1,
      February 1973, pp 4-9

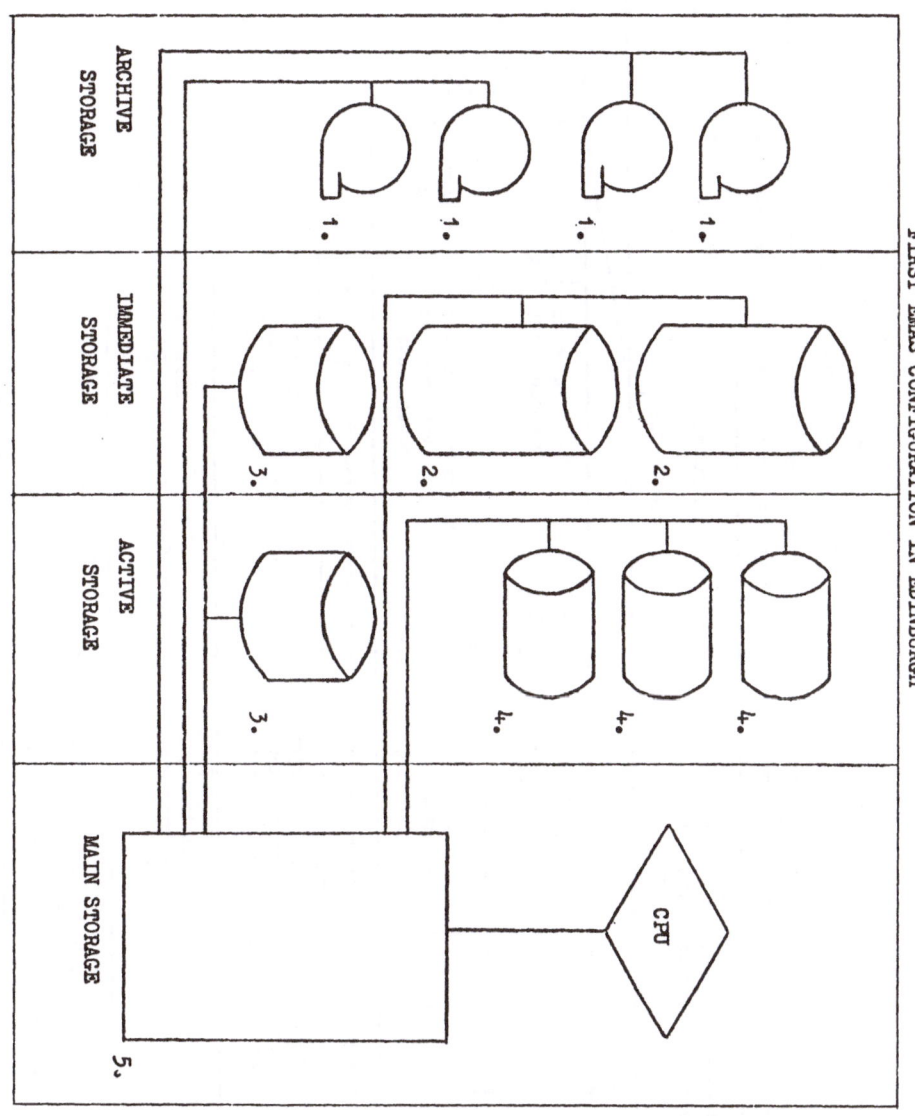

FIRST EMAS CONFIGURATION IN EDINBURGH

1. 1600 BPI. Tape
2. 350 Megabyte Disk
3. 6 Megabyte Disk
4. 2 Megabyte Drum
5. 1 Megabyte Core

figure 1

CATEGORY	LEVEL	INVOKED BY	FUNCTIONS PERFORMED	CODE
RESIDENT SUPERVISOR	KERNEL	Interrupts, routine calls, returns from MAIN processes.	Inter-process message switching. Privileged hardware instructions. Interrupt-message conversion. Process dispatching.	10 k.bytes
RESIDENT SUPERVISOR	VIRTUAL PROCESSOR SUPPORT	Inter-process message.	Active and Main storage allocation. Virtual processor scheduling and contingency handling.	32 k.bytes
RESIDENT SUPERVISOR	DEVICE HANDLERS	Inter-process message.	I/O device control. Paged I/O scheduling and error recovery. Interactive communications device control.	52 k.bytes
VIRTUAL / REAL BOUNDARY				
DIRECTOR	VIRTUAL MEMORY MAPPING	Inter-process message, and Master Page entries.	Association of virtual memory addresses and immediate memory sites. User process Signal mechanism.	4 k.bytes
DIRECTOR	SUB-PROCESSES	Inter-process message.	Interactive communication. File system maintenance. File transfer for I/O.	46 k.bytes
EXEC	EXECUTIVE USER PROCESSES	Inter-process message.	Unit record device spooling. Batch scheduler. Archive memory control. Engineering test programmes.	69 k. + 16 k. + 75 k.bytes
SOFTWARE PRIVILEGED / NON-PRIVILEGED BOUNDARY				
NORMAL USER	STANDARD SUBSYSTEM	Inter-process message and routine calls.	File definition. Object file layout, linking and loading. Logical I/O mapping.	110 k.bytes
NORMAL USER	PROGRAMMES	Routine calls.	Editors, Compilers, Utilities and User provided routines and programmes.	450 k.+ user code bytes

figure 2

```
record format CAT LAY (byte integer CATEGORY, PRIORITY, STORE, c
                ASPERD, ASMAX, ASMIN, c
                NCY1, NCY2, NCY3, NCY4, c
                integer CPU TIME, STROBE TIME)
!
! NCY1 is next category if process runs out of core.
! NCY2 is next category if process exceeds time limit.
! NCY3 as ncy2 but core used less than next smallest core limit.
! NCY4 is category if process goes to sleep.
! ASMIN is the unconditional allocation of active store.
! ASMAX is the largest amount of active store that can be held.
! ASPERD is the number of MPS residency periods before recomputing WS.
!
!           hexadecimal constants are bracketed by X' and '.
!
! CPU TIME is cpu allocation in 8 microsecond units. X'00020000'=1 sec.
! STROBE TIME is the period over which the main storage WS is computed.
!

const record array CAT TAB(1:20) (CAT LAY) = c
   1,  1,  42,   20,   80,  64,   17, 15, 11, 14,  X'00020000', X'00004000',
   2,  1,  16,   20,   80,  64,    3,  2,  0,  2,  X'00010000', X'00010000',
   3,  1,  24,   20,   80,  64,    4,  3,  2,  3,  X'00020000', X'00020000',
   4,  1,  42,   20,   80,  64,    4,  4,  3,  4,  X'00040000', X'00010000',
   5,  1,  16,   40,   80,  64,    8,  6,  0,  5,  X'00010000', X'00010000',
   6,  4,  16,   20,   80,  64,   10,  7,  0,  5,  X'00080000', X'00020000',
   7,  5,  16,   20,   80,  64,   10,  7,  0,  5,  X'00140000', X'00020000',
   8,  1,  24,   40,   80,  64,   11,  9,  5,  8,  X'00020000', X'00010000',
   9,  4,  24,   10,   80,  64,   13, 10,  6,  8,  X'00140000', X'00020000',
  10,  4,  24,   10,   80,  64,   13, 10,  7,  8,  X'000C0000', X'00020000',
  11,  2,  32,   40,   80,  64,   14, 12,  8, 11,  X'00020000', X'00020000',
  12,  4,  32,   10,   80,  64,   16, 13,  9, 11,  X'00140000', X'00020000',
  13,  5,  32,   10,   80,  64,   16, 13, 10, 11,  X'00180000', X'00020000',
  14,  2,  42,   20,   80,  64,   17, 15, 11, 14,  X'00020000', X'00020000',
  15,  4,  42,   10,   80,  64,   19, 16, 12, 14,  X'00140000', X'00020000',
  16,  5,  42,   10,   80,  64,   19, 16, 13, 14,  X'00140000', X'00020000',
  17,  3,  52,   20,  128,  80,   20, 18, 14, 17,  X'00040000', X'00010000',
  18,  4,  52,    5,  128,  80,   20, 19, 15, 17,  X'000E0000', X'00010000',
  19,  5,  52,    5,  128,  80,   20, 19, 16, 17,  X'000A0000', X'00020000',
  20,  3,  52,   20,  128,  80,   20, 18, 15, 17,  X'00040000', X'00008000'

!
const byte integer array CHOICE(0:63) = c
          5,1,2,1,2,1,2,1,1,2,1,1,2,1,3,1,
          2,1,1,4,1,1,2,1,2,1,1,2,1,1,3,1,
          1,2,1,1,2,1,2,1,4,1,1,2,1,1,3,1,
          1,2,1,1,2,1,2,1,1,3,1,2,1,2,1,1
!
```

figure 3

EMAS VERSN 781A   DATE: 05/03/74   TIME: 14.31.01

CATEGORY TABLE MOVEMENT

					TO					
		1	2	3	4	5	6	7	8	9	10
F R O M	1	396	0	0	0	0	0	0	5	0	0
	2	0	2323	892	0	0	0	0	0	0	0
	3	0	894	1911	470	0	0	0	0	0	0
	4	0	0	472	600	0	0	0	0	0	0
	5	0	0	0	0	14694	115	0	2666	0	0
	6	0	0	0	0	8	0	5	0	0	151
	7	0	0	0	0	0	0	171	0	0	80
	8	0	0	0	0	2683	50	0	9169	38	0
	9	0	0	0	0	0	0	2	9	0	4
	10	0	0	0	0	122	0	73	39	0	167
	11	0	0	0	0	0	0	0	3874	37	0
	12	0	0	0	0	0	0	0	24	0	15
	13	0	0	0	0	0	0	0	57	0	35
	14	0	0	0	0	0	0	0	13	0	0
	15	0	0	0	0	0	0	0	0	0	0
	16	0	0	0	0	0	0	0	0	0	0
	17	0	0	0	0	0	0	0	3	0	0
	18	0	0	0	0	0	0	0	0	0	0
	19	0	0	0	0	0	0	0	0	0	0
	20	0	0	0	0	0	0	0	3	0	0

					TO					
		11	12	13	14	15	16	17	18	19	20
F R O M	1	2	0	0	0	0	0	388	0	0	0
	2	0	0	0	0	0	0	0	0	0	0
	3	0	0	0	0	0	0	0	0	0	0
	4	0	0	0	0	0	0	0	0	0	0
	5	1	0	0	0	0	0	0	0	0	0
	6	0	0	0	0	0	0	0	0	0	0
	7	0	0	0	0	0	0	0	0	0	0
	8	3842	0	0	0	0	0	0	0	0	0
	9	1	0	59	0	0	0	0	0	0	0
	10	2	0	49	0	0	0	0	0	0	0
	11	4124	111	0	4678	0	0	0	0	0	0
	12	34	20	14	0	0	101	0	0	0	0
	13	25	0	90	0	0	139	0	0	0	0
	14	4779	77	0	3105	120	0	1850	0	0	0
	15	68	0	57	21	544	26	0	0	300	0
	16	122	0	57	22	0	933	0	0	320	0
	17	11	0	0	1325	145	0	951	146	0	766
	18	2	0	0	3	0	18	7	297	55	250
	19	15	0	0	145	0	237	28	0	2417	250
	20	16	0	0	125	207	0	130	183	0	2113

figure 4

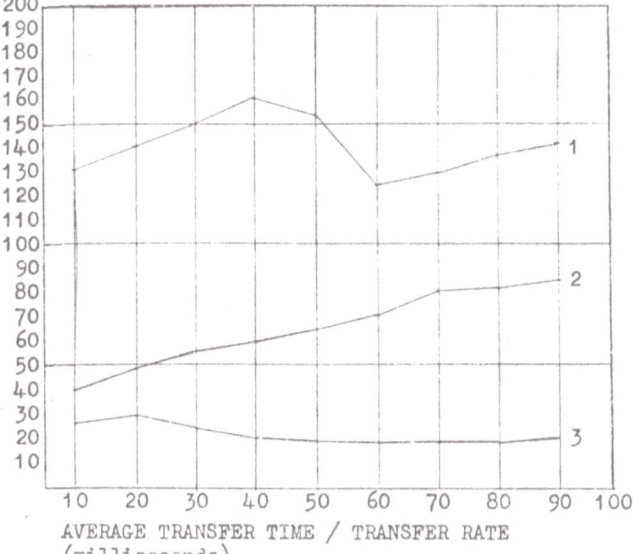

AVERAGE TRANSFER TIME / TRANSFER RATE
(milliseconds)

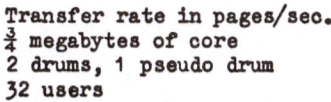

Transfer rate in pages/sec.
¾ megabytes of core
2 drums, 1 pseudo drum
32 users

16 minute sample

KEY

1. Diskfile demand reads.

2. Drum and pseudo drum
   demand reads.

3. Drum and pseudo drum
   prepage reads.

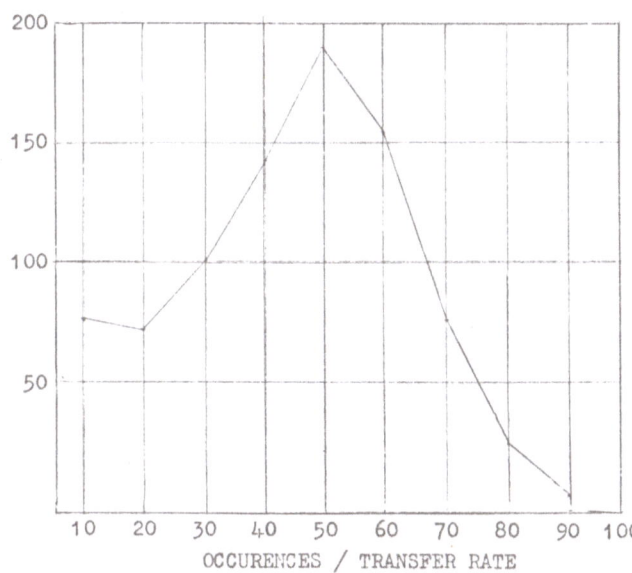

OCCURENCES / TRANSFER RATE

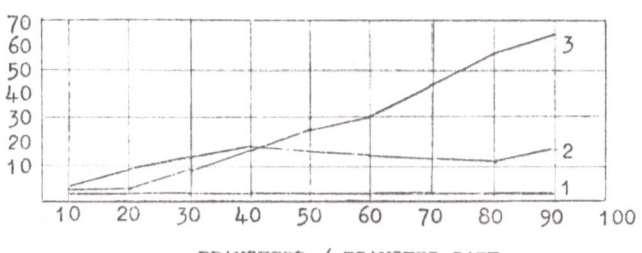

TRANSFERS / TRANSFER RATE

figure 5

MACHINE A

201 allocatable pages
3 drums and 1 pseudo drum

from: 23:28 on: 27/02/74
  to: 23:18 on: 28/02/74

Queues sampled every ten seconds.
Each point represents 1000 samples.

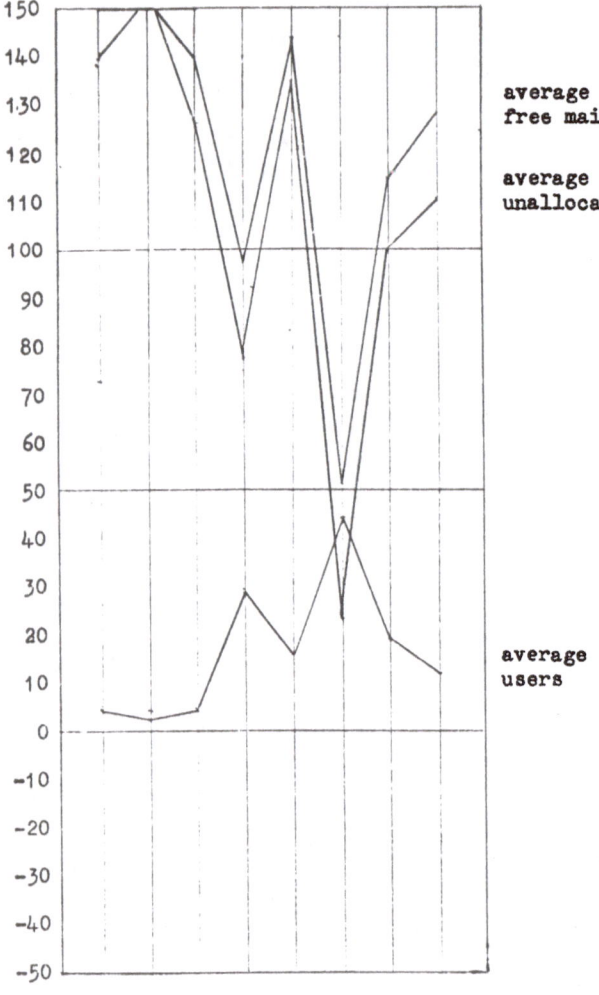

average
free main store

average
unallocated main store

average
users

figure 6

Lecture Notes in Economics and Mathematical Systems